British Strategy & War Aims
1914~1916

British Strategy & War Aims

1914~1916

DAVID FRENCH

Lecturer in History, University College, London

London
ALLEN & UNWIN

Boston   Sydney

Allen & Unwin (Publishers) Ltd,
40 Museum Street, London WC1A 1LU, UK

Allen & Unwin (Publishers) Ltd,
Park Lane, Hemel Hempstead, Herts HP2 4TE, UK

Allen & Unwin, Inc.,
8 Winchester Place, Winchester, Mass. 01890, USA

Allen & Unwin (Australia) Ltd,
8 Napier Street, North Sydney, NSW 2060, Australia

First published in 1986

British Library Cataloguing in Publication Data

French, David
  British strategy and war aims, 1914–16
1. World War, 1914–1918 – Great Britain
I. Title
940–4′012   D517
ISBN 0–04–942197–2

Library of Congress Cataloging-in-Publication Data

French, David, 1954–
  British strategy and war aims, 1914–16.
Bibliography: p.
Includes index.
1. World War, 1914–1918 – Diplomatic history.
2. Great Britain – Foreign relations – Europe. 3. Europe – Foreign
relations – Great Britain. 4. Great Britain – Politics and government –
1910–1936. I. Title.
D621.G7F74   1986   940.4′012   86–1186
ISBN 0–04–942197–2 (alk. paper)

Set in 10 on 12 point Bembo by Computape (Pickering) Limited,
Pickering, Yorkshire
and printed in Great Britain by Anchor Brendon Ltd,
Tiptree, Essex

Contents

Acknowledgements

I WOULD like to thank the following people for their advice and encouragement during the writing of this book. Dr Kathleen Burk and Dr Keith Neilson have shared with me over many years their knowledge of Anglo-American and Anglo-Russian relations during the First World War and Keith kindly read the entire manuscript. Professor M. R. D. Foot, Dr Robin Prior and Dr Stevan Pavlowitch each gave me important insights into the Balkan Wars and the Dardanelles campaign and Dr Keith Grieves greatly assisted my understanding of the British government's manpower policy. The members of the Military History Seminar of the Institute of Historical Research, particularly Mr Brian Bond, Dr Michael Dockrill, Mr John Ferris and Dr Brian Holden Reid, made several valuable criticisms of some of my wilder ideas about the development of British strategy during the war. Parts of this book have been given as seminar papers to audiences at London, Oxford and Sheffield and I am most grateful for the comments of those who were present. If I have on occasions differed from them in my interpretation of events I hope they will forgive my stubbornness. None of the aforementioned are responsible for what appears here and all errors of fact or judgement are my own.

The following individuals and institutions have kindly given me permission to quote from material to which they own the copyright: the Rt Hon Julian Amery MP; Brigadier A. F. L. Clive; Dr Paul Howell; Viscount Simon; the Trustees of the National Library of Scotland and the holder of the copyright of Field Marshal Earl Haig; Newcastle University Library; the Trustees of the Liddell Hart Centre for Military Archives, King's College, London; Mr David McKenna; the Trustees of the Imperial War Museum; the Trevelyan family; the *Spectator*; Viscount Selborne; Colonel R. St G. Kirke; the Master, Fellows and Scholars of Churchill College, Cambridge in the University of Cambridge; the Clerk of the Records, the House of Lords Record Office; Lord Gainford; Vice-Admiral Hogg; Viscount Esher; Mr Mark Bonham-Carter; the Bodleian Library; Colonel Tony Aylmer; Lord Robertson; Mr. A. J. P. Taylor and the Trustees of the Beaverbrook Foundation; Mr A. Grant C. R. and Mr Ian Crum Hamilton; Mr John Montgomery-Massingberd;

the Library of Congress, Washington; the National Trust for Places of Historic Interest or National Beauty. Crown copyright material is reproduced by permission of the Controller of Her Majesty's Stationery Office. Material from letters by the Prime Minister to His Majesty King George V is reproduced by gracious permission of Her Majesty the Queen. If I have unwittingly infringed anyone's copyright I hope that they will accept my apologies.

It would have been impossible to write this book without the unfailing help and courtesy of numerous librarians and archivists and I would especially like to thank the staff of the following institutions for their assistance: the history library of University College, London; Senate House library of the University of London; the Institute of Historical Research of the University of London; the Liddell Hart Centre for Military Archives, King's College, London; the Department of Western Manuscripts of the Bodleian Library, Oxford; the Department of Manuscripts of the National Library of Scotland; the University of Newcastle upon Tyne library; the Department of Documents of the Imperial War Museum; the Archives of Churchill College, Cambridge; the House of Lords Record Office.

My greatest debt is once again to my parents to whom this book is dedicated.

Introduction

THIS IS THE first of two volumes about the development of British strategy and war aims during the First World War. These books are not another attempt to write the domestic political history of Britain between 1914 and 1918, a task already accomplished by far sharper pens than mine. Rather they will seek to analyse the connections between British military policy and the development of its war aims during the First World War, and they will only include such references to domestic politics as are necessary to make this story intelligible. This volume will examine the policies of the wartime administrations under H. H. Asquith between 1914 and 1916. A subsequent volume will deal with the Lloyd George coalition of 1916–18.

The sheer enormity of the scale of the war and the casualties which the combatants suffered has numbed the imaginations of subsequent generations, and many observers have simply abandoned the task of trying to understand what the war was about. One reviewer, writing in June 1983, was struck by the awful horror of the Somme, and could only lament, 'You work at it and find the horror is too much. The mind jams at its inability to make sense of it all. And then you realise that you will never make sense of it, because it does not make sense.'[1] The purpose of this book is to demonstrate that at least for the policy-making elite the war did make sense. They fought the war for two reasons. The most obvious was to preserve their country's independence and status as a great power by preventing Britain and its empire from falling under the domination of the Central Powers. But their second purpose, one often obscured by their public rhetoric and only made plain by some of their private deliberations, was to gain a peace settlement on terms which would also provide Britain and its empire with security against its allies.

The most widely accepted picture of the strategic debate inside the British government was that it was conducted between two sharply different schools. 'Westerners' like Sir William Robertson, the Chief of the Imperial General Staff (CIGS) from 1915 to 1918 and Sir Douglas Haig, the Commander-in-Chief (C.-in-C.) of the British Expeditionary Force (BEF) in France between 1915 and 1918, condemned hundreds of thousands of men to their deaths by their insistence that the war could only be won in costly battles of attrition like the Somme and the Third Battle of Ypres. By contrast 'Easterners', like Winston Churchill and David Lloyd George, maintained that they had discovered a cheaper and quicker road to victory in the East, either at the Dardanelles or in the Balkans, but that they were prevented from taking it by colleagues too timid, too foolish or just too stupid to go against the advice of their professional advisers.

This sharply defined division into two separate schools of thought was a caricature of the debate about war policy conducted within the British government between 1914 and 1916 and cannot be sustained by the evidence which is now available. It was created by the memoirs and biographies of the participants which were published in the 1920s and 1930s. Books like *Sir Douglas Haig's Command, December 19th., 1915 to November 11th., 1918*, written by the journalist G. A. B. Dewar and Haig's own former private secretary J. H. Boraston in 1922, Churchill's *The World Crisis, 1911–1918*, written between 1919 and 1926, Sir William Robertson's *From Private to Field Marshal* (1921) and *Soldiers and Statesmen 1914–1918* (1926), Sir Charles Callwell's edition of Sir Henry Wilson's diaries, *Field Marshal Sir Henry Wilson: His Life and Diaries* (1927) and Lloyd George's *War Memoirs*, first published between 1933–6, were not attempts to present a dispassionate history of events. They were pieces of polemical literature in which their authors sought to prove that they had been right and that their enemies had been wrong. Churchill wrote his book largely to disprove the charges which had been laid against him as the man who had masterminded the Dardanelles fiasco.[2] Haig encouraged Boraston and Dewar because he believed that Lloyd George and others had denigrated the part played by the BEF in winning the war and Dewar himself wanted a measure of revenge for the unfair criticisms he believed the government had levelled against him for his reports of the Battle of Cambrai in 1917.[3] Wilson had been outspoken about soldiers and politicians alike in the privacy of his diaries, but Callwell's own particular axe was made clear in a letter written to Boraston in 1926 when he wrote that 'as far as I am concerned, the politicians must take their chance. On the other hand I want to present the position as regards our soldiers reasonably impartially and not to accept all that H[enry] W[ilson] says without comment.'[4] Lloyd George wrote his memoirs to restore his reputation as the man who had won the war and to settle some scores with former friends who had since become enemies. In April 1934 he explained to his former Cabinet secretary, Sir Maurice Hankey

> I hope that the panjundrums will remember that I am on my defence, that for 15 years I have borne with a stream of criticism polluted with much poisonous antagonism, that the books published by Generals and

Admirals and their minions have all quoted – or summarised views unfairly – official secret documents. My shelves here groan under their mutilated, bowdlerised, distorted quotations.[5]

In seeking to destroy the reputations of their opponents both sides of the argument were guilty of myth-making and plundering the past for their own polemical purposes. None of them gave full weight to the cardinal fact that Britain did not fight the war alone but as a member of the Entente alliance. In a lecture to the Royal United Services Institute in 1931 the distinguished historian B. H. Liddell Hart, who gave Lloyd George considerable help in the composition of his *War Memoirs*, argued that Britain had been wrong to abandon its traditional maritime strategy in favour of committing a large army to the continent. His argument was flawed on four counts. Britain had not traditionally avoided continental commitments. Whenever it had an ally in the Low Countries it habitually dispatched an army to give assistance. The historical analogy Liddell Hart drew between the First World War and the Napoleonic Wars was no longer valid by 1914. The invention of the railway meant that for the first time great land powers like Germany could move troops across Europe more quickly than the British could move their forces by sea. Thirdly, the effectiveness of economic pressure was strictly limited against an enemy like Germany, again largely due to the coming of the railway. Germany commanded not only its own economic resources but by conquest it could add to them those of a large part of the rest of Europe.[6] And finally, the Entente alliance was not simply a military arrangement. Liddell Hart's suggestion that if the British had sent their New Armies to the East in 1915–16 the French would have been compelled to remain on the defensive supposes that the British had absolute control over the alliance's policies.

They did not. The Entente alliance existed on four levels, political, military, economic and naval. Only in the naval sphere was Britain the undisputed leader of the alliance from the start to the finish of the war. It began the war with the smallest army of the three great-power members of the alliance and did not achieve a rough military parity with the French or Russians until 1916. The cost of doing so was a significant diminution of its economic power. In August 1914 it was the strongest economic power within the Entente and quickly assumed the role of banker to the alliance. But by late 1915 it was becoming apparent that Britain would not be able to sustain indefinitely this role of paymaster to the allies and provide a continental-scale army. Britain, therefore, never enjoyed the overwhelming preponderance of power within the Entente alliance which might have enabled it to disregard the wishes of its major allies and force them to conform to a purely British policy. In November 1914 the Germans recognized that their initial plan to achieve a quick victory in a two-front war had failed. They therefore began to extend peace feelers to each of Britain's allies in the hope that they could persuade them to break with the Entente and conclude a separate peace. The British were aware of this and, sometimes reluctantly, had to shape their policies accordingly. If they did not meet their allies' wishes over certain crucial issues they were afraid that the latter might decide they had more to gain by accepting one of the German offers than by continuing the war in the company of the British.

In 1914–16 the real division between the British policy-makers did not lie between 'Easterners' and 'Westerners'. All policy-makers were agreed that measures had to be taken to protect the British empire in the East and that Britain had to assist its Russian ally. What they could not agree upon was how best to do this. The party of caution, led by McKenna and Runciman, were ready to continue the war for a decade if necessary. They were ready to overlook French and Russian importunities for more military assistance and hoped that simply by imitating what they believed had been their predecessors' policies during the Napoleonic Wars, that is husbanding Britain's manpower, subsidizing their allies and exploiting their naval power, they could defeat the Central Powers. Their opponents, Lloyd George, Robertson and most senior Unionist ministers with the exception of Balfour were temperamentally unsuited to pursuing a fabian-like policy, disbelieved in its efficacy, and were afraid that if they pursued it one or more of their continental allies might desert them.

Before 1914 Britain's relationship with its Entente partners had not run smoothly and these tensions continued, and to some extent even increased, once the war started. Mutual misunderstandings and suspicions were perhaps inevitable. At a personal level many members of the decision-making elite in Britain had difficulty communicating with representatives of their allies. Some could not speak French and very few could speak Russian. On a political level many of them lacked sympathy for the autocratic regime of tsarist Russia. The resources which each ally brought to the alliance were unbalanced. The importance of British naval power was little understood by nations without a strong naval tradition of their own. Some of the allies resented Britain's role as the economic powerhouse of the alliance, seeing it as an attempt by the British to get rich at the expense of its allies. More fundamentally, Britain had a long tradition of hostility to Russia and France and, by contrast, until the late nineteenth century none at all with Germany. In the minds of many members of the policy-making elite, the rise of the Anglo-German antagonism had only overlaid, but had not abolished, Britain's quarrels with France and Russia. Membership of the alliance undoubtedly added to Britain's security but it also brought with it the extra burden of having to fight not only to achieve its own aims, but those of its allies as well. The two sets of goals were not always compatible.

British policy-makers between 1914 and 1916 had three goals. They sought to hold the Entente alliance together, to vanquish the Central Powers, more especially Germany, and to ensure that when the time to make peace arrived Britain was the strongest of all of the belligerents and was able to impose its terms on enemies and allies alike. They began the war hoping that it would be possible to do this at comparatively little cost to Britain. They intended that Britain's part in the alliance would be confined to blockading the Central Powers, supplying its allies with money and munitions and dispatching a small army to northern France as a token of Britain's good intent. They were drawn into operations outside of France before the Western front had become stalemated because of the need to protect Britain's own imperial possessions. Kitchener raised the New Armies in 1914–15 to ensure that Britain would be the strongest military power at the peace conference. They were intended not only to win the war for the Entente alliance but also to win the peace for Britain.

Britain launched the Dardanelles campaign in 1915 to assist Russia and to persuade Italy and the Balkan neutrals to join the Entente. It persisted with it throughout 1915 at least in part because some of its policy-makers, not only in London but also in Cairo and Delhi, were afraid that if Britain scuttled ignominiously from the Gallipoli peninsula its prestige in the East, the foundations upon which they believed the whole empire rested, would crumble. The British did not participate in the Salonika campaign because they sought to avoid their obligations to their allies to pay the blood tax of a continental war but because France and Russia asked them to do so. The policy of attrition was devised by Kitchener at the beginning of 1915 as a way of conserving British soldiers' lives. He intended that the French and Russian armies would bear the brunt of wearing down the enemies' military manpower in 1915–16 so that the British army could administer the final blow in early 1917. However the very heavy losses the Germans had inflicted on the French since the start of the war and the Russian 'Great Retreat' of the summer of 1915 indicated that it might be difficult to keep to this time-scale. Between the summer of 1915 and the spring of 1916 a majority of British policy-makers reluctantly concluded that the future of the Entente alliance depended on Britain's readiness to play a major role in the continental land war. The Battle of Loos in September 1915 marked the halfway point in their conversion. Loos was a political offensive, designed to bolster faltering French and Russian morale.

At the beginning of 1916 some ministers, notably McKenna, Runciman and Balfour, still believed that the policy of holding back the great bulk of the New Armies from active offensive operations on the Western front until the Germans were on the point of collapse was practicable. But by April the majority were reluctantly persuaded by Robertson and Kitchener that the war might end in an indecisive peace, or worse still a German victory. One or more of the allies might abandon the Entente alliance if the British did not participate to the fullest possible extent in the combined allied offensive which had been planned by the allied military representatives at the Chantilly conference in December 1915. The BEF's part in this offensive, the Battle of the Somme, was an enormous gamble. Haig's army was only able to mount the battle because in January and April, despite the warnings of the Treasury and the Board of Trade that it might bankrupt Britain, the government introduced conscription. Ministers agreed to the battle in the almost certain knowledge that if the Entente did not force the Central Powers to sue for peace by the end of the year Britain might have passed the peak of its strength. For a few weeks in August and September, and despite the heavy losses Haig's troops sustained, the success of the Brusilov offensive and Romania's entry into the war on the side of the Entente enabled the policy-makers to believe that their gamble had succeeded and some officials and ministers began to give serious consideration to detailed war aims. But by the late autumn their hopes had been dashed. The Central Powers had recovered. They still remained in occupation of large tracts of allied territory, whilst the economic consequences of the British government's temerity were starting to come home to roost. By the time the Asquith coalition collapsed in December 1916 it was apparent that only American credit could sustain Britain and its allies into 1917.

Notes

1   Richard Boston in the *Guardian*, 18 June 1983.
2   See R. Prior, *Churchill's World Crisis as History* (London: Croom Helm, 1983).
3   D. French, 'Sir Douglas Haig's reputation, 1918–1928: A note', *Historical Journal*, vol. 28, no. 4 (1985), pp. 953–60.
4   Callwell to Boraston, 24 June 1926, Boraston mss, 71/13/2.
5   Lloyd George to Hankey, 18 April 1934, Lloyd George mss, box G/212.
6   Captain B. H. Liddell Hart, 'Economic pressure or continental victories', *Journal of the Royal United Services Institute*, vol. 76 (1931), pp. 486–503; for some recent criticisms of Liddell Hart's ideas see M. Howard, 'The British way in warfare – a reappraisal', in M. Howard, *The Causes of War* (London: Temple Smith, 1983), pp. 169–186; B. J. Bond, *Liddell Hart: A Study of his Military Thought* (London: Cassell, 1977), pp. 65–80; P. M. Kennedy, *The Rise and Fall of British Naval Mastery* (London: Allen Lane, 1976), pp. 177–204, 239–66.

1

The Ententes and the Security of the British Empire

BRITISH foreign and defence policy was made by a small elite before 1914. At its apex was a small number of Cabinet ministers. First among them was the Prime Minister between 1908 and 1916, H. H. Asquith. Those who worked with him frequently remarked on his great judicial ability and his rapid grasp of even the most intricate problems. But he also had some of the defects of his virtues. He managed to hold together a very talented team of ministers for nearly eight years but he was not a man of great initiative himself. Nor was he an inspiring war leader. The war filled him with sadness and he disliked the public adulation which greeted him in the early days of the conflict. His contempt for attacks on his person was coupled with an indifference to public opinion which eventually weakened his position as a wartime Prime Minister. He delighted too much in his ability to compose arguments in Cabinet with a form of words. Too often after August 1914 this meant that he simply skirted around real divisions of opinion to the fury of some of his colleagues. Before the war his authority over his colleagues was undisputed and remained so during the opening months of the war. Charles Hobhouse, the Postmaster General, wrote of him in March 1915 that 'The P.M.'s abilities are as transcendent as ever: his qualities more noticeable. Temper, tact, courage quite marvellous.'[1] But after the formation of the coalition his power began to decline. The Unionist party in the country never had any confidence in him and the confidence of some Liberals began to wane because of the problems raised by his mishandling of conscription and Ireland.[2]

Asquith's closest confidants before 1914 were Sir Edward Grey, the Foreign Secretary and Lord Crewe, Secretary of State for India between 1910–15, Lord President of the Council 1915–16 and President of the Board of Education in 1916. Asquith believed that Crewe had the soundest judgement of all of his ministers. His admiration for him may have been based on the fact that, unlike some of his other colleagues, he never spoke at unnecessary length. He was, according to Lord Selborne who sat with them both in Cabinet in 1915–16, 'a replica of the P.M.' only less able.[3] Grey lived much less in the Prime Minister's shadow. Between 1905 and 1914 there was general agreement between Grey and his professional advisers about foreign policy. He listened to their advice but ultimately he made policy.[4] Grey's first experience of foreign affairs had been as under secretary in the 1890s when he had been unpleasantly struck by the way in which Germany tried to exploit Britain's differences with France and Russia to force it to make concessions. Grey was a Liberal Imperialist although he did not give the empire the same close attention as his Unionist predecessor, Lord Lansdowne. But he believed that if Britain abandoned its empire it would pass under the control of other powers and Britain would cease to be a great power. He was opposed to further imperial expansion because he recognized that British resources were already dangerously overextended in defending what it already held. He welcomed the Anglo-French Entente of 1904 because it reduced Britain's liabilities and since 1895 he had sought a similar agreement with Russia. Germany's behaviour during the Boer War had served only to convince him further of its hostility. Under his guidance the centre of British diplomatic policy shifted to Europe and he was ready to sacrifice some Indian and colonial interests for the sake of preserving good relations with Britain's Entente partners.[5] He impressed everyone before 1914 with his apparent honesty. His speech of 3 August 1914 urging that Britain should stand by its Entente partners made him a symbol of Britain's determination to fight the war second only to Kitchener. He went into partial eclipse after August 1914, depressed by his inability to prevent the outbreak of war and by his failing eyesight. But he had his own ideas about policy, and naturally obstinate, he was not prepared to follow blindly the lead of the military.[6]

R. B. (later Lord) Haldane was Secretary of State for War between 1906 and 1912. He was a close associate of both Asquith and Grey before the war, but by February 1915 Asquith only rated his judgement as about average in the Cabinet. Many Liberals were repelled by his propensity for intrigue and many Unionists believed that he was pro-German. Winston Churchill, First Lord of the Admiralty 1911–15, aroused deep distrust. 'Churchill is ill mannered, boastful, unprincipled, without any redeeming qualities except his amazing ability and industry', wrote one Liberal.[7] The Unionists thought he was a renegade who had crossed the floor of the House of Commons to join the Liberals. Many Liberals were perpetually afraid that he might be about to make the return journey. But none could deny his political courage. 'I would go out tiger shooting with him any time', wrote Selborne, 'but I could never trust him in the absence of the tiger, because the motive power is always "self" and I don't think he has any principles.' His colleagues resented the way in which he squandered their time in Cabinet by delivering lengthy harangues. At his worst he could be 'noisy, rhetorical, tactless, & temperless – or -full'. Most Liberals were horrified by the war but he was both repelled and fascinated by it.[8] In contrast his closest associate in the Cabinet, the Chancellor of the Exchequer, David Lloyd George, showed little interest in preparations for war before 1914. He was Churchill's equal in energy and ability and in temperament. Therein lies the reason for their estrangement from their Liberal colleagues in 1915–16. They were both impatient of delay and anxious to see things done quickly.

By the Agadir crisis in 1911 this group of ministers were agreed that British policy had to be based on the continuation of the Triple Entente. In July 1911 Grey explained to C. P. Scott, the editor of the Liberal *Manchester Guardian*, that the foundation of his policy

> was to give France such support as would prevent her from falling under the virtual control of Germany and estrangement from us. This would mean the break up of the triple Entente and if France retired Russia would at once do the same and we should again be faced with the old troubles about the frontiers of India. It would also mean the complete ascendancy of Germany in Europe and some fine day we might have the First Lord of the Admiralty coming to us and saying that instead of building against two powers we had to build against six.[9]

They were also prepared to commit the small British regular army to the continent to support France. They believed that Britain could limit its participation in a land war to a token force of a handful of divisions. In February 1912 Lloyd George, looking back to the Agadir crisis, believed that

> the French Government had thrown away the finest opportunity they had ever had or were ever likely to have again, to try conclusions with Germany. They had the certainty of our armed support. The aid of 150,000 English soldiers would have had a great moral effect. Our Navy would have cut off Germany commercially from the West, Russia would have put pressure on the Eastern frontier of Germany, there would have been shortness of food and famine prices in Germany, commercial stagnation and financial disaster. He did not think that France would have crushed Germany as Germany had France in 1870, but it would have brought home to the Germans that they could not ride rough shod over Europe as they appeared to think.[10]

Their readiness during the Agadir crisis to participate in a European land war to preserve the balance of power set them apart from the rest of the Cabinet and Liberal party. In 1858 John Bright had condemned the balance of power as 'neither more nor less than a gigantic system of outdoor relief for the aristocracy of Great Britain'.[11] Many members of the radical wing of the Liberal Party and the Labour Party rejected both the balance of power and conscription as being inherently evil. They welcomed the Anglo-French Entente as a sign of good relations between the two countries but objected to the Anglo-Russian Entente because they disliked being associated with the repressive tsarist regime. They objected to Britain entering into peacetime alliances because they prevented it from performing its proper role as an international pacificator. They objected to conscription because the navy could protect Britain from invasion and because they feared it would encourage governments to embark on expensive foreign adventures against the wishes of the people. The idea of a conscript army also ran counter to their preference for voluntarism and they feared that it might be used by a future government as a tool of domestic repression. The way in which some Unionists supported conscription before 1914 only made Labour doubly suspicious that it was on a par with landlordism and capitalism. Grey continually had to look over his shoulder to appease radical suspicions. In December 1911 about eighty back-benchers formed the Liberal Foreign Affairs Committee to stop what they saw as Grey's tendency to move too close to Russia and France at the expense of a better understanding with Germany. More than any other group they were instrumental in ensuring that the Ententes did not blossom into alliances before 1914.[12]

The number of really committed radicals who simply wanted to ignore the balance of power was quite small. In the prewar Cabinet they were represented by Lord Loreburn, who resigned as Lord Chancellor in 1912, John Burns and Lord Morley, both of whom resigned in August 1914 rather than support Britain's entry into the war. Other radicals realized that although they might be the heirs of Bright, they were also the heirs of Gladstone. Whilst they were not prepared to intervene on the continent to uphold the balance of power they might be ready to do so to preserve the rights of small nations against aggression. The German invasion of Belgium allowed most of them to support the government with a more or less clear conscience in 1914. This group helped to bridge the gap between the out-and-out radicals and those ready to use force to preserve the Ententes.

One of them was Walter Runciman, President of the Board of Agriculture between 1911 and 1914 and President of the Board of Trade from the outbreak of war until the fall of the Asquith coalition. He was generally reckoned to be an able and hardworking departmental minister but lacking Churchill's political genius or Lloyd George's charm. That alone was enough to make him liked and respected by those Unionists who worked with him in 1915–16 even if they did not agree with his opposition to the Military Service Acts. Like his close friend Reginald McKenna, First Lord of the Admiralty from 1908 to 1911, Home Secretary 1911–15 and finally Chancellor of the Exchequer in the Asquith coalition, he made no secret of the fact that he disliked Lloyd George.

When McKenna was at the Home Office before the war his colleagues believed him to be an able administrator. Asquith rated his political courage and his intelligence very highly. But by early 1915 his handling of the aliens question and the bill to disestablish the Anglican church in Wales had made him one of the most unpopular men in the Cabinet and he was heartily loathed by the Unionists who entered the government in May 1915. Selborne described him as 'a bigoted Cobdenite radical with a narrow technical mind ... and the appearance of a cocksparrow'.[13] During the coalition period he was probably the Prime Minister's closest Liberal confidant.

During the Agadir crisis in 1911 Runciman and McKenna opposed the dispatch of troops to the continent but they were ready to support France by other means. Runciman explained their position when he wrote in September 1911 that

> What I have been most anxious about has been that this week which is critical should not pass without the French knowing that whatever support we may have to give her, it cannot be by six divisions, or four, or one on the Continent. The sea is our natural element and the sooner they realise that we are not going to land troops the better will be the chances of preserving Europe's peace.[14]

In 1912 they were instrumental in engineering the dispatch of Haldane to Berlin in an attempt to improve Anglo-German relations. Between 1912 and 1914 one of their number, the Colonial Secretary, Lewis Harcourt, did all he could to mend Britain's fences with Germany by helping to engineer agreements with it about outstanding colonial differences in Africa and the Middle East.[15]

The Cabinet received information and advice from several groups of advisers. Grey's senior officials were highly experienced diplomatists. Ambassadors were usually middle-aged men of wide experience. Sir George Buchanan, for example, had been a diplomat for 34 years before becoming ambassador to St Petersburg in 1910. In London Grey's most senior advisers, apart from his two successive permanent under secretaries, Sir Charles Hardinge (1905–10 and 1916–20) and Sir Arthur Nicolson (1910–16) were probably Sir William Tyrrell, his principal private secretary from 1907 to 1915 and Sir Eyre Crowe, promoted to assistant under secretary of state in 1912 and given responsibility for the Eastern and Western departments of the Foreign Office which dealt with relations with all the major and most of the minor European states. Tyrrell was 'a puckish and mundane Catholic with no zest for groundwork but strong on the wings of flair and forecast'. Crowe, by contrast was noted for his application to detail and prodigious hard work.[16]

Grey and his professional advisers had two other things in common apart from their shared suspicion of Germany. They insisted that the conduct of foreign affairs required a high degree of freedom from public scrutiny. Before the war, although there were some unofficial links between the Foreign Office and certain privileged London newspapers, there was never any attempt systematically to educate the public about foreign affairs. On a certain range of issues the Foreign Office simply believed that the public would react in a certain manner. Their policies were therefore sometimes subject to a good deal of ill-informed criticism, but in 1914 they correctly predicted that war over Serbia would be unpopular but that war over Belgium would not.[17] They also believed that, in the conduct of foreign affairs, personalities counted for just as much as ideologies and that foreign policy-making in other countries was not an autonomous activity but the product of domestic political circumstances. They based their recommendations concerning the future trends of French or Russian policy on a close analysis of public opinion as expressed in the press, by political meetings and in conversation with the various political personalities with whom they came into contact. As Harold Nicolson, who received his diplomatic education in the Foreign Office before 1914 wrote, diplomacy was very sensitive to 'any shifting in the incidence of sovereignty'.[18]

The men who guided British policy after 1906 belonged to one generation. Most had been born in the 1850s and 1860s and reached maturity in the 1880s. As young men they had learnt to recognize France and Russia as Britain's two major rivals long before Germany had usurped that role, and it was a lesson which they never quite forgot. The Anglo-French Entente of 1904 originated in the desire of the Unionist government to settle Britain's colonial differences with France lest they find themselves dragged into a war neither of them wanted by their allies Japan and Russia.[19] It was not initially directed against Germany. Colonial and economic rivalry had been a feature of Anglo-German relations in the late nineteenth century and by 1902 the growth of the new German navy had convinced many of the government's professional advisers at the Foreign Office, War Office and Admiralty, that Germany rather than France and Russia was Britain's most immediate and dangerous rival. The Entente was therefore welcomed because it lessened Britain's need to look to Germany for diplomatic support and the German attempt to destroy it during the Moroccan crisis of 1905 only served to drive Britain and France closer together. In 1907 fear of German penetration in the Ottoman empire, coupled with the realization that the British simply could not defend India if a Russian army entered Afghanistan, led Grey to sign a second Entente with Russia. Ostensibly it was no more than a settlement of colonial differences. But Grey hoped that it would persuade the Russians to turn their attention towards Europe and to act as a makeweight against Germany.[20]

The Ententes had to be carefully nurtured. They did not eliminate all imperial rivalries between the signatories. The British had continued disagreements with the French about Egypt, the French arms trade in the Persian Gulf and above all over Morocco. For the sake of the Entente, Unionist journalists voiced their criticisms of French imperialism in Morocco in private but their Liberal colleagues had no such compunction. However, these were as nothing compared to the criticisms directed at the workings of the Anglo-Russian Entente. The Russians were criticized by the left and the right. Unionists like the ex-Viceroy of India, Lord Curzon, believed that Grey had conceded too much to the Russians. Radical Liberal and Labour MPs disliked the whole idea of their government co-operating with the autocratic tsarist regime, sometimes preferring themselves to work with emigre opponents of the tsar.[21] By 1912 Russian power was reviving after the Russo-Japanese war and the 1905 revolution. They had resumed their penetration into Tibet, Mongolia and Chinese Turkestan and Persia. Nicolson believed that when the Russians realized they could confront Germany without British support, they might abandon the Entente. Persia became the main touchstone of Anglo-Russian relations. For the sake of their continued friendship he was ready to sacrifice future British interests in Persia by partitioning the neutral zone and to transform the Entente into an alliance.[22] But the India Office objected that permitting the Russians to come even nearer to the frontier of India was too high a price to pay. Tyrrell agreed that Russian power was advancing rapidly but dismissed the idea of a Russo-German *rapprochement* as most unlikely and insisted that the British could adopt a firm stand in Persia without threatening the Entente. Grey agreed with his private secretary and up to 1914 he continued to temporize with the Russians in the hope of avoiding an awkward question which could become a divisive issue within his party.[23]

After 1905 the Anglo-German antagonism in Europe took precedence over the continued threats to Britain's imperial position in the Middle East and around the frontiers of India. But the outbreak of war in August 1914 did not cause the Entente partners to forget their prewar differences. At one and the same time the British were careful not to offend the susceptibilities of their Entente partners but they also moved to protect their own interests. When the whole Eastern Question was opened up in 1914–15 by the apparently imminent collapse of Turkey, British desiderata were chosen not only with an eye towards securing Britain's postwar position against Germany but also against France and Russia.

The British were not the only people who believed that the prewar Ententes were less than perfect. They were criticized in France and Russia by two different groups, those who did not think that Britain was a worthwhile friend and wished to strengthen their relationship before a real crisis arose, and those who thought that the British were the wrong partners entirely and wanted an agreement with Germany instead. The British listened to the first group because they were the best friends of the Entente. Many Frenchmen believed that until Britain introduced conscription and could field a continental-scale army, its help would not be worth having. In December 1907, for example, the Germanophobe Georges Clemenceau told the British ambassador Sir Francis Bertie that 'he considers it to be a grave error for England to rely entirely on her ships. The day may and probably will come perhaps soon or in the course of ten or twenty years hence when it will be essential for the welfare of England and of Europe that She [*sic*] should have a respectable military force for operations on the continent.'[24] Senior French generals agreed with him. In April 1911 General Foch told the British military attaché that he hoped the British would send their army to France at the very start of the war because of the uplift it would give to French morale if they saw the British fighting side by side with them.[25] The British were too ready to dismiss such sentiments as further proof of the instability of the 'Latin temperament'. The French were more aware than the British of the importance of such psychological factors in sustaining national morale. The French General Staff were dismissive of the British reply that what they lacked in land power they could more than make up for in warships. In February 1913 General Joffre, the French Commander-in-Chief thought that the Royal Navy would be worth only a single soldier in a land war against Germany.[26] From 1906 the Anglo-French Entente was accompanied by intermittent staff talks between the General Staffs of the two countries.[27] But Grey never gave the French what they most wanted, a binding promise of British military support in the event of a Franco-German war. This equivocation in British policy was a major source of tension in the Entente before 1914.

Doubts also grew in Russia about the nature of their loosely-defined relationship with Britain. By the end of 1913 the Russian foreign minister, S. D. Sazonov, was convinced that Germany did not especially fear the Franco-Russian alliance, but that it would be much more wary of engaging in any dangerous foreign adventures if the British were more firmly associated with them. Grey would not agree to a formal peacetime alliance and so the tsar suggested that naval staff talks might be conducted instead as a second best. Grey's response was cautious and equivocal. He minuted that 'If the French agreed we might let the Russians know what has passed between military and naval authorities on each side but we had better postpone discussions of anything as long as we can'.[28] The French did agree. They were concerned that unless something was done the Russians might drift into the German camp. In April 1914 Grey agreed to open naval conversations with the Russians. But he added a series of provisos which all but nullified his agreement, insisting that Britain still had no definite engagements with either France or Russia, pointing out that whether or not Britain engaged in a continental war would depend on the state of public opinion and adding that close relations with Russia were made especially difficult by the repressive reputation the tsarist regime had in Britain.[29]

The Foreign Office had to pay equal attention to the second group of critics, those who preferred a *rapprochement* with Germany to an Entente with Britain, because one day they might come to power and be able to implement their policy. Outwardly the governments of the Third Republic appeared to be very unstable. France had no less than twelve governments between 1910 and 1914. The British overlooked the fact that behind the rapid coming and going of governments some continuity was provided by the fact that the same ministers often sat in successive Cabinets. Many British observers were baffled by French politics and shared the opinion of Lord Loreburn who dismissed the French government in July 1911 as 'a tinpot Government. Germany has but to stamp her foot and they will give way.'[30] Some Frenchmen concluded that Britain's unwillingness to become a major land power meant that it was only a fair-weather friend and that France should therefore mend its fences with Germany rather than become Britain's continental catspaw.[31] Between 1907 and 1911, under the acquiescent foreign minister Stephen Pichon, the French ambassador at Berlin, Jules Cambon, worked unobtrusively for a Franco-German detente. In 1909, for example, he privately urged Pichon that in any future negotiations the question of Alsace–Lorraine, which had divided France and Germany since 1871, should be laid aside as the Germans would never be prepared to surender them. He was thwarted by a combination of the Germanophobe bureaucrats of the French foreign ministry and the policies of the Prime Minister, later President, Raymond Poincaré. Poincaré was determined to maintain the Franco-Russian alliance and the Anglo-French Entente and to keep the two power blocs of the Triple Alliance and the Triple Entente firmly separate.[32]

While those who thought like Poincaré were in power in France the British could be reasonably certain that, despite some grumbles, the French would maintain the Entente. The real threat to its continuation, however, sprang from the fact that some French politicians wanted to follow Cambon's course. The man most feared and distrusted by the Foreign Office was Joseph Caillaux, the French premier during the Agadir crisis. When Joffe told him that France did not have a 70 per cent chance of winning a Franco-German war he decided to negotiate. He did so by circumventing his own foreign ministry officials in Paris. When the Foreign Office in London heard of this they were alarmed. They believed that Caillaux might be a very able finance minister but he was otherwise a crook. Crowe denounced him in January 1912 as 'the instigator and promoter of the policy of general co-operation with Germany'. Sir

Edward Goschen, the British ambassador to Berlin, thought that 'there seems to have been a lot of shady work in France'.[33] Shortly after the conclusion of the crisis Caillaux fell from power, but in 1913 he became the leader of the largest party in the Chamber of Deputies, the Radicals. In the years immediately preceding the war, France experienced a nationalist revival. But it was comparatively weak, being confined to the national political leadership and to the youth of Paris. It was counterbalanced by the rapid growth of the French Socialist party, the SFIO, and the main trade union federation, the CGT, both of which were publicly pledged to take collective action to prevent war. The Radicals and the Socialists opposed the introduction of the Three Year Service Law in 1913 and contemporaries believed that the general election of 1914 demonstrated substantial opposition not only to the law but also to Poincaré's diplo-macy. One authority has stated that 'It was widely feared, not least in government, that French opinion lacked the cohesion needed to see it through a war'.[34] The possibility that Caillaux might return to power and resume negotiations with the Germans was a constant source of concern for many British policy-makers after the war began.

Before 1914 Grey did everything he could within the limits of the domestic political constraints within which he was forced to operate to avoid upsetting the French. He welcomed Poincaré's determination to uphold the Entente but that meant he was also a more demanding partner than his predecessor. In an effort to stifle French fears that the Haldane mission to Berlin in 1912 heralded a major Anglo–German *rapprochement* at France's expense, the British agreed to sign the Mediterranean agree-ment with France. Henceforth the French fleet was concentrated in the Mediterranean and the Royal Navy was concentrated in the North Sea. The agreement contained a preamble to the effect that it was not to be politically binding on either government in the event of war. But a politically binding agreement was just what Poincaré wanted. In July 1912 Bertie reported that he believed that 'If the Entente does not mean that England will come to the aid of France in the event of Germany attacking the French ports its value to France is not great, so says Poincaré'.[35] By 1913 the Foreign Office knew that the British were not meeting France's expectations. In October 1913 Nicolson wrote to Hardinge that 'I fear that France is beginning to have some doubts as to whether in case of need she could really count upon us with absolute certainty, and even whether the assistance we might be disposed to render would be of any great benefit'.[36]

Interpreting any 'shifting in the incidence of sovereignty' in Russia was even more difficult.[37] The Foreign Office paid very careful attention to even the most trivial events to try to ascertain who really wielded power in St Petersburg. Russian ministers were responsible personally to the tsar, not collectively or individually to the Duma. As Cecil Spring-Rice, who was secretary of the embassy at St Petersburg between 1903 and 1906 explained, 'There is no Cabinet – each minister reports separately to the Emperor. Consequently no one considers himself to be bound by anything another minister says.'[38] The British quickly developed their favourite and their not-so-favourite Russian politicians. The former included men like A. P. Isvolskii, the foreign minister from 1906 to 1910 and, crucially, S. D. Sazonov, his successor from 1910 to 1916. Both were believed to be strongly in favour of close relations with France and Britain. Similarly the British recognized that Russian liberals inside and outside the Duma supported the Entente. They looked to liberal Britain as their mentor and blamed many of the illiberal aspects of the tsarist regime on German influence.[39] Conversely the British recognized that 'reactionary' circles around the Russian court and the parties of the right in the Duma and the right-wing press remembered that Prussia had been Russia's long-standing ally and looked to the Kaiser as the strongest supporter of autocracy in Europe. Members of these groups deprecated the French alliance because France was anti-clerical and republican and they were afraid that it might drag Russia into a war with Germany simply to recover the lost provinces of Alsace–Lorraine. They disliked the Entente with Britain because it appeared to give Russia too little compensation in Persia or Asia and because the British had been reluctant to support them during the Bosnian crisis of 1908–9. One of their leaders before 1914 was the Russian elder statesman S. Witte, the mastermind of Russia's rapid industrialization in the late nineteenth century.[40]

Grey believed that Russian policy depended upon who had the tsar's ear. In theory the tsar had complete control over Russian foreign and defence policy. The Duma might refuse to vote funds but if they did so he could dissolve them. Nicholas II was not susceptible to public opinion. He lived outside St Petersburg and had little contact with his people. His isolation made it difficult for the British to predict how his policies might develop. Buchanan's contacts with him were correct but never intimate. The Foreign Office believed that Nicholas's own inclinations were in favour of the Franco-Russian alliance and the Anglo-Russian Entente but it was impossible to ascertain just how much influence the reactionaries and pro-Germans might be able to exert over him. Grey described him as 'an honourable and conscientious man but not one of such ability and grasp as to be beyond the influence of suggestion or misrepresentation'.[41] When the tsar met the Kaiser at Potsdam in November 1910 both Buchanan and Nicolson were afraid that their meeting might be the first step towards the reconstruction of the *Dreikaiserbund* and the end of the Entente.[42] A particular *bête noir* of the British was the tsarina, formerly a German princess. As the war progressed they believed that she exerted an increasingly pernicious influence over the course of Russian politics by using her influence to find places for pro-Germans in the administration.

In March 1914 Witte publicly demanded an alliance between France, Russia and Germany. He denounced Britain as Russia's enemy, blaming it for Russia's defeat during the Russo-Japanese war. Buchanan found this ominous. 'There has always been a German party at Court', he wrote to Grey, 'and there can be no doubt that persons in the immediate entourage of the Emperor not infrequently contrast the material advantages to be derived from an understanding with Germany with the very problematic ones which the Anglo-Russian understanding has to offer.'[43] Witte died in late 1914 but the policy he represented did not die with him and the British were never able to ignore the possibility that eventually the Russians might find an accommodation with Germany more comfortable than the Entente with Britain.

On the eve of war the British had an alliance with neither France nor Russia. Nor did it have a continental-scale conscript army which could intervene decisively in a European land war. These facts were deprecated by its friends in the Entente countries and deplored by its enemies. There were also some voices in Britain raised in favour of a continental policy of alliances and conscription. The National Service League was established in 1902. In public, it campaigned for conscription for home defence but, in private, some of its leaders like Lord Roberts saw that as only the first step towards creating the conscript army they believed the British would have to raise to support France in a war against Germany. This conviction was shared by the General Staff's Director of Military Operations (DMO) between 1910 and 1914, Brigadier-General Henry Wilson. During the Agadir crisis he wanted a defensive alliance with France, Russia, Belgium and Denmark. Churchill liked the idea and pressed it on Grey. But Sir William Nicholson, the CIGS, and Haldane, poured scorn on it. Britain simply did not have enough troops to assist Belgium and Denmark. The Belgian government were unresponsive and the idea was dropped. But Wilson had shown Churchill the need to seek allies among the smaller powers, and this was a quest into which he was to fling himself with a will once the war had started.[44]

Many British soldiers had a high opinion of the French and Russian armies. British officers had observed French and German military manoeuvres and had come away with certain fixed opinions about the two armies. French qualities of dash and *élan* and superior French tactics were thought to make them more than a match for the rather wooden Germans.[45] British soldiers, perpetually concerned with the defence of the North West Frontier of India, had overestimated Russia's military potential for nearly a century and the Russo-Japanese war did not cause many of them to alter their ideas. They blamed Russia's defeat on a few incompetent generals and, like the French, believed that by the eve of war the Russians had learnt from their past mistakes and put their house in order. After the Agadir crisis the Germans began to increase the size of their army and the Russians retaliated by inaugurating their own 'Great Programme'. By 1917 they intended to double the strength of their peacetime army to 2,245,000 men. Their active army would then be larger than the combined forces of the Triple Alliance. Furthermore as the Russians only trained 25 per cent of potential recruits compared to 52 per cent in Germany and 80 per cent in France it appeared to some Foreign Office officials that the Russians had the potential to become the most formidable military power in Europe.[46] The British propensity to base their estimates of Russian power on a simple counting of heads had two effects on British policy in 1914. In the first instance it blinded them to some of the fundamental weakness of the Russian economy which served to vitiate their war effort and secondly the need to counterbalance any great accretion of power to Russia after Germany had been defeated was one of the constant themes underlying the development of British war aims after 1914.

But although the Russians might win in the East because of their superior numbers, morale would count for as much as manpower in the West. Wilson wanted to send British troops to the continent both to sustain French morale and to give the Entente a crucial numerical advantage in northern France.[47] He was a conscriptionist because he thought that history had overtaken the voluntary system. In the eighteenth century, European armies had been small and so Britain had been able to maintain the balance of power with a small army. But in 1914 European armies were much larger and victory would go to the big battalions. A professional army might be able to match a conscript army at the start of a war but it lacked the large trained reserves that only conscription could provide to enable it to make good its losses in a prolonged war.[48] Several Foreign Office officials would have welcomed a defensive alliance with France and Russia but few, except Nicolson, agreed with Wilson that Britain needed a conscript army to maintain the European balance. A large navy and a small professional army had brought Britain great rewards in the past and they were loath to abandon it. Eyre Crowe described sea power as being always more potent than land power and Goschen thought that only the Royal Navy stood between Europe and German hegemony.[49] The Admiralty's operational plans revolved around two concepts. They intended to blockade Germany's ports to bring about the collapse of its economy and they contemplated combined operations against its coastline in an effort to force Germany to divert large numbers of troops away from the French frontier. In making these recommendations they ignored the fact that Germany did not depend on overseas trade for its economic survival and that its trade could still be carried on through contiguous neutrals. The Admiralty could not predict how long it would take before a blockade really began to bite and since 1902 the army had become increasingly reluctant to be dragged into combined operations, if for no other reason than that the German railway network would make it easy for them to concentrate enough troops to crush any landing. Britain still needed a large navy to defend its own shores and ensure the safe arrival of imports but the exponents of sea power as a decisive offensive weapon were living in the past. They did not fully understand the revolutionary implications that the coming of the railways had on the exercise of sea power. As ships became ever bigger and better armed observers were too willing to extrapolate their greater tactical power on to the strategic plane. They were misled by the comparative ease with which, in the nineteenth century, European navies had on occasion been able to overawe non-industrial powers into believing that sea power could be a decisive weapon against a continental land power.[50]

The Liberal government opted for a compromise between the policies advocated by the General Staff, the Admiralty and Foreign Office. Grey rejected a defensive alliance with France or Russia. The major row which erupted in his party and Cabinet in November 1911 over his strongly pro-French stance during the Agadir crisis demonstrated that his party would not accept a binding military commitment to the French.[51] Moreover he never entirely abandoned the hope of a *rapprochement* with Germany, provided that it did not threaten the existing Ententes, and that *rapprochement* would become even more improbable if he was bound to France and Russia by a treaty of alliance. The government also refused to introduce conscription. By 1913–14 those ministers who concerned themselves with contingency planning had drifted into believing that if the Cabinet did decide to intervene in a war between France and Russia on the one hand and Germany and Austria–Hungary on the other, Britain would only make a token contribution to the land war. Instinctively their thoughts went back to the Napoleonic Wars which they thought Britain had won because the navy had made it absolutely secure against invasion while small amphibious operations had encouraged continental allies to coalesce and defeat the French on land.[52] If the British did support France and Russia, its major contribution to the war effort would be in the shape of the Royal Navy. It would keep Britain's own sea lanes open and blockade Germany. British manufacturers would make good their lost German markets by 'capturing' Germany's extra-European trade and by supplying France and Russia with the material they needed to win the land war. Whatever the public may have believed in 1914 about the war being over by Christmas, the government before 1914 did not assume that a European war would necessarily be over quickly provided that the initial economic dislocation caused by the outbreak of hostilities did not produce total economic collapse. In March 1912 the Committee of Imperial Defence asked the General Staff to estimate the likely duration of a war against Germany. They refused to predict the likely maximum duration, merely giving them the delphic response that 'it would not be safe to calculate the war lasting less than six months'.[53] If the war was anything other than very short, Britain's economic potential would become very significant. In a war between the Dual Alliance and the Triple Alliance (minus Italy), the latter would have a much larger economic base. But if Britain joined the French and Russians the balance of economic advantage would shift clearly to the Entente.[54] The enemy would be defeated by a combination of British gold and French and Russian soldiers. The strategy of 'business as usual' had the inestimable advantage to the British that they would not have to pay the heavy blood tax of a continental land war. But whether it would suffice in a prolonged struggle in which Britain's allies suffered heavy casualties but won few victories was another matter. One lesson of the Napoleonic Wars which the exponents of 'business as usual' had overlooked was that the exercise of British sea power had not only annoyed its enemies but it had also upset its allies. The day of the professional mercenary was past. By 1914 men expected to fight for a cause and they also expected their allies to make an equal sacrifice. Dying in the cause of making the British richer might have little appeal to French or Russian soldiers.

'Business as usual' would also minimize the domestic disruption that the war would cause. No one anticipated that Kitchener would be able to raise a huge volunteer army. Hence there was no need for the state to plan to take command of economic resources to support the war effort. The army was believed to have enough ammunition stockpiled to last it for six months, by which time the government's ordnance factories and the private arms manufacturers would have taken their reserve machinery out of mothballs and would be able to supply the army's modest wants in the usual way. The economic planning conducted by the Committee of Imperial Defence before 1914 was not designed to mobilize the economy for war but to prevent the outbreak of war causing economic collapse. To reduce that possibility they planned to act around the margins of the economy to ensure the continued movement of trade. In their domestic social policy the Liberal government had demonstrated that they believed that judicious piecemeal reforms could produce a better educated, better housed, more sober and fitter population which would therefore be more economically productive. In the wartime emergency they intended to adopt the same approach. They did not plan to pursue a policy of *laissez-faire* but nor did they plan to establish a command economy. Ensuring the arrival of adequate quantities of supplies was their first priority, keeping prices down was only a secondary consideration. They planned to take over the war risk insurance market and the railways to ensure the continued importation and transportation of food and raw materials. The professional brokers and managers would become *de facto* civil servants for the duration of the war. This pattern of co-opting businessmen into government as quasi civil servants was to be followed on countless occasions throughout the war.[55]

Notes

1   Edward David (ed.), *Inside Asquith's Cabinet: From the Diaries of Charles Hobhouse* (London: John Murray, 1977), p. 229.
2   Lord Selborne, The War Cabinet, *c.* July 1916, Selborne mss, file 80, ff. 285–90; C. Hazlehurst, 'Asquith as Prime Minister, 1908–1916', *English Historical Review*, vol. 85, no. 336 (1970), pp. 502–31.
3   Selborne, The War Cabinet; Michael and Eleanor Brock (eds), *H. H. Asquith: Letters to Venetia Stanley* (London: Oxford University Press, 1982), pp. 452, 545; David (ed.), *Inside Asquith's Cabinet*, p. 120.
4   Zara Steiner, 'The Foreign Office, 1905–1914', in F. H. Hinsley (ed.), *British Foreign Policy under Sir Edward Grey* (Cambridge: Cambridge University Press, 1977), pp. 24–5.
5   K. Robbins, 'Sir Edward Grey and the British Empire', *Journal of Imperial and Commonwealth History*, vol. 1, no. 2 (1972–3), pp. 213–21; C. J. Lowe and M. L. Dockrill, *The Mirage of Power: British Foreign Policy 1902–1914*, Vol. 1 (London: Routledge & Kegan Paul, 1972), p. 18; K. M. Wilson, 'Imperial interests in the British decision for war, 1914: the defence of India in Central Asia', *Review of International Studies*, vol. 10, no. 3 (1984), pp. 189–90.
6   David (ed.), *Inside Asquith's Cabinet*, pp. 120, 230; Lord Hankey, *The Supreme Command 1914–1918*, Vol. 1 (London: Allen & Unwin, 1961), pp. 184–5.
7   David (ed.), *Inside Asquith's Cabinet*, p. 120.
8   Selborne, The War Cabinet; David (ed.), *Inside Asquith's Cabinet*, p. 231; Brock (eds), *H. H. Asquith*, pp. 415, 449; R. S. Churchill, *Winston S. Churchill*, Vol. 2, *Companion*, pt 2, *1907–1911* (London: Heinemann, 1969), p. 912; Sir A. Fitzroy, *Memoirs* (London: Hutchinson, 1923), p. 594.
9   T. Wilson (ed.), *The Political Diaries of C. P. Scott, 1911–1928* (London: Collins, 1970), p. 51; see also G. P. Gooch and H. W. V. Temperley (eds), *British Documents on the Origins of the War, 1898–1914*, Vol. 6 (London: HMSO, 1932), p. 784 (henceforth BDOW); Churchill to Lloyd George, 31 August 1911, Lloyd George mss, C/3/15/7.
10   Lowe and Dockrill, *Mirage of Power*, Vol. 3, p. 452; Public Record Office (henceforth PRO) FO 800/100, Asquith to Grey, 7 September 1908.
11   M. Howard, *War and the Liberal Conscience* (London: Temple Smith, 1978), p. 43.
12   *Hansard*, 51 HC Deb., 5s. cols 1533, 1591–3, 11 April 1913; F. Eyck, *G. P. Gooch: A Study in History and Politics* (London: Macmillan, 1982), p. 232; D. French, *British Economic and Strategic Planning, 1905–1915* (London: Allen & Unwin, 1982), pp. 25–6; A. Clinton, 'Trade Councils during the First World War', *International Review of Social History*, vol. 15 (1970), pp. 215–16.
13   Selborne, The War Cabinet.
14   Runciman to Harcourt, 4 September 1911, Runciman mss, WR 63.
15   R. Langhorne, 'Anglo-German negotiations concerning the future of the Portuguese colonies, 1911–1914', *Historical Journal*, vol. 16 no. 24 (1973), pp. 386–7; Zara Steiner, *Britain and the Origins of the First World War* (London: Macmillan, 1977), pp. 105–9.
16   R. G. Vansittart, First Baron Vansittart, *The Mist Procession: The Auto-*

biography of Lord Vansittart (London: Hutchinson, 1958), p, 45; R. A. Jones, *The British Diplomatic Service 1815–1914* (Gerrards Cross: Colin Smythe, 1983).

17 K. M. Wilson, 'The Foreign Office and the "education" of public opinion before the First World War', *Historical Journal*, vol. 26, no. 2 (1983), pp. 403–10; M. Sanders and P. M. Taylor, *British Propaganda during the First World War 1914–1918* (London: Macmillan, 1982), pp. 1–12.

18 H. Nicolson, *Diplomacy* (London: Oxford University Press, 1939/1969), p. 35; Sir G. Buchanan, *My Mission to Russia and other Diplomatic Memories*, Vol. 1 (London: Cassell, 1923), pp. 107–8.

19 G. Monger, *The End of Isolation: British Foreign Policy 1900–1907* (London: Nelson, 1963), pp. 104–46.

20 ibid., pp. 99–102; P. M. Kennedy, *The Rise of the Anglo-German Antagonism, 1860–1914* (London: Allen & Unwin, 1980).

21 D. B. Saunders, 'Stepniak and the London emigration. Letters to Robert Spence Watson, 1887–1890', *Oxford Slavonic Papers*, vol. 13 (1980), pp. 80–93; A. J. A. Morris, *The Scaremongers: The Advocacy of War and Rearmament 1896–1914* (London: Routledge & Kegan Paul, 1984), pp. 286–7.

22 E. Corp, 'Sir William Tyrrell: The eminence grise of the British Foreign Office, 1912–1915', *Historical Journal*, vol. 25, no. 3 (1982), p. 702; Wilson, 'Imperial interests in the British decision for war, 1914', pp. 193–4.

23 Corp, 'Sir William Tyrrell', pp. 700–5.

24 *BDOW*, Vol. 8, pp. 156–7; *BDOW*, Vol. 6, pp. 149, 168; K. A. Hamilton, 'Great Britain and France, 1905–1911', in F. H. Hinsley (ed.), *British Foreign Policy under Sir Edward Grey* (Cambridge: Cambridge University Press, 1977), pp. 113–131.

25 *BDOW*, Vol. 6, pp. 617–19; see also Sir G. Arthur, *Not Worth Reading* (London: Longman Green, 1938), p. 177.

26 Sir C. E. Callwell, *Field Marshal Sir Henry Wilson: His Life and Diaries*, Vol. 1 (London: Cassell, 1927), p. 122.

27 S. R. Williamson, *The Politics of Grand Strategy: Britain and France Prepare for War 1904–1914* (Cambridge, Mass: Harvard University Press, 1969).

28 *BDOW*, Vol. 10, pt 2, pp. 777–83; D. C. B. Lieven, *Russia and the Origins of the First World War* (London: Macmillan, 1983), pp. 48–9.

29 PRO FO 800/94, Grey to Bertie, 1 May 1914; Viscount Grey, *Twenty-Five Years, 1892–1916*, Vol. 1 (London: Hodder & Stoughton, 1925), pp. 282–6.

30 T. Wilson (Ed.), *The Political Diaries of C. P. Scott*, pp. 43–4; N. Stone, *Europe Transformed, 1878–1919* (London: Fontana, 1983), pp. 272–4.

31 *BDOW*. Vol. 6, pp. 149, 168.

32 J. F. Keiger, *France and the Origins of the First World War* (London: Macmillan, 1983); J. F. Keiger, 'Jules Cambon and Franco-German detente, 1907–1914', *Historical Journal*, vol. 26, no. 3 (1983), pp. 641–6.

33 C. H. D. Howard (ed.), *The Diary of Sir Edward Goschen 1900–1914* (London: Royal Historical Society, 1980), p. 258; *BDOW*, Vol. 7, p. 821; Keiger, *France*, p. 35.

34 D. Stevenson, *French War Aims against Germany 1914–1919* (Oxford: Clarendon Press, 1982), p. 7; Keiger, *France*, pp. 141–2; N. Papayanis, 'Collaboration and Pacifism in France during World War One', *Francia*, vol. 5 (1977), pp. 426–8; *BDOW*, Vol. 10, pt 2, pp. 674–5.

35 *BDOW*, Vol. 10, pt 2, p. 607; Lowe and Dockrill, *Mirage of Power*, Vol. 3, p. 457.

36 *BDOW*, Vol. 10, pt 1, p. 51.

37 Nicolson, *Diplomacy*, p. 35.

38   Spring-Rice to St Loe Strachey, 4 April 1904, St Loe Strachey mss, S/13/14/12.
39   Lieven, *Russia*, pp. 124–30.
40   K. Neilson, 'Wishful thinking; The Foreign Office and Russia, 1907–1917', in B. J. C. McKercher and D. J. Moss (eds), *Shadow and Substance in British Foreign Policy 1895–1935. Memorial Essays Honouring C. J. Lowe* (Edmonton, Alberta: University of Alberta Press, 1984), pp. 152–9; D. C. B. Lieven, 'Pro-Germans and Russian foreign policy 1890–1914', *International History Review*, vol. 2, no. 1 (1980), pp. 34–53.
41   Grey, *Twenty-Five Years*, Vol. 1, p. 286; Lieven, *Russia*, pp. 50–7; Buchanan, *My Mission*, pp. 170–5.
42   *BDOW*, Vol. 10, pt 2, pp. 589–90, 599–600.
43   *BDOW*, Vol. 10, pt 2, pp. 769–80, 777–90.
44   Callwell, *Sir Henry Wilson*, Vol. 1, p. 102; K. M. Wilson, 'The War Office, Churchill and the Belgium option, August to December 1911', *Bulletin of the Institute of Historical Research*, vol. 50 (1977), pp. 218–28; Churchill, *Companion*, Vol. 2, pt 2, pp. 1116–17.
45   P. Towle, 'The European balance of power in 1914', *Army Quarterly and Defence Journal*, vol. 104 (1974), pp. 333–42; Maxse to Wilson, 1 June 1914, Wilson mss, 73/1/81; General Staff, War Office, *Report on Foreign Manoeuvres* (1907), pp. 28–35, 52, 66–7; (1912), p. 49; (1913), pp. 24, 56.
46   General Staff, War Office, *Report on Foreign Manoeuvres* (1910), pp. 198; (1912), p. 111; (1913), pp. 79–80; British Military Attaché, St Petersburg to Buchanan, 20 December 1911, Wilson mss, 73/1/24.
47   J. Gooch, *The Plans of War: The General Staff and British Military Strategy, c. 1900–1916* (London: Routledge & Kegan Paul, 1974), pp. 278–95; N. d'Ombraine, *War Machinery and High Policy* (Oxford: Clarendon Press, 1973), pp. 81–9; H. Wilson, Appreciation of the political and military situation in Europe, 20 September 1911, Wilson mss, 73/1/24; PRO WO 33/364, War Office, Records of a strategic war game, 1905; PRO WO 106/46/E2/1, Callwell to Ballard, 3 October 1905; PRO WO 106/47/E2/17, General Staff, British military policy in a war between France and Germany, 26 November 1908; PRO WO 106/47/E2/23, H. Wilson, The necessity for co-operation with France in the event of war between it and Germany, 11 August 1911; PRO WO 106/47/E2/25, H. Wilson, Examination of conditions of a war between France and Germany and the role of the BEF, 12 August 1911; K. M. Wilson, 'To the western front: British war plans and the "military entente" with France before the First World War', *British Journal of International Studies*, Vol. 3, no. 2 (1977), p. 156.
48   H. Wilson, Standard of Efficiency – Lecture II, 25 November 1907, Wilson mss, 73/1/17; H. Wilson, Is conscription necessary?, 1 November 1909, Wilson mss, 73/1/17.
49   Callwell, *Sir H. Wilson*, Vol. 1, p. 93; *BDOW*, Vol. 6, p. 536.
50   A. J. Marder, *The Anatomy of British Sea Power: A History of British Naval Policy in the Pre-Dreadnought Era 1880–1905* (Hamden, Conn.: Archon reprints, 1964), pp. 504–6; P. Haggie, 'The royal navy and war planning in the Fisher era', *Journal of Contemporary History*, vol. 8, no. 3 (1973), pp. 118–21; P. Kemp (ed.), *The Papers of Admiral Sir John Fisher*, Vol. 2 (London: Navy Records Society, 1964), pp. 315–60; P. M. Kennedy, *The Rise and Fall of British Naval Mastery* (London: Allen Lane, 1976), pp. 253–5; G. Hardach, *The First World War 1914–1918* (London: Allen Lane, 1977), p. 32; C. I. Hamilton, 'Naval power and diplomacy in the nineteenth century', *Journal of Strategic Studies*, vol. 3, no. 1 (1980), pp. 74–86.

51 David (ed.), *Inside Asquith's Cabinet*, pp. 107–8; Gainford mss, diary entries, 24 October and 1 November 1911; Haldane to Elizabeth Haldane, 13 and 16 November 1911, Haldane mss, 6011.

52 See, for example, Charles Trevelyan to Runciman [n.d. but *c*. 1911–12], Trevelyan mss, CPT 30.

53 PRO CAB 16/18B, Note by the General Staff, Standing sub-committee of the Committee of Imperial Defence. Inquiry regarding trading with the enemy, 14 March 1912.

54 P. M. Kennedy, 'The First World War and the international power system', *International Security*, vol. 9, no. 1 (1984), pp. 7–40.

55 French, *British Economic and Strategic Planning*, pp. 22–84.

2

Maritime Operations,
August–October 1914

THE CABINET'S decision to intervene in the war in August 1914 and the policies they pursued in the next two months did not represent any fundamental departure from the strategic or political principles they had evolved before the war. The outbreak of war did not eradicate the prewar tensions which had existed between Britain and its Entente partners. Nor did it lead to a common agreement about how to fight the war. This was at least partly due to the fact that behind all the rhetoric about the need to uphold the public law of Europe and to maintain the rights of small nations against aggression, there remained real confusion about why Britain had entered the conflict. Neither the dispatch of the British Expeditionary Force (BEF) to France nor the raising of the New Armies meant that all the Cabinet accepted the need to maintain the balance of power in Europe by committing a powerful army to the continent. The dispatch of the BEF was regarded by most Cabinet ministers as an amphibious operation which could be rapidly terminated if it appeared that the force was in serious danger. Kitchener's New Armies were not designed to play a major part in the land fighting. He raised them to ensure that Britain won the peace. British strategy in the opening months of the war bore marked similarities to the policies pursued by Pitt the Younger in the 1790s. Asquith and his colleagues launched a series of expeditions to capture Germany's colonies both to protect Britain's overseas possessions and trade routes and in the hope that they would be able to use them as bargaining counters at the peace conference. They sought allies, in Scandinavia, in the Mediterranean and the Balkans in order to isolate the Central Powers and in the hope of throwing the burden of the land war still further on to the shoulders of others. But German successes in Belgium and France forced them to turn their attention back to northern France. It was the Russians, worried lest the French capitulate if Paris fell, not the British, who turned the Entente into an alliance in September 1914 by insisting upon Britain signing the Pact of London. The British did not completely commit themselves to playing a full part in the continental land war until the spring of 1916.

At the end of July the Cabinet viewed the prospect of war with revulsion and it seemed for some days that Britain might be able to stand aloof. On 29 July ministers agreed that if the Germans did violate Belgium's neutrality Britain should act only if it was deemed to be in its political interests to do so. It was under no moral or treaty obligation to defend Belgium's neutrality if it was threatened by another one of the signatories of the Treaty of London.[1] But they were divided on the wider question of what to do if the French asked for British help. Only Asquith, Grey, Haldane, Churchill and Crewe were in favour of offering it. The French and Russians declared that a firm British pledge of support for them would deter the Germans but the majority of the Cabinet refused to give it. Some, like Morley, Burns and Sir John Simon, the Attorney General, wanted to declare that Britain would remain neutral under all circumstances. Many of the remainder shared Lloyd George's sympathy for France but recognized that the strategic argument for standing up to the Germans would carry little weight inside their party. Few Liberals wanted anything to do with a war in eastern Europe which they feared would only be fought to aggrandize Russia. But the waverers in the Cabinet knew that opinion might change if the Germans actually did invade Belgium.[2]

The Cabinet meetings of 2 August were decisive. For the first time there was some concrete discussion of how British interests might be affected by a Franco-German war. From them emerged some agreement on a very narrow definition of British interests. Grey argued that Britain had to act to uphold the balance of power because if it did not it would eventually find itself isolated and overwhelmed by a German-dominated continental combination. Only Asquith, Haldane, Churchill and Crewe frankly accepted this argument.[3] And even they did not believe that the immediate dispatch of the Expeditionary Force to the continent would serve any useful purpose.[4] However, Grey's second contention, that the presence of a German fleet in the Channel, attacking France's North Sea coast, would menace British security, gained a wider measure of agreement. J. A. Pease, the President of the Board of Education wrote that 'Our interests in English trade, protection of our own food supplies, are such that we can't afford to allow the Germans to occupy the French coast in the English Channel. If these conditions will not be observed, we may get into War.'[5] Even so Asquith was afraid that three-quarters of his own party would oppose intervention. Two things rescued him from this dilemma, a letter written on 2 August by the Unionist leaders Bonar Law and Lansdowne promising him their support if Britain went to war to assist France and the German invasion of Belgium on 3 August. Only two

Liberal ministers, Morley and Burns actually resigned. The remainder recognized that, even if they did resign, Britain would still go to war under a Liberal–Unionist coalition and that a war to defend Belgian neutrality would be acceptable to the public and their party alike.[6] The significance of this for future British strategy was that none of the waverers was won over to intervention by Grey's argument that British security demanded that it support its Entente partners and uphold the balance of power. They went to war accepting a much narrower definition of what constituted British interests, namely the independence of Belgium and the exclusion of the Germans from the Channel ports. For a considerable time this enabled them to bask in the illusion that Britain could achieve its aims and yet still remain largely aloof from the continental land war.

But in fact British war aims quickly extended far beyond the confines of the Channel coast. Even before the war some Liberals had been suspicious of Germany's growing power because they believed that its government was unchecked by the electorate. It was not ruled by a democratic government but by 'a military and bureaucratic oligarchy supported by a powerful Junker landlord class'.[7] However, after 1912 there had been an apparent improvement in Anglo-German relations and Germany's decision to go to war therefore shocked the British. They explained this turn-about in German policy by suggesting that its government was torn between a peace party and a war party. The latter was in the hands of the Crown Prince, Tirpitz and the army, and had deliberately sought war. In their public speeches ministers denied that they were fighting the war in order to expand the British empire. In public and private they insisted they were fighting a crusade to free Belgium from German domination, to uphold the rights of small nations and to eradicate Prussian militarism from the fabric of German politics. As Lloyd George wrote to his wife on 11 August, 'Beat the German Junker but no war on the German people'.[8] This formula struck a receptive chord in the nonconformist conscience of the left in a way that no discussion about rearranging the frontiers of Europe could ever have done. The press quickly took it up and it therefore served to minimize opposition to the war.[9]

Opponents of the war in the Labour movement, like Keir Hardie and Ramsay MacDonald, found themselves comparatively isolated. They joined with a handful of dissident Liberals led by C. P. Trevelyan and Arthur Ponsonby to form the Union of Democratic Control (UDC). The UDC called for an end to the kind of secret diplomacy which they believed that Grey had practised and which they argued had involved Britain in an unnecessary war. Yet they remained a secret organization themselves until September when their manifesto was leaked to the *Morning Post*.[10] Most trade unionists accepted the government's formula, perhaps because they had more immediate concerns. They were afraid that the burden of maintaining the large numbers of unemployed the war might produce would bankrupt them. On 27 August they reached a concordat with the government. The unions promised to forgo the right to strike for the duration of the war and the government promised to provide more funds to support the unemployed. Arthur Henderson lived down his Quaker–Radical background and led the pro-war majority of the movement.[11] After this apparent capitulation by organized labour the government was able in the early months of the war to ignore pressure from trades councils, the anti-war Independent Labour Party (ILP) and umbrella organizations like the War Emergency Workers National Committee (WEWNC) that they should mitigate the hardships faced by the poor during the war by fixing the prices of basic necessities. Instead, from September onwards, the Treasury deliberately allowed prices to rise as a way of persuading workers to seek higher earnings in war-related industries. Initially the British economy was mobilized through inflation. The Liberal, Labour and Unionist parties agreed to a political truce of sorts. It was confined to by-elections. They still anticipated and planned for a general election in 1915. Asquith knew that the election could not be postponed beyond the end of 1915 but he was determined to fight the war on the basis of the normal party system. The truce only put a slight brake on party politics. In September the Unionists were incensed when the Liberals went ahead with contentious legislation over Irish Home Rule and Welsh Disestablishment, and Unionist back-benchers and their press began to retaliate by accusing the government of pacifism and want of patriotism.[12]

But the longer-term significance of fighting to destroy Prussian militarism was even more important. As John Gooch has persuasively argued, Asquith and his political colleagues were committed to securing victories over Germany of such magnitude that the Germans would overthrow their existing rulers and establish in their place a more democratic constitution. As Kitchener explained to the American ambassador in March 1916, 'the only really satisfactory termination of the war would be brought about by an internal revolution in Germany'.[13] It was unlikely that a nation as powerful as Germany and governed by a ruling class who had always demonstrated a tenacious grip on power, would be ready to accept such humiliating terms at the hands of their enemies unless forced to do so by a catastrophic defeat. However, Asquith and his political colleagues were not prepared to will the means to achieve these ends. In 1914–15 they sought to carry out these aims by employing strictly limited means, by relying on economic pressure and their allies to defeat the enemy whilst Britain itself stood largely aloof from the land war. This contradiction between limited means and total ends was to bedevil British war policy.

In August 1914 the government's official advisers were temporarily eclipsed. The control of policy-making remained firmly in the hands of a small number of ministers, Asquith, Grey, Churchill, and the new Secretary of State for War, Lord Kitchener. Except for the ageing Lord Roberts, Kitchener was the empire's most distinguished soldier. He rapidly became the living embodiment of the British war effort. His Cabinet colleagues, perhaps a little shocked by the outbreak of war, were initially ready to defer to him over most military matters. But his unwillingness to talk freely with those outside of his personal staff and his obvious dislike of the give and take of Cabinet debate meant he was a difficult colleague to work with.[14] Most of the prewar General Staff accompanied the BEF to France. Those who took their place were 'dug-outs', retired officers recalled to duty for the duration of the war. For a long time Kitchener bypassed them. Neither the CIGS, Sir Charles Douglas, known as 'Sunny Jim' behind his back, nor the DMO, Sir Charles Callwell, were even told what Sir John French's orders were when the BEF went to France. Douglas died in September 1914 and was replaced by Sir James Wolfe-Murray, a Scot who lacked the force of character to stand up to Kitchener.[15] The First Sea Lord, Prince Louis of Battenberg, was similarly ineffective. In 1913 he was widely regarded as the outstanding admiral on the active list. But in 1914 he was handicapped by his German ancestry and in October was driven from office by the anti-German hysteria which swept the country. Sir John Jellicoe became the C.-in-C. of the Grand Fleet at the start of the war but he was no Nelson. He realized all too clearly that if he made one wrong decision he could lose the war in an afternoon. He was determined to maintain his fleet in being in the knowledge that as long as he did so the Entente and not the Central Powers, would control the oceans. The Foreign Office also suffered a drop in its prestige and power. In August 1914 a new War Department was established by amalgamating the Eastern and Western departments. Its second head, George Clerk, became one of Grey's closest advisers. But by early 1915 several senior officials like Tyrrell and Nicolson were suffering too severely from strain and overwork to be of much real use to Grey. Grey himself was depressed by the outbreak of war and as the war progressed his sight seriously deteriorated, compelling him to take frequent holidays.[16] But when he was at the office he still managed to get through an enormous amount of work and retained most major policy decisions in his own hands. He was never prepared simply to be the tool of the soldiers.

In 1914 Kitchener dominated the government's discussions of war policy. As early as 1909 he had decided that an Anglo–German war would last at least three years. He knew nothing of the prewar deliberations of the Committee of Imperial Defence (CID) which had pointed towards the possibility that the war might be quickly ended by general economic collapse. In the 1880s and 1890s he had fought successfully in Egypt and the Sudan on a financial shoe-string and believed that 'No financial pressure has ever yet stopped a war in progress'.[17] A careful weighing of the resources available to both sides and a shrewd appreciation of the enemy's determination not to be beaten meant that he never believed that 'business as usual' and the French and Russian armies would be enough to win the war. The Russians had large reserves of manpower but 'had untried and unproved offensive powers'.[18] The French, who trained 80 per cent of their manpower in peacetime compared to just over 50 per cent in Germany, had already placed most of their men in the field. The Germans were a formidable nation of 70 million people with large reserves of military manpower and 'it should be assumed that before Germany relinquishes the struggle, she will have exhausted every possible supply of men and material'.[19] Kitchener's vision went far beyond the end of this war. Like other ministers and officials he feared that at the end of the war, if Germany was defeated, Russian power would be enormously enhanced and it would emerge as a new threat to British security. As Sir Francis Bertie wrote on 7 August, 'The German Military Power has been a curse to the world: may it come to an end and not be replaced by that of another Power such as Russia'.[20] The government was, in Lloyd George's words, 'dead against carrying on a war of conquest to crush Germany for the sake of Russia'.[21] Therein lay the key to Kitchener's decision to raise the New Armies and the reason why his colleagues allowed him to act without protest even though his new creation undermined many of the precepts of 'business as usual'. The New Armies were not just intended to win the war for the Entente but to win the peace for Britain. Kitchener wanted the British army to reach its maximum strength in early 1917. In the meantime the Central Powers and Britain's continental allies would have fought each other to a standstill. The British, with their manpower reserves almost untapped, would then be the strongest of all the belligerents. They would be able to deliver the final blow against the Germans and allow the British to dictate their peace terms to allies and enemies alike. For, as he told Lieut.-Col. Repington of *The Times* early in August 1914, there must 'be no question of peace except on our own terms'.[22]

Every crusade needs crusaders and Kitchener found them in hitherto undreamt of numbers. The extent of the nation's willingness to fight was amply demonstrated by the response to his call for recruits. The army's recruiting machinery was quickly swamped and by mid-August the War Office had to enlist the voluntary services of municipal authorities. Recruits were drawn from all social classes. Enlistments were equally heavy in industrial and agricultural areas, although heavier still from the commercial and distributive trades. In late August Kitchener told the Cabinet he wished to enlist 700,000 men by April 1915. In fact by Christmas 1914 over one million had volunteered. The Kitchener armies were one of the last great voluntary efforts of Victorian Britain.[23] But they created unprecedented problems for the government. Kitchener's military critics, lacking his broad vision, were initially scathing about them behind his back. They resented the way in which officers and NCOs were held back from the front to train the new recruits.[24] Perhaps a more valid criticism of the government's policy is the way in which his political colleagues reacted. Overawed by his personality, and perhaps a little doubtful of success, they gave him a free hand to proceed. But the sudden removal of a large number of men from the workforce and the sudden sharp increase in the demand for war-related goods did at least as much as the outbreak of war to disrupt the normal functioning of the economy. The Cabinet still thought that conscription was politically impossible and so recruits had to be taken as and when they were prepared to enlist. It was therefore impossible for the government to prepare a rational manpower budget and allocate resources between civilian and military needs.

In the opening months of the war Asquith's government devoted much time and effort to securing their control of the sea lanes by mounting attacks on Germany's colonies. Possession of them would also give Britain useful bargaining counters at the peace conference. They began to subsidize some of their poorer continental allies and they sent a small amphibious expeditionary force to the continent as a visible token of their commitment to the Entente's war effort.

Until 4 August the Cabinet were reluctant even to contemplate sending the BEF abroad.[25] Two *ad hoc* war councils on 5 and 6 August gave the Cabinet conflicting advice. Henry Wilson wanted the force sent to France as soon as possible but Sir John French, the C.-in-C. of the BEF, wavered between accepting his advice and landing at Antwerp instead. Like Battenberg, French had a reputation as a highly competent professional officer. But some of those who worked closely with him doubted whether his mercurial temperament meant that he was really fitted to hold a high command in wartime. His behaviour was to prove them correct. With the fleet already mobilized the Admiralty thought that a sudden German invasion was impossible. But Asquith wanted to retain some regular troops at home to deal with civil disturbances if the economy collapsed.[26] On 6 August the Cabinet finally decided to send the BEF to northern France. Most ministers believed they were only sanctioning a limited amphibious operation that could quickly be liquidated. The BEF would be deployed on the extreme left of the French and could retreat to the coast if the French were overwhelmed.[27] Kitchener, however, recognized that such a course was politically impossible. If the BEF were evacuated it would have a disastrous effect on the solidarity of the Entente and he was determined that it would not leave France until the Germans had been defeated.[28] Sir John's orders reflected the Cabinet's decision to preserve the BEF intact. He was reminded that there were few trained drafts to replace casualties and so if he found himself thrust forward by General Joffre, the French C.-in-C., without strong French support, he was enjoined not to expose his troops to a superior enemy force without first consulting London. He was instructed to co-operate with Joffre, but he was not placed under his command. These orders were not properly explained to Joffre and they were to bedevil the relationship between the two generals.[29]

The Cabinet's policy of 'business as usual' was summarized by J. A. Pease when he wrote to his brother that

> we decided that we could win through by holding the sea, maintaining our credit, keeping our people employed & our own industries going – By economic pressure, destroying Germany's trade cutting off her supplies. We would gradually secure victory. This policy is steadily pursued – We have never thought we could successfully afford to compete with her by maintaining also a continental army on her scale – Our Navy, finance & trade was our life's blood, & we must see to it that these are maintained.[30]

The blockade came into operation on the outbreak of war and German overseas commerce was quickly driven from the oceans. After the set-back of the Battle of Coronel in November 1914 had been avenged in December at the Battle of the Falklands, German surface raiders were all but eliminated. The last of them was interned in April 1915. They had accounted for little more than 2 per cent of British tonnage, losses so small as to be of no real consequence.[31] The blockade did not bring the Central Powers to their knees but it did deprive them of access to extra-European sources of supply and in the long run the Entente's access to such sources was to be of crucial importance in allowing Britain to continue fighting.

The government did not seek out Germany's colonies simply to add more territory to the British empire. In 1912 Churchill had predicted that in the event of war Germany's colonies would become British hostages. It was necessary to eliminate them to prevent the Germans using them as bases and intelligence-gathering sources for their commerce raiders. On 5 August a new Offensive sub-committee of the Committee of Imperial Defence recommended that the government of India should dispatch troops to German East Africa to ensure the protection of British possessions and shipping in the Indian ocean.[32] British forces in the Gold Coast were similarly required to destroy German wireless installations in West Africa and the Australian and New Zealand governments were asked to occupy the German wireless and cable stations on the Pacific islands of Yap, German New Guinea, Samoa and Naru. The next day the Cabinet, looking according to Asquith, 'more like a gang of Elizabethan buccaneers than a meek collection of black-coated Liberal Ministers' agreed, and Harcourt belied his pacifistic reputation by enthusiastically drafting the telegrams to the colonial governments himself.[33] Togoland fell on 26 August and by the end of September Australian and New Zealand forces had occupied their objectives. German South West Africa was occupied by South African troops in July 1915 and the Cameroons fell in February 1916. Only in German East Africa was German resistance prolonged and the local German commander did not surrender until after the armistice in November 1918. On 7 August Grey asked the Japanese for limited naval help to hunt down the German cruisers known to be in Far Eastern waters but the Japanese insisted that they could not confine their action to naval operations alone and that they would also have to attack German bases. In November, with only very limited British assistance, they captured Tsingtau, the main German naval base in China. The operation under-lined the extent to which Britain's imperial security in the Far East now rested on Japanese co-operation.

The British quickly discovered that occupying Germany's possessions was one thing, but disposing of them was a more difficult problem. The Offensive sub-committee soon recognized that if Britain and its Domin-ions were seen to be gobbling up all of Germany's colonies they would excite the jealousy of France and also perhaps of Russia. Local British commanders were therefore ordered not to announce the formal annexa-tion of any occupied territory.[34] This was not difficult to do in Africa but it aroused suspicions in the Pacific. Neither the Chinese, the Americans nor the Australians or New Zealanders welcomed Japanese military activities in China and the Pacific especially when, in October 1914, the Japanese let it be known that they did not intend to relinquish their gains. In Australia this provoked much talk of the Japanese 'Yellow Peril'. Grey could only equivocate, allowing the Japanese to remain in occupation of their gains for the duration of the war but insisting that his agreement would not prejudice their ultimate disposal.[35] The Anglo-Japanese relationship during the war never really recovered from the mutual suspicion that this episode aroused.

The search for allies and alternative fronts began with the outbreak of war, several months before military stalemate descended on the Western front. The first exponents of using Britain's diplomatic and economic resources to entice other powers into the war were Churchill, Battenberg and also Crowe, who for a short time was the first head of the Foreign Office's War Department. The Admiralty wanted an alliance with Norway, Holland and Belgium as a way of tightening the blockade,[36] and on 5 August Crowe minuted

> I presume there can be no doubt that it would be to our advantage to obtain the active cooperation of as many states as possible. It should be our endeavour to bring into a system of fighting alliance a ring of Powers surrounding the enemies. With Sweden, Norway, and Holland

neutral (at least neutral) we should, and I am convinced we could, bring into line with us Portugal and Spain, and I should not despair of winning over Italy, Greece and possibly Turkey. Even leaving out Turkey, there would be a solid force shutting off Germany and Austria from the rest of the world on practically all sides.

If this is the policy to be aimed at, we should set about at once offering such terms to the several Powers as might be required to win their cooperation. The terms would have to include effective financial assistance and supplies of war material and guns, which could no doubt if necessary be obtained or ordered from America.[37]

Britain's search for allies in August and September failed for several reasons. Because of its geographical position the Foreign Office had written off Denmark as falling within Germany's sphere of influence even before the war. The Norwegians were more sympathetic to the British but were concerned at the attitude of the royalist, pro-German and anti-Russian government of their neighbour Sweden. Most Swedes wanted to remain neutral but the court favoured intervention on Germany's behalf and the conservative government wanted to aid Germany although they hesitated actually to go to war.[38] Grey offered the Norwegians and Dutch the vague prospect of 'common action' if Germany threatened them but both preferred a policy of strict neutrality. The Norwegians, believing that the Royal Navy would be unable to protect them against Germany, tried to insure themselves by signing a secret agreement with the Swedes that both would remain netural. Faced by a *fait accompli* Grey accepted this as a second best and stopped trying to pursuade them to join the Entente.[39]

Balked of success in northern Europe the Foreign Office turned their attention to Italy. Its behaviour during the July crisis seemed to justify its reputation for perfidy. But as the Germans and Austrians kept their partners completely in the dark about their policies during the crisis the Italians were perfectly entitled to remain aloof. Once the war had started most of the Italian ruling class accepted that if Italy wanted to remain a great power it would have to participate on the winning side. The problem facing them was to decide which was the winning side. Immediate intervention was impossible because the Italian army was not prepared for war and public opinion was divided over the merits of the two sides. The leaders of the movement for intervention in support of the Entente were liberal lawyers, journalists and intellectuals. They hoped that participation in the war would promote British-style liberalism in Italy and looked to France as the enemy of authoritarianism and the home of revolution. Conversely many members of the conservative upper classes felt more sympathy with the authoritarian German and Austrian empires. The foreign ministry was torn between their fear of Germany's military superiority and fear of what the Royal Navy might do to Italy's coastal cities if they joined the Central Powers. Neutrality, coupled with preparations for war, therefore seemed the best policy.[40] There was also a further problem. The Italians were worried that, if the Entente won, the Serbs would get the outlet to the Adriatic they sought and would menace the whole of Italy's long and vulnerable Adriatic coast. Any negotiations to bring Italy into the war were thus bound to involve long and complex territorial negotiations to balance their rival claims. On 15 August the Italian foreign minister announced that Italy would not join the Central Powers but was not yet ready to join the Entente. Grey saw little point in embarking on detailed negotiations about any future territorial settlement until the Italians were ready to enter the war. A premature *démarche* might only persuade them to turn to the Central Powers to ascertain if they would make them a better offer.[41]

The leading exponents of creating a Balkan confederation to help the Entente were Churchill and Lloyd George. They were drawn to the Balkans by two things. Liberal sympathies for the former subject nationalities of the Turkish empire in Europe dated from Gladstone's espousal of Bulgaria's cause in the 1870s. And since 1905 British estimates of their military potential had increased markedly. The General Staff had carefully tabulated the growing strength of their armies and as early as 1910 had estimated that if the Serbs and Bulgars united 'it would be unwise to predict an easy victory for Austria–Hungary, history might repeat itself in the shape of a Bulgarian Moscow or a southern slav ulcer'.[42] The speed with which the Balkan states destroyed Turkish power in Europe during the first Balkan War of 1912–13 further increased British estimations of their power. In November 1912 G. H. Fitzmaurice, the chief dragoman at the British embassy in Constantinople, believed that the 'Confederated Balkan States really constituted a new Great Power in the Near East, a fact which Austria seemed to be taking into account'.[43] Sir Thomas Cunninghame, the British military attaché at Vienna, suggested that if the armies of the confederation were mobilized against Austria–Hungary they would profoundly alter the entire European balance of power in the Entente's favour. The Austrians would be forced to divert troops from their common frontier with Russia and the Germans would then have to make good the deficit on the Eastern front by reducing their forces in the West.[44] It is thus easy to see why the British thought them desirable allies in 1914–15.

But in fact most British policy-makers failed to grasp the realities of the situation in the Balkans. Britain had more diplomatic and consular officials in Chile than in the whole of the Balkans. The British exaggerated both the weakness of the Turks and the strength of the Balkan states. The Turkish army had not been decisively defeated in the first Balkan War. It had simply retreated without a fight but reports like those of Sir

R. Paget, the British minister in Belgrade, pointing this out were over-looked amidst the rejoicing that the Turks had almost been driven from Europe bag and baggage.[45] The Balkan states may have been able to put a quantity of peasant soldiers into the field but none of them had the industrial infrastructure to supply them and they were therefore dependent on outside suppliers for arms and munitions. But above all the Balkan confederation was inherently unstable and had already broken up before August 1914. The original confederation had been no more than a series of bilateral arrangements. It had never been a multilateral treaty binding all parties to a single policy. None of the bilateral treaties contained clear proposals for the division of the territorial spoils once the Turks had been defeated. After the first Balkan War, the Great Powers intervened and insisted on the creation of an independent Albania. If Serbia and perhaps Greece had been allowed to expand into Albania then Bulgaria could have satisfied itself in central Macedonia. But as an independent Albania was established, the Serbs were still left without an outlet to the Adriatic and the Bulgarians refused to give up any of their claims in Macedonia. In June 1913 the Christian powers began to fight amongst themselves over the division of the spoils. The Bulgars suffered a total military débâcle as they faced not only the Serbs and Greeks but the Turks as well. The Serbs took the contested zone of Macedonia as well as the uncontested zone which they had promised to Bulgaria in 1912. The Greeks took Kavalla and its hinterland, the Romanians gained the southern part of the Dobrogea and the Turks regained Thrace and Adrianople. Henceforth few of the Balkan armies were in any shape to face another war, the Bulgarians were bent on revenge and all the other Balkan powers distrusted them.[46]

The first British attempt to create a Balkan confederation failed for the same reasons that subsequent attempts failed. The British belief that a Balkan confederation could be recreated was based on the erroneous assumption that the national rivalries of the Balkan states were soluble by pragmatic compromises between the interested parties where no such solution could in fact be found. The mutual suspicions and rivalries generated by the Balkan Wars persisted. On 10 August E. Venizelos, the liberal Greek Prime Minister, who had been seeking a British guarantee of Greece's gains during the Balkan Wars since January 1914, offered to forge a Balkan confederation to fight for the Entente. The members would compensate themselves at Austria's expense. Churchill and Lloyd George enthusiastically pursued his offer. On 11 August, a day before they formally declared war on Austria–Hungary, the Cabinet agreed to back the members with British credit.[47] Crowe and Clerk preferred it to Russia's efforts to persuade the Romanians to attack Austria which they were afraid would only cause the Bulgarians and Turks to join the enemy. But Nicolson was more cautious and realistic. He agreed with Sir Henry Bax-Ironside, the British minister to Bulgaria, who had reported that

Bulgaria had been exhausted by the Balkan Wars and that Bulgarian politicians were about evenly divided between those who looked to Austria and those who looked to Russia. On the eve of war he had informed Nicolson that King Ferdinand secretly welcomed the prospect of Serbia receiving a drubbing at Austria's hands and 'whatever statements she [Bulgaria] may make officially, she will wait to see which way the cat jumps before taking any decisive action'.[48] Nicolson therefore dismissed the possibility of Bulgaria joining any confederation, and if Bulgaria remained aloof the other states would not dare turn their backs on it by attacking the Central Powers.[49] He was right. King Carol of Romania, a south German prince linked to the Triple Alliance by a secret treaty dating back thirty years, wanted to join the Central Powers. But he could not follow his own inclinations because it was widely feared in Romania that an Austro-Serbian war would lead to the aggrandisement of Bulgaria and the thwarting of Romania's own ambitions to unite the Romanian populations of the Austrian provinces of Transylvania and Bukovina with the mother country. On 3 August the king was overruled and Romania declared its neutrality. A few days later they rejected a Russian offer, made with British and French agreement, of Transylvania if they joined the Entente. The Greeks were similarly divided. King Constantine, married to the Kaiser's sister, was personally sympathetic to Germany and was reluctant to commit his small country to the war until he could identify the winning side. Venizelos needed far more than the promise of British financial help to persuade the cautious king to plump for the Entente, especially when the Russians told him that the Bulgarians were unlikely to join any confederation until the Greeks surrendered Kavalla to them.[50]

The British were also hamstrung in the offers they could make to the Balkan neutrals because the Cabinet wanted to avoid war with Turkey. On 2 August the Turks and Germans had signed a treaty of alliance. An open pointer to Turkey's attitude was given on 10 August when it gave sanctuary at Constantinople to the German cruisers *Goeben* and *Breslau* which were fleeing from allied pursuers in the Mediterranean. Shortly afterwards the Turks purchased them, although retaining their German crews. After the Balkan Wars the British had a poor opinion of the Turkish army. In 1914 they did not think that it had recovered from its defeats and they believed that another war would be unpopular in Turkey.[51] But although they had no doubt of their ability to defeat the Turks quickly they wished to avoid war with them if they possibly could. A second war on their southern frontier would force the Russians to divert troops away from Germany and Austria–Hungary and it might cause very serious unrest among the Muslim population of India and Egypt.

Ever since the Indian Mutiny the British had been aware that they could not hope to rule their Eastern empire by force alone. The material basis of their rule in India and Egypt was tenuous. At least 300m Indians were ruled by only 1,200 members of the Indian Civil Service and about 77,000 British troops. In Egypt, with a population of about 13m, the British garrison numbered only about 5000.[52] British colonial government rested on the active collaboration of a large number of natives who worked in the lower reaches of the civil administration and the army, and the passive acquiescence of the rest of the population. The British believed that their rule was only as strong as those they governed thought it was and the colonial regimes were therefore constantly concerned to maintain British prestige in the eyes of the natives. Prestige was an amalgam of private and public virtues and its maintenance became almost an end in itself. The British had to ensure that their native subjects saw them as being better rulers than any possible native alternative. British rule had to be seen as fair and just. The mask of British moral superiority could never be allowed to slip and intimate relations between the races was frowned upon. Taxes had to be as light as possible and justice had to be administered fairly. Like every aristocratic regime they used displays of conspicuous consumption to demonstrate their wealth and power. Demonstrations of physical force were held in reserve and, for most of the time, the British hoped that the mere knowledge that they would be used would suffice. But above all the British had to retain a reputation for military invincibility. Minor military set-backs were only tolerable if they were swiftly reversed.

The Mutiny and the Mahdist rebellion in the Sudan, had taught the British that the greatest threat to their rule was the spread of Panislamic nationalism. Their fears were encouraged by the Sultan Abdul-hamid II of Turkey who sedulously encouraged the spread of Panislamic ideas in the last quarter of the nineteenth century, both as a way of holding together his ramshackle empire and as a threat to deter further depredations against it by France, Russia and Britain. The situation became acute in 1914. The Viceroy of India, Lord Hardinge, feared that war with Turkey would provoke a crisis of conscience in the minds of Indian Muslims, forcing them to choose between their temporal rulers, the British, and the Sultan-Caliph, the supreme political embodiment of their religion. The British chargé d'affaires in Egypt reported that native feeling was broadly pro-German and would certainly deteriorate in the event of war against Turkey. Sir Beauchamp Duff, the C.-in-C. of the Indian Army, was afraid that if too many troops were taken from India, the Afghans would proclaim a jihad, there would be attacks along the North West Frontier and unrest might affect the Muslim units of his own army.[53] Their fears had a receptive audience in London where there was a small but influential Indo-Egyptian party in the Cabinet consisting of men like Kitchener, who had been Consul General in Cairo between 1911 and 1914, Crewe, the

Secretary of State for India, and Grey, who as Foreign Secretary was ultimately responsible for the British administration in Cairo.

On 14 August Nicolson and Grey decided that if the Greeks could not re-establish the Balkan confederation, it would be better for everyone if the Balkan states and Turkey remained neutral.[54] They suggested to France and Russia that they should offer the Turks a joint guarantee of their integrity in return for their neutrality. Churchill, angry at the escape of the two German cruisers, wanted to send destroyers through the Dardanelles to sink them but the Cabinet firmly quashed the suggestion on the grounds that it would enrage Muslim opinion in India and Egypt.[55] Venizelos's offer made on 18 August to bring Greece into the war against Turkey or against Bulgaria if it attacked Serbia and if the Serbs invoked their treaty of alliance with the Greeks, received a polite but negative reply from both the British and the French.[56]

The final and perhaps overriding reason why the neutrals were not willing to join the Entente in August 1914 was that they were not certain that the Entente would win. Germany's spectacular advance in Belgium and northern France in August made it seem likely that Paris would quickly fall and France might make a separate peace. In 1911 Henry Wilson had predicted that the Germans would deploy the bulk of their forces in the West and that the Russians would attack Germany as soon as possible after the declaration of war in order to relieve the pressure on their ally.[57] There was little real co-ordination between the Anglo-French and the Russian armies in the opening weeks of the war and it was not until March 1915 that the Russian C.-in-C. the Grand Duke Nicholas, and Joffre had a safe cipher for their communications. The Russians regarded the BEF as no more than a minor adjunct to the French army. Military co-operation between the Russians and Britain began with Grey's vague promise of 5 August that 'we shall, of course, not restrict our action, but shall take offensive by every means in our power' and a Russian reply that they would invade East Prussia on 15 August. But by late August, as the Germans repulsed Joffre's initial offensive and wheeled through Belgium, the first strains became apparent within the Entente. The Belgian king, his own army in retreat, resented the fact that the French had not come to his aid more quickly. The French begged the Russians to speed up their advance into East Prussia. On 23 August the BEF had its first serious encounter with the Germans at Mons in Belgium. News of the rapid fall of the supposedly impregnable Belgian fortress of Namur coupled with Sir John's retreat from Mons caused consternation in the Cabinet. Asquith thought that the French plan of campaign had been bungled and some ministers began to visualize the possibility of Sir John constructing a latter-day example of the lines of Torres Vedras by retreating to a fortified position across the Cherbourg peninsula.[58]

French public opinion had accepted the war as inevitable and rallied to the 'Union Sacré' proclaimed on 4 August. Mobilization was greeted calmly but with no great enthusiasm. The war was expected to be short and Parliament decided that its patriotic duty lay in deferring to the executive and the army high command. On 4 August the Chamber adjourned itself and 200 deputies went away to do military service. On 26 August the Cabinet reacted to the prospect that the Germans might soon enter Paris, by carrying out a reshuffle and created a government of national unity. Viviani, who had become Prime Minister in June 1914, remained in office. Alexandre Millerand became minister of war and Théophile Delcassé, the French architect of the Entente Cordiale and a fervent supporter of the Russian alliance, became foreign minister.[59] They asked the Russians to send three or four corps to the Western front via Siberia and Archangel. The latter were scornful. On 1 September news of the Russian defeat at Tannenberg, which ended the possibility of a rapid Russian advance on Berlin, reached London and Paris.[60] In France Anglo-French military co-operation almost broke down. Sir John, adhering to the letter of his orders not to risk the destruction of his small force, wanted to withdraw from the line for eight days rest and refitting at the very moment when Joffre wanted him to co-operate in an operation to save Paris. The British Cabinet were alarmed when they heard of Sir John's wishes. They realized that if he did retire the French and Russians would accuse the British of deserting them at their hour of greatest need. On 1 September a small conclave of ministers decided that Kitchener should go to GHQ 'to put the fear of God into them all' and make Sir John conform to Joffre's plan.[61] He did so, the BEF participated in the Battle of the Marne, and helped to save Paris. But the episode was the first of several which soured Sir John's relations with Kitchener.

The Russians welcomed the formation of the new French government but Joffre's retreat and the French government's decision to leave Paris for Bordeaux on 2 September rekindled their fears that in the face of a full scale German onslaught the French would collapse and leave them in the lurch. The British shared some of these apprehensions. They had already heard rumours that the Germans hoped to make a quick peace with the French. From Stockholm the British minister reported that a prominent banker who had just returned from Berlin had said that the Germans hoped that 'after one or two crushing victories against France to be able to induce [the] latter to accept "moderate" terms of peace, that England then would also make peace and that Russia would be obliged to follow in due course'.[62] In several neutral capitals the Germans were trying to tempt their hosts to join them by claiming that they had already won the war. Sazonov was the first to suggest that the best way to counter the German policy was for the Entente partners to place their relationship on a more public and formal footing. On 1 September he suggested that Britain,

France and Russia should sign an agreement promising not to make a separate peace with Germany and to record this by an exchange of notes which could be published. Grey was under no illusions as to why he made the proposal. The Russians did not trust the French and British to continue the war if Paris fell. In addition public declarations of solidarity might persuade the neutrals that the Entente was not yet finished.[63] Crowe and Nicolson greeted the proposal warmly, Nicolson minuting, 'There is no objection to giving the assurance that we would not make a separate peace, in fact there is a positive advantage in doing so. Unless we all stand together we shall assuredly fall & we could not give greater pleasure to Germany than by declining to sign.' But the British were wary about committing themselves to all of their allies' detailed war aims. Asquith insisted on adding a clause to Sazonov's formula that when the time came to consider detailed peace terms no single ally would press for conditions which had not previously been agreed by both their partners. The French and Russians agreed and the Pact of London was signed on 5 September.[64] The ambiguities of the prewar Ententes now gave way to a formal alliance.

None of the lesser members of the coalition were consulted by the British before they signed the pact. The British believed that under the terms of the Anglo-Japanese alliance the Japanese were already bound not to make a separate peace with the Germans, an interpretation which, for the time being, the Japanese were content to accept. Belgian wartime diplomacy has been described as 'schizophrenic'. On the one hand they realized that they would only regain their independence if they co-operated with France and Britain. But on the other they resented the obligations imposed on them by membership of a coalition. For the time being they were not interested in conducting separate peace negotiations with the Germans and in September German feelers were sharply rebuffed.[65] The pact tried to regulate the political relations of the allies. It ensured that the war would not end quickly, because if any ally faltered it could always look to its partners for support. But it did not lay down terms for military or economic co-operation between them. These were left to evolve under the pressure of circumstances. The allies wanted Britain to give them all the men and money that it could. The British wanted to give them only what it thought they needed and what it could provide. As the military situation moved towards a stalemate in the autumn and winter of 1914–15 the gap between the allies' expectations and what Britain could or would provide became a cause for tension and ill-feeling between them.

Notes

1   Samuel to his mother, 26 and 30 July 1914, Samuel mss, A/156/466 and 467.
2   Michael and Eleanor Brock (eds), *H. H. Asquith: Letters to Venetia Stanley*

(London: Oxford University Press, 1982), pp. 138–9; Pease diary, 29 and 31 July, 2 August 1914, Gainford mss, box 39; Samuel to his wife, 1 August 1914; PRO FO 371/2160/35370, Grey to Bertie, 1 August 1914.

3   Samuel to his wife, 2 August 1914, Samuel mss, A/157/697; Lord Haldane, Memorandum of events between 1906–1915 [c. April 1916], Haldane mss, 6109 (II).

4   Asquith to Bonar Law, 2 August 1914, Bonar Law mss, 34/3/3; PRO FO 371/2160/35412, Grey to Bertie, 2 August 1914.

5   Pease to his wife, 2 August 1914, Gainford mss, box 521; Pease diary, 2 August 1914, Gainford mss, box 39; Runciman, Cabinet – Sunday 2 August, Runciman mss, WR 135; Brock (eds), *H. H. Asquith*, pp. 145–6.

6   C. Hazlehurst, *Politicians at War, July 1914 to May 1915: A Prologue to the Triumph of Lloyd George* (London: Cape, 1971), pp. 103–16; T. Wilson, 'Britain's "moral commitment" to France in August 1914', *History*, Vol. 64, no. 212 (1979), p. 388; Runciman, Cabinet – Sunday 2 August, Runciman mss, WR 135; McKenna, Memoranda supplied by Mr McKenna on 20 March 1927, Beaverbrook mss, box 3, folder 7; Samuel, The Cabinet in the days preceding the war, 25 October 1924, Samuel mss, A/45; Pease diary, 3 August 1914, Gainford mss, box 39; K. M. Wilson, 'The British Cabinet's decision for war, 2 August 1914', *British Journal of International Studies*, Vol. 1, no. 2 (1975), pp. 148–56.

7   R. S. Churchill (ed.), *Winston S. Churchill*, Vol. 2, *Companion*, pt 2, *1907–1911* (London: Heinemann, 1969), p. 1360; in general see P. M. Kennedy, *The Rise of the Anglo-German Antagonism, 1860–1914* (London: Allen & Unwin, 1980), ch. 9 *passim*.

8   J. Grigg, *Lloyd George: From Peace to War, 1912–1916* (London: Methuen, 1985), p. 169; L. S. Jaffe, *The Decision to Disarm Germany* (London: Allen & Unwin, 1985), pp. 6–11.

9   See, for example, C. Haste, *Keep the Home Fires Burning: Propaganda in the First World War* (London: Allen Lane, 1977), pp. 2, 21–2; A. F. Havighurst, *Radical Journalist: H. W. Massingham (1860–1924)* (Cambridge: Cambridge University Press, 1974), pp. 228–30.

10 H. Hanak, 'The Union of Democratic Control during the First World War', *Bulletin of the Institute of Historical Research*, vol. 36, no. 94 (1963), pp. 168–72; T. Wilson, *The Downfall of the Liberal Party, 1914–1935* (London: Fontana, 1968), pp. 30–3; M. Swartz, *The Union of Democratic Control in British Politics during the First World War* (Oxford: Clarendon Press, 1971), pp. 28–35.

11 C. Howard, 'MacDonald, Henderson and the outbreak of the war, 1914', *Historical Journal*, vol. 20, no. 4 (1977), pp. 871–5; Notes of deputation from the Trades Union Congress, 27 August 1914, Asquith mss, vol. 89.

12 Hazlehurst, *Politicians*, pp. 135–42; S. Koss, *The Rise and Fall of the Political Press in Britain*, Vol. 2, *The Twentieth Century* (London: Hamish Hamilton, 1984), pp. 254–6.

13 A. S. Link (ed.), *The Papers of Woodrow Wilson*, Vol. 36 (Princeton, NJ: Princeton University Press), p. 437; J. Gooch, 'Soldiers, strategy and war aims in Britain 1914–1918', in B. Hunt and A. Preston (eds), *War Aims and Strategic Policy in the Great War 1914–1918* (London: Croom Helm, 1977), p. 24; see also T. Wilson (ed.), *The Political Diaries of C. P. Scott, 1911–1928* (London: Collins, 1970), pp. 96–9; *Hansard*, 65 HC Deb., 5s, cols 1822–4 (Grey) and 2074–80 (Asquith); V. H. Rothwell, *British War Aims and Peace Diplomacy, 1914–1918* (Oxford: Clarendon Press, 1971), pp. 18–20; PRO FO 800/377, Nicolson to Buchanan, 8 January 1915 and 3 May 1915.

14 Lord Hankey, *The Supreme Command, 1914–1918*, Vol. 1 (London: Allen &

Unwin, 1961), p. 186; E. David (ed.), *Inside Asquith's Cabinet: From the Diaries of Charles Hobhouse* (London: John Murray, 1977), p. 231; Lord Selborne, The War Cabinet, *c.* July 1916, Selborne mss, file 80, ff. 285–90.

15 J. Gooch, *The Plans of War: The General Staff and British Military Strategy, c.* 1900–1916 (London: Routledge & Kegan Paul, 1974), pp. 301–4; Callwell to Wilson, 26 August and 4 September 1914, Wilson mss, box 73/1/18.

16 Zara Steiner, 'The Foreign Office at war', in F. H. Hinsley (ed.), *British Foreign Policy under Sir Edward Grey* (Cambridge: Cambridge University Press, 1977), pp. 516–19.

17 Esher diary entry, 9 October 1914, Esher mss, 2/3.

18 Lieut.-Col. C. à Court Repington, *The First World War, 1914–1918* (London: Constable, 1920), p. 21.

19 Esher diary entry, 9 October 1914, Esher mss, 2/3.

20 Lady Algernon Gordon Lennox (ed.), *The Diary of Lord Bertie of Thame 1914–1918*, Vol. 1 (London: Hodder & Stoughton, 1924), p. 12.

21 Grigg, *Lloyd George*, p. 169.

22 PRO CAB 37/127/34, Lord Kitchener, The future relations of the Great Powers, 21 April 1915; Sir R. Storrs, *Orientations* (London: Ivor Nicholson & Watson, 1937), p. 148; Brock (eds), *H. H. Asquith*, p. 138; D. French, *British Economic and Strategic Planning, 1905–1915* (London: Allen & Unwin, 1982), pp. 124–5; Sir G. Arthur, *Not Worth Reading* (London: Longman, Green, 1938), pp. 192, 244.

23 Brock (eds), *H. H. Asquith*, pp. 190–1; P. E. Dewey, 'Military recruiting and the British labour force during the First World War', *Historical Journal*, vol. 27, no. 1 (1984), pp. 199–223; J. M. Osborne, *The Voluntary Recruiting Movement in Britain, 1914–1916* (London and New York: Garland, 1982), pp. 7–29; J. M. Winter, 'Britain's "Lost Generation" of the First World War', *Population Studies*, Vol. 31, no. 3 (1977), pp. 450–6.

24 Sir H. Wilson, Memorandum from the Aisne Valley, 22 September 1914 and L. Maxse to Wilson, 26 September 1914, both in Wilson mss, box 73/1/81.

25 PRO FO 800/166, Bertie to Grey, 3 August 1914.

26 Gooch, *Plans*, p. 301; R. Blake (ed.), *The Private Papers of Douglas Haig 1914–1919* (London: Eyre & Spottiswoode, 1952), pp. 68–9; Haig to Haldane, 4 August 1914, Haldane mss, 5910; Sir Charles Callwell, *Field Marshal Sir Henry Wilson: His Life and Diaries*, Vol. 1 (London: Cassell, 1927), pp. 158–9; Balfour to Bonar Law, 5 August 1914, Bonar Law mss, 117/1/2; Lord Newton, *Lord Lansdowne. A Biography* (London: Macmillan, 1929), pp. 440–1; PRO CAB 42/1/2 and PRO CAB 42/1/3, Secretary's notes of a War Council held at 10, Downing Street on 5 and 6 August 1914; A. J. Murray to C. Deedes, 18 December 1930; Spears mss, 2/3/79.

27 Pease diary, 6 August 1914, Gainford mss, box 39.

28 PRO WO 79/62, A. J. Murray, Note of conversation with Lord Kitchener, Wellesley House, Aldershot, 14 August 1914.

29 R. Holmes, *The Little Field Marshal: Sir John French* (London: Cape, 1981), pp. 200–1.

30 Pease to Sir A. Pease, 28 August 1914, Gainford mss, box 145.

31 A. J. Marder, *From the Dreadnought to Scapa Flow: The Royal Navy in the Fisher Era, 1904–1919*, Vol. 2 (London: Oxford University Press, 1965), pp. 126–7.

32 PRO CAB 21/3, Joint naval and military committee for the consideration of combined operations in foreign territory, Hankey to PM, 5 August 1914; Maj.-Gen. Sir C. E. Callwell, *Experiences of a Dug-Out* (London: Constable, 1920), pp. 171–3; PRO CAB 17/102B, Report on the opening of the War. CID Historical Section, 1 November 1914; G. Smith, 'The British Govern-

ment and the disposition of the German colonies in Africa, 1914–1918', in P. Gifford and Wm. Roger Louis (eds), *Britain and Germany in Africa: Imperial Rivalry and Colonial Rule* (New Haven, Conn.: Yale University Press, 1967), pp. 276–7; M. Gilbert, *Winston S. Churchill, 1914–16*, Vol. 3 (London: Heinemann, 1971), p. 75.

33 Brock (eds), *H. H. Asquith*, p. 158; Hankey, *Supreme Command*, Vol. 1, p. 168; R. R. James (ed.), *Memoirs of a Conservative: J. C. C. Davidson's Memoirs and Papers, 1910–1937* (London: Weidenfeld & Nicolson, 1969), p. 21.

34 PRO CAB 21/3, Proceedings . . . foreign territory, 14 and 17 August 1914.

35 I. Nish, *Alliance in Decline: A Study in Anglo-Japanese Relations 1908–1923* (London: Athlone Press, 1972), pp. 134–44; Wm. Roger Louis, 'Australia and the German colonies in the Pacific, 1914–1919', *Journal of Modern History*, vol. 38, no. 4 (1966), pp. 407–11.

36 PRO FO 800/88, Churchill, Battenberg and Sturdee to Asquith and Grey, 3 August 1914.

37 PRO FO 371/2162/36542, Minute by E. A. Crowe, 5 August 1914.

38 F. D. Scott, 'Gustaf V and Swedish attitudes towards Germany, 1915', *Journal of Modern History*, Vol. 39, no. 2 (1967), pp. 113–18; S. Koblik, *Sweden: The Neutral Victor. Sweden and the Western Powers, 1917–1918. A Study in Anglo-American-Swedish Relations* (Laromedelsforlagen: Scandinavian University Books, 1972), pp. 11–20; N. Rose, *Vansittart: Study of a Diplomat* (London: Heinemann, 1978), pp. 39–40; T. Kaarsted, *Great Britain and Denmark, 1914–1920* (Odense: Odense University Press, 1979), pp. 36–40.

39 PRO FO 371/2161/35797 and /35799, Grey to Villiers, Findlay and Chilton, 4 August 1914; PRO FO 371/2163/36829, Findlay to Grey, 7 August 1914, and Grey to Findlay, 8 August 1914; PRO FO 371/2163/36887, Howard to Grey, 7 August 1914; PRO 371/2163/37384, Grey to Chilton, 11 August 1914.

40 Brock (eds), *H. H. Asquith*, pp. 125–6; R. Bosworth, *Italy and the Approach of the First World War* (London: Macmillan, 1983), pp. 121–30; A. J. de Grand, 'The Italian nationalist association in the period of Italian neutrality, August 1914–May 1915', *Journal of Modern History*, vol. 43, no. 3 (1971), pp. 395–401; PRO FO 800/65, Rodd to Grey, 3, 9 and 22 August, 8 September 1914.

41 C. J. Lowe, 'Britain and Italian intervention, 1914–1915', *Historical Journal*, Vol. 12, no. 3 (1969), pp. 533–5; PRO FO 800/65, Grey to Rodd, 18 September 1914; PRO FO 371/2161/36484, Grey to Buchanan, 6 August 1914; PRO FO 371/2163/36808, Buchanan to Grey, 7 August 1914, and Grey to Buchanan, 9 August 1914 and (37523) Rodd to Grey, 9 August 1914; PRO FO 371/2171/3884, Grey to Rodd, 12 August 1914 and (38538), Rodd to Grey, 15 August 1914.

42 General Staff, *Handbooks of the Armies of Bulgaria, Greece, Montenegro, Rumania and Servia* (1904); *Handbook of the Rumanian Army* (1907 and 1910); *Handbook of the Bulgarian Army* (1909 and 1910); *Handbook of the Servian Army* (1909) (London: War Office).

43 Gooch and Temperley (eds), *BDOW*, Vol. 9, pt 2, pp. 210, 339–41.

44 *BDOW*, Vol. 9, pt 2, pp. 343–8, 540.

45 *BDOW*, Vol. 9, pt 2, p. 66.

46 R. J. Crampton, *The Hollow Detente: Anglo-German Relations in the Balkans, 1911–1914* (London: George Prior, 1979), pp. 48, 54–5, 63–6, 98–102.

47 Brock (eds), *H. H. Asquith*, pp. 165–6; PRO FO 371/2164/37861, Barclay to Foreign Office, 10 August 1914, Erskine to Foreign Office, 10 August 1914; (37903), Bax-Ironside to Foreign Office, 10 August 1914; (3844), Grey to Bertie, 12 August 1914; PRO FO 800/63, Churchill to Grey, 8 August 1914;

M. G. Fry, *Lloyd George and Foreign Policy*. Vol. 1, *The Education of a Statesman* (Montreal and London: McGill University Press, 1977), p. 281.

48   PRO FO 800/375, Bax-Ironside to Nicolson, 29 July 1914.

49   PRO FO 371/2164/37861, Minute by Nicolson on Barclay to Foreign Office, 10 August 1914; K. Robbins, 'British diplomacy and Bulgaria, 1914–1915', *Slavonic and East European Studies Review*, vol. 49, no. 117 (1971), p. 565–6.

50   PRO FO 371/2163/37466, Grey to Barclay, 9 August 1914; PRO FO 371/2164/38415, Bertie to Foreign Office, 12 August 1914 and (38473), Buchanan to Foreign Office, 12 August 1914 and (38476), Buchanan to Foreign Office, 12 August 1914; G. E. Torrey, 'Rumania and the belligerents 1914–1916', *Journal of Contemporary History*, vol. 1, no. 3 (1966), pp. 171–2.

51   Marder, *From the Dreadnought*, Vol. 2, pp. 20–31; U. Trumpener, 'Turkey's entry into World War One: An assessment of responsibilities', *Journal of Modern History*, vol. 34, no. 4 (1962), pp. 369–71; H. S. W. Corrigan, 'German-Turkish relations and the outbreak of war in 1914: a reassessment', *Past and Present*, no. 36 (1967), pp. 144–52; Brock (eds), *H. H. Asquith*, p. 168; PRO FO 371/2169/56661, Buchanan to Foreign Office, 6 October 1914 and (37824), Capt. W. H. Deedes, Report on a journey from Constantinople, through Rumania, Hungary and Germany to London, 10 August 1914; PRO FO 371/2170/39200, Beaumont to Foreign Office, 13 August 1914.

52   Judith Brown, 'War and the colonial relationship: Britain, India and the war of 1914–1918', in M. R. D. Foot (ed.), *War and Society. Historical Essays in Honour and Memory of J. R. Western, 1928–1971* (London: Paul Elek, 1973), pp. 89–90.

53   PRO FO 371/2162/36525, Cheetham to Foreign Office, 6 August 1914; PRO FO 371/2169/44613, Cheetham to Foreign Office, 29 August 1914.

54   PRO FO 371/2164/38465, Minute by Nicolson on Erskine to Foreign Office, 12 August 1914, and Grey to Erskine, Bertie and Buchanan, 14 August 1914.

55   Brock (eds), *H. H. Asquith*, p. 171; J. Heller, 'Sir Louis Mallet and the Ottoman Empire: The road to war', *Middle Eastern Studies*, vol. 12, no. 1 (1976), pp. 3–9; C. Jay Smith, 'Great Britain and the 1914–1915 Straits agreement with Russia: The British promise of November 1914', *American Historical Review*, vol. 70, no. 4 (1964–5) pp. 1015–19.

56   Brock (eds), *H. H. Asquith*,. pp. 181–2; PRO FO 800/100, Note by Asquith [20] August 1914; PRO FO 371/2172/40993, Erskine to Foreign Office, 19 August 1914, Grey to Erskine, 20 August 1914; Grey to Bertie and Buchanan, 20 August 1914.

57   PRO FO 371/2161/35946, Grey to Buchanan, 5 August 1914; H. Wilson, Note on a meeting at Chantilly, 29 March 1915, Sir H. Wilson mss, box 73/1/19; M. O. 3 (b), The strategical aspect of a war between Germany and Russia, 18 December 1911, Sir H. Wilson mss, box 73/1/24. On Anglo-Russian relations between 1914–17, K. Neilson, *Strategy and Supply: The Anglo-Russian Alliance 1914–1917* (London: Allen & Unwin, 1984) is indispensable.

58   E. David (ed.), *Inside Asquith's Cabinet*, p. 184; Brock (eds), *H. H. Asquith*, pp. 192–7; Samuel to his wife, 24 August 1914, Samuel mss, A/157/725; PRO FO 371/2164/41420, Villiers to Foreign Office, 20 August 1914; PRO FO 371/2095/41804, Buchanan to Grey, 22 August 1914.

59   P. Renouvin, 'L'opinion publique en France pendant la guerre 1914–1918', *Revue d'histoire Diplomatique*, Vol. 84, no. 4 (1970), pp. 291–8; J. C. King, *Generals and Politicians. Conflict between France's High Command, Parliament and Government, 1914–1918* (Berkeley, Calif.: University of California Press, 1951), pp. 11–24.

60 Brock (eds), *H. H. Asquith*, pp. 204–5, 208–10; Holmes, *The Little Field Marshal*, pp. 227–32; PRO FO 371/2170/45399, Buchanan to Foreign Office, 1 September 1914; PRO FO 371/2173/44502, Grey to Buchanan, 29 August 1914 and (44774), Bertie to Grey, 30 August 1914 and (44895), Buchanan to Foreign Office, 30 August 1914.

61 Brock (eds) *H. H. Asquith*, pp. 208–9, 213; Holmes, *The Little Field Marshal*, pp. 232–4; PRO FO 371/2167/45032, Bertie to Foreign Office, 31 August 1914 and (45087), 31 August 1914.

62 PRO FO 371/2165/43561, Howard to Foreign Office, 26 August 1914 and (44218), Rodd to Foreign Office, 28 August 1914 and (44609), Mallet to Foreign Office, 29 August 1914 and (44611), Barclay to Foreign Office, 29 August 1914; B. J. Hendrick (ed.), *The Life and Letters of Walter Hines Page* (London: Heinemann, 1930), pp. 401–2.

63 Viscount Grey, *Twenty-Five Years, 1892–1916*, Vol. 2 (London: Hodder and Stoughton, 1925), pp. 158–60.

64 PRO FO 371/2173/46060, Nicolson to Grey, 2 September 1914 and (45394), Buchanan to Foreign Office, 1 September 1914 and Grey to Buchanan, 3 September 1914 and (46456), Buchanan to Foreign Office, 5 September 1914.

65 D. Stevenson, 'Belgium, Luxemburg and the defence of Western Europe, 1914–1920', *International History Review*, vol. 4, no. 4 (1982), p. 506; PRO FO 371/2174/49602, Villiers to Foreign Office, 11 September 1914.

3

Russia, Turkey and the Balkans, September–December 1914

IN THE AUTUMN of 1914 British hopes that the war might be over by Christmas evaporated and the Pact of London was placed under growing strain. In November the Turks finally decided to join the Central Powers. That compelled the British to open up two new military fronts, along the Suez Canal and in Mesopotamia. It also confronted them with the possibility that they would have to counter a major campaign of political subversion waged by their enemies among their Muslim populations. And it raised a possible bone of contention with the Russians over the ultimate disposal of Constantinople and the Straits. At the same time the allies also began to demand that the British fulfil their role as the banker and supplier of the Entente. None of this would have mattered very much if only the French and Russian armies had been advancing towards Berlin. But they were not. By December the Anglo–French forces in the West had stabilized the line, leaving the Germans in occupation of most of Belgium and much of northern France. The Russians had suffered a series of defeats at the hands of the Germans and the Russian 'steamroller' was in no condition to roll towards Berlin.

The Germans began to encourage Muslim agitators in Egypt and India even before the war began. On 31 July the Kaiser wrote that 'our consuls in Turkey and India, etc., must get a conflagration going throughout the whole Mohammedan world against this hated, unscrupulous dishonest nation of shopkeepers – since if we are going to bleed to death, England must at least lose India'.[1] A day later the Turko–German treaty of alliance was signed and in the autumn of 1914 several mixed German–Turkish missions were dispatched to Persia, India, Afghanistan, Libya and Morocco to stir up disaffection among the Muslim populations of Germany's enemies and compel them to divert men away from the main fronts in Europe. In Persia the Germans tried to establish a coalition of tribes to fight the British and in Afghanistan they sought to persuade the Emir to support a jihad against the British along the North West Frontier of India.[2] Throughout August the British made repeated attempts to persuade the Turks to repatriate the German crews of the *Goeben* and *Breslau*, but by early September it was apparent that they had no intention of doing so and the British ambassador at Constantinople concluded that all he could do was to postpone an open breach for as long as possible.[3] Churchill, still hankering after a Balkan confederation, pressed the Cabinet to break the deadlock in the Balkans by abandoning the formula of Ottoman integrity and promising the Bulgarians the territory they had lost during the second Balkan War if they agreed to re-establish the confederation. The Cabinet remained hesitant but finally agreed to threaten the Turks that if they did not put an end to Germany's growing influence in Constantinople, Britain would adopt a hostile attitude towards Turkey.

This was to no avail for on 1 October the Turks closed the Straits. The Russians were alarmed because at a stroke the Turks had shut-off half of their export trade. On 2 October the British Cabinet retaliated by abandoning their support for Ottoman integrity. But even that did not pave the way for a Balkan confederation brought into existence by promises of Turkish territory.[4] The Russian victory against the Austrians at Lemberg in early September had increased enthusiasm for the Entente among politically articulate Romanians (always in a minority in a country where 80 per cent of the population were unenfranchised peasants). But the dying King Carol still opposed intervention against the Central Powers and although the prime minister, Bratiano, was convinced by the Battle of the Marne that the Entente would be the ultimate winners and wished to use the war to complete Romania's national unity, he was also well aware that the Romanian army was not yet ready for war. On 23 September he signed an agreement with the Italians providing for consultation and joint action. His expectation that this would significantly enhance Romania's bargaining position with the Entente was rapidly fulfilled. On 2 October, without consulting the British, Sazonov promised Romania much of what it might expect if it joined the Entente (Transylvania and part of Bukovina) merely for staying neutral. This is one illustration of why Britain's Balkan diplomacy failed in the autumn of 1914. With the possible exception of Greece, with its long and vulnerable coastline, Britain had no significant influence in the Balkans. Conversely the Russians wielded considerable influence and used it without consulting their Entente partners. Grey could only remonstrate, for although he wanted to create a Balkan confederation his first priority was to maintain the loyalty of existing allies. It would benefit the British nothing if, in gaining Bulgaria, Greece and Romania, they alienated Russia. He could, therefore, do no more than allow the Russians to lead.[5]

The dependence of the Western allies on the Russian army grew in September and October. Bertie estimated the French had lost 360,000 men in August and September. The British and French armies had pursued the Germans from the Marne to the Aisne but were then brought to a standstill. They therefore looked to Russia to break the deadlock. But news from Russia was sketchy and late. On 13 September Buchanan reported that the Russians had suffered a setback at Tannenberg but believed that their victories in Galicia against Austria meant that the Austrian army would remain a negligible force for the remainder of the war.[6] The Western allies were dismayed to hear that enemy troop concentrations near Cracow meant that the Grand Duke would have to postpone his advance on Berlin. The possibility of a long pause before the next Russian offensive was doubly disquieting because of intelligence reports the British began to receive in late September of German plans to launch an invasion of Britain from the Belgian Channel ports. In fact these were false rumours deliberately spread by the Germans to conceal the movement of troops from France and Belgium to the Eastern front. However, the British secret intelligence services were largely improvised after the outbreak of war and did not detect this.[7] Kitchener took the possibility of invasion very seriously and on 4 October telegraphed to Buchanan that

> It is most important that we should be kept informed as to the real progress of the fighting on the Eastern frontier of Germany in the next few weeks. Upon this will depend the critical decision that we shall have to take as regards sending troops abroad or keeping them at home.
>
> If the Russians defeat or continue to press back the Germans we can with safety send troops abroad to help France and Belgium.
>
> But if there is deadlock between Russian and Germans forces such as there had been in France for last 3 weeks and the Germans are able to maintain a defensive line we must be prepared for an attempt to land German troops in England and if we are misled as to real situation that developed between Russians and Germans and denude this country of regular troops in the winter we may suddenly be confronted with a situation at home that would not only be critical but fatal.[8]

Kitchener's telegram elicited little actual news. Throughout October the War Office and Cabinet remained largely ignorant of what was happening on the Russian front.

They were, therefore, all the more concerned that the Russians might divert troops away from the Eastern front towards Turkey because of the closure of the Straits. In the course of a casual conversation with Buchanan and the French ambassador Paléologue on 12 September, Sazonov mentioned that at the end of the war he hoped that the Straits question would be settled according to the interests of Russia and

Romania and that the principle of nationality, applied against the Germans, would guide the territorial settlement in Europe. Russia might acquire the mouth of the Nieman, Posen and the Polish-speaking areas of Silesia would be combined with Russian Poland. The Dual Monarchy should be trisected into the three kingdoms of Austria, Hungary and Bohemia. Serbia should gain Bosnia, Herzegovina and parts of Dalmatia. Schleswig–Holstein should be ceded to Denmark, France should regain Alsace–Lorraine and Britain would be allowed to retain the German colonies it had captured. This indicated that Sazonov at least was committed to the vigorous prosecution of the war until the Entente could impose their aims on the Central Powers. Such an extensive rearrangement of the territorial map of Europe would never come about by negotiation. But his musings did not represent a definitive Russian war aims programme. Buchanan reported it in a private letter to Nicolson, not in an official telegram, and the British made no immediate response.[9]

A month later Buchanan sent home a more disquieting report of rumours circulating in Petrograd that a group of officials in the Russian foreign ministry were working for some kind of negotiated settlement between Germany and Russia. The British already knew that Witte had opposed Russia's entry into the war because he did not think that it was in any way prepared for war and now Buchanan reported that he was conducting 'a mischievous campaign against views and policy of Russian Government and also of His Majesty's Government in regard to the war'.[10] In early November rumours reached Buchanan that Witte was seeing an American lawyer and legal adviser to the American State Department and it was possible that they were considering ways of ending the war by mediation. Grey was pleased to hear that Witte's opinions were not representative of the Russian government, but even so he believed that he had to do something to encourage the pro-war party in Russia. Turkey's action on 29 October in allowing the *Goeben* and *Breslau* to attack Russia's Black Sea coast offered him the perfect opportunity. Sazonov told Buchanan that Turkey's entry into the war would be welcomed in Russia because it would entail the final settlement of the Straits question. 'For this reason', he concluded, 'war is likely to be welcomed by a large section of the Russian public who were afraid that Russia would gain no solid advantages from the war with Austria and Germany.'[11]

Grey realized that the reactionaries might be reluctant to continue the war simply to crush their fellow autocrats in Berlin and Vienna but war for Constantinople would be attractive to reactionary and liberal Russians alike. The British had no option other than to declare war on Turkey on 4 November for had they held aloof they would have placed an intolerable strain upon the Russian alliance and the Cabinet had no objection to going a long way towards meeting Russia's wishes over Constantinople.

Asquith privately believed that at the end of the war Turkey ought to be driven from Europe once and for all, and that Constantinople ought to become either a free port or a Russian city. On 12 November, therefore, Grey assured Sazonov that after Germany had been defeated the final disposal of Constantinople would be settled in accordance with Russia's desires.[12] This was the first, but certainly not the last occasion on which the British offered their allies the tempting prospect of territorial gains after the war to ensure that they continued fighting.

Turkey's entry into the war posed a direct threat to the security of Britain's empire in the Middle East and India. By early October it was apparent that war with Turkey was probably only a matter of weeks away. The British did not fear the Turks' military or naval power. Since the Young Turk revolution of 1908, British opinion of the Turks' military prowess had steadily diminished as the Directorate of Military Operations collected intelligence showing that experienced senior officers were being dismissed and were replaced by ill-trained juniors. The Balkan Wars only seemed to confirm that the Turks were finished as a military power. But they were afraid that war against the Caliph would encourage disaffection among the Muslims of India and Egypt and their policies in the opening months of the war were designed to minimize that disaffection. The Russians reported that at the end of October the Turks had 88,000 men in Syria and Palestine poised to attack the Suez Canal. The British C.-in-C. in Egypt, Sir John Maxwell, did not think that the Turks would be able to send a large force across the Sinai peninsula to attack the Suez Canal, but then they might not have to. The European population was already afraid of a Turkish attack, 'and the natives know jolly well the funk they are in'.[13] The Turkish Press was busy inciting religious feeling against the British, and Egyptian nationalist politicians blamed the British for the problems the local cotton-growers faced in selling their crops. The British administration retaliated by secretly inserting pro-British and anti-Turkish articles in the local press. British and Russian intelligence confirmed that the Khedive, who was visiting Constantinople, had thrown in his lot with the Committee of Union and Progress.[14] In India the Viceroy, Lord Hardinge, believed that as long as great care was taken not to offend the religious susceptibilities of the Muslim population the country would remain quiet. The state of the army, however, was of paramount importance, not least because it contained a disproportion-ately large number of Muslims. He preferred to have as many of them out of the country as possible because, if they did mutiny, it would be safer for India if they did so abroad. But his C.-in-C. in India, Sir Beauchamp Duff, was equally afraid that if too many troops were taken away from the North West Frontier the Afghans would be encouraged to start trouble.[15]

On 14 November the Caliph declared a jihad against Britain, France and Russia. In Egypt the call fell flat. Two days before the war started Maxwell had declared martial law, the garrison was reinforced by Indian and later by Australian and New Zealand troops, and British intelligence officers uncovered a number of German and Turkish plots. In the Sudan the governor, Sir Reginald Wingate, discovered that several native officers were sympathetic to the Turks and Germans and at least one was caught spying. A ship was wrecked off the coast carrying copies of a proclamation calling for a jihad. Most important of all, the British ensured the loyalty of the ordinary Egyptian peasant by buying his cotton crop.[16] The anomalous position of the Khedive and of Egypt itself, still technically one of the Sultan's domains although now a major military base of one of his enemies, was also overcome. Grey had considered deposing the Khedive even before the war and replacing him with his more pliant and pro-British uncle. The Foreign Secretary now wanted to annex Egypt outright. But Sir Miles Cheetham, the acting Consul-General, opposed annexation because it would infuriate Egyptian opinion. Ronald Storrs, the oriental secretary at the British consulate, proposed that as a compromise Egypt should be declared a kingdom and the Khedive's uncle should be placed on the throne. He also attached much importance to giving the new ruler the title of Sultan. Those Egyptians who had qualms about living under British occupation in a war against the Sultan in Constantinople might rally to their own Sultan in Cairo.[17]

Storr's advice was accepted. Egypt was declared a British protectorate and on 19 December the new Sultan mounted his throne in the course of a ceremony carefully stage-managed by the British and designed to give the impression of maximum support for the new regime. Quite who the Cairo authorities thought they were fooling is unclear. After the event Storrs wrote that 'On the surface there is complete calm and general acquiescence both in the Protectorate and the Sultanate, but one is all the same vaguely aware of occasional mutterings and rumblings which necessitate pretty continuous watchfulness'.[18]

Maxwell was prepared to defend Egypt along the line of the Suez Canal but hoped that it would not be necessary to try to do so. Instead he proposed that a British force should land on the Syrian coast, behind the Turks, and sever their communications with Constantinople. Kitchener liked the idea but Grey did not. Just as the Russians were sensitive about the postwar status of Constantinople, so the French were sensitive about Syria. French diplomats and colonialists were divided about the future of the Turkish empire. Some still hoped that it could be preserved more or less intact but others accepted that partition was now inevitable and wanted France to grab what it could. None of them wanted to see Britain establish itself in Syria.[19] The cause of allied harmony meant, therefore, that Maxwell had to wait for the Turks along the Canal.

In 1911 Sir Douglas Haig, then Chief of the General Staff in India, had complained that Hardinge was blind to the danger of German penetration via Baghdad into Persia and Afghanistan. Hardinge had also turned down Haig's suggestion that India should have a properly equipped expeditionary force capable of taking part in a European war. By 1914 the Indian army was ill-prepared for anything more serious than a war on the North West Frontier of India.[20] Even so in 1914 Kitchener used the Indian army as an imperial fire brigade. A complete Indian corps was dispatched to the Mediterranean and thence to the Western front where it suffered very heavy casualties. Other units were sent to Egypt and an expeditionary force was dispatched to German East Africa. To Duff's pleas that these and other overseas commitments left his forces on the frontier dangerously thin, Kitchener replied that

> I do not think you quite realise in India what the war is going to be. If we lose it, it will be worse for India than any success of internal revolution, of frontier attacks, for there will be no one to reconquer India after it is over, so it will be better for India to see that we win.[21]

But the government of India and the India Office were not only concerned about immediate prospects on the frontier. Britain's supremacy in the Persian Gulf rested on command of the sea and the network of political relations it had established with the local sheikhs on either side of the Shatt-al-Arab. On 11 August the Turks began to mobilize their Baghdad army and to seize British property. The India Office was afraid that if they allowed the lion's tail to be twisted in this fashion the Gulf rulers and the whole of Arabia would join the Turks. The Sharif of Mecca, the guardian of the Muslim holy places in Arabia, might endorse the Caliph's call for a jihad and Persia and ultimately Afghanistan would rise against the British. To counter this, on 26 September the military secretary of the India Office, Sir Edmund Barrow, suggested that a British force should be landed at the head of the Gulf to encourage the sheikhs to remain loyal.[22] On 2 October the Cabinet agreed but, in order not to provoke the Turks, insisted that no troops should land on Turkish territory until after war had been declared. British consular representatives in the gulf reassured the local rulers that the troops had been sent to protect them from the Turks.[23] The best Indian divisions had already gone overseas and the troops who made up Force D and were sent to the Gulf, the sixth Division under Sir Arthur Barrett, were not fit for war against a European enemy but were thought to be adequate to carry out what was conceived of as being little more than a flag-waving expedition.[24]

The demonstration in the Gulf began on 1 November and by 23 November Barrett had occupied the major town of Basra at the head of the Gulf. But his political adviser, Sir Percy Cox, believed that unless the momentum of the British advance was maintained the Turks would still be able to subvert the Arabs and Persians. He therefore suggested that, with a single division, Barrett should advance nearly 400 miles up the River Tigris to Baghdad.[25] Cox and Hardinge wanted to couple this with a proclamation annexing Basra in order to reassure the Arabs that they would never be returned to Turkish rule. Realism increased with distance from Basra. Crewe, the Secretary of State for India and the minister responsible for operations in Mesopotamia, immediately ruled out annexation as being a violation of the Pact of London. Barrow agreed that the British had to maintain their momentum but that an advance on Baghdad with only one division was premature and dangerous. He recommended a more modest proposal, the occupation of Qurna, situated fifty miles up the Tigris at its confluence with the River Euphrates. Once there the British would control the navigable waterways and be better able to prevent German–Turkish attacks on the Persian oilfields just across the border. Crewe agreed and Qurna was occupied on 9 December. He then forbade any further advance.[26] Force D appeared to have achieved its objectives at remarkably little cost.

The signing of the Pact of London had done nothing to regulate Britain's economic relations with its allies. Before 1914 it had been taken for granted that, as the world's leading creditor nation, Britain would easily be able to finance its allies. No thought had been given to the limits of Britain's financial resources or how the necessary money might be raised. No plans had been prepared to show how Britain would allocate the goods and services like shipping that it might employ to assist its allies. Such was the confidence in Britain's world economic leadership that all this was left to be improvised under the pressure of events. In August the Treasury took the first tentative step towards organizing Britain's financial resources to help the allies by preventing British capital escaping to neutral countries when they banned all foreign capital issues except those made with their express permission. The War Office also began to look to the USA, the only major industrial country not already involved in the war, as a possible source of supplies. And on 18 August the British and French established the first of many inter-allied economic agencies, the Commission Internationale de Ravitaillement (CIR). Composed originally of officials of the War Office, the Board of Trade and the Admiralty and representatives of the French government, its purpose was to co-ordinate the purchase of supplies for the French armed forces in Britain and abroad. By co-operating they hoped to avoid bidding against each other and forcing up prices. The Belgians joined the CIR on 1 September, the Russians a few days later, the Serbs on 6 November and the Japanese and Italians in June 1915. However, the CIR did not solve all the problems associated with allied purchasing. Several Russian government departments ignored it and continued their prewar system by which foreign contracts were placed according to bureaucratic fiat and often only after lucrative bribes had been paid to some of the officials concerned.[27] Britain also started to send arms to its allies in mid-August. The first Austrian invasion of Serbia began on 12 August. Four days later Crowe suggested that the British ought to give the Serbs and Montenegrins money and arms. Grey was willing to help but was once again wary of acting unilaterally in the Balkans without first consulting the Russians. They had already given the Serbs £600,000 and 50,000 rifles but welcomed the British offer of more money. On 2 September the Cabinet agreed to lend the Serbs £800,000. A week later, without consulting anyone, they granted a loan of £10m to Belgium. At the beginning of December the Belgians returned, asking for a second loan of £60m. The Cabinet agreed to give them half of this sum, on the assumption that the French would supply the remainder. But the French could not. Even before the war the French government had been borrowing quite small sums at what the British considered to be ruinously high interest rates. Hitherto, because the French kept large gold reserves, the British had assumed that their credit was good. But at the end of November the French government asked to be allowed to float a loan of £8–10m on the London money market backed by a British government guarantee. They hoped that, by raising the money in the world's premier money market, they would prove to their own investors that their credit was sound. The Treasury was reluctant to agree as it would drain gold from London but, as the matter was so vital to French credit, they could not refuse. Lloyd George was downcast by the whole episode and afraid that it might indicate that the French would not be able to go on fighting beyond June 1915.[28]

But a worse shock was soon to follow and one which was to indicate that the Entente would have to do more not only to co-ordinate their economic policies but their military policies as well. The Russians were granted their first loan of £20m at the end of September and they returned in December asking for another £100m. On 16 December the War Council, which began a series of intermittent meetings in late November, only agreed to £40m and then under strict conditions. The loan was to be repaid at 5 per cent interest, it was only to be spent in Britain and the Russians were to ship gold to London to cover it. These strings caused great indignation in Russian financial circles and Hugh O'Beirne, the councillor at the British embassy in Petrograd, advised Tyrrell that unless the Russians were granted the loan on roughly the terms they sought, there would be a period when M. Bark, the Russian finance minister, 'will be at his wits end to find money to carry on the war with'.[29] That prediction could not have come at a more significant moment. Turkey's entry into the war had done nothing to convince the Balkan neutrals that they ought to join the Entente. On 7 November the British, French and

Russians offered the Bulgarians all the territory it had lost to Turkey during the second Balkan War but Ferdinand would not budge. He also wanted a large part of Serbian Macedonia. The Serbs, who loathed the Bulgarians almost as much as the Austrians and who had already successfully repulsed one Austrian invasion, refused to concede any-thing.[30] At the end of November, Bax-Ironside reported that both the Bulgarian court and cabinet were hostile to Britain and looked forward to war with Serbia. The Austrians then mounted a second invasion of Serbia and for two weeks occupied Belgrade until the Serbs again drove them back across the border. Lloyd George and Churchill wanted to offer Bulgaria the whole of Macedonia simply to refrain from attacking Serbia when it was at its weakest. But Grey's common sense prevailed. 'Bulgaria would not be bought by the size of the promise, but would consider which group would most probably be in a position to redeem its promises.'[31]

The only ally with any real influence in the Balkans was Russia but by the end of 1914 it was hardly in a position to exert it. Throughout November Buchanan reported news of large German troop movements towards Russia together with a German attack to the west of Warsaw and predicted that it would be some time before the Russians mounted another invasion of Germany, but most decision-makers in London remained optimistic about the situation on the Russian front. No one doubted that the Russian army was the allies' trump card. Nicolson wrote that in the spring of 1915 Russia 'will be the power to give the deciding stroke in the campaign, and we are all much beholden to her'.[32] But on 4 December, the Grand Duke informed his Western counterparts that unless they took the offensive, the Germans would be able to continue to move troops to the Russian front and his men would have to halt where they were. This news shocked the government out of some of its complacency. The DMO, Sir Charles Callwell, now thought that the Russians could only just hold their own on the Eastern front. Buchanan then reported that there was a growing feeling amongst the Russian public that the Western allies, and especially Britain, had left them in the lurch. Some Moscow merchants, usually among Britain's warmest admirers, had coined the phrase that 'England will fight till the last Russian soldier'.[33] Buchanan thought that Witte was behind the whole campaign and Arthur Balfour, the former Unionist Prime Minister who was now a member of the War Council, was certain that there were powerful influences at work in Russia in favour of a speedy negotiated peace with Germany.[34] Despite reports of German troop movements eastwards, Grey was afraid that if the Russian front remained inactive the Germans would switch their forces back to the West for a major offensive. There was little immediate military help the British could offer. The first New Army would not be ready until March 1915. The Grand Duke blamed Russia's inactivity on shortages of rifles and shells and warned that only quick deliveries would allow him to resume the offensive in the spring. For the time being the government realized that all it could do was to seek more clarification of the situation. Kitchener and Grey decided that it was vital to have more information about the real state of the Russian army and its munitions supplies. They also asked Sir John French and Joffre to provide a joint assessment of the situation for their governments so that all three allies could try to co-ordinate their policies.

Between August and November 1914 the British entered not one but two wars, against Germany and Austria–Hungary in Europe and Germany and Turkey in the Middle East. In both cases they expected France and Russia to bear the brunt of the fighting on land, whilst they provided them with money and supplies. The events of the opening months of the war presented them with a series of surprises. None of the belligerents collapsed under the economic dislocation caused by the outbreak of war. In Egypt and India war against Turkey did not ignite a second Indian Mutiny, although the fear of one persisted and was a major factor underlying Britain's policy in the Middle East throughout 1915. In Europe, despite numerous British blandishments, the smaller powers who had not been invaded remained neutral. The French and British abandoned most of Belgium and large parts of northern France to the Germans but stopped them from capturing Paris. In the East the Serbs repulsed the Austrians but the Russians, despite some considerable success against the Austrians, failed to reach Berlin. By December the Eastern and Western fronts were in deadlock and the British government was beginning to recognize that it was engaged in a war between two coalitions and would have to do much more to co-ordinate its economic, political and military policies with its allies.

Notes

1   M. Balfour, *The Kaiser and his Times* (London: Cresset Press, 1964), p. 352.
2   E. Burk, 'Moroccan resistance, pan-islam and German war strategy, 1914–1918', *Francia*, vol. 3 (1975), pp. 434–64; U. Trumpener, 'Suez, Baku and Gallipoli: the military dimensions of the German–Ottoman coalition, 1914–1918', in K. Neilson and R. A. Prete (eds), *Coalition Warfare: An Uneasy Accord* (Waterloo, Ontario: Wilfred Laurier Press, 1984), pp. 40–1.
3   J. Heller, 'Sir Louis Mallet and the Ottoman empire: The road to war', *Middle Eastern Studies*, vol. 12, no. 1 (1976), pp. 3–17.
4   C. Jay Smith, 'Great Britain and the 1915–1915 Straits agreement with Russia: The British promise of November 1914', *American Historical Review*, vol. 70, no. 4 (1964–5), pp. 1021–6; PRO FO 800/88, Churchill to Grey, 23 September 1914.

5   K. Neilson, *Strategy and Supply: The Anglo-Russian Alliance, 1914–1917* (London: Allen & Unwin, 1984), pp. 46–7; C. J. Lowe, 'The failure of British diplomacy in the Balkans, 1914–1916', *Canadian Journal of History*, vol. 4, no. 1 (1969), pp. 77, 81–2; G. E. Torrey, 'Rumania and the belligerents, 1914–1916', *Journal of Contemporary History*, vol. 1, no. 3 (1966), pp. 177–9.

6   PRO FO 800/375, Buchanan to Nicolson, 13 September 1914; PRO FO 800/56A, Bertie to Grey, 21 September 1914; PRO FO 371/2170/47612, Buchanan to Foreign Office, 8 September 1914.

7   D. French, 'Sir John French's secret service on the Western front, 1914–1915', *Journal of Strategic Studies*, vol. 7, no. 4 (1984), pp. 423–40; PRO FO 371/2165/51967, Grant Duff to Foreign Office, 22 September 1914; PRO FO 371/2095/52753, Buchanan to Foreign Office, 24 September 1914.

8   PRO FO 371/2095/55811, Kitchener to Buchanan, 4 October 1914; K. Neilson, 'Kitchener: A reputation refurbished?', *Canadian Journal of History*, vol. 15, no. 2 (1980), pp. 207–8; E. David (ed.), *Inside Asquith's Cabinet: From the Diaries of Charles Hobhouse* (London: John Murray, 1977), p. 200.

9   PRO FO 800/275, Buchanan to Nicolson, 13 September 1914; W. A. Renzi, 'Who composed "Sazonov's Thirteen Points"? A re-examination of Russia's war aims of 1914', *American Historical Review*, vol. 88, no. 2 (1983), pp. 347–57.

10 PRO FO 371/2176/69090, Bertie to Foreign Office, 9 November 1914 and (70275), Foreign Office to Buchanan, 11 November 1914 and (70439), Buchanan to Foreign Office, 12 November 1914; G. Katkov, *Russia 1917: The February Revolution* (London: Longman, 1967), pp. 64–6; Lady Algernon Gordon Lennox (ed.), *The Diary of Lord Bertie of Thame, 1914–1918*, Vol. 1 (London: Hodder & Stoughton, 1924), p. 7.

11 Buchanan to Grey, 29 October 1914, quoted in Martin Gilbert (ed.), *Winston S. Churchill*, Vol. 3, *Companion*, pt 1 (London: Heinemann, 1971), p. 234.

12 Neilson, *Strategy*, pp. 49–50; W. A. Renzi, 'Great Britain, Russia and the Straits, 1914–1915', *Journal of Modern History*, vol. 42, no. 1 (1970), p. 5, PRO CAB 19/33, Minutes of evidence of the Dardanelles Commission, Q. 791 (Grey).

13 PRO 30/57/45/QQ/45, Maxwell to Kitchener, 5 October 1914; PRO FO 371/2170/62322, Buchanan to Foreign Office, 22 October 1914 (65336), Buchanan to Grey, 30 October 1914; St Loe Strachey to Gertrude Bell, 9 October 1914, St Loe Strachey mss, S/18/1/8; Sir R. Storrs, *Orientations* (London: Ivor Nicholson & Watson, 1939), pp. 151, 153–5; D. French, 'The origins of the Dardanelles campaign reconsidered', *History*, vol. 68, no. 223 (1983), pp. 211–14.

14 PRO 30/57/45/QQ/49, Graham to Kitchener, 24 October 1914; PRO FO 371/2172/63870, Grey to Cheetham, 27 October 1914.

15 PRO FO 800/375, Hardinge to Nicolson, 5 October 1914; PRO CAB 19/8, Mesopotamian Commission, Duff to Kitchener, 30 August and 24 September 1914.

16 PRO 30/57/45/QQ/44, Wingate to Fitzgerald, 28 September 1914 and (QQ/54), Wingate to Clayton, 7 November 1914 and (QQ/58), Graham to Kitchener, 8 November 1914 and (QQ/62), Note by Storrs, 7 November 1914 and (QQ763), Storrs to Fitzgerald, 29 November 1914.

17 J. Darwin, *Britain, Egypt and the Middle East. Imperial Policy in the Aftermath of War, 1918–1922* (London: Macmillan, 1981), pp. 60–2; PRO 30/57/45/QQ/62, Note by Storrs, 7 November 1914.

18 PRO 30/57/45/QQ/73, Storrs to Fitzgerald, 28 December 1914; PRO FO 633/24A, Herbert to Cromer, 2 January 1915.

19   PRO FO 800/102, Kitchener to Grey and minute by Grey [n.d. but *c.* 11 November 1914]; Jukka Nevakivi, *Britain, France and the Arab Middle East, 1914–1920* (London: Athlone Press, 1969), p. 14; C. M. Andrew and A. S. Kanya-Forstner, *France Overseas. The Great War and the Climax of French Imperial Expansion* (London: Thames & Hudson, 1981), pp. 40–9.

20   Haig to Wilson, 19 April 1911, Sir H. Wilson mss, box 73/1/17; [Cd. 8610.] *Mesopotamian Commission Report*, 1917, pp. 10–11; J. D. Goold, 'Lord Hardinge and the Mesopotamian expedition and inquiry, 1914–1917', *Historical Journal*, vol. 19, no. 4 (1976), pp. 920–3; J. S. Galbraith, 'No man's child: the campaign in Mesopotamia, 1914–1916', *International History Review*, vol. 6, no. 3 (1984), p. 376.

21   PRO CAB 19/8, Mesopotamian Commission, Kitchener to Duff, 24 September 1914.

22   PRO CAB 19/8, Mesopotamian Commission. Proceedings, Q. 9 (Barrow); PRO WO 106/877, Precis of correspondence regarding the Mesopotamian expedition: its genesis and development. Sir G. Barrow. The role of India in a Turkish War, 26 September 1914; B. C. Busch, *Britain, India and the Arabs, 1914–1921* (Berkeley, Calif.: University of California Press, 1971), pp. 3–10; S. A. Cohen, 'The genesis of the British campaign in Mesopotamia, 1914', *Middle Eastern Studies*, vol. 12, no. 2 (1976), pp. 119–26.

23   PRO WO 106/877, Crewe to Hardinge, 26 September, 2, 3, 5 and 8 October 1914; Busche, *Britain, India*, p. 15; PRO FO 800/375, Hardinge to Nicolson, 5 October 1914.

24   Callwell to Wilson, 26 September 1914, Sir H. Wilson mss, box 73/1/18.

25   PRO WO 106/877, Hardinge to Crewe and enc. from Cox, 25 November 1914.

26   PRO WO 106/877, Minute by the Military Secretary, India Office (Barrow), 27 November 1914; Crewe to Hardinge, 27 and 30 November 1914; Busch, *Britain, India*, pp. 23–6.

27   K. M. Burk, 'The Treasury: from impotence to power', in K. M. Burk (ed.), *War and the State: The Transformation of British Government, 1914–1919* (London: Allen & Unwin, 1982), pp. 86–7; K. Neilson, 'Russian foreign purchasing in the Great War: a test case', *Slavonic and East European Studies Review*, vol. 60, no. 4 (1982), p. 573–4; Neilson, *Strategy*, pp. 51–4; *History of the Ministry of Munitions*, Vol. 2, pt 8 (London: HMSO, 1920), pp. 5–7.

28   D. French, *British Economic and Strategic Planning, 1905–1915* (London: Allen & Unwin, 1982), pp. 151–2; PRO FO 371/2172/40156, Minute by Crowe, 16 August 1914 and Grey to Buchanan, 17 August 1914 and (41426), Buchanan to Grey, 20 August 1914; PRO FO 800/101, Lloyd George to Belgian Minister of Finance, 2 December 1914; PRO FO 800/56A, Bertie to Grey, 28 September 1914; PRO T 170/83, Memo by Bradbury, [n.d. but *c.* December 1914] and Memo by I. R., 1 December 1914.

29   PRO FO 800/74, O'Beirne to Tyrrell, 8 December 1914; PRO FO 800/101, Bradbury to Tyrrell, 26 September 1914; Neilson, *Strategy*, pp. 54–7.

30   PRO FO 800/376, Bax-Ironside to Nicolson, 2 and 22 November 1914 and C. de Graz to Nicolson, 27 November 1914 and Barclay to Nicolson, 14 November 1914; PRO CAB 37/123/30, Bax-Ironside to Grey, 30 November 1914; K. Robbins, 'British diplomacy and Bulgaria, 1914–1915', *Slavonic and East European Studies Review*, vol. 49, no. 117 (1971), pp. 569–70.

31   David (ed.), *Inside Asquith's Cabinet*, p. 208; PRO FO 800/376, Nicolson to Hardinge, 1 and 31 December 1914.

32   PRO FO 800/376, Nicolson to Hardinge, 1 December 1914; PRO FO 371/2171/71/71269, Buchanan to Foreign Office, 14 November 1914 and

(73481), Buchanan to Grey, 20 November 1914; Haldane to his mother, 7, 24, 26 November 1914, Haldane mss, 5992.

33   PRO FO 800/376, Buchanan to Nicolson, 10 December 1914 and enc., Bayley to Buchanan, 8 December 1914; PRO FO 371/2095/78627, Buchanan to Foreign Office, 4 December 1914 and (82761), Buchanan to Foreign Office, 15 December 1914; PRO FO 371/2096/79390, Buchanan to Foreign Office, 6 December 1914.

34   PRO FO 800/376, Balfour to Nicolson, 21 December 1914.

4

The Search for an Entente Strategy, December 1914 – February 1915

THE PACT OF London had been signed, at Russia's insistence, when France seemed to be on the point of defeat and when Russia appeared to be the strongest military power within the Entente. By the end of 1914 these circumstances had altered. The line in the West had stabilized and there was no immediate danger of Paris falling. Although the New Armies were a long way from being ready the British were transforming themselves into a major land power. In time the balance of military power within the alliance might swing towards them. Conversely, although the Russians still had very large manpower reserves, they had lost a very large proportion of their trained men and lacked the rifles, guns and ammunition to enable them to re-equip their forces rapidly. By November the Germans faced the nightmare prospect of a two-front war against a powerful enemy coalition. Their prewar plan, to knock France out of the war within six weeks and then to turn on Russia, had failed. They identified Britian as the centre of the Entente and their most implacable opponent. In 1915–16 they tried to break up the Entente coalition by persuading either the French or the Russians to make a separate peace. The British quickly discovered this and recognized that they could not hope to win the war without French and Russian support. Their very first objective, therefore, became to preserve the cohesion of the Entente alliance.

On 2 December 1914, Lord Esher, who had acted as Kitchener's private factotum in France since September, told Kitchener that the greatest problem confronting the Entente was that

> Perfect frankness is wanting between the highest authorities engaged in conducting the war on behalf of England, France and Russia. The problem of obtaining intimate touch with Russia is very difficult: the

enormous distances, the Romanoff reserve of the Grand Duke and his repugnance to employing diplomatic channels, render the situation a very difficult one. But with regard to France, it would be comparatively simple to establish ties of intimacy. This is an essential condition to carrying on a war with a highly organised and concentrated military power such as Germany. We cannot afford to procrastinate and muddle along, owing to the enormous strain upon France, a strain which is not felt to the same extent in this country, and owing to the psychology of Russia, an Empire that before now, under Alexander a hundred years ago, and in the Crimea sixty years ago, and the other day in Manchuria, suddenly and for no obvious reason, collapsed.[1]

The Germans believed that they were fighting a war of self-defence and that their survival as a world power depended upon their being able to establish a large economic and territorial base within Europe. As their armies moved into enemy territory they sought to erect a series of buffer zones around Germany. That alone was sufficient to ensure a long war. The nation states of early-twentieth-century Europe were extremely sensitive to any attacks on their sovereignty. France and Russia were not ready to allow the Germans to seize their provinces while they had the ability to resist and allies to help them. By late November, with the German failure to take Ypres in the West and Lodz in the East, the early realization of their grandiloquent dreams was dashed. In December the German Chancellor, Bethmann-Hollweg, wrote that 'for us everything depends on shattering the [enemy] coalition, i.e. on [concluding] a separate peace with one of our enemies'.[2] Germany, therefore, began a series of secret approaches to people in Russia, France and Belgium, whom they thought might be susceptible to a negotiated peace. They hoped that their military victories would create a mood of defeatism among the Entente powers which would finally make them ready to negotiate.

The prospect of a long war was unwelcome in Britain but most decision-makers realized that the magnitude of the issues at stake now pointed to a prolonged conflict.[3] In the opening months of the war the Entente's armies had suffered fearful casualties. By December the Russian army had lost about 1·8m casualties, approximately half of its prewar trained manpower. In the winter and spring of 1915 they were replaced but the new recruits went to the front with only 4–6 weeks training and often without rifles. Even so, the British still had enormous faith in Russian numbers if only they could be armed.[4] The Serbs' success in recapturing Belgrade in mid-December was greeted with delight but it was apparent that if the Russians could not contain the bulk of the Central Powers' forces on the Eastern front, Serbia's days would be numbered and so would any possibility of the Balkan neutrals or Italy joining the

Entente.[5] The French had suffered over 200,000 casualties in August alone, a rate of loss probably never again reached by any other army throughout the war. The Germans had occupied large parts of northern France, including some of the most important engineering centres which were lost to the Entente for the duration of the war. The French government sought unsuccessfully to make good some of their own manpower losses by trying to persuade the Japanese to send troops to France. Although the BEF was the smallest of all the armies of the major belligerents in 1914 they too had not escaped the holocaust. By the end of the First Battle of Ypres in November Sir John French's army had suffered 89,000 casualties, nearly 60 per cent of the original force, and at least three times as high as the General Staff's prewar estimates of its likely losses.

Against this background of stalemate and heavy casualties dissatisfaction began to grow among the allies about the size of Britain's contribution to the land war. Some Russians were beginning to whisper that the British intended to fight the war until the last Russian. The French public, many of whom had probably never seen a British soldier, began to question the value of the British army; and Grey and Kitchener, perhaps foolishly, refused to allow French journalists to visit the BEF to publicize its work. French businessmen were jealous at Britian's alleged success in capturing German trade in neutral markets. One correspondent reported that 'the cry of "Perfide Albion" could be heard'.[6] However, although each of the Entente powers had suffered grievously in the opening months of the war none of their governments was disposed to accept a negotiated peace.

Indeed their losses, both of men and territory, made them only more determined to continue fighting. They were not yet exhausted and only victory and the imposition of their own terms on the Central Powers could justify such losses. But, in the knowledge that the precise delineation of territorial war aims was bound to cause dissension, each government tried to refrain from opening the Pandora's box for as long as possible. For example, on 7 November Sazonov rejected an offer to mediate peace made by the Italian ambassador and, after Grey's promise of 12 November concerning Constantinople, the Russian government were content for the time being to leave precise war aims unstated. Grey and Buchanan agreed that, as the allied armies were still a long way from Berlin, anything more would be premature. Even when pressed to be more precise by the French ambassador, Maurice Paléologue, who was probably acting entirely on his own initiative, Sazonov would only stoop to generalities, insisting that the allies had to continue fighting until they could impose their own terms on the Central Powers. On 21 November the tsar was a little more specific but the French ambassador may have given free reign to his novelist's imagination in reporting the tsar's territorial desiderata to his government.[7]

The French foreign minister, Delcassé, agreed that a patched up peace brought about by neutral mediation would only be an armed truce which would be no guarantee of France's future security. On 22 December, when Parliament reconvened in Paris the Prime Minister, Viviani, announced that France would continue fighting until it had extracted indemnities from Germany to reconstruct the devastated areas and would not make peace until it had driven Germany from the occupied provinces, restored Belgium's independence and destroyed Prussian militarism. In January 1915 Delcassé spoke vaguely in private to Bertie about the desirability of dissolving the German empire, ending German rule over the Rhenish provinces and dividing Asia Minor between the Entente powers, and in February Viviani added the liberation of Alsace–Lorraine to the list of French war aims.[8]

French and Russian reluctance to accept neutral mediation while the Germans were in occupation of parts of their country presented Grey with a diplomatic problem. The Entente, and especially Britain, could not afford to give serious offence to President Wilson of the United States. For a decade before 1914 Anglo-American relations, based upon a common language and culture, had been cordial if somewhat distant. There were no major sources of Anglo-American conflict before 1914 and once the European war had begun both governments regarded an Anglo-American war as a disaster which neither of them could afford. British politicians saw America as an adolescent, perhaps a little gauche but likely soon to become a mature and respectable neighbour. They had a low regard for American politicians and the wisdom of American governments. Few Englishmen understood the informality of decision-making in Washington and they thought that most American governments were ignorant of European affairs. The Wilson administration was no exception to this generalization. The British ambassador in Washington, Sir Cecil Spring-Rice, may have been a little handicapped by having too many close friends who were Republicans when a Democrat administration was in the White House, but before the war at least, he more than made up for that by his close relations with Colonel E. M. House, Wilson's friend and confidant. However, as the war progressed and Spring-Rice's temper worsened, he was increasingly ignored by Wilson, who preferred to communicate with Grey through House.[9]

Grey regarded Wilson's attempts to mediate as the work of a well-intentioned meddler who really ought to mind his own business. But it was precisely because the Entente rapidly became dependent on American business that he could not say so and reject Wilson's approaches out of hand. The Entente not only welcomed American moral support, they also required its material assistance in the shape of money, food, raw materials and munitions. Grey's handling of the negotiations with Wilson and House were significant not only because he succeeded in maintaining their benevolent neutrality but also because they compelled him to formulate more clearly than he did anywhere else exactly what his government meant by victory and upon what conditions it was prepared to make peace. Grey knew that not all Americans were Anglophiles and that the Irish and especially the German communities in the USA might try to push Wilson towards a pro-German policy. If the Entente appeared to be unreasonable in rejecting Wilson's offers of mediation or if the blockade of the Central Powers caused too much annoyance in the USA, there was always the possibility that Wilson might try to make the Entente see American reason by placing an embargo on trade with the allies. In order to present the Entente in the best possible light Grey carefully stressed the unselfish aspects of the allies' war aims, such as the paramount need to restore Belgium's independence and to create after the war a permanent agreement between nations which would prevent any one power upsetting the peace of the world.[10]

The first American mediation attempt was an unofficial effort made in the middle of the Battle of the Marne. Oscar Strauss, a German–American lawyer, a former ambassador to Turkey and a member of the Permanent Court of Arbitration at the Hague, suggested to the German ambassador in Washington, Count Bernstorff, that as France had been defeated, the Germans should accept American mediation through an ambassadors' conference. The Germans had no intention of allowing the Americans to save Paris but nor did they wish to incur the odium of rejecting an offer they assumed came from Wilson himself. Bernstorff, therefore, replied that Germany would agree to Strauss's offer but only if the other belligerents also did so, thus leaving 'the odium of rejection on our enemies'.[11] Jules Jusserand, the French ambassador, immediately rejected the offer and henceforth the French government did all it could to stop American mediation. The French could afford to be more brusque than the British. They did not have to bear the lion's share of the odium of imposing the blockade against American trade. Grey and Spring-Rice were more careful to explain fully their reasons for continuing the war. The Entente, they insisted, were not just fighting for their own physical security but because Germany's invasion of Belgium demonstrated that even its most solemn promises offered no guarantee of a lasting peace. Strauss's attempt finally collapsed on 16 September when the Germans replied that they were not ready to negotiate but only to accept the Entente's application for peace. Spring-Rice rejected Bernstorff's subsequent attempt to arrange a secret meeting with him as a crude ploy to sow divisions among the allies. Under no circumstances would the British negotiate with Germany without their allies. As Grey insisted, 'When Germany really wishes for peace she should approach all the Allies or make her wish for mediation known to President Wilson who could then communicate with all the Allies fairly and straightforwardly who would together take the situation into consideration.'[12]

The second American mediation attempt began in December when the German and Austrian ambassadors in Washington asked Wilson to send House to Europe to mediate. As an inducement they even agreed to evacuate and compensate Belgium before negotiations started. Wilson was under considerable domestic pressure to intervene from the cotton states of the South whose trade had been adversely affected by the allied blockade. The Foreign Office was privately wary and impatient of Wilsonian intervention. Eric Drummond minuted that 'The real danger is that Mr. Wilson is quite capable of thinking out a bold stroke of policy, and perhaps we should not forget that in dealing with him we are dealing with a man who is almost, if not quite, a statesman'. Or, as Nicolson explained, 'People in the U.S. have nothing at stake. We and our Allies have our political independence at stake.'[13] In the absence of any confirmation from Berlin, Grey simply did not believe that the Germans would evacuate Belgium and thought this was yet another attempt to divide the Entente.

But again Grey tried not to give offence in Washington. In a private letter to House he explained that he could make no definite reply until he had consulted his allies. But he was frankly sceptical as to whether Germany's notion of a durable peace matched that of the allies. The Germans wanted to place Western Europe under German domination. 'We would rather perish than submit to that.' The Entente did not seek a durable peace by physically crushing Germany, an objective which would probably never be achieved in any case, but they did hope that by inflicting a series of military defeats on it, Germany would become 'a democratic State emancipated from the rule of the Prussian military party'.[14] The best hope for a lasting peace lay in an agreement reached by all the powers, including USA, to safeguard their mutual security by promising to use force against any aggressor. Grey hoped that this would not only appeal to Wilson's idealism but that it would be a long time before he could persuade Congress to underwrite the postwar European settlement and in the meantime the allies might have some peace from American interference.[15]

But Wilson was undeterred by the allies' collective insistence that Germany was not sincere in its search for peace, and House arrived in Britain on 6 February. Irritation with Wilson's persistence in the face of this discouragement led the British to doubt the purity of his motives. A presidential election was due in November 1916 and Spring-Rice believed that 'The President's credit here evidently depends on his acting as mediator successfully. His personal sympathies no doubt are with us, but he wants re-election.' House was wasting his time. Grey carefully repeated his earlier formula and Asquith concluded that his ideas about postwar disarmament and a league of nations to preserve world peace were millennial. House received a similar polite refusal to negotiate in Paris and Grey's scepticism about the Germans' unwillingness to negotiate on the Entente's terms was entirely confirmed by House's visit to Berlin.[16]

From mid-November the British received excellent intelligence through diplomatic channels about the German peace feeler to Belgium, France and Russia designed to divide the Entente.[17] The Germans tried to use the Prime Minister of Luxembourg and the Swiss President to offer favourable terms to the Belgians if they would abandon the Entente. Belgium's defection, by removing the ostensible cause for which Britain had gone to war, might have made it more difficult for the British government to justify their continued participation in the conflict, but France's defection would have been a fatal blow. Germany's policy towards a separate peace with France was coloured by a good deal of wishful thinking. On the eve of war France had been divided by the debate on the Three Year Service Law and a scandal involving the ex-premier Caillaux, whose wife had shot the editor of a Paris paper who was threatening to ruin her husband's reputation. Caillaux had also been one of the leaders of the opposition to the new law and the Germans convinced themselves that France was on the eve of a socialist revolution and so they therefore directed their efforts towards Caillaux and the French left. Bertie had reported in August that if Caillaux had been in power he would have made peace by granting the Germans an indemnity to leave France. The French government were equally suspicious and sent him off on a mission to Brazil to get him out of the way.[18] But in 1914–15 the Germans made their most sustained efforts to secure a separate peace with Russia. They exploited a variety of contacts. These included Witte's former under secretary in the Russian ministry of finance who was married to a German lady and was living in Sweden, the Grand Duchess of Baden, the Danish King Christian, who they hoped might be able to influence the dowager tsarina who was a Danish princess, and Etatsrat Andersen, a director of the Danish East Asiatic Shipping Company. Andersen was a close friend of the Danish king and believed that successful Danish mediation would enormously increase the monarchy's prestige. In the autumn of 1914 he paid two visits to Grey to suggest mediation and Grey again refused to negotiate without France or Russia. In November Andersen contacted the Kaiser through their mutual friend the German shipowner Albert Ballin. The Kaiser refused his offer of general mediation but asked him to open negotiations with the Russians.[19]

Most professional diplomats took a realistic view of rumours that one or other of the allied governments might make a separate peace. They discounted them for what they were, crude German attempts to divide the alliance. But their advice was now at a discount both with their political masters and with some generals at the front. Diplomats and diplomacy had been discredited in August 1914. They were blamed for allowing the war to start in the first place. British politicians operated within a pluralist society in which groups with different aims competed for power. They assumed that their counterparts among the allies worked in a similar environment. Existing governments might be committed to the continued prosecution of the war. But more costly military defeats might spread defeatism among the allied populations and bring to power other politicians more willing to listen to German blandishments. Bertie noted in December that 'Grey did not seem sure of a complete victory not from want of determination on our part but on account of French weakness'.[20] The politicians could not risk the possibility that their more sanguine diplomatic advisers were wrong. The generals in the field were more conscious than anyone of Britain's relatively weak military position and its dependence on its allies. Sir John French's mercurial temperament made him a bad judge of allied prospects but, by early 1915, in his more depressed moods he was doubtful whether either France or Russia could endure a war lasting three or four years.[21] Both politicians and generals were also subject to direct pressure from their colleagues among the allies who were not above exploiting these fears to persuade the sometimes reluctant British to fall in with their strategic wishes.

In December the British government began to consider its policy for 1915. The main forum of discussion was the War Council, established at the end of November when Asquith finally realized that the full Cabinet was too large to discuss matters of strategy. Its original members were Asquith, Kitchener, Churchill, Crewe, Lloyd George, Fisher, and Sir James Wolfe Murray. However, the latter was so much in awe of Kitchener that he never spoke. The new body had certain distinct advantages over the full Cabinet, not the least of which was that it had a secretary, Lt.-Col. Maurice Hankey, who had also been the secretary of the Committee of Imperial Defence. Hankey was one of the outstanding successes of the war and in the absence of a fully-functioning General Staff in London he offered a great deal of often very sound strategic advice in 1915. However, it was not always taken and the new organization had many defects. It had no executive authority although in practice most of its decisions were rubber-stamped, after sometimes rather protracted discussion, by the full Cabinet.[22] Its ability to reach coherent and realistic decisions depended greatly on the quality of the intelligence it received. The political intelligence it was given by the Foreign Office was on the whole accurate and timely. The prewar diplomatic service continued to function, except in enemy countries, and it had not been severely disrupted by the outbreak of the war. The same was not true of British military or naval intelligence. Although the Admiralty and War Office had realized before 1914 that in wartime they would depend heavily on covert intelligence sources they had done little to prepare them. The small secret intelligence network they had created in Germany, Belgium and Holland before 1914 was practically destroyed in August, and only the Dutch network survived. Several new secret services were improvised from scratch in the autumn and winter of 1914–15. Similarly, both the War Office and the Admiralty also improvised their own signals intelligence organizations.

These new organizations were remarkably successful within a short time in supplying the War Council with information about German troop and shipping movements.[23] But the assessment of this material depended on the strategic preoccupations and preconceptions the assessors brought to their work. In the winter of 1914–15 two prewar preoccupations were still so paramount that they gave the decision-makers a distorted image of reality. Before 1914 the Committee of Imperial Defence had conducted no less than three separate inquiries into the possibility that a German invasion force could evade the Royal Navy and land troops on the British mainland. By 1914 they had decided that while a full-scale invasion was bound to be detected a raid might succeed.[24] In the autumn of 1914 the Germans began to move large numbers of troops to the Eastern front in order to assist Austria–Hungary and inflict such a serious military defeat on Russia that it would be willing to listen to German offers of a separate peace. They concealed the movement of their troops by spreading false rumours through their embassies in neutral countries that they were in fact concentrating troops in the West. Kitchener and some other ministers, although not Sir John French or his own intelligence staff, took the rumours at their face value. Interpreting them in the light of their prewar preoccupations, the War Council believed they indicated that the Germans might try to break the military stalemate on the Western front by a sudden descent on Britain, coupled with another offensive in the West.[25] Kitchener's preoccupation with these two possibilities coloured all his thinking early in 1915 and in particular it made him reluctant to embark on any distant military adventures requiring him to dispatch a force larger than a single brigade.

The second prewar preconception which persisted after August 1914 was the belief that a long war between industrial nations would be impossible because their economies would collapse under the dislocation and exhaustion caused by the outbreak of war. In August 1914 Sir Archibald Murray, the chief of staff of the BEF, thought that the war would last between three to eight months. After that the belligerents would have exhausted their supplies of money and food. However, all of the belligerents survived the economic dislocation that attended the opening of the war and although exhaustion took a very long time to begin, the belief that it would ultimately end the war persisted. Food and money might not run short but manpower would. Casualties in the summer and autumn of 1914 were much heavier than had been predicted before the war. The notion soon gained currency that no matter how high allied losses were, German losses were always higher. In December 1914 Kitchener ordered Callwell to write a memorandum for the War Council estimating when the Central Powers would run out of men. Callwell privately thought the exercise was quite worthless, writing that 'One must be a mug indeed if one cannot prove anything with figures as counters'.[26] He predicted that the Germans would begin to run short of men within six months, well before any of the allies.

This statistical sleight of hand was based on several fallacies. He assumed that German monthly casualties were at least twice and perhaps three times as heavy as those suffered by France. He made no allowance for the new classes of recruits only just reaching military age and he took no account of the possibility of the closing down of non-essential industries or the use of substitutes to enable the Germans to take men from industry. He assumed that the Austro-Hungarians, with their much smaller army had ample manpower reserves but believed that they would not be able to raise more divisions. The French could probably keep their army up to strength for at least the whole of 1915 and, estimating that Russia had 20 million men of military age, he concluded that 'the question whether there is any possibility of the military forces running short of men disappears'. All that was needed to make them effective was more weapons. Kitchener's colleagues were delighted with Callwell's conclusions and vied with each other in predicting when the Germans would exhaust their manpower reserves. Asquith plumped for the end of the summer, Sir John French for October or November. But Kitchener, more realistically believed that they would not be exhausted until 1917. Callwell's memorandum was of seminal importance for future British policy. Swallowed whole, his conclusions meant that time and numbers were on the Entente's side. They pointed the way towards and justified the policy of attrition which the British pursued and tried to persuade their allies to pursue in 1915. French manpower reserves were adequate and Russia's were practically limitless while that of their enemies were finite. The Entente would win if Britain supplied its allies with money and munitions and if they conducted military operations to wear down the enemies' manpower reserves until they reached such a point that they could not find enough men to keep their armies up to establishment and their factories working.[27]

There was no shortage of ideas about how the British might assist their allies in bringing the Central Powers to the point of exhaustion. GHQ believed that, as the allied line in the West was impregnable, in the winter the Germans might mount a limited offensive in the East to drive the Russians back across the Vistula and the San, thus safeguarding both East Prussia and Hungary. To assist the Russians, Joffre began his own winter offensive on 16 December. Sir John French, short of men and ammunition and facing appalling weather, gave him only half-hearted support. His mind was elsewhere. He was much attracted by Churchill's proposal that the army should take part in a combined operation with the navy to advance up the Belgian coast to capture Ostend and Zeebrugge. French therefore asked Kitchener to send out New Army battalions, shells and heavy guns to reinforce his army as quickly as possible.[28]

Joffre disliked this plan because it would divert troops away from his next major operation, a two-pronged offensive near Arras and Rheims designed to pinch out the great bulge formed by the German line in France. Joffre's planned spring offensive found little favour with Hankey, Churchill or Lloyd George. They were all temperamentally unsuited to participating in a lengthy and costly land war. Churchill and Lloyd George were politicians impatient of delay and Hankey was a marine who never really thought that the government was giving British sea-power a fair chance to win the war. Each took the opportunity offered by the Christmas holiday to write long memoranda explaining their ideas about how best the British could assist their allies at the least cost to Britain. Churchill had been looking for ways in which the navy might carry out a spectacular coup, and one which might revitalize his own flagging reputation, long before the Western front had become stalemated. In August he had suggested to the Russians that if the Grand Fleet could decisively defeat the German High Seas Fleet, they could then convoy a Russian army through the mine and torpedo-infested waters of the Baltic to land on the German coast. In December, together with his Zeebrugge scheme, he suggested that as a first step in April or May 1915 the navy should seize the island of Borkum off the German coast. Possession of it would make a German invasion of Britain impossible and light craft could attack the German fleet in harbour. It might also force them to come out and do battle with Jellicoe's forces. Fisher's suggestion that the plan should be modelled on an operation carried out by the Russians in 1761 was an indication of the state of the Admiralty's staff planning.[29]

Hankey dismissed the possibility of a rapid Russian advance on Berlin and doubted whether the Entente would be able to invade Germany within the foreseeable future. He recommended that nothing should be done to lessen Britain's commitment to the land war in France and suggested that research should begin on what eventually evolved into the tank in order to break the tactical stalemate in the West. But he also insisted that 'we should endeavour by the means proposed to get assets into our hands wherewith to supplement the tremendous asset of sea

power and its resultant economic pressure, wherewith to ensure favourable terms of peace when the enemy had had enough of the war'.[30] The
implication of Hankey's comments was that whilst the Entente might not
be able to defeat the Germans outright the British should ensure that they
were able to win the peace. He wanted the British to mount a land
campaign against the Turks, the weakest of the Central Powers. If they
used three corps of the Kitchener armies they would be able to induce the
Bulgars and Greeks to co-operate in a military campaign to take Constantinople. Once the city was captured the Russians would merely have
to co-ordinate their advance with the Serbs and Romanians in order to
occupy Hungary and force Austria to sue for peace.[31]

Lloyd George wrote his memorandum because he was angered by the
apparent lack of foresight shown by the War Office. In October he had
bullied them into greatly increasing their orders for guns and munitions in
order to expedite deliveries. French and Russian requests for loans made
him see that the Entente would have to work together more closely. He
was afraid that if the Western allies did not help Russia the Germans
would knock it out of the war in 1915. He was averse to sending the New
Armies to attack in France because a recent trip to France convinced him
that the Western front was stalemated. Futile and expensive assaults in the
West would have a serious impact on civilian morale. He and Hankey
agreed that military or naval victories were a political necessity. They
were much more sensitive than most generals to the fact that the civilian
population of democracies like France and Britain would not endure
indefinitely being separated from their loved ones by a war which offered
them ever lengthening casualty lists but no tangible victories which could
be reported in the press.[32] Lloyd George's attention was drawn to the
Balkans by three things, the advice he received from the Bulgarophile
brothers Charles and Noel Buxton that a Balkan confederation could be
constructed, the apparently desperate plight of Serbia and finally indications reaching London that the Austrians might be ready to make peace.

The British felt no particular bitterness towards the Austrians when
they went to war with them in August. Indeed they were only nominal
enemies. The burden of fighting the Dual Monarchy fell on Russia. In
August the Russians issued a proclamation to all Poles living under
German and Austrian rule promising them autonomy after the war. It
was good propaganda and the proclamation appeared to have broken the
common interest in keeping Poland divided, which the three Eastern
monarchies had shared since the end of the eighteenth century. In
September Bertie reported that some Austrians were trying to make peace
independently of Germany through the mediation of neutral Spain. In
November and December more reports arrived of strains in Austro-
German relations and by 21 December Asquith believed that there were
good reasons for believing that Austria wanted to come to terms. Grey,

therefore, told the Russians that the British would welcome a separate peace with Austria if one could be achieved on terms acceptable to Russia. Lloyd George recommended two separate operations. The first was an attack on Austria–Hungary via either Salonika or the Dalmatian coast, mounted by 600,000 men in conjunction with the Serbs, Romanians and Greeks. The threat of a military disaster would further hasten the Austrians' desire to leave the war. The second was a landing by 100,000 men on the Syrian coast. This would not only cut off the Turkish troops menacing Egypt but the occupation of Syria, with its biblical associations, was sure to appeal to the British public. Lloyd George painted his plans with very broad brush strokes. He claimed too much when he suggested that if both operations were mounted they would result in 'bringing Germany down by the process of knocking the props under her'.[33] Balfour wrote a short critique of Hankey's memorandum which could be applied equally to Lloyd George's proposals. It would take months of negotiations to allay the mutual jealousies of the Balkan states to the point where they would be ready to attack Turkey or Austria. Germany was the centre of the enemy coalition. It was Germany who, increasingly as the war progressed, propped up Turkey and Austria, not the other way around.[34] Balfour might have added that Lloyd George and Hankey both ignored the very difficult logistical problems of moving a large army through the mountainous Balkans.

Asquith agreed that, as the first of the New Army divisions would be ready in a few months, it was time to consider new departures. 'I am profoundly dissatisfied with the immediate prospect – an enormous waste of life & money day after day with no appreciable progress.'[35] All concerned agreed that any new plan had to be devised in concert with the French and the Russians. The strategic alternatives which were considered by the War Council in a series of meetings in January 1915 were not designed to permit the British to evade their responsibilities to their allies but to allow them to fulfil them with their still limited military resources.

In 1906 a joint Admiralty–War Office Committee investigating the defence of Egypt suggested that the successful passage of a British fleet through the Dardanelles to Constantinople would cause the collapse of the Turkish government. But they deprecated actually carrying out such an operation. The Director of Naval Intelligence argued that a purely naval assault would involve heavy losses from the batteries protecting the Straits. The General Staff argued that a combined operation would have to be mounted involving the landing of troops on the Gallipoli peninsula to silence the batteries but by the time a sufficiently large body of troops to do this had been assembled in the eastern Mediterranean the Turks would have reinforced their garrisons and the landing would fail. The political repercussions of failure would be horrendous. It would destroy

Britain's reputation for invincibility in the Muslim east and 'would be followed by a general uprising against British authority throughout the East'.[36] The Dardanelles were best left alone.

However, that did not stop Churchill raising the idea again in August and September 1914. Smarting under the humiliation of the escape of the *Goeben* and *Breslau* he seized upon an offer made by Venizelos that the Greek army and the Royal Navy should combine in an amphibious assault against the Gallipoli peninsula. Nothing came of this. Callwell objected that it was impractical not only because the Greeks lacked siege artillery and therefore the Turks' defences were too strong but also because the Greek offer was conditional upon a Bulgarian promise to remain neutral which was not forthcoming.[37] When the Turks did finally go to war against Russia, Churchill's interest again centred on the Dardanelles and on 3 November British ships under Vice-Admiral Carden conducted a short bombardment of the forts at the mouth of the Dardanelles. The purpose of the operation was probably to ascertain the range of the new Krupp heavy guns the Germans were rumoured to have mounted there. Churchill's critics have claimed that the operation was foolish as it merely alerted the Turks to their vulnerability. But it is doubtful whether they needed to be reminded of the very obvious fact that the Dardanelles defences protected the only sea route to their capital from the Mediterranean.[38]

By December Russian troops in the Caucasus were already under some pressure from the Turks and on 2 January the Grand Duke asked the British if they could mount a naval or military demonstration to draw Turkish forces away from the Caucasus. How serious the Russian plight really was is unclear. Two days later they crushed the Turks at Sarikamish. The Grand Duke may have made the request to distract allied attention from his inability to attack on the Eastern front.[39] However, the British took his request seriously. A military demonstration was impossible because Kitchener had only one spare division, the Twenty-Ninth, and he refused to dispatch that to the Mediterranean lest the Germans should attack in France or try to invade Britain. But he and Churchill agreed that a purely naval demonstration, combined with rumours that Constantinople was to be attacked, might be feasible.[40] Fisher did not. He had led the marine landing-parties during the bombardment of Alexandria in 1882 and knew that naval gun-fire alone could not permanently silence shore batteries. Although he wrote that an attack on the Dardanelles 'holds the field', he hedged his agreement around with so many impossible conditions that he made it clear that he had no confidence in the Churchill–Kitchener scheme. He insisted that, if it was to succeed, it had to be mounted at once and as a combined operation involving 75,000 British troops taken from France, assisted by the Greek and Bulgarian armies and timed to coincide with a Russian, Serbian and Romanian offensive against Austria.[41] But Churchill was not to be balked. He suggested quite erroneously that in Lloyd George's memorandum, Fisher's letter and Kitchener's suggestion there was a convergence of opinion in favour of an operation at the Dardanelles. There was no such convergence and Churchill saw agreement where there was none. Abandoning the idea of a mere demonstration he telegraphed to Carden asking him whether it would be possible actually to force the Dardanelles by ships alone. Carden replied cautiously that while it would not be possible to rush the Dardanelles it might be possible to force a passage by mounting a prolonged and methodical operation. His grudging acceptance that the operation might be successful was enough to persuade Churchill that it was feasible.[42]

But for the time being Churchill's major concern was the attack on Borkum. On 7 January the War Council decided in principle that it should be taken by an amphibious force consisting of a single division. French's offensive along the Belgian coast was quashed because Kitchener refused to release the necessary troops.[43] The next day the Council turned its attention to other theatres. Lloyd George suggested landing at Ragusa or Salonika to attack Austria–Hungary, only to be told by Kitchener that his suggestion was not feasible because both lacked adequate communications inland and his plan would require the co-operation of neutrals, Italy and Greece, who had not yet joined the Entente. He also deprecated attacking the Dardanelles because it would require 150,000 troops in addition to the navy. The War Council either had to find some troops or discover a plan which did not require any.[44] Churchill seized upon Carden's plan, to bombard the Dardanelles defences methodically for a month and clear the minefields in the Straits, as a way out of this dilemma. The only soldiers necessary would be some small marine landing parties.[45] Both Churchill and the Admiralty War Staff had been too impressed by the ease with which the Germans had destroyed the Belgian forts of Liège and Namur in August 1914 to question the feasibility of ships destroying shore batteries. They did not recognize that although warships might just conceivably be able to silence the forts they would have much greater difficulty in destroying the concealed howitzer batteries which the Turks had deployed on the Gallipoli peninsula. Unless they could be silenced, the unarmoured merchant ships which the fleet relied upon for its supplies would not be able to follow the warships to Constantinople and Carden's ships would soon have to return for want of coal and ammunition.

A largely inconclusive War Council was held on 13 January. The Dardanelles was still only one among several options considered. French extracted an agreement that he should be permitted to prepare an operation to advance along the Belgian coast but a firm decision to do so was postponed until February. Kitchener suggested landing Australian and New Zealand troops stationed in Egypt at Alexandretta to cut off the Turkish troops menacing Egypt, but continuing French objections made it impossible. The Council agreed that preparations might commence along the lines Carden had outlined. Churchill saw it as an option which might be tried but which could be terminated if there was a setback.[46] Lloyd George continued to lobby for his Balkan option and in the next few weeks it loomed much larger in the government's consideration than the Dardanelles. The Buxton brothers, just returned from a trip to the Balkans, persuaded Asquith and the Chancellor that if the Entente promised Bulgaria those parts of Macedonia it had lost to Serbia in 1913, compensated Serbia with Bosnia and part of the Dalmatian coast, gave Transylvania to Romania, southern Albania, Rhodes and possibly Smyrna to Greece, they would all join the Entente. Asquith liked the plan, insisting that it was 'of the first importance that, one way or the other, they should all be brought in'.[47] He realized that the main stumbling block would be to persuade the Serbs to surrender territory they already occupied in Macedonia in return for promises of Austrian territory at the end of the war.[48] But the pressure of events might compel them to accept their neighbours' help whatever the price. In January 1915 ominous reports reached London that a large Austro-German force was about to mount another invasion of Serbia. The War Council were determined that Serbia would not be crushed. If it were, then all hope of neutrals joining the Entente would be ended. Kitchener abandoned the Alexandretta operation, French was told to postpone his offensive along the Belgian coast and Grey promised the Greeks and Romanians British troops if they aided Serbia.

However, they reckoned without the French. Joffre wanted every British soldier he could get in France both in order to ward off an expected German attack and to take over more of the line to free French troops for his projected offensive. The French minister of war, Millerand, arrived in London on 22 January to put Joffre's views forcefully to the British.[49] Asquith and Lloyd George were incensed at what they thought were Joffre's quite unreasonable demands.[50] Fisher caused further complications. He became increasingly opposed to both the Dardanelles and the Zeebrugge operations. He had never favoured a purely naval adventure in the eastern Mediterranean and became even less enthusiastic for it as, throughout early 1915, the Admiralty's signals intelligence unit, Room 40, intercepted signals indicating that the High Seas Fleet was about to launch an invasion of Britain. He wanted to keep the Grand Fleet's margin of superiority in the North Sea as wide as possible.[51] But he was now an old and tired man. In discussion with Asquith on 28 January the First Sea Lord failed to press his objections in the face of Churchill's insistence that the Battle of the Dogger Bank, fought on 22 January, demonstrated that Jellicoe now enjoyed a greater superiority over the High Seas Fleet than he had in August 1914. Asquith, ever in search of a compromise, agreed that the Zeebrugge operation would be dropped if Fisher ceased his objections to the Dardanelles.[52]

The full War Council met twice on 28 January. The Zeebrugge project was formally abandoned and it was agreed that a naval assault at the Dardanelles should be launched in mid-February. High hopes were expressed about what success would mean. Kitchener compared it to a successful campaign mounted by the New Armies. Balfour thought that it would free the Russian wheat crop and open the mouth of the Danube to the allies. Grey believed that it would finally persuade Bulgaria to join the Entente and the other Balkan neutrals would follow in its wake. But they did not believe that they were irrevocably committed to pursuing the operation if it met with an initial setback. 'One merit of the scheme', as Kitchener said, 'was that, if satisfactory progress was not made, the attack could be broken off.' But the obverse was also true even if left unsaid. To break off the operation would be to dash all these hopes and would be a severe blow to Britain's reputation in the East for invincibility.[53] In the afternoon a sub-committee considered a General Staff paper on possible destinations for the New Armies in the spring. Churchill and Lloyd George urged the dispatch of the two territorial divisions, formerly earmarked for the Zeebrugge operation, to Salonika. Venizelos had privately agreed to co-operate in this if the Bulgarians promised to remain neutral, if the Romanians joined Greece and if the British and French landed two corps.[54] Kitchener was hesitant, wishing to keep his promise to Millerand to send all the men he could to France. This provoked an angry exchange at the reconvened War Council. Churchill insisted that the French should rest content with the military aid the British had already given them because it was far more than they had promised before the war. Grey replied, with more than a grain of truth, that 'the question could not be discussed from the standpoint of a commercial bargain'. Kitchener agreed to compromise. He was still concerned about the possibility of a German invasion. The troops in question could be retained in Britain, to be sent to France if needed and to Salonika if they were not. In the meantime the Greeks were to be asked if a force of 5,000 men would be of any value to them as a token of what might come in the future.[55]

The War Council also agreed that Lloyd George, who was to go to Paris on 1 February for a conference of allied finance ministers, should informally raise with them the question of how the allies might co-ordinate their military operations more closely. Lloyd George understood that to mean that he had *carte blanche* to persuade the French to agree to send troops to Salonika. The need to do something to save Serbia became more urgent at the beginning of February when the Bulgarians gave a very clear indication of where their sympathies lay by accepting a large loan from Germany. Kitchener continued to delude himself by suggesting that this only meant that Ferdinand and his government were pro-German, but Bax-Ironside, who was much nearer to the reality of Balkan politics, gloomily concluded that it meant that 'Our enemies are on top now'. Sir Arther Paget, who had been sent to the Balkans by Kitchener, reported that if the Serbs were attacked by more than 400,000 men they would be overwhelmed.[56] In Paris Lloyd George was disgusted to discover that Millerand had not reported the substance of his conversation about the Balkans to his colleagues probably because he knew that some ministers, especially Briand and Delcassé, favoured a Balkan adventure. In November 1914, much to Joffre's disgust, Briand had suggested landing 400,000 French troops at Salonika. France had extensive economic interests in the Balkans which it hoped to further and to use to facilitate its postwar economic recovery. They were also antagonistic to the idea of Russia establishing its hegemony in the region.[57] They accepted Lloyd George's plan and agreed to send two divisions to Salonika just as soon as Joffre and Sir John French were ready to release them. Sir John claimed that although he did not oppose the plan in principle he did not have the troops to spare to support it. They then consulted Sir William Robertson, Murray's successor as Sir John's chief of staff. Given Robertson's notorious opposition to the whole Salonika theatre after he became CIGS in December 1915, Lloyd George's claim that he believed it was 'good strategy' must be taken with a pinch of salt. Bertie, who was present during the Chancellor's conversation with Delcassé and Briand, believed that Lloyd George had doctored his account of their talks by exaggerating the degree of French support for his proposal and he may have done the same in reporting his talk with Robertson.[58]

The War Council met again on 9 February. Sir John insisted that Serbia was in no danger because intelligence reports indicating a German–Austrian troop concentration near the Serbian frontier were false and were really intended to prevent the Russians from breaking through the Carpathian frontier. No one else agreed and the meeting decided that they would send their last remaining regular division in Britain, the Twenty-Ninth, to Salonika, and Sir John would have to make do with a good Territorial division in its place. They also decided to tell the Greeks that they were honour bound to assist Serbia and that the French and Russians were each going to send a division. In fact the Russians had already intimated that they could only spare a single Cossack regiment. Although Venizelos might have been tempted by these terms he was still unable to overcome the opposition of the king and queen and the General Staff. The queen was the Kaiser's sister and the General Staff were convinced that the Central Powers would win the war. As if to confirm the correctness of their belief, on 7 February the Germans opened an initially successful offensive against the Russians in Poland and on 15 February the Greeks refused their co-operation. The Serbian and Syrian options were for the time being closed and, in Asquith's words, 'So one's eyes are now fixed on the Dardanelles . . . '[59]

Notes

1   O. Esher (ed.), *Journals and Letters of Reginald Viscount Esher*, Vol. 3 (London: Ivor Nicholson & Watson, 1938), p. 200; P. Fraser, *Lord Esher: A Political Biography* (London: Hart-Davis, 1973), pp. 266–7.
2   L. L. Farrar, *Divide and Conquer. German Efforts to Conclude a Separate Peace, 1914–1918* (New York: Columbia University Press and East European Quarterly, 1978), p. 105; G. Ritter, *Sword and Scepter. The Problem of Militarism in Germany*, Vol. 3 (Coral Gables, Fla: University of Miami Press, 1972), pp. 24–46.
3   PRO FO 800/376, Nicholson to Hardinge, 3 December 1914.
4   A. K. Wildman, *The End of the Russian Imperial Army: The Old Army and the Soldiers' Revolt (March–April 1917)* (Princeton, NJ: Princeton University Press, 1980), pp. 85–8.
5   Callwell to Wilson, 8, 12 and 21 December 1914, Sir H. Wilson mss, box 73/1/18; PRO CAB 37/123/17 and /18, Grey to Bertie and Buchanan, 9 January 1915; V. Rothwell, 'The British government and Japanese military assistance, 1914–1918', *History*, vol. 57, no. 186 (1971), pp. 37–8; Michael and Eleanor Brock (eds), *H. H. Asquith: Letters to Venetia Stanley* (London: Oxford University Press, 1982), pp. 342, 348–9; PRO WO 32/8813, F. W. Stopford. Wastage in war, 26 April 1906.
6   PRO FO 800/167, W. E. Pease to Grey, 12 February 1915; Northcliffe to Asquith, 1 January 1915 and Brade to Drummond, 4 January 1915 and Tyrrell to Drummond, 6 January 1915, Asquith mss, vol. 14, ff. 1–6; Note by Wilson, Talk with Capel, 3 February 1915, Sir H. Wilson mss, box 73/1/19.
7   PRO FO 371/2174/71776, Buchanan to Foreign Office, 15 November 1914 and Grey to Buchanan, 16 November 1914 and (74460), Buchanan to Foreign Office, 23 November 1914 and (74460), Grey to Buchanan, 25 November 1914 and (79919), Telegram left by M. Cambon giving summary of audience of M. Paléologue with the tzar regarding terms of peace, 2 December 1914; see also PRO FO 371/2176/68563 and 68925, Rodd to Foreign Office and Note communicated by M. de Etter, 7 November 1914; M. Paléologue, *An Ambassador's Memoirs*, Vol. 1 (London: Hutchinson, 1923), pp. 189–98.
8   D. Stevenson, *French War Aims against Germany, 1914–1919* (Oxford: Clarendon Press, 1982), p. 17; PRO FO 371/1984/87257, Granville to Foreign Office, 28 December 1914; PRO FO 371/2506/44508, Bertie to Grey, 13 January 1915; PRO FO 800/181, Bertie to Grey, 10 November 1914; PRO FO 800/56A, Bertie to Foreign Office, 22 November 1914; PRO FO 800/166, Memo by Bertie, 18 December 1914.
9   P. A. R. Calvert, 'Great Britain and the New World', in F. H. Hinsley (ed.), *British Foreign Policy under Sir Edward Grey* (Cambridge: Cambridge University Press, 1977), pp. 382–94; D. C. Watt, *Succeeding John Bull: America in Britain's Place, 1900–1975* (Cambridge: Cambridge University Press, 1984), pp. 24–8; Mary R. Kihl, 'A failure of ambassadorial diplomacy', *Journal of American History*, vol. 57, no. 3 (1970), pp. 636–53.

10 C. M. Mason, 'Anglo-American relations: Mediation and "permanent peace"', in F. H. Hinsley (ed.), *British Foreign Policy*, pp. 466–9; PRO FO 800/84, Spring-Rice to Grey, 25 August, 6, 8, 28 September and 6 October 1914, Grey to Spring-Rice, 8 September 1914.

11 A. S. Link (ed.), *The Papers of Woodrow Wilson*, Vol. 31 (Princeton, NJ: Princeton University Press, 1980), p. 10.

12 PRO FO 800/84, Grey to Spring-Rice, 22 and 23 September 1914; Link (ed.), *Wilson's Papers*, Vol. 31, pp. 15–16, 21–2; Viscount Grey, *Twenty-Five Years, 1892–1916*, Vol. 2 (London: Hodder & Stoughton, 1925), pp. 115–17.

13 PRO FO 371/2176/80506, Minutes by Drummond and Nicolson on Spring-Rice to Foreign Office, 27 November 1914.

14 PRO FO 800/84, Grey to Spring-Rice, 22 December 1914 and Spring-Rice to Grey, 18, 21, 24 December 1914 and Spring-Rice to Tyrrell, 29 December 1914; PRO FO 800/166, Memo. by Bertie, 18 December 1914.

15 PRO FO 800/85, Grey to Spring-Rice, 2 January 1915.

16 C. Seymour (ed.), *The Intimate Papers of Colonel House*, Vol. 1 (London: Ernest Benn, 1926), pp. 347–404; PRO FO 800/171, Grey to Bertie and Buchanan, 12 February 1915; Brock (eds), *H. H. Asquith*, pp. 434–5.

17 PRO FO 371/2173/51130, Rodd to Foreign Office, 19 September 1914; PRO FO 371/2176/85789, Findlay to Foreign Office, 21 December 1914; PRO FO 800/65, Rodd to Grey, 26 December 1914 and 13 February 1915; PRO WO 159/3, Memo, annon., Present Condition in Germany, 9 February 1915.

18 L. L. Farrar, 'Peace through exhaustion: German diplomatic motivations for the Verdun campaign', *Revue Internationale d'Histoire Militaire*, vol. 8, no. 2 (1972–5), p. 480; PRO FO 800/56A, Bertie to Grey, 1 December 1914.

19 F. Fischer, *Germany's Aims in the First World War* (London: Chatto & Windus, 1967), pp. 185–92; T. Kaarsted, *Great Britain and Denmark, 1914–1920* (Odense: Odense University Press, 1979), pp. 81–91; PRO CAB 37/124/11, Howard to Grey, 8 February 1915; PRO FO 371/2505/10809, Howard to Foreign Office, 22 January 1915 and (10409), Howard to Foreign Office, 27 January 1915 and (21481), Grant Duff to Foreign Office, 17 February 1915 and (22758), Grant Duff to Foreign Office, 18 February 1915 and (23892), Grant Duff to Foreign Office, 25 February 1915; PRO FO 800/75, Grey to Buchanan, 29 January 1915.

20 PRO FO 800/166, Memo by Bertie, 18 December 1914.

21 Seymour (ed.), *Papers of Colonel House*, Vol. 1, pp. 360–1; PRO FO 800/167, Memo by Bertie, 21 January 1915.

22 D. French, *British Economic and Strategic Planning, 1905–1915* (London: Allen & Unwin, 1982), pp. 176–7.

23 D. French, 'Sir John French's secret service on the Western front, 1914–1915', *Journal of Strategic Studies*, vol. 7, no. 4 (1984), pp. 423–40; P. Beesly, *Room 40: British Naval Intelligence, 1914–1918* (London: Hamish Hamilton, 1982), pp. 1–62.

24 J. Gooch, *The Plans of War: The General Staff and British Military Strategy c. 1900–1916* (London: Routledge & Kegan Paul, 1974), pp. 278–95.

25 Brock (eds), *H. H. Asquith*, pp. 266, 281, 331; E. David (ed.), *Inside Asquith's Cabinet: From the Diaries of Charles Hobhouse* (London: John Murray, 1977), pp. 200–1; PRO CAB 42/1/12, Minutes of a meeting of the War Council, 8 January 1915; PRO FO 800/102, Grey to Kitchener, 20 November 1914; PRO FO 371/2166/74302, Maxse to Foreign Office, 23 November 1914; W. Kirke to Maj.-Gen. F. S. G. Pigott and (enc.), Lt.-Gen. Sir G. MacDonogh, 29 July 1947, Kirk mss, WMK 13.

26 Callwell to Wilson, 2 January 1915, Sir H. Wilson mss, box 73/1/18.

27   PRO CAB 42/1/10, The War Office, A comparison of the Belligerent Forces, War Office, 6 January 1915. For German manpower policy, see G. D. Feldman, *Army, Industry and Labour in Germany* (Princeton: Princeton University Press, 1966), pp. 64–73; Brock (eds), *H. H. Asquith*, pp. 378, 398; Sir J. French, diary entry, 13 January 1915, French mss, vol. H.; PRO CAB 42/1/38, Kitchener, Remarks by the Secretary of State for War on the Chancellor of the Exchequer's Memorandum (G–7) on the conduct of the war, 25 February 1915.

28   R. Holmes, *The Little Field Marshal: Sir John French* (London: Cape, 1981), pp. 259–63; French, diary entry, 27 December 1914, French mss, vol. G; PRO CAB 42/1/9, Sir J. French, Relative strengths of the opposing forces on either side of the European theatre of war, 3 January 1915.

29   R. Prior, *Churchill's World Crisis as History* (London: Croom Helm, 1983), pp. 46–9; M. Gilbert (ed.), *Winston S. Churchill*, Vol. 3, *Companion*, pt 1 (London: Heinemann, 1971), pp. 284–7, 343–5.

30   PRO CAB 37/122/194, Memo. by Hankey, 28 December 1914.

31   ibid.

32   For Hankey on this point see PRO CAB 42/1/8, M. P. A. Hankey, The War – attack on the Dardanelles, 2 February 1915.

33   PRO CAB 42/1/8, D. Lloyd George, The War – Suggestions as to the military situation, 1 January 1915; Brock (eds), *H. H. Asquith*, p. 334; W. B. Fest, *Peace or Partition. The Habsburg Monarchy and British Policy 1914–1918* (London: George Prior, 1978), pp. 24–5; K. J. Calder, *Britain and the Origins of the New Europe* (Cambridge: Cambridge University Press, 1976), p. 22; PRO FO 371/2505/1500, Grey to Rodd and Sir H. Howard, 5 January 1915 and (25220), Sir H. Howard to Foreign Office, 7 January 1915 and (5262), Sir H. Howard to Foreign Office, 14 January 1915; Callwell to Wilson, 21 December 1914, Sir H. Wilson mss, box 73/1/18; PRO FO 800/95, Memo. by Grey, 6 January 1915.

34   Gilbert (ed.), *Companion*, Vol. 3, pt 1, pp. 363–4.

35   Brock (eds), *H. H. Asquith*, p. 346.

36   CID, Paper 92 B, N. G. L[yttleton], The possibility of a joint naval and military attack upon the Dardanelles – Memorandum by the General Staff, 19 December 1906, Hamilton mss, 17/7/22.

37   Prior, *World Crisis*, pp. 44–5; PRO CAB 19/28, Dardanelles Inquiry – Statements of evidence. First phase, Appendix A1. Churchill to Sir C. Douglas; PRO CAB 19/28, Dardanelles ... Appendix 2, Maj.-Gen. Callwell, Memo, 3 September 1914; PRO CAB 19/33, Dardanelles Commission. Minutes of Evidence, Q. 1111 (Churchill); PRO FO 800/63, Foreign Office to Elliot, 4 September 1914.

38   Prior, *World Crisis*, p. 45; Gilbert (ed.), *Companion*, Vol. 3, pt 1, p. 243; for an account of the bombardment see Capt. F. W. Kennedy, Account of the first bombardment of the Dardanelles, November 1914, Kennedy mss, vol. 5.

39   PRO FO 371/2504/540, Buchanan to Foreign Office, 2 January 1915.

40   PRO FO 371/2504/540, Grey to Buchanan, 2 January 1915; PRO CAB 19/28, Dardanelles Inquiry. Statement by Mr. Churchill upon the Dardanelles Operation to the end of the first phase, Kitchener to Churchill, 2 January 1915; PRO CAB 19/33, Dardanelles Commission. Minutes of evidence, Q. 5793 (Asquith).

41   Gilbert (ed.), *Companion*, Vol. 3, pt 1, pp. 367–8.

42   Prior, *World Crisis*, pp. 53–4; PRO CAB 17/123, Churchill to Carden, 3 and 6 January 1915 and Carden to Churchill, 5 January 1915.

43 Brock (eds), *H. H. Asquith*, pp. 364–5; PRO CAB 42/1/11, Minutes of the War Council, 7 January 1915.

44 PRO CAB 42/1/12, Minutes of the War Council, 8 January 1915.

45 PRO CAB 17/123, Carden to Churchill, 11 January 1915.

46 PRO CAB 42/1/16, Minutes of the War Council, 13 January 1915; PRO CAB 19/28, Dardanelles Inquiry. Statement . . . phase, Churchill to Kitchener, 20 January 1915.

47 Brock (eds), *H. H. Asquith*, p. 384.

48 Brock (eds), *H. H. Asquith*, p. 380; PRO FO 800/100, Asquith to Grey, 17 January 1915.

49 Brock (eds), *H. H. Asquith*, p. 391; H. Wilson, Precis of note from Gen. Joffre to Sir J. French, 19 January 1915 and H. Wilson, Chantilly, 21 January 1915, Sir H. Wilson mss, box 73/1/19; O. Esher (ed.) *Journals*, Vol. 3, pp. 208–9.

50 Brock (eds), *H. H. Asquith*, p. 393; Lloyd George to Churchill, 29 January 1915, Lloyd George mss C/3/16/17.

51 R. F. Mackay, *Fisher of Kilverstone* (Oxford: Clarendon Press, 1973), pp. 477–87; Beesly, *Room 40*, pp. 63–4; Gilbert (ed.), *Companion*, Vol. 3, pt 1, pp. 429–30, 451–3, 460.

52 MacKay, *Fisher*, pp. 388–9.

53 PRO CAB 42/1/25, Minutes of the War Council, held at 11.30 a.m., 28 January 1915.

54 PRO CAB 42/1/26, Minutes of the War Council held at 4 p.m., 28 January 1915; PRO FO 800/63, Elliot to Grey, 25 and 31 January 1915 and Grey to Elliot, 26 January 1915.

55 PRO CAB 42/1/27, Minutes of the War Council held at 6 p.m., 28 January 1915.

56 PRO FO 800/377, Bax-Ironside to Nicolson, 12 February 1915; PRO WO 32/5836, Sir A. Paget, Report on the situation in the Balkans, 9 February 1915; PRO CAB 19/29, Bax-Ironside to Foreign Office, 6 February 1915.

57 G. H. Cassar, *The French and the Dardanelles* (London: Allen & Unwin, 1971), pp. 34–40; G. B. Leon, *Greece and the Great Powers, 1914–1917* (Thessaloniki: Institute of Balkan Studies, 1974), pp. 101–2; D. Dutton, 'The Balkan campaign and French war aims in the Great War', *English Historical Review*, vol. 94, no. 370 (1979), pp. 100–1.

58 PRO FO 800/57, Bertie to Grey and enc., 7 February 1915; D. R. Woodward, *Lloyd George and the Generals*, (Newark: University of Delaware Press, 1983), pp. 37–8.

59 Brock (eds),. *H. H. Asquith*, pp. 423–4, 433; PRO CAB 42/1/29, Minutes of the War Council, 9 February 1915; PRO CAB 19/29, Buchanan to Grey, 7 February 1915; Leon, *Greece and the Great Powers*, pp. 109–16; N. Stone, *The Eastern Front, 1914–1917* (London: Hodder & Stoughton, 1975), pp. 116–19; K. Neilson, *Strategy and Supply: The Anglo-Russian Alliance, 1914–1917* (London: Allen & Unwin, 1984), pp. 68–9.

5

The Constantinople Agreement, Italy and the Collapse of the Asquith Government, February–May 1915

THE ASQUITH government has been severely criticized because of its failure in the spring of 1915 to co-ordinate its diplomatic and military initiatives at the Dardanelles and in the Balkans. But this failure was more apparent than real. Such criticisms presupposed two things, that success at the Dardanelles would have significantly influenced the Balkan states and that the British had a free hand to negotiate whatever terms they chose with the neutrals regardless of the wishes of its existing allies. But Russia had no intention of allowing any other state to acquire Constantinople and Russia, not Britain, held the key to the Balkans. If its armies were successful against Germany and Austria–Hungary the Balkan states, and more particularly Bulgaria, might have just been persuaded to sink their differences and join the Entente. As long as Bulgaria remained watchfully neutral even the prospect of the imminent fall of Constantinople would probably not have been enough to shift the Greek king or the Romanian prime minister from their self-imposed neutrality. Probably nothing less than a decisive Russian victory would have caused Ferdinand to join the Entente. Only Italy, with its long coastline, was susceptible to British influence, and it alone joined the Entente in 1915. This was the strategic situation which provided the background to the collapse of the Asquith government in mid-May. There is no mastery about why Asquith formed a coalition government. The failure of the Anglo-French spring offensive to break the German line and the resulting 'shell-scandal', the failure of the Dardanelles campaign to bring in the Balkan neutrals, the German breakthrough at Gorlice-Tarnow taken together made Asquith realize that the war would not be over before the end of 1915. A wartime general election was inescapable unless he adopted his one remaining expedient and formed a coalition government with the Unionists.

The beginning of Carden's bombardment of the Dardanelles' defences on 19 February coincided with a series of diplomatic initiatives in the eastern Mediterranean and with the start of a successful German offensive in Poland which went far towards neutralizing any political effect it might have had in the Balkans. On 13 February, with Sazonov's agreement, Grey told the Bulgarians that, while the allies would not offer them territory before they knew how the offer would be received for fear of needlessly offending the Serbs, once the Bulgarians declared their willingness to co-operate with the Entente, they would promise them the Enos-Midia line and the contested zone of Macedonia. The Bulgarian response was reserved.[1] The second British initiative was at Constantinople. The British believed that Turkey's entry into the war had been engineered by a small and unpopular group of pro-German zealots belonging to the Committee of Union and Progress. They thought that the war was widely unpopular in Turkey and that no more than a small externally administered shock would be needed to start a revolution at Constantinople which would topple the existing regime and replace it with a pro-British government willing to make peace. The almost casual way in which the British went about mounting the Dardanelles expedition can only be understood in the light of their belief that the Turks were not a first class Western power but a backward oriental despotism which would collapse immediately the first shots were fired. Too many British decision-makers simply did not believe that the lengthy military preparations necessary to confront a European power like Germany would be necessary in a campaign against the Turks.[2] In January 1915 the Director of Naval Intelligence, Captain W. R. Hall, sent three agents to Athens to open secret negotiations with dissident members of the Turkish government. News of this was kept secret from all but a handful of British ministers until 16 February when the Cabinet were told that 'we are promised a military rising and ultimate revolution on the fall of the first forts'.[3]

But not everyone was so sanguine. By 19 February several voices, including those of Hankey and Vice-Admiral Sir Henry Jackson, then employed on special duties at the Admiralty, had been raised in favour of sending troops to accompany the expedition. They were afraid that if the optimists were wrong and the fall of the first forts did not lead to a pro-British revolution then the whole enterprise might fail. Warships might be able to silence the enemy's fixed batteries, sail through the Dardanelles and reach the Bosphorus and Constantinople, but there was no guarantee that they would also be able to silence the mobile howitzer batteries which the Turks had deployed on both sides of the Straits. If these remained intact they would be able to prevent unarmoured merchant vessels reaching the fleet to resupply it.[4] On 9 February Kitchener had casually promised that 'if the Navy required the assistance of the land forces at a later stage, that assistance would be forthcoming'.[5] The cancellation of the Salonika expedition meant that if the navy did need help, the Twenth-Ninth Division together with the ANZAC forces in Egypt, could be earmarked to assist them. On 17 February the French, anxious to protect their own claims in the eastern Mediterranean, also agreed to send a division if it were needed. These units were not intended to form an amphibious assault force to take the Gallipoli peninsula by storm. They were merely to land after the navy had silenced the Turkish batteries and occupy them to prevent their crews returning once the fleet had sailed past them.[6] However, German success in Poland meant that the decision actually to send them to the Dardanelles was postponed for another three weeks. Both Kitchener and Joffre were afraid that after making limited gains in Poland the Germans might bring their forces back to the West and launch another attack on Paris or the Channel ports. It was not until 10 March, when the Russian position had stabilized and they had begun their own offensive in the Carpathians, and after a prolonged wrangle in the War Council, that Kitchener finally allowed the Twenty-Ninth Division to leave Britain.[7]

In the meantime the fine weather at the Dardanelles broke on 20 February and the bombardment was not recommenced until 26 February. It then continued without interruption until 2 March. The outer forts were silenced and the fleet was able to operate 6 miles inside the Straits. This success encouraged Churchill to give the operation wide publicity. In doing so he committed the British to seeing it through, come what may. Withdrawal would be a damaging blow to British prestige in the East and, as Kitchener remarked on 24 February, 'The effect of a defeat in the Orient would be very serious. There could be no going back. The publicity of the announcement has committed us.'[8]

As the ships worked their way slowly up the Straits, the British tried to extract the maximum diplomatic advantage from their progress. They negotiated to try to get the Turks out of the war and the Greeks into it. All they succeeded in doing was to arouse Russian suspicions and force themselves into a position where they could only allay them by signing away Constantinople. In January the Russians had sharply rebuffed approaches by dissident members of the Turkish government seeking a separate peace.[9] In the wake of the German successes in Poland, rumours continued to reach London of German efforts to reach a separate peace with Russia. The Foreign Office professionals were still sceptical that the tsar would listen to them but Grey was anxious, in the face of Russia's defeats, not to do anything which might diminish its enthusiasm for the war.[10] He therefore had to keep his promise of November 1914 that the

Russians could do as they pleased with Constantinople at the end of the war. Since January the Foreign Office had known that the Turkish dissidents would not act unless the allies promised that Turkey would not be dismembered.[11] Until early March it seemed possible that some compromise between their determination to retain Constantinople and Russia's determination that it would have free passage through the Straits might be possible. Grey's pledge in November had not specified any particular territorial arrangements. But the bombardment had electrified Venizelos. He believed that if Greece acted quickly it might occupy Constantinople and the eastern Mediterranean would become a Greek lake. On 1 March, to the delight of Asquith and Kitchener, he offered to land three divisions on the Gallipoli peninsula and threatened the king with his resignation if he did not agree. His initiative failed. For a short time Constantine wavered, tantalized by the prospect of marching into the city of St Sophia at the head of his army. But the General Staff were still afraid that the Bulgarians would stab Greece in the back if it attacked Turkey. Venizelos's plan was rejected and on 6 March he resigned.

In the face of these divisions within the Greek government the possibility of it joining the Entente was both remote and short-lived but it had been enough to alarm the Russians. On 2 March the British had accepted Venizelos's offer, subject to Russia's concurrence. The Russians would not give it. Under no circumstances were they willing to allow the Straits to·fall under the control of another power. Their own offensive against Austria–Hungary had just begun and it seemed that they might be able to create their own Balkan bloc on their own terms. Some members of the War Council hoped to avoid the problem by sticking strictly to the letter of the Pact of London and insisting that any agreement on the final disposal of Constantinople should wait until the peace conference, but Grey insisted that procrastination was impossible. 'It was very important', he insisted on 3 March, 'to avoid anything in the nature of a breach with Russia, or any action which would incite Russia to make a separate peace.'[12] On 4 March Sazonov made his demands known: Constantinople, the western shores of the Bosphorus, the Sea of Marmara, the Dardanelles, southern Thrace up to the Enos-Midia line and the islands of Imbros and Tenedos. In return he promised to extend to the British and French every consideration when they presented their list of desiderata. Sazonov hinted that unless they agreed he might be replaced by someone who supported a return to the *Dreikaiserbund*.[13] The War Council were very bitter that Sazonov had effectively vetoed Greece's entry but no one disagreed when Grey said that 'he would prefer to have all the Balkan states in opposition rather [than] alienate Russia at this crisis'.[14] They accepted the Russian demands but insisted in return that the present neutral zone in Persia should become part of the British sphere of influence, that there should be free passage through the Straits for all commerce, and that whatever happened to the rest of the Turkish empire, Arabia and the Holy Places had to remain under Muslim control. It would never do for the British to be seen as the despoilers of Islam. But above all the agreement had to be kept secret for fear of alienating the Balkan neutrals and the Russians had to drop their objections to them joining the Entente.[15]

The Constantinople agreement meant that the allies could no longer postpone consideration of their territorial war aims until hostilities were over. The French and British now had to consider their own desiderata in the Turkish empire. They had only accepted the agreement grudgingly and now tried to protect their own postwar interests. The French were afraid that Russian predominance at Constantinople would threaten their considerable investments in the Turkish empire. Even before the agreement was signed, Poincaré and Briand had been considering seeking compensation in Syria and Cilicia. In early February Delcassé said that if the Turkish empire was partitioned France must have Syria and Alexandretta.[16]

Some members of the British government had also begun to consider their objectives before the Constantinople agreement was signed. In January Herbert Samuel, the President of the Local Government Board, wrote a memorandum suggesting that Britain should annex Palestine at the end of the war. This would serve three purposes. The public would naturally desire some tangible territorial spoils as a reward for their sacrifices. Annexing Turkish Palestine would be preferable to annexing German colonies because the latter would create a source of permanent enmity between Britain and Germany and make a lasting peace impossible. Possession of Palestine would also add to the security of the British empire after the war. Like Kitchener, Samuel did not think that the present grouping of the powers would be permanent. France and Russia had been Britain's rivals in the past and, with Germany defeated, they might be so again in the future. If Palestine were annexed by the British it would act as a buffer between French territory to the north and British-dominated Egypt to the south.[17]

The same considerations, the need for some tangible territorial rewards to please the public, the need to do everything possible to reach a territorial settlement which would not create lasting enmity with the Germans, and the need to secure the British empire against France and Russia after the war, dominated the War Council's discussions of war aims in March. The general consensus of opinion was against fighting the war in order to crush Germany. Churchill and Kitchener thought that Britain would be secure against the Germans once the German fleet were destroyed, the Kiel Canal removed from German control and a large indemnity imposed to make it impossible for them to build a new fleet. A moderately powerful Germany in the centre of Europe was both inevitable, given its economic strength, and in Britain's interest as it would counterbalance Russia. As Lloyd George said on 19 March, 'She would always be a very powerful nation, and it might eventually be desirable to have her in a position to prevent Russia becoming too predominant.'[18] Unless the Dominions and the Japanese insisted on retaining them, the War Council agreed that it would be a mistake to keep too many German colonies. Like Lloyd George, Kitchener was also more concerned about the threat which Russia and to a lesser extent France, rather than Germany, might pose to the British empire. He wanted to safeguard Britain's position in the Middle East and satisfy the public's desire for territorial spoils by annexing Mesopotamia together with either Alexandretta or Aleppo as its Mediterranean outlet. The rump of Turkey in Asia, stretching from Anatolia to the Persian border, would provide a convenient buffer between Mesopotamia and Russia. The Admiralty and the India Office also coveted Mesopotamia. The navy needed Middle Eastern oil and the India Office and the government of India hoped that with proper irrigation, Mesopotamia (which they defined as running from the Gulf of Alexandretta to the Persian Gulf) would provide India with corn and an outlet for its surplus population.[19]

But others felt that this was hardly the time to make it plain to the allies that Britain distrusted their postwar ambitions. In the light of France's demands for Cilicia, Syria and Palestine, the suggestion to annex Meso-potamia met with a lukewarm response. While Asquith agreed that Britain had to protect its interests against France and Russia and probably Italy and Greece as well, it already possessed as much territory as 'we are able to hold'.[20] Sir Edmund Barrow, the military secretary at the India Office, pointed out that Britain lacked the troops necessary to garrison such a vast area. Lewis Harcourt, the Colonial Secretary, dissented in another direction. The German colonies were not Britain's to give back. The Dominions and Japan had captured most of them and intended to retain them. However, there was general agreement that they had to preserve some kind of independent Muslim state in the Middle East because, as Grey explained, they had 'to take into account the very strong feelings in the Moslem world that Mohammedanism ought to have a political as well as a religious existence'.[21] The War Council therefore decided to try to postpone discussing with the allies the future partition of Turkey in Asia for as long as possible in the hope that something would turn up. The ideal solution, at least for the British, was proposed at the end of June by an inter-departmental committee under Sir Maurice de Bunsen, the former British ambassador to Vienna. De Bunsen and his colleagues suggested that the Turkish empire, minus Constantinople and its hinterland, should be preserved intact. Each of the empire's constituent parts should be granted its own autonomous government and each of them would be free to appoint foreign 'advisers'. British 'advisers' would serve in Palestine and Mesopotamia and by this means they would pass into the orbit of Britain's informal empire.[22]

As long as the Constantinople agreement remained secret there was still a possibility that success at the Dardanelles or in the Carpathians might induce the Balkan states to join the Entente. For a short time in March the situation in Romania and Bulgaria looked auspicious. Sir George Barclay thought that the Romanian king was increasingly veering towards the Entente, while in Bulgaria both Bax-Ironside and Sir Arthur Paget reported that if Constantinople fell, Ferdinand would be unable to prevent his country joining the Entente.[23] But if there were still grounds for hope in the Balkans there was none at Constantinople. Early in March Hall's agents held secret discussions with Talaat Pasha, a senior member of the Committee of Union and Progress. The discussions reached a climax on 15–16 March. The British wanted the Turks to withdraw from their alliance with Germany, end the war and open the Dardenelles. They had expected to do business with a traitor who was ready to sell his country for gold and offered Talaat a bribe of £4m. But Talaat was a patriot who simply wanted to reverse a political error. The negotiations collapsed when Hall's agents could give him no assurance that Constantinople would remain the capital of Turkey after the war. The Constantinople agreement made a negotiated peace with Turkey impossible.[24]

The Entente's only major diplomatic success in the spring of 1915 was the entry of Italy into the war. With its long Adriatic coastline vulnerable to Austrian naval attack, Italy was perhaps the most susceptible of all the neutrals to the lure of British sea power. In November 1914 the new Italian foreign minister, Sidney Sonnino, had hinted to Grey that although Italy's military preparations were incomplete he would like to discuss the terms of its eventual entry. But the Russians were as opposed to its entry as they were to that of Greece. They were determined that at the end of the war their client Serbia, and not Italy, would control the Dalmatian coast. Grey therefore refused to negotiate unless the Italians first gave a definite promise that they would join the Entente and its entry hung fire throughout the winter of 1914–15.[25] The Germans worked hard to keep it neutral. In December 1914 Bethmann-Hollweg sent the former chancellor, Prince von Bulow, to Rome to work for Italian neutrality by offering it concessions at Austria–Hungary's expense. He was, however, handicapped by his own government's refusal to put sufficient pressure on the Austrians to make enough concessions.[26] On 4 March Sonnino finally told Grey that he was ready to join the Entente and presented a very long list of territorial demands, including the Trentino, the Cisalpine Tyrol, Trieste, Istria and the Istrian islands, Dalmatia and the Dalmatian islands and, if the Turkish empire was partitioned those provinces washed by the Mediterranean contiguous to Adelia. He also insisted that the French and British fleets would have to co-operate with the Italian navy in destroying the Austrian Adriatic fleet, that the Russians would have to mount an offensive against Austria to cover Italy's mobilization, and that the British would have to lend Italy money to pay for its war effort.[27] Grey and Asquith believed that Italy's entry into the war was too big a prize to miss. If the Italians came in they believed that Romania would not be far behind.[28] But the Russians objected to the Italians' claims in the Adriatic, and it was their objections, and the deep divisions within Italian society, rather than the inability of the allied fleet to carry the Dardanelles which delayed Italy's entry into the war until May.

The breaking-off of the talks withi Talaat Pasha meant that the allied fleet had to continue to work its way up the Straits. As the operation proceeded Carden's enthusiasm for it waned. Mines and concealed howitzers made it apparent that the purely naval enterprise was a more dangerous undertaking than it had appeared to be in January. On 11 March the Admiralty War Group told Carden that the potential results of the operation justified his pressing on regardless of losses. The next day he received intelligence that the Turks' heavy batteries were very short of ammunition. Carden agreed to continue but insisted that considerble numbers of troops would have to be landed to silence the concealed howitzers and secure his lines of communication into the Sea of Marmara. Kitchener agreed that troops should be concentrated at Mudros on the Greek island of Lemnos in the Aegean but he still did not expect that they would have to be used in an amphibious assault. Before Carden could carry out his orders he fell ill and was replaced by Vice-Admiral de Robeck. De Robeck mounted the final purely naval attack on 18 March. The Turks fired most of their remaining heavy gun ammunition and the allied fleet sailed into a minefield and lost three battleships sunk and another three crippled. The manner in which the Turks stuck to their batteries convinced de Robeck that the fleet's high velocity guns would not be able to silence them permanently, that the garrison would not bolt from the peninsula even if the fleet passed them by and that there would not be a revolution in Constantinople even if he did get through. On 22 March he met the newly-appointed army commander, General Sir Ian Hamilton, and they agreed that the army would have to land on the peninsula to clear a way for the fleet and its unarmoured supply vessels.[29] Their decision added to the growing feeling in London that the operation had been bungled. Churchill, Asquith and Kitchener initially wanted de Robeck to renew his naval assault, but the views of the Admiralty War Group and the men on the spot prevailed. On 23 March the Cabinet agreed that the next step ought to be an amphibious landing. The fears of Fisher and the other Sea Lords, that this would represent a serious drain on the Grand Fleet's reserves, were ignored.[30]

Hamilton could not land until mid-April because he had to await the arrival of the Twenty-Ninth Division and his transports had to be reloaded for an assault landing. But this was not the obstacle which delayed Italy's entry into the war. The real reason why it took until the end of April before Italy could be induced to sign the Treaty of London was the difficulty in finding a compromise between Russian and Italian ambitions on the shores of the Adriatic. The Italians wanted to control the entire Dalmatian coast because otherwise their own coastline would be vulnerable to any hostile naval power opposite them. As the Italian ambassador in London explained, 'It would not be worth Italy's while to fight simply to substitute a Slav for an Austrian position in the Adriatic'.[31] But the Serbs did not want to see Austria replaced by Italy as the predominant power in the Adriatic. Asquith was disgusted at the Italians' greed but the Russians were the key to the situation. As long as they supported Serbia, deadlock resulted. It was not broken by British diplomacy but by the collapse of Russia's offensive against Austria. On 6 April this had ground to a halt and the Grand Duke told Sazonov that Russia itself now needed Italian assistance. After further haggling Sazonov finally assented to Italy's revised terms on 21 April and Italy signed the Treaty of London on 26 April.[32] The treaty marked a significant step in the development of British war aims policy. The Pact of London had bound Britain to continue the war in common with its allies. It was as much a guarantee that they would not desert Britain as that Britain would not desert them. It had not committed the British to fighting to achieve any particular territorial settlement. They recognized that France wanted to regain Alsace–Lorraine at the end of the war, but the British government had made no formal pledge to them that Britain would fight on until they had occupied the lost provinces. Similarly, the Constantinople agreement only committed the British to allow Russia to occupy Constantinople if the Entente had first won the war. But the territorial clauses of the Treaty of London meant that, for the first time, the British were bound to continue the war to fulfil the territorial war aims of one of their allies. Italy's war aims had become Britain's war aims.[33]

Hamilton's troops landed on the Gallipoli peninsula on 25 April. The Turks were not routed and there was no revolution in Constantinople. They resisted stoutly and Hamilton's forces barely got beyond the beaches. Hamilton quickly realized that he was not fighting a backward oriental despotism but a still great military power and began to call for reinforcements and all the paraphernalia of modern war, especially heavy guns and high explosive ammunition, so he could blast his way through the enemy's trenches. They were not available and by mid-May the Gallipoli front was stalemated.[34] But even if Hamilton had taken the peninsula in a single bound Italy's entry into the war would probably still have been postponed for another month.

The Italian government had signed the treaty on the understanding that they would be given a month's grace in which to prepare Italian public opinion for war against their ostensible ally, Austria. Italian opinion was seriously divided. The professional, upper and landed classes were sympathetic to the Central Powers, fearing that an Entente victory would mean the triumph of socialism and republicanism in Italy. The British were particularly concerned at the way in which the Vatican tried to manipulate public opinion. The clerical press openly favoured the Central Powers and Pope Benedict XV opposed Italy joining the war, partly from humanitarian considerations and partly because he wished to see Catholic Austria remain a great power. The Germans encouraged the Vatican with grants of money channelled through the German Catholic politician Matthias Erzberger and the papal chamberlain, Monsignor Rudolf Gerlach.[35] As late as the end of April probably a majority of deputies and a large segment of the public were in favour of remaining neutral and the government had to work hard to create pro-war sentiments. On 12 May the British ambassador in Rome reported that there was a real possibility that the Italians might renege on the Treaty of London, 'such is [the] timidity of many of this nation that they clutch at any excuse for not accepting the issue of war like drowning men at straws'.[36] The government's basic conservatism made it reluctant to rest its case on the support of street demonstrations organized by the minority of interventionists. On 13 May the Prime Minister, Salandra, resigned. The situation was saved for the Entente only because the leader of the neutralists, Giolitti, hesitated to return to Rome and while he did so the interventionists managed to increase the numbers and violence of the pro-war demonstrations in Rome and in other cities. A crowd in Rome broke into the Chamber and attacked some of Giolitti's principal lieutenants. The king therefore recalled Salandra and on 20 May the Chamber voted for war by 407 votes to 74.[37] The manner of Italy's entry into the war did not augur well for the future. Its army was poorly prepared and its society was clearly divided. Enthusiasm which had been aroused so quickly could evaporate just as quickly.

On 30 March Asquith predicted that if the allies broke through at the Dardanelles and Italy and the Balkan neutrals then joined the Entente, the war would be over by June. His optimism was fed by the fact that the possibility of the Balkan states joining the Entente, coupled with the Russians' initial successes in the Carpathians, had forced some Hungarians to inquire about terms. The Hungarian Independence Party, who did not think that a German victory would be in Hungary's interests, conducted desultory discussions with Rodd and Sonnino between January and May. Rumours that the Austrians might also want to seek terms with the Russians emanated from the Vatican, Switzerland and the

Austrian ambassador at Berlin. The day after the Italians signed the Treaty of London, Grey made another approach to the Bulgarians and repeated his formula of 13 February and Bax-Ironside reported that the Bulgarian prime minister seemed interested. On 8 May he tentatively offered to join the Entente in return for the contested and uncontested zones of Macedonia and the towns of Kavalla, Seres and Drama. On 3 May the Romanians presented their terms to the Russians and the Greek king hinted that even he might be about to change his mind.[38] But Italy's entry into the war was not the catalyst which set the Balkans on the march for the Entente. Two things saved the Austro–Hungarian empire. The terms the Independence Party sought were unacceptable to the Russians. The Hungarians insisted on retaining Transylvania but Russia had already promised that to Romania. And, of much greater consequence, at the beginning of May the Germans began an offensive which, by the end of the summer, cost the Russians Warsaw and most of Poland and which more than cancelled out the impact of Italy's entry into the war. By the end of May both the Bulgarians and the Greeks had returned to their policies of watchful neutrality and the British were no nearer to inducing the Balkans to join the Entente than they had been in February.[39]

The allies had equally little success in breaking the German line in the West. After the War Council had vetoed the Zeebrugge operation, Sir John French agreed to Joffre's plan to strike at the shoulders of the bulge formed by the German line in Artois and the Champagne. On 16 February Joffre asked Sir John to co-operate by seizing Aubers Ridge while the French Tenth Army took Vimy Ridge a little to the south. However that plan fell through when the Twenty-Ninth Division was diverted to the Mediterranean. The British were then left to attack at Neuve Chapelle alone. The Battle of Neuve Chapelle was a tactical success in as much as Haig's First Army did break through the German front positions on 10 March. But they were unable to exploit their success and two days later the troops were ordered to dig-in where they stood.[40] The dispatch of the Twenty-Ninth Division to the Dardanelles had caused much ill-feeling among the French, who were afraid that Kitchener meant to send the New Armies to Constantinople rather than France.[41] In fact Kitchener was reluctant to send the New Armies anywhere. There was not enough ammunition for them and he still adhered to his original plan that they ought not to be used until their commitment was certain to end the war. On 29 March he told Joffre and French that apart from two divisions already earmarked for the BEF, he would not send any more divisions to France until the allies had actually broken the German line.[42] But Joffre was determined to mount a general offensive. The British role in this began on 9 May when Haig's First Army assaulted Aubers Ridge. The BEF had learnt some of the lessons of Neuve Chapelle but the Germans had learnt far more. Haig assaulted a much stronger enemy position and suffered proportionately heavier casualties.[43]

The episode might have ended there but for three things. French's relations with Kitchener had been steadily worsening since September 1914. By May Sir John believed that Kitchener planned to supplant him and take command of the New Armies himself when they were ready. French was also deeply upset by the heavy casualties his troops had suffered. He blamed his losses and his inability to break the German line on the inadequate supplies of artillery ammunition, and particularly of high explosive shells, he was receiving. And finally Kitchener had hinted that if he could not break through, the New Armies might be sent elsewhere. The last straw came on 10 May when French received a telegram from the War Office ordering him to send 20,000 rounds of artillery ammunition to Hamilton. It seemed to portend that his army was about to be starved of resources to serve the Dardanelles. Encouraged by members of his personal staff, French unleashed a vicious attack on Kitchener's apparent mishandling of munitions supply through *The Times* military correspondent, Lieut.-Col. Charles à Court Repington, who was then a guest at his headquarters, and through members of his staff who recounted Sir John's side of the story to sympathetic politicians.[44] When the news broke in London it formed but one part of the crisis which engulfed the Liberal government in the middle of May.

The shell crisis of the spring of 1915 was an expression of the government's inability to improvise a successful war economy in the face of Kitchener's creation of the New Armies. Kitchener's call for men had produced over one million volunteers by December 1914. Reliance on the voluntary system and the need to take recruits as and when they presented themselves made it impossible for the government to prepare a rational plan to mobilize industry to equip the new forces. Some production bottle-necks and inflation were perhaps inevitable but they were probably made worse by Lloyd George's financial policies. He was not a successful war chancellor. He had little interest in the details of budgetary policy. His response at the Treasury to Kitchener's innovations was inadequate. From the very beginning of the war detailed parliamentary scrutiny of the estimates was abandoned as a security measure. The cost of the war was met by a series of votes of credit. In October 1914 the Chancellor insisted on an arbitrary increase in munitions orders in excess of the number of men Kitchener had raised. In January 1915, to encourage manufacturers to lay down more plant as rapidly as possible, he abandoned the system of contracting for munitions by competitive tender. His alternative was to inject large amounts of cash into the munitions industry in the hope that this would expedite deliveries – and incidentally make up for the deficiencies in the industry caused in part by the Treasury's prewar parsimony. This may have been necessary to ensure the more prompt delivery of orders but it was highly inflationary.[45]

Lloyd George might have been able to restrain inflation through his first war budget but his fiscal policy only added to it. Basil Blackett, one of his Treasury advisers, had warned him in August that the best way to pay for the war would be out of current taxation but he did not heed this advice. In the light of the fiasco of his April 1914 budget, Lloyd George had to summon up all his political courage even to introduce the mild measures that he did bring forward in November 1914. With the war already costing £900,000 per day he was content to double direct taxes for the last quarter of the financial year. He toyed with the idea of reducing working-class spending power by reducing the income tax threshold from £160 to £50 p.a. but rejected it because of its obvious political unpopularity. Instead he taxed the poor – and raised their cost of living – by increasing duties on beer, tobacco, tea and sugar.[46]

This provided only a fraction of the cost of the war to the end of the financial year. To raise the remainder he resorted to loans. The first war loan was issued in November on terms which were extremely generous to the joint stock banks. While funds for this were being subscribed the government resorted to the sale of Treasury bills to meet its immediate needs. In April 1915 these were issued as tap stock for the first time, enabling the Treasury to keep domestic interest rates high enough to attract foreign deposits to London.[47] The Treasury had already issued large sums of paper money without the backing of gold to overcome the financial crisis of August 1914. Lloyd George's policy only served further to inflate the currency. Most of the bills were bought by the banks, who thereby increased their reserves and so were able to lend more money to their customers. It was a recipe for currency inflation.[48] Thanks to a combination of higher transport costs, increased world demand and currency inflation, the Board of Trade's retail price index rose by 22 per cent between August 1914 and February 1915.[49] A little remarked innovation of January 1915 marked a clear break with the free trade policies of the past. Before 1914 Lloyd George had encouraged the free export of British capital in an attempt to provide markets and cheap imports for British exports. The demands of war forced him to curb this policy. In September 1914 the Treasury began to subsidize the allies and it became necessary to prevent capital leaving the country indiscriminately and to channel it into the war effort. Henceforth fresh domestic capital issues were only permitted if they were in the national interest, colonial issues were only allowed if they were urgently necessary, and foreign issues were not normally allowed at all. This marked a clearer break with free trade orthodoxy than the largely symbolic McKenna duties of September 1915.[50]

The government's policy of ensuring adequate deliveries of food supplies worked, in as much as calorific intake per head was not threatened until 1916.[51] But inflation brought with it obvious social and political problems. In January and February 1915 the War Emergency Workers National Committee and similar bodies organized a series of public protests against rising prices. Allegations that shipowners and millers were making abnormally high profits were rife.[52] Asquith and Runciman only further angered the government's critics when they blandly assured the Commons that they had no intention of interfering in the free market. They were hiding the truth. Public disclosure of the large meat contracts they had signed with the Argentinian government was inadvisable because it would embarrass the Argentinians. News that the government was also secretly buying large quantities of grain with the intention of releasing it on to the open market at less than the prevailing market price if retail prices rose too steeply would have been counter-productive. It would simply have caused private importers to go on strike. Indeed that was exactly what did happen when news of the government's activities leaked out.[53]

The first major strike in a war-related industry occurred on Clydeside in February. The strikers were bought off with a war bonus and other groups of workers had some of their demands met.[54] But in mid-March the Cabinet and Treasury agreed that the granting of war bonuses only made inflation worse. Consequently Lloyd George and Runciman, acting on the advice of Sir John Bradbury, joint permanent secretary of the Treasury and Edwin Montagu, the Financial Secretary, hatched a plan to impose austerity on the working classes. Private consumption would be reduced and inflation checked if the government refused to sanction further wage rises. In return for going short of goods and clothing the working classes were to be persuaded 'to submit to the necessary sacrifices' by the government taking steps to limit the profits of war manufacturers.[55] The result was a very one-sided bargain. Munitions firms were asked to agree to limit their profits to a figure 20 per cent above their peacetime profits. By contrast, under the terms of the Treasury agreement negotiated by Lloyd George and Runciman with national union leaders in March, organized labour was asked to forgo the right to strike for the duration of the war, to submit all disputes to arbitration, and to accept the dilution of skilled labour. In return all they received was a promise to return to the status quo ante bellum.[56]

Lloyd George had begun to play a key role in mobilizing the British economy to support the Entente's war effort in late February. Since January he had seen all his hopes come to naught apparently because the British lacked the resources to carry them out. He was afraid that the allies were still pursuing a policy of drift. The British were tackling neither the Dardanelles nor his own Salonika scheme with energy and determination. Little was known about the Russians except that they were being beaten because they lacked rifles, guns and shells. On 22 February he wrote an epoch-making Cabinet memorandum designed to remedy this. He insisted that the three major allies had to hold a joint military conference to co-ordinate their plans. Britain and its empire had to throw their full weight into the alliance. Britain should abandon the idea of fighting the war on limited liability principles, mobilize the whole of its engineering industry to manufacture war goods and adopt a total war economy in which only the basic minimum of resources were left aside to meet essential civilian needs. He placed himself squarely behind Kitchener's drive to create a continental-scale army. Britain had to raise up to another one and a half million men on top of the troops it had already recruited. But mobilization on such a scale would not be complete until the beginning of 1916. In the meantime the Entente must look to Italy and the Balkans for an immediate increase in their forces.[57]

This remained the essential basis of Lloyd George's policies throughout 1915–16. Unlike McKenna and Runciman, who began to emerge as the champions of 'business as usual' in the spring and summer of 1915, Lloyd George had abandoned the radical-navalist belief that the blockade and the military strength of France and Russia would be sufficient to win the war. But there was a lacuna in Lloyd George's thinking. He did not really understand how important financial management would be in a long war and he completely failed to frame his May 1915 budget as if he expected a prolonged and testing conflict. He formulated his budget against an apparently hopeful military background, just after Italy had signed the Treaty of London, just before Hamilton failed to carry the Dardanelles at one bound and just when it was easy to imagine that Constantinople was about to fall and a Balkan alliance was about to be constructed. On 4 May he announced that his proposals were intended only as an interim measure and the only significant new impost was a sharp increase in the duty on alcohol, designed to restrict consumption rather than raise revenue.[58]

Since the autumn of 1914 the Unionists had become increasingly critical of the government.[59] Unionist back-benchers resented the silence imposed on them by the party truce and in January 1915 twenty-five of them formed the Unionist Business Committee as a pressure group to criticize the Liberal administration. Like the Unionist press, they believed that the government contained some pacifists and feared that they might be ready to make a compromise peace. There was no real possibility of this. Only a small and isolated group of Liberals like Lord Loreburn, John Burns and F. W. Hirst, the editor of the *Economist*, wanted a negotiated peace in the spring of 1915. In March 1915 the Bryce group, a mixture of young intellectuals and elder statesmen like Lord Bryce and Lord Loreburn began to discuss the possibility of a peace based on reconciliation and national self-determination rather than on conquest. They argued that the war had not been started by Prussian militarism but was a product of an anarchic international system which would only be tamed if all the powers joined a peace league. If it went on, the whole future of liberal civilization would be placed at risk. G. Lowes Dickinson, one of the leaders of the group, believed that in every belligerent nation there was a conflict between

> those who want to fasten upon the world militarism, war, and class domination; and those who want peace and the continued development of democracy and social justice. We in England were told, and believed, that we are fighting to destroy militarism and to confirm freedom. Since then, *The Times* has frankly insisted that we are really fighting for the balance of power and our own interests; and the *Morning Post* daily pours contempt on democracy, freedom, and peace.[60]

They had little influence in the Liberal Party and none in the Cabinet. The public heard little of their ideas and it is doubtful if they would have been particularly receptive to them. The war made public discussion of anything other than military victory very difficult and it was safer for the Bryce group and similar organizations like the UDC to remain quiet rather than be accused of helping the enemy. The Foreign Office was confident that most members of the working classes had accepted that Britain had a moral duty to fight for Belgium's independence. Stories of German atrocities, given spurious confirmation by the evidence collected by a committee presided over by Bryce himself, the Germans' use of poison gas at Ypres in April and the sinking of the *Lusitania* in May, only gave added cogency to the notion that Britain was engaged in a crusade against the evil Hun.

It was not until 3 May that those in favour of a peace of reconciliation took their first major public step by establishing the League of Nations Society. Like the UDC and the ILP, the society was not a 'stop the war' body. Each of these groups believed that future wars could be prevented if members of the League agreed to support each other against any aggressor. They wanted to ensure that Britain's war aims were just because, if they were, a negotiated peace between peoples would be possible. As a first step they began to ask the government to define its territorial war aims.[61] Grey's impatience with them verged on contempt. Officially he still maintained a discreet silence. Privately he believed that 'If these people were likely to be open to reason I would reply that the restoration of Belgian independence with an indemnity cannot be called a policy of vengeance and that the policy outlined [?] in the resolution would in the present state of German opinion strengthen the military party there'.[62] Grey clung to the belief that the real issue at stake was Britain's survival as an independent nation and that was not a subject for negotiation. On 10 March he explained to Ambassador Page that the political issues at stake were too great to make an early compromise peace possible.

> If we [i.e. the British] are defeated, it will be worse with us than it can be with Germany if she is defeated. The German people in any event will remain – remain on land that can practically feed them. We – if Germany shd. [*sic*] win – wd. [*sic*] have our overseas dominions cut off and we shd. [*sic*] be an island people without the means of self-support – utter obliteration of Great Britain and of English influence.[63]

By the same token the Germans were not likely to give in until they were completely defeated. 'When you have a great nation like Germany', wrote Nicolson, 'with its wonderful organisation and patriotism, engaged in a struggle for what is practically her existence as a great nation, one cannot expect that she will surrender until she had been brought down to the very last of her resources.'[64]

A negotiated peace was anathema to the Unionists. Lord Curzon told Colonel House that he wanted 'to make peace in Berlin no matter how long it takes to get there'.[65] As self-appointed spokesmen for the opposition, the Unionist press and the Business Committee saw their job as being to urge the government towards a more vigorous prosecution of the war – if possible at maximum cost to their political principles.[66] By the beginning of May many Unionists believed that Churchill had bungled the Dardanelles and they were angry that the government was not doing all that it should to support the army in France with men and munitions.[67] Bonar Law privately agreed with many of their criticisms but hesitated to criticize the government too strongly in public for fear of tarnishing the Unionists' reputation as the patriotic party. The only alternatives to his policy of 'patriotic criticism' were to remain silent or to establish a formal coalition with the government and, as he told Lord Curzon in January 1915, 'The latter proposal I should certainly be against'.[68]

But in mid-May Bonar Law was no longer able to restrain his followers. All the government's failures came home to roost. On 20 April Asquith had told an audience in Newcastle that the army had sufficient shells for its needs. On 14 May *The Times* published Repington's dispatch blaming Sir John French's failure at Aubers Ridge on a shortage of shells. A day later Fisher resigned, citing as his reason the fact that the Dardanelles campaign was draining the Grand Fleet of the ships it needed to ensure the safety of the British Isles.[69] Initially the Unionist front bench decided simply to make private representations to the government. This infuriated W. A. Hewins, a leader of the Unionist Business Committee. On 17 May he warned Asquith and Bonar Law that he would table a question in the House making Fisher's resignation public. Bonar Law's policy of patriotic opposition was about to collapse. But Asquith recognized a marvellous opportunity. The revelations of 14–17 May did not cause the collapse of the Liberal government, they only provided the occasion for it. Asquith still had a working majority in the Commons and could have weathered any debate with little difficulty. His subsequent claim that he was worried about the effect a parliamentary debate on Fisher's resignation and the shell crisis might have on the still wavering Italians does not stand up to close scrutiny.[70] If a mere debate might deter the Italians from joining the Entente, a full-scale government crisis involving the resignation of one government followed by a lengthy period of confusion during which he had to construct a new coalition Cabinet was even more likely to convince them that the British were not stable allies upon whom they could rely. His concern for Italy was a smoke-screen to hide his real reason for bringing about the collapse of his own government. Asquith had gone to war banking on a short conflict. A general election was due at the end of 1915 and if he could present the Liberals as the party who had won the war they might also win the election. But the blockade and 'business as usual' had not brought the Germans to their knees. The allies' failure to break through on the Western front and at the Dardanelles, the Russian collapse and the fast receding prospect of a Balkan confederation all pointed to the fact that the war would last well into 1916. The Dardanelles had done little to help Russia and the allies were increasingly resentful that they were bearing the brunt of the land war while British industry seemed to be waxing rich. A wartime general election would divide the nation and probably lead to the Liberals being trounced. Only a coalition would enable them to avoid the awful political fate awaiting them. To a man, the Unionist leaders loathed the idea of entering a coalition. But they had no option. Asquith had called their bluff. As Lord Selborne wrote, 'This coalition is damnable but of course we could not say no when asked *Pro Patria*'.[71]

Notes

1. PRO CAB 19/29, Dardanelles Commission. Statements of Evidence. Note for evidence on the attempt to secure assistance by diplomatic efforts to help the position in the Peninsula [n.d. but *c.* 1916].
2. D. French, 'The origins of the Dardanelles campaign reconsidered', *History*, Vol. 68, no. 223 (1983), pp. 213–5; see also Callwell to Wilson, 23 December 1914, Sir H. Wilson mss, box 73/1/18.
3. E. David (ed.), *Inside Asquith's Cabinet: From the Diaries of Charles Hobhouse* (London: John Murray, 1977), p. 222.
4. PRO CAB 42/1/8, M. P. A. Hankey, The War – attack on the Dardanelles, 2 February 1915; M. Gilbert (ed.), *Winston S. Churchill*, Vol. 3, *Companion*, pt 1 (London: Heinemann, 1971), pp. 500, 506–12.
5. PRO CAB 42/1/29, Minutes of the War Council, 9 February 1915.
6. R. R. James, *Gallipoli* (London: Pan, 1974), pp. 39–40; PRO CAB 42/1/33, 34 and 42, Minutes and Conclusions of the War Council, 16, 19 and 24 February 1915; PRO WO 106/1538, Directorate of Military Operations,

Dardanelles Operations [n.d. but *c.* early February 1915]; Gilbert, *Companion*, Vol. 3, pt 1, pp. 563–4.

7   M. and E. Brock (eds), *H. H. Asquith: Letters to Venetia Stanley* (London: Oxford University Press, 1982), pp. 436, 446, 449; Sir G. Arthur, *Not Worth Reading* (London: Longman, Green, 1938), p. 230; PRO CAB 42/1/34, Minutes of the War Council, 19 February 1915.

8   PRO CAB 42/1/42, Minutes of the War Council, 24 February 1915.

9   PRO FO 371/2482/10108, Minute by G. R. Clerk, 23 January 1915 and Grey to Buchanan, 26 January 1915.

10 PRO FO 371/2449/21523, Findlay to Foreign Office, 23 February 1915 and minutes by Clark and Nicolson, 24 February 1915; PRO FO 371/2505/22758, Grant Duff to Foreign Office, 18 February 1915 and (23892), Grant Duff to Foreign Office, 25 February 1915; PRO FO 800/377, Buchanan to Nicolson, 24 February 1915.

11 PRO FO 371/2482/13895, Grant Duff to Foreign Office, 29 January 1915.

12 PRO CAB 42/2/3, Minutes of the War Council, 3 March 1915.

13 PRO CAB 37/125/19, Buchanan to Grey, 4 March 1915; PRO CAB 37/125/29, Grey to the Cabinet, 10 March 1915; PRO CAB 37/126/2, Note by Count Beckendorff; W. A. Renzi, 'Great Britain, Russia and the Straits, 1914–1915', *Journal of Modern History*, Vol. 42, no. 1 (1970), pp. 1–19; E. David (ed.), *Inside Asquith's Cabinet*, pp. 225–6.

14 E. David (ed.), *Inside Asquith's Cabinet*, p. 227; Brock (eds), *H. H. Asquith*, pp. 460–3; PRO FO 800/57, Grey to Buchanan, 4 March 1915.

15 PRO CAB 42/2/5, Minutes of the War Council, 10 March 1915; PRO CAB 37/125/28, Asquith to H.M. the King, 9 March 1915; PRO CAB 37/126/3, Grey to Buchanan, 11 March 1915; PRO CAB 37/126/5, Buchanan to Grey, 13 March 1915; PRO CAB 37/126/33, Buchanan to Grey, 13 March 1915 and enc.; PRO CAB 37/126/18, Memorandum communicated by Count Beckendorff, 22 March 1915.

16 C. Andrew and A. S. Kanya-Forstner, *France Overseas. The Great War and the Climax of French Imperial Expansion* (London: Thames & Hudson, 1981), pp. 71–4; D. Dutton, 'The Balkan campaign and French war aims in the Great War', *English Historical Review*, vol. 94, no. 370 (1979), pp. 103–4.

17 PRO CAB 37/123/43; H. Samuel, The future of Palestine, 21 January 1915; PRO CAB 37/126/1, H. Samuel, Palestine, 11 March 1915; I. Friedman, *The Question of Palestine, 1914–1918. British–Jewish–Arab Relations* (London: Routledge & Kegan Paul, 1973), pp. 8–14.

18 J. Grigg, *Lloyd George: From Peace to War, 1912–1916* (London: Methuen, 1985), p. 211.

19 Jukka Nevakivi, *Britain, France and the Arab Middle East, 1914–1920* (London: Athlone Press, 1969), pp. 15–18; PRO FO 800/377, Hardinge to Nicolson, 6 January 1915 and Chirol to Nicolson, 2 February 1915; M. Gilbert (ed.), *Companion*, Vol. 3, pt 1, pp. 785–6; PRO CAB 37/126/14, Sir A. Hirtzel, Note by the secretary, political department, India Office, 14 March 1915; PRO CAB 42/2/9, Sir A. K. Wilson, Russia and Constantinople, 15 March 1915; PRO CAB 42/2/10, Kitchener, Alexandretta and Mesopotamia, 16 March 1915; PRO CAB 37/127/34, Kitchener, The future relations of the Great Powers, 21 April 1915; PRO CAB 42/2/11, The Admiralty, Alexandretta and Mesopotamia, 17 March 1915; PRO CAB 42/2/18, H. B. Jackson, Alexandretta. Its importance as a future base, 18 March 1915.

20 PRO CAB 42/2/14, Minutes of the War Council, 19 March 1915; Brock (eds), *H. H. Asquith*, pp. 509–10; Friedman, *Question of Palestine*, pp. 18–19.

21 PRO CAB 37/126/14, Sir E. Barrow, Note by Sir E. Barrow on the defence

of Mesopotamia, 16 March 1915; PRO CAB 37/126/27, L. Harcourt, The Spoils, 25 March 1915; G. Smith, 'The British government and the disposition of the German colonies in Africa, 1914–1918', in P. Gifford and Wm. Roger Louis (eds), *Britain and Germany in Africa: Imperial Rivalry and Colonial Rule* (New Haven, Conn.: Yale University Press, 1967), pp. 277–80.

22 PRO CAB 42/3/12, Asiatic Turkey. Report of a Committee, 30 June 1915.

23 M. Gilbert (ed.), *Companion*, Vol. 3, pt 1, pp. 674, 704; PRO CAB 19/29, Dardanelles Commission. Statements of Evidence. Notes . . . position in the Peninsula [n.d. but *c.* 1916]; PRO FO 371/2449/27139, Barclay to Foreign Office, 8 March 1915; PRO FO 800/57, Bertie to Grey, 13 March 1915; PRO FO 800/377, Barclay to Nicolson, 14 March 1915 and Bax-Ironside to Nicolson, 8 March 1915.

24 Hankey diary entry, 4 March 1915, Hankey mss, 1/1; French 'Origins . . . reconsidered', p. 218.

25 PRO FO 800/65, Rodd to Grey, 7 November 1914; PRO FO 800/74, Buchanan to Grey and Grey to Buchanan, 9 November 1914.

26 R. Bosworth, *Italy and the Approach of the First World War* (London: Macmillan, 1983), p. 131.

27 PRO FO 371/2507/28275, Grey, Memorandum, 4 March 1915; W. A. Renzi, 'Italy's neutrality and entry into the Great War: A re-examination', *American Historical Review*, vol. 73, no. 2 (1967–8), pp. 1426–30.

28 Brock (ed), *H. H. Asquith*, pp. 462–3, 501; PRO FO 371/2507/28275, Grey to Bertie and Buchanan, 9 March 1915; PRO FO 800/377, Buchanan to Nicholson, 30 March 1915; C. J. Lowe, 'Britain and Italian intervention, 1914–15', *Historical Journal*, vol. 12, no. 3 (1969), pp. 541–7.

29 PRO CAB 19/33, Dardanelles Commission. Minutes of evidence, QQ. 2730, 2776–82 (de Robeck), QQ. 4318–20, 4344, 4352 (Hamilton); Hamilton to Kitchener, 19 and 23 March 1915, Hamilton mss, 15/17; Hamilton to Asquith, 25 March 1915, Asquith mss, vol. 14, ff. 18–21A; Gilbert (ed.), *Companion*, Vol. 3, pt 1, pp. 752–3; P. G. Halpern (ed.), *The Keyes Papers; Selections from the Private and Official Correspondence of Admiral of the Fleet Baron Keyes of Zeebrugge*, Vol. 1 (London: Navy Records Society, 1972), p. 113; R. R. James, *Gallipoli*, pp. 60–70.

30 Brock (eds), *H. H. Asquith*, pp. 488, 500–1, 506–7; Gilbert (ed.), *Companion*, Vol. 3, pt 1, pp. 700–1, 754, 781–4; PRO CAB 19/33, Dardanelles Commission. Minutes of evidence, QQ. 3598–603, 3641 (Callwell); French, 'Origins . . . reconsidered', p. 220.

31 PRO FO 371/2507/33540, Grey to Buchanan and Bertie, 22 March 1915; PRO FO 800/377, de Graz to Nicolson, 4 April 1915.

32 Brock (eds), *H. H. Asquith*, pp. 518–19, 524–8, 535, 562–4; PRO FO 371/2508/44480, Grey to Bertie and Buchanan, 14 April 1915 (46420), 18 April 1915 (46726), Grey to Buchanan, 19 April 1915 (46987), Buchanan to Grey, 20 April 1915 (47618), Buchanan to Grey, 21 April 1915 (50797), Grey to Rodd, Bertie and Buchanan, 26 April 1915; David (ed.), *Inside Asquith's Cabinet*, p. 234; C. J. Lowe, 'Italy and the Balkans, 1914–1915', in F. H. Hinsley (ed.), *British Foreign Policy under Sir Edward Grey* (Cambridge: Cambridge University Press, 1977), pp. 419–21.

33 PRO FO 371/2508/42860, Nicolson to Grey and Asquith, 10 April 1915.

34 Hamilton to Kitchener, 28 April, 9, 10 and 17 May 1915, Hamilton mss, 15/17; Hamilton to War Office, 16 June 1915, Hamilton mss, 5/4; Gilbert (ed.), *Companion*, Vol. 3, pt 2, p. 952.

35 De Grand, 'The Italian nationalist association in the period of Italian neutrality, August 1914 to May 1915', *Journal of Modern History*, vol. 43, no.

3 (1971), pp. 408–9; W. A. Renzi, 'The Entente and the Vatican during the period of Italian neutrality, August 1914–May 1915', *Historical Journal*, vol. 13, no. 3 (1970), pp. 491–506; J. D. Gregory, *On the Edge of Diplomacy* (London: Hutchinson, 1928), pp. 87–102; Bagot to St Loe Strachey, 7 April 1915, St Loe Strachey mss, S/18/2/10.

36   PRO FO 800/65, Rodd to Grey, 12 May 1915; PRO FO 371/2508/55802, Rodd to Foreign Office, 8 May 1915 (57152), Howard to Foreign Office, 9 May 1915 (58432), Rodd to Foreign Office, 11 May 1915 (59740), Rodd to Foreign Office, 13 May 1915; PRO FO 371/2509/614000, Rodd to Foreign Office, 11 May 1915; W. A. Renzi, 'Italy's neutrality and entry into the Great War', pp. 1430–1.

37   Bosworth, *Italy*, pp. 137–8; PRO FO 371/2509/64437, Rodd to Foreign Office, 17 May 1915; De Grand, 'The Italian nationalist association', pp. 411–12.

38   PRO FO 371/2508/50797, Grey to Barclay, 27 April 1915; W. B. Fest, *Peace or Partition. The Habsburg Monarchy and British Policy 1914–1918* (London: George Prior, 1978), pp. 33–6, PRO FO 800/378, Bax-Ironside to Nicolson, 12 May 1915; PRO CAB 19/29, Dardanelles Commission. Statement of evidence, Note for evidence . . . in the Peninsula [n.d. but *c.* 1916]; G. E. Torrey, 'Rumania and the belligerents 1914–1916', *Journal of Contemporary History*, vol. 1, no. 3 (1966), pp. 182–3.

39   PRO CAB 19/29, Dardanelles Commission. Statement of evidence. Note for evidence . . . in the Peninsula [n.d. but *c.* 1916]; K. Robbins, 'British diplomacy and Bulgaria 1914–1915', *Slavonic and East European Studies Review*, vol. 49, no. 117 (1971), pp. 573–6.

40   R. Holmes, *The Little Field Marshal: Sir John French* (London: Cape, 1981), pp. 268–70.

41   PRO 30/57/57, Joffre to Kitchener, May 1915; PRO 30/57/59, Esher to Kitchener, 22 March 1915; PRO 30/57/76/WR/14, Asquith to Kitchener, 22 March 1915; PRO FO 800/57, Memo. by Grey, 28 February 1915.

42   H. Wilson, Note of a meeting at Chantilly, 29 March 1915, Wilson mss 73/1/19.

43   D. French, 'The military background to the "shell crisis" of May 1915', *Journal of Strategic Studies*, vol. 2, no. 2 (1979), p. 202.

44   Diary entries, 10 and 12 May, French mss, Vol. K.

45   D. French, *British Economic and Strategic Planning 1905–1915* (London: Allen & Unwin, 1982), pp. 134–5.

46   French, *Strategic Planning*, p. 106; E. V. Morgan, *Studies in British Financial Policy, 1914–1925* (London: Macmillan, 1952), pp. 89–90; A. J. P. Taylor (ed.), *Lloyd George: A Diary by Frances Stevenson* (London: Hutchinson, 1971), pp. 11–12.

47   Morgan, *Financial Policy*, pp. 106–8; Kathleen Burk, 'The Treasury: From impotence to power', in Kathleen Burk (ed.), *War and the State: The Transformation of British Government, 1914–1919* (London: Allen & Unwin, 1982), p. 88.

48   French, *Strategic Planning*, pp. 106–7.

49   D. W. French, 'Some aspects of social and economic planning for war in Great Britain, *c.* 1905–1915', PhD thesis, London University, 1978, pp. 164–7.

50   Morgan, *Financial Policy*, pp. 262–3; J. Atkin, 'Official regulation of British overseas investment, 1914–1931', *Economic History Review*, vol. 23, no. 2 (1970), pp. 324–5.

51   P. E. Dewey, 'Food Production and Policy in the United Kingdom,

1914–1918', *Transactions of the Royal Historical Society*, 5th series, vol. 30 (1980), p. 71.

52   C. E. Fayle, *The War and the Shipping Industry* (London: Oxford University Press, 1927), pp. 126–7; PRO 30/69/1231, Leicester Daily Post – Conference held at the Secular Hall, Leicester, by the War Emergency Workers National Committee, 15 February 1915.

53   French, *Strategic Planning*, pp. 102–3; PRO 30/69/1231, J. A. Cross to Mac-Donald, 16 February 1915.

54   French, *Strategic Planning* pp. 108–9; J. Hinton, *The First Shop Stewards' Movement* (London: Allen & Unwin, 1973), pp. 103–5.

55   PRO CAB 37/126/12, J. B[radbury], The War and Finance, 17 March 1915.

56   French, *Strategic Planning*, pp. 162–3.

57   PRO CAB 37/124/40, Lloyd George, Some further considerations on the conduct of the war, 22 February 1915.

58   Morgan, *Financial Policy*, p. 91.

59   Bonar Law to Cecil, 30 October 1914, Bonar Law mss, 37/4/25.

60   PRO FO 371/2509/46016, G. L. Dickinson to Grey, 16 April 1915.

61   T. Wilson (ed.), *The Political Diaries of C. P. Scott* (London: Collins, 1970), p. 115; D. S. Birn, *The League of Nations Union, 1918–1945* (Oxford: Clarendon Press, 1981), pp. 6–7; PRO 30/69/1238, MacDonald to Simon, 16 April 1915; A. S. Link (ed.), *The Papers of Woodrow Wilson*, Vol. 32 (Princeton, NJ: Princeton University Press, 1980), p. 350; ibid., Vol. 33, pp. 100–101.

62   PRO FO 371/2505/44511, Minute by Grey on resolution by the Carlisle branch of the ILP, 7 April 1915.

63   Link (ed.), *Wilson's Papers*, Vol. 32, p. 361.

64   PRO FO 800/377, Nicolson to Hardinge, 31 March 1915.

65   C. Seymour (ed.), *The Intimate Papers of Colonel House*, Vol. 1 (London: Ernest Benn, 1926), p. 393.

66   S. Koss, *The Rise and Fall of the Political Press in Britain*, Vol. 2: *The Twentieth Century* (London: Hamish Hamilton), pp. 255–6, 270–1.

67   See, for example, Long to B. H. Fitzgerald, 4 January 1915, Talbot to Fitzgerald, 3 March 1915, Selborne to Fitzgerald, 21 March 1915, Fitzgerald mss (microfilm); Long to Bonar Law, 21 and 23 December 1914, Bonar Law mss, 35/5/55.

68   Bonar Law to Curzon, 29 January 1915, Bonar Law mss, 37/5/6; Bonar Law to Cecil, 10 November 1914, Bonar Law mss, 37/4/27 and Bonar Law to Oliver, 18 December 1914, Bonar Law mss, 37/4/39.

69   French, *Strategic Planning*, pp. 146–7; R. F. Mackay, *Fisher of Kilverstone* (Oxford: Clarendon Press, 1973), pp. 493–7.

70   Lansdowne to Bonar Law, 14 May 1915, Bonar Law mss, 117/1/8; PRO CAB 37/128/19, Asquith to the Cabinet, 17 May 1915; M. D. Pugh, 'Asquith, Bonar Law and the first coalition', *Historical Journal*, vol. 17, no. 4 (1974), pp. 813–36.

71   Selborne to Fitzgerald, 21 May 1915, Fitzgerald mss (microfilm); Chamberlain to Bonar Law, 17 May 1915, Bonar Law mss 37/2/37; Long to Gwynne, 20 May 1915, and Beresford to Bonar Law, 17 May 1915, Gwynne mss, box 18.

6

The Asquith Coalition and the Policy of Attrition, May–August 1915

TWO QUESTIONS dominated the early months of the Asquith coalition, how was the government to extricate itself from the Dardanelles and how was it to respond to Russia's increasingly strident calls for help as its army was driven back towards Warsaw. Between May and August British policies were reversed. The failure of the May offensive only further convinced Kitchener that it would be wrong to commit the New Armies to France until they were fully equipped and trained. The Cabinet agreed and Sir John French was instructed to resume the war of attrition. He was ordered to strengthen the British line and to wait for the Germans to wear themselves out by attacking him. In the meantime Hamilton's forces at the Dardanelles were reinforced and a second landing was planned to carry the peninsula. But the expected German attack in France never came. Throughout the summer the Germans concentrated their forces in the East, drove the Russians eastwards, and in August captured Warsaw. Simultaneously Hamilton's second landing failed. It then became apparent that if the British did not participate in a major offensive in the West both the French and Russian governments might collapse and their successors might seek peace. Consequently, the Cabinet reluctantly agreed to mount the Loos offensive more as a political gesture to their allies rather than in the hope that it would achieve a tangible military victory.

The manner in which Asquith distributed offices between the parties in the coalition government demonstrated that he was still very much in command of the political situation. With the exception of Balfour, Curzon and perhaps Bonar Law, Asquith had a low opinion of the Unionists and he was determined to retain as much power as possible in Liberal hands.[1] He made only the barest minimum of concessions to the Unionists. McKenna quitted the Home Office because of Unionist criticisms of his handling of the question of the internment of enemy aliens. But he was rewarded with the Treasury and replaced by another Liberal, the former Attorney General Sir John Simon.[2] Churchill's removal from the Admiralty and demotion to the Duchy of Lancaster was as welcome to many Liberals as it was to the Unionists.[3] By contrast the Liberals resented Haldane's exclusion from the Woolsack because of the Unionists' dislike of his supposedly pro-German views. Twenty-two ministers sat in the new government, twelve Liberals, eight Unionists, one Labour member (Arthur Henderson, nominally included as President of the Board of Education but in reality as the representative of organized labour) and one non-party minister, Kitchener.[4]

The Liberals' preponderance was even greater than their numbers suggest for they retained most of the key portfolios. Asquith and Grey kept their old offices. Lloyd George was transferred to the Ministry of Munitions. Runciman stayed at the Board of Trade where he and the new chancellor could keep a wary Liberal eye on taxation and tariffs. Birrell remained at the Irish Office to ensure that the unionists could not interfere with the Liberals' Home Rule policy. Kitchener remained at the War Office because the vicious attacks made on him by the Northcliffe press had made him fire-proof. The Unionists had to make do with the slim pickings that remained. Bonar Law's colleagues believed that he ought to have had the Ministry of Munitions or the Treasury but the Liberals would not agree. Asquith skilfully isolated him by giving Balfour, Bonar Law's predecessor as Unionist leader, the Admiralty and then insisting that the Unionists could not hold both service ministries and Law was eventually fobbed off with the Colonial Office.[5] Law's two rivals for the Unionist leadership in 1910, Austen Chamberlain and Walter Long, were both given more powerful and prestigious posts, the India Office – which was effectively running its own war in Mesopotamia – and the Local Government Board – which was to become responsible for the organization of manpower. Curzon became Lord President of the Council, Lansdowne became Minister without Portfolio, Lord Selborne became President of the Board of Agriculture and Sir Edward Carson became Attorney General. Several of them felt slighted.[6] Their only consolation, and one which had not yet become apparent, was that much power devolved down from the Cabinet on to smaller committees on which they were better represented.

The new Cabinet was not a harmonious body. The Unionists loathed Asquith, McKenna and Churchill. They also had their own intra-party feuds. Curzon, Selborne and Chamberlain thought that Bonar Law and Lansdowne, their nominal leaders, lacked drive and political courage. Long's opinions seemed to change almost daily.[7] Kitchener's relations with Curzon had been poor since 1905 when they had enjoyed an epic row which culminated in Curzon's resignation as Viceroy, and by September

1915 Kitchener believed that Asquith and Balfour were the only honest and capable ministers in the Cabinet. Curzon's pomposity irritated his colleagues and Carson was soon depressed at 'the present system of governing by 22 gabblers round a table with an old procrastinator in the chair'. Hankey dismissed him as 'a veritable dismal Jimmy'.[8] The Liberals disliked the coalition just as much. Runciman and McKenna were careful to ascertain before they joined it that Asquith had made no promises to Bonar Law about tariffs or conscription. They comforted themselves with the thought that it was unlikely to last for long and they would soon be reunited with colleagues who had been excluded from office.[9] The new government never enjoyed much political popularity. The circumstances of its formation made it appear to be a conspiracy of the two front benches against their own supporters. Lord Milner, who emerged as one of its bitterest critics, damned it as 'a Government of the united mandarins'.[10] The Unionist press disliked it because it bore little resemblance to the independent Unionist government they craved. Many Unionists outside the government would have preferred a general election followed by a coalition formed on Unionist terms which would have given them a fairer share of offices. The Liberal press, like many Liberal back-benchers and supporters in the country, were baffled as to why Asquith had formed a coalition in the first place, and Asquith did little to enlighten them beyond appealing to their personal loyalty and by making vague generalizations about 'national necessity'. It was little wonder that they thought the whole episode was the result of a conspiracy by the Northcliffe press.[11]

Like its predecessor the new Cabinet was incapable of taking swift decisions about policy or strategy. A dozen powerful personalities, with perhaps five or six different opinions, had to be consulted on every issue. Decisions were reached only after prolonged discussions and were often no more than unsatisfactory compromises. Bonar Law said of the coalition that 'no one expected it to last. It had been regarded merely as a stop-gap arrangement and both parties were watching each other closely all the time.'[12] As a token of this, all three parties continued their preparations for a general election. It was not until 9 December that a bill was introduced to extend the life of Parliament, in the first instance for a year but this was later reduced at the committee stage to only eight months.[13] What was surprising was not that the coalition collapsed after only eighteen months, but that it lasted so long. Its longevity can be explained only by the fact that there was, for so long, no credible alternative.

The establishment of the new government was not immediately marked by any new departures in policy because early in June it took two decisions which confirmed the course already set by its predecessor. It agreed to continue Kitchener's policy of attrition on the Western front and it agreed that reinforcements should be sent to the Dardanelles so that Hamilton could launch another offensive.

Sir John's failure to break through in May and the Russian retreat reinforced Kitchener's belief that it would still be premature to commit the New Armies to a major offensive in France. In the spring he had, against his own better judgement, met Sir John's requests for more infantry even though he did not have enough guns or shells to support them. As a result he had been pilloried by the Northcliffe press for the 'shell scandal'. Kitchener was now determined not to bow to French's importunities. Another Western offensive would simply play into the Germans' hands. He therefore decided that the British would postpone any major operation in the West for an unspecified time so that they could build up their stocks of ammunition. In the meantime they would strengthen their line and 'continue for the present the war of attrition in the hope that the Germans will continue to break themselves up by costly attempts to shatter our lines – attempts which can never succeed as long as we keep proper reserves in hand to meet them'.[14] This did not seem to be an entirely unrealistic possibility. In the summer, GHQ intelligence staff reported that the Germans had concentrated a number of newly-raised divisions on the Western front. French believed that they presaged another German offensive in the West and it was only subsequently discovered that they were there solely for training.[15]

At the end of May Kitchener informed Sir John and Joffre that he would send no more than three new divisions to France in the immediate future.[16] Sir John was disgusted and remonstrated that although GHQ had not expected instant success, they had broken the Germans' first line and still believed that, with sufficient men, guns and shells, including those which were apparently being frittered away at the Dardanelles, they could break through in France.[17] Joffre was equally impatient. He already believed that the British had let him down in May and now he informed Kitchener that with 2·2 million men in the field France had reached the limit of its manpower. He wanted fifteen New Army divisions to be sent to France by the end of June to relieve his divisions north of Ypres and south of Arras.[18] On 22 May the Grand Duke had asked 'whether we intended to "Attack" [sic] in the West or rely on a policy of "attrition"'.[19] Joffre had replied that their policy was 'active et agressive'.[20] But Kitchener's preference for attrition meant that Sir John could only give Joffre minimal co-operation and by 20 June the allies' Western offensive had been halted.[21]

The Cabinet agreed with Kitchener. On 2 June Asquith had visited GHQ and conferred with French and Joffre. He was not impressed by their arguments, which was not surprising as even Sir John admitted that the French commanders 'appear to throw all logical argument to the winds when their ideas are in the least degree opposed'.[22] Asquith concluded by asking for an immediate report on the state of the British defences in France followed by a conference in London with Sir John, and a joint conference with the French. The Cabinet agreed that the BEF would take over another ten miles of the line but insisted that attrition was the right policy in France because, as Balfour explained, 'There is no prospect, I believe, of the Allies obtaining an old-fashioned victory over the Germans at this stage of the war'.[23] When Joffre's personal emissaries arrived in London on 8 June to plead for twelve divisions by mid-July, Kitchener gave them scant comfort beyond expressing the hope that he might be able to send them half that number by 15 August.[24]

The French found this refusal all the more annoying in the face of Kitchener's readiness to reinforce Hamilton.[25] Hamilton's initial failure to carry the Gallipoli peninsula left the War Council with a dilemma. Kitchener could see no way in which Hamilton could succeed quickly, especially as fear of U-boats had led the Admiralty to order the withdrawal of the battle cruiser *Queen Elizabeth*. But he was loath to order an evacuation. It would end all possibility of the Balkans joining the Entente, it would mean that the allies would forfeit the glittering prize of Constantinople and that the Germans would be able to proceed with their 'Drang nach dem Osten' and it might deal British prestige in the Muslim world a terrible blow. Hamilton's own appreciation reached London in the middle of the political crisis. The Turks, he insisted, were not the backward oriental despotism so many had expected them to be.

> Here we are after all, only an expeditionary force, though a strong one, fairly lodged within easy striking distance of the enemy's capital and head-power. This enemy, though much fallen away from his former high state, is still a great empire on a continental scale possessing vast resources.[26]

If the Turks were left undisturbed to reinforce their garrison he wanted reinforcements of two corps. If the Russians attacked them or if the Balkan neutrals came in, one corps plus drafts would suffice. In either case he also needed a liberal supply of high explosive shells.[27] Initially Kitchener was as reluctant to send reinforcements to Hamilton as he was to French and for the same reason. They might be needed in Britain to repulse a German invasion or in France to counter an attempt to break the allied line. He therefore recommended that Hamilton should remain where he was in the hope that the Turks would run out of ammunition.[28]

The final decision was left to the War Council's successor, the Dardanelles Committee. Its original members were Kitchener, together with three Liberals, Asquith, Crewe and Churchill, and five Unionists, Curzon, Selborne, Bonar Law, Balfour and Lansdowne. The Unionists were not blind opponents of the Dardanelles. On 1 March Bonar Law had welcomed the naval attack in the House of Commons, claiming that 'it is going to have a great effect on the ultimate issue of the war'.[29] But after 18 March Unionist support dwindled and gave way to criticism when it became apparent that the government had failed to ensure that sufficient troops were on hand to support the navy. When the new government was formed, many Unionists agreed with Henry Wilson that every man sent to the Dardanelles was wasted.[30] However, Selborne played a crucial role in persuading his colleagues to reject Kitchener's advice and instead to reinforce Hamilton. Since February he had favoured an attack on Constantinople, provided it was mounted with a large enough naval and military force and he still wanted to proceed with the operation in the hope that it would assist Russia and bring in the Balkan neutrals. He agreed with Kitchener that evacuation would free Turkish troops to attack Mesopotamia and Egypt and 'The blow to our prestige in the Near East and the Far East would be so serious that it is scarcely possible to measure it'.[31] On 7 June the Dardanelles Committee agreed, with some reluctance, to send Hamilton three new divisions and naval reinforcements and to mount a second major landing in mid-July. Some members, including Bonar Law, felt little enthusiasm for it and only allowed themselves to be persuaded because of their self-confessed ignorance of military matters. Others were not so diffident and, in Cabinet the next day Carson argued in favour of evacuating the entire force. But he was overruled and Churchill was delighted, believing that the Cabinet 'have adopted my policy & taken all the steps that I was pressing for & more'.[32]

By mid-June the Cabinet was committed to the policy of attrition. There would be no major offensive in the West in 1915. The Russians would have to bear the brunt of the land war. The French would be encouraged to husband their manpower. Men, guns and munitions for the New Armies were to be prepared, the Dardanelles would be cleared, the Balkan neutrals persuaded to join the Entente and Russia would be resupplied. Only in 1916 would the allies be able to mount a combined offensive on all the major fronts which would bring the war to a climax in 1916–17.[33]

However, no sooner had the Cabinet agreed to this than they were subject to pressure to change their minds. It was problematic for how long the Rusians could continue to resist the Central Powers without massive assistance from their allies. On 14 June Sir John Hanbury Williams, the head of the British military mission in Russia, reported that 'The shortage of shells is extremely serious and there is an acute lack of rifles'.[34] There was more than the simple desire to expel the Germans from French soil behind Joffre's requests for the New Armies to be sent to France. The French public believed that the Dardanelles expedition was the product of Britain's selfish desire to increase its empire in the Middle East and by May some small signs of war weariness began to appear in

France.[35] The newspaper of the federation of metal workers carried an article by the federation's secretary denouncing France's insistence that it had to recover Alsace–Lorraine. This was only a straw in the wind, but it was not one which could be ignored by the British high command in France, especially as their French counterparts took special care to bring evidence like this to their attention. On 14 June an officer on Joffre's staff told Haig that

> the French people are getting tired of the war. The tremendous cost of the war, the occupation of a very wealthy part of France by the enemy and the cessation of trade and farming operations were effecting them. Everything was practically at a standstill and the whole of the manhood of the nation was concentrated on this frontier. There was a general wish that a vigorous effort should be made to end the war by the autumn.[36]

Many Frenchmen resented Lloyd George's budget speech of 4 May because it appeared to show that the British were still wedded to 'business as usual'. The French explained Britain's reluctance to attack in the West by alleging that the latter had put the need to capture German trade before the provision of adequate munitions for their armies. The Board of Trade tried to dampen down this resentment with a cold douche of facts, insisting that Britain's exports had sunk to well below their prewar levels, but even the Foreign Office was not satisfied. Clerk minuted that 'There is already a sufficiently unfortunate feeling abroad in France and it is needless to dilate upon the disastrous consequences of giving it substantial grounds'.[37] According to Henry Wilson, Foch put the same message more succinctly, claiming that the French 'may grow restless & nasty if we don't play up'.[38] There were also growing criticisms of Joffre and Millerand and a movement afoot amongst the Radicals and Socialists in the Chamber to replace Joffre, who had failed to shift the Germans from France, by General Galliéni, the governor of Paris. Bertie reported that the critics might soon turn their attention to the two strongest supporters of the Entente, Poincaré and Delcassé.[39]

This placed the British high command in a dilemma. They did not want to undertake an offensive before they had sufficient men and guns to achieve success, but nor did they want to see a growing peace movement in France and they thought that the only way to stop it was to make visible progress before the winter in driving the Germans eastwards. On 19–20 June representatives of GHQ and the French and British ministries of munitions met at Boulogne to discuss the BEF's future requirements. Sir John asked for another 1090 heavy guns and howitzers, an order which could not possibly be fulfilled until 1916.[40] But at Chantilly on 24 June he agreed with Joffre that a passive defence on the Western front was out of the question. Joffre insisted that 'A policy such as the British Cabinet appeared to favour was one which, by making sure of a Russian defeat, would make certain of our defeat in our turn'.[41] The two generals agreed to mount a major Anglo-French offensive in August, although the exact role the BEF was to play was left vague. The French had already suggested an attack by Haig's First Army near Loos but, after examining the slag heaps and miners' cottages which littered the ground, Haig was most unenthusiastic about it.

The conference which Asquith had requested with Sir John French was held on 2–3 July. French, Robertson and Wilson presented GHQ's case for reinforcements and an August offensive, but met with only mixed success. Bertie took a realistic view of rumours of growing war weariness in France. He believed that they were deliberately exaggerated by the French high command because Joffre and Millerand badly needed British support to achieve a military victory in order to sustain their own positions.[42] But the Cabinet were much more cautious and agreed that the French had to be given a tangible token of support. Kitchener therefore agreed to send the Second New Army to France at once and promised the French a total of twenty-five new divisions by December 1915. But ministers would not budge from their position that attrition was the correct policy to pursue. The new divisions would take over more of the line to free French troops for an offensive but they would not be used to mount a major and costly British offensive. Two days later, to underline their commitment to open the Dardanelles, another two Territorial divisions were sent to Hamilton.[43]

The first Anglo-French summit conference to discuss strategy met at Calais on 6 July. Its organization was chaotic. No secretaries were employed to record its decisions and consequently both sides left believing that they had carried the day. Kitchener met Joffre privately before the full conference and thought that he had persuaded him to postpone his Western offensive until Hamilton had tried once more to take Gallipoli. He also gave Joffre a programme of reinforcements, but made it clear that although the French could attack if they wished the British were still so short of ammuniton that they would be able to do little to support them. At the end of the conference Asquith believed that both parties had agreed that the Dardanelles were to be pursued to a successful conclusion and that, on the Western front, 'The main policy [is] to be to continue the war of attrition'. He agreed to small local offensives designed to demoralize the enemy but he would not sanction any large-scale operations which, if they failed, would cripple the allies.[44] However, Joffre put his case for a full-scale offensive most vigorously and Sir John French believed that it had been accepted 'with the proviso that he must exercise prudence & caution.'[45] The next day they tried to take his embryonic episode in allied co-operation a stage further by agreeing with the military attachés of Italy, Serbia and Russia that they would try to mount a simultaneous allied offensive. But in practice this was little more than an expression of mutual goodwill as they could not agree on a generally acceptable date.

In the first half of August the British policy of attrition collapsed. Hamilton's landing at Suvla Bay failed to carry the peninsula. The Russians lost Warsaw and the Greeks and Bulgarians remained neutral. Finally two political crises in France and Russia frightened the Cabinet into believing that the stability of the Entente alliance was threatened and forced them reluctantly to sanction British participation in an autumn offensive in the West.

In June the Dardanelles Committee had toyed with the idea of committing the new divisions they were sending to the Dardanelles to a landing across the neck of the Gallipoli peninsula at Bulair. But Kitchener and Hamilton objected that the beaches were not suitable, that troops landed there would be out of direct contact with the main force to the south and that they would be exposed to Turkish counter-attacks from both the north and south. The idea was dropped and it was agreed instead to land at Suvla Bay, to the north of Anzac cove. Neither the commander of the landing force nor the troops themselves were ideally suited to the operation. The commander of the Ninth Corps, Sir Frederick Stopford, had retired in 1909 and had been brought out of retirement in 1914 to command an army in England. He was described by a staff officer who lunched with him just before the landing as 'deprecating, courteous, fatherly, anything except the Commander of an Army Corps which had been entrusted with a major operation that might change the whole course of the war in twenty-four hours'.[46] Hamilton had asked for one of two younger corps commanders from the Western front, Sir Henry Rawlinson or Sir Julian Byng, but French refused to release either of them. Stopford's troops, three New Army divisions, had never before been in action and one of their divisional commanders had suffered a breakdown in 1912 and 'was not the font of energy and confidence a Commander should be'.[47] Hamilton could only do his best with the commanders he was given but the absence of decisive leadership was to be a fundamental reason why the operation failed. He decided that two of the new divisions would land at Suvla Bay and the third at Anzac from whence the main thrust, designed to capture the Sari Bair ridge and so dominate the peninsula, was to be launched.

The British again tried to co-ordinate their forthcoming military offensive with a diplomatic *démarche* to the Bulgarians. In an ironic reversal of priorities Kitchener now insisted that Bulgarian help was necessary to ensure success at the Dardanelles. On 29 May the Entente had offered Bulgaria the Enos-Midia line and a large part of Macedonia. The Serbs were outraged that their allies were about to give away part of their territory and the Serbian Crown Prince even hinted that he would prefer to make peace rather than cede territory to Bulgaria.[48] The other obvious drawback of this policy was that 'Offers of future territorial acquisitions can really have very little weight with the people to whom you offer them', wrote Nicolson, 'as they are by no means certain as to whether you would be in a position to eventually fulfil your promise'.[49] In any case the Austrians soon trumped the Entente's offer by promising King Ferdinand the whole of Macedonia simply for remaining neutral. Ferdinand had no intention of moving until he was absolutely certain which side was going to win the war. His minister in Paris told a British officer that they still bore a deep grudge against the French and Russians for deserting them in 1913 and would not join the Entente until they agreed to tear up the Treaty of Bucharest and allow Bulgaria to dictate its own terms.

Their procrastinations bred resentment in London.[50] Lord Robert Cecil, the new Unionist under secretary at the Foreign Office, insisted that Bulgaria's intransigence was due to the incompetence of the British minister at Sofia, Sir Henry Bax-Ironside, who seemed to be incapable of making the Bulgars realize the latent power of Britain and Russia, and he was replaced at Sofia by Hugh O'Beirne, formerly the counsellor at the British embassy in Petrograd. This smacked a little of shooting the messenger who brought the bad news. Grey and Crewe, who intermittently deputized for the former at the Foreign Office, were much nearer to the truth when they insisted that any diplomatic *démarche* would end in fiasco unless it was accompanied by an end to the Russian retreat, a successful Russian counter-attack and a breakthrough at the Dardanelles.[51] On the advice of their ministers at Sofia the Entente powers agreed that the only way to induce the Bulgars to join them was by placing pressure on the Serbs and Greeks to force them to make the territorial concessions the Bulgarians demanded. But the Serbs remained intransigent and, furthermore, when news of this leaked in Greece it did the Entente's cause no good at all. Vanizelos had won a majority in the Greek elections in mid-June but before Parliament met, his opponents had got wind of the Entente's proposals and used them to stir up neutralist opinion.[52]

The Entente's offer to the Bulgarians was delivered on 3 August and Hamilton's offensive began on 6 August. By 17 August he was compelled to admit that it had failed. However it is doubtful whether either the Greeks or Bulgarians would have joined the Entente even if Hamilton had succeeded because on 5 August the Germans entered Warsaw. It would have benefited the neutrals nothing if, just as they were swallowing up Turkey, the Central powers in turn swallowed them up. Grey's riposte to the Germans' victory, a diplomatic note to Sofia, Athens and Nish sent on 13 August asking them to sink their differences in the face of the threat posed by the Central Powers, was a tacit admission of the magnitude of the Germans' achievement and had a distinctly hollow ring about it.[53]

These military and diplomatic defeats provoked increasing criticism in France and Russia about Britain's inactivity. They also helped to ignite in both countries political crises which finally convinced the cabinet that although Kitchener's policy of attrition was eminently desirable, it was no longer politically possible. In late July and early August the Germans extended peace feelers to both France and Russia. They were rebuffed and the British, who learnt of them from their allies, were reassured that the existing French and Russian governments would continue the war.[54] But there was no guarantee that either government would remain in power indefinitely and some possibility that they might be replaced by groups who would be more receptive to German offers. At the end of July left-wing attacks on Millerand and Joffre increased sharply when Joffre sacked one of the few left-wing generals in the French army, General Sarrail. Ministers in London were especially alarmed that if a real political crisis blew up it might open the way for Caillaux to return to power. On 28 July Henry Wilson was summoned home to report on the increase in anti-British feeling in France and discovered that Asquith was much preoccupied with Caillaux. By 12 August there were rumours in Paris that the Socialists might soon leave the Cabinet and destroy the Union Sacré unless Millerand were sacked. Two days later the French government decided to ask the Chamber for a vote of confidence.[55]

The growing political crisis in Russia was seen to be even more serious. Between April and September the Russians had lost two million men. The scale of the catastrophe led many Russians to believe that the retreat was due to treason in high places. The chief culprits were thought to be those Russians of German descent who had gained high places in the bureaucracy and army. The tsarina was a German and there were men with German names like Fredericks, Sturmer and Bark at the court and in the bureaucracy.[56] Second only to the 'internal enemy' as the culprit for Russia's disaster were the allies who had failed to help Russia in its hour of need. British diplomats and journalists reported that civilians and soldiers alike bitterly resented the inactivity of the French and British on the Western front and contrasted it unfavourably with the way Russia had gone to their aid in August 1914. In addition the British had failed to deliver the shells they had promised. After a lengthy prorogation the Duma met on 1 August and Sazonov insisted that Russia would not make peace until the war was won. Buchanan was not entirely reassured.[57] On 15 August the government released news of the fall of Warsaw. The Germans were moving towards Riga and if that city fell they might be able to occupy Petrograd itself. Buchanan reported that some people in the capital including even certain members of the Duma, appear to regard situation as lost and are talking of separate peace. I am told many reactionaries are in favour of peace, and that German influences at Court are working in the same direction and warning the Emperor of the danger of revolution.[58]

Under pressure not only from GHQ but from the allies as well, Kitchener gave in. On 17 August Hamilton had asked for drafts and reinforcements totalling 95,000 men. Kitchener turned his request down.[59] He had little confidence that an autumn offensive in the West would produce a tangible military victory but he was now convinced that 'if we remained as we were, there was some chance of the Russians and French making separate terms of peace in October'.[60] Hamilton was informed that he might expect a trickle of drafts but no major reinforcements. On 20 August a reluctant and apprehensive Cabinet finally agreed to the BEF participating in Joffre's autumn offensive.[61] Their policy of attrition in the West coupled with a determined effort to knock Turkey out of the war in 1915 had collapsed.

Neither Kitchener nor Sir John thought that Joffre's offensive could expel the Germans from France by the end of 1915. On 28 July French had reluctantly agreed to Joffre's plan that his forces would attack at Loos even though both he and Haig still thought the ground was too difficult. Sir John shared Kitchener's concern for the future of the alliance but his doubts about the feasibility of the Loos offensive persisted.[62] He did not believe that the allies could break the German line and get their cavalry through, and he was carrying a heavy psychological burden of guilt because of the heavy losses his troops had already sustained. He was afraid that Loos might only result in another huge butcher's bill for little real gain. He therefore tried to minimize casualties by keeping his main reserve forces, Lt.-Gen. Sir Richard Haking's Eleventh Corps and the British and Indian Cavalry Corps, well back from Haig's start line and under his own control.[63] This was to have portentous consequences both for the conduct of the battle and for French's own career. Neither French nor Haig thought that they had sufficient guns or ammunition for a decisive attack. In June and July Haig had explained to Asquith and Lloyd George that such an operation would require thirty-six divisions attacking along a 25–30 mile front supported by 1150 heavy guns. At Loos Sir John committed a total of seventeen divisions and Haig estimated that he had only enough heavy guns to support two of his six assault divisions. But both men were able to convince themselves that an operation which had been impossible in June or July was practicable in September because they hoped to make good their deficiencies in artillery by employing poison gas discharged by gas cylinders and carried to the German trenches by the wind.[64]

Shortly before the battle began Kitchener told Haig that 'it is of great political importance to gain a success at the present time'.[65] His hopes were disappointed. The battle began on 25 September. It was a military and political failure. Haig's First Army lost heavily in return for few tangible gains. The subsequent recriminations about the dispositions of the reserves wrecked French's career in France. The effort came too late to save the French and Russian governments from crisis and the losses the BEF sustained provided further ammunition for the conscriptionists in Britain whose campaign was shortly to rock Asquith's own government. Loos did not represent the beginning of Britain's total commitment to the Western front but its mid-point. The process by which the British became committed to the European land war began in July when Kitchener promised the French large-scale reinforcements by Christmas but withheld agreement on an all-out offensive. Loos was a political gesture designed to reassure the allies of Britain's support for them. The decision to take part in Joffre's autumn offensive was hedged around with all kinds of political and tactical reservations which the Cabinet did not shed until April 1916 when they finally agreed to mount the Somme campaign as part of a combined allied offensive designed to win the war by the end of 1916.

Notes

1   Hankey diary entry, 21 May 1915, Hankey mss, 1/1; Memoranda supplied by Mr McKenna on 20 March 1927, Beaverbrook mss, box 3, folder 7.
2   Long to Bonar Law, 23 May 1915, Bonar Law mss, 50/3/39; Simon to Asquith, 18 May 1915 and Asquith to Simon, 25 May 1915, Simon mss, box 50.
3   W. M. R. Pringle to Asquith, 20 May 1915, Asquith mss, vol. 27, f. 178.
4   Steel-Maitland to Bonar Law, 21 May 1915, Bonar Law mss, 50/3/25.
5   Chamberlain to Bonar Law, 20 May 1915, Bonar Law mss 50/3/9; Asquith to Bonar Law, 21 May 1915, Bonar Law mss, 50/3/15; Memorandum by Asquith, 26 May 1915, Asquith mss, vol. 27, f. 216.
6   Long to Bonar Law, 23 May 1915, Bonar Law mss, 50/3/39; Lansdowne to Long, 23 May 1915, Bonar Law mss, 50/3/39.
7   Selborne, The War Cabinet, [n.d. but *c.* July 1916], Selborne mss, file 80, ff. 285–90.
8   J. Barnes and D. Nicholson (eds), *The Leo Amery Diaries*, Vol. 1, *1896–1929* (London: Hutchinson, 1980), p. 123; Hankey diary entries, 3 and 11 September 1915, Hankey mss, 1/1.
9   Runciman to McKenna, 19 May 1915, McKenna mss, 5/8; Runciman to Samuel, 26 May 1915, Samuel mss, A48/6.
10 Barnes and Nicholson, *Amery*, p. 118.
11 Long to Bonar Law and enc., 13 June 1915, Bonar Law mss, 50/4/27; Asquith to Gulland, 28 May 1915, Pease mss; Masterman to Samuel, 26 May 1915, Samuel mss, A/48/11; S. Koss, *The Rise and Fall of the Political Press in Britain*, Vol. 2, *The Twentieth Century* (London: Hamish Hamilton, 1984), pp. 279–82.

12 Lord Hankey, *The Supreme Command 1914–1918*, Vol. 1 (London: Allen & Unwin, 1961), p. 319; E. David (ed.), *Inside Asquith's Cabinet: From the diaries of Sir Charles Hobhouse* (London: John Murray, 1977), pp. 248–9; M. Gilbert (ed.), *Winston S. Churchill*, Vol. 4, *Companion*, pt 1 (London: Heinemann, 1977), p. 7.

13 M. D. Pugh, *Electoral Reform in War and Peace, 1906–1918* (London: Routledge & Kegan Paul, 1978), pp. 56–60.

14 PRO WO 159/7, Hankey to Kitchener, 29 May 1915; PRO CAB 42/2/19, Secretary's notes of a War Council ... 14 May 1915; Hankey, *Supreme Command*, Vol. 1, p. 338.

15 Kirke diary entries, 14 and 16 July 1915, Kirke mss; French diary entries, 14 and 18 July 1915, French mss, vol. L; Wilson diary entry, 14 July 1915, Wilson mss (microfilm) reel 6.

16 Wilson diary entries 17 and 18 May 1915, Wilson mss (microfilm) reel 6; French diary entries, 16 and 18 May 1915; PRO WO 159/7, Kitchener to Yarde-Buller, 29 May 1915; PRO 30/57/59, Esher to Kitchener, 23 May 1915.

17 R. Holmes, *The Little Field Marshal: Sir John French* (London: Cape, 1981), pp. 293–4; PR 30/57/50, French to Kitchener, 11 June 1915; Robertson to Callwell, 31 May 1915, Robertson mss, I/8/23; Maurice to his wife, 23 May 1915, Maurice mss, 3/1/4/167.

18 Clive diary entries, 16 and 26 May 1915, Clive mss, II/1; PRO CAB 37/129/12, Asquith to Cabinet and enc., 4 June 1915; Le Roy Lewis to Callwell, 1 June 1915, Wilson mss, 73/1/18.

19 French diary entry, 22 May 1915, French mss, vol. K.

20 Wilson diary entry, 22 May 1915, Wilson mss (microfilm) reel 6.

21 Wilson diary entry, 20 June 1915, Wilson mss (microfilm) reel 6.

22 French diary entry, 2 June 1915, French mss, vol. L; Wilson diary entry, 2 June 1915, Wilson mss (microfilm) reel 6.

23 PRO 30/57/78/WV/49, Balfour to Kitchener, 6 June 1915; Asquith, Note prepared after visit to Sir J. French, June 1915, Asquith mss, vol. 27, f. 266.

24 PRO WO 159/7, Notes of meeting held at War Office, 8 June 1915 and note by Kitchener, 9 June 1915.

25 PRO 30/57/77/WU/27, Nicolson to Grey, 15 March 1915.

26 M. Gilbert (ed.), *Winston S. Churchill*, Vol. 3, *Companion*, pt 2 (London: Heinemann, 1972), p. 952; Kitchener to Hamilton, 18 May 1915, Hamilton mss, 15/17; PRO CAB 37/128/27, Kitchener, The Dardanelles. Note by the War Office, 28 May 1915.

27 Hamilton to Kitchener, 27 May 1915, Hamilton mss, 15/17.

28 PRO CAB 37/128/27, Kitchener, The Dardanelles ... 28 May 1915.

29 *Hansard*, 70 HC Deb., 5s. col. 604, 1 March 1915.

30 Bonar Law to Wilson, Bonar Law mss, 37/5/17.

31 PRO CAB 37/129/10, Selborne, The Dardanelles, 4 June 1915; Selborne to Fitzgerald, 28 February 1915, Fitzgerald mss (microfilm).

32 Gilbert (ed.), *Churchill*, Vol. 4, *Companion*, pt 1, p. 5; Bonar Law to Selborne, 8 June 1915, Selborne mss, file 80, ff. 8–11; PRO CAB 42/3/1, Conclusions of a meeting of the Dardanelles Committee, 7 June 1915; PRO CAB 19/33, Dardanelles Commission. Minutes of evidence, QQ. 21695 (Crewe), 23107 (Curzon), 22526 (Carson).

33 See for example, PRO WO 159/4, Kitchener, An appreciation of the military situation in the future, 26 June 1915, PRO CAB 37/130/26, Hankey, The future policy of the war, 24 June 1915; S. Roskill, *Hankey: Man of Secrets*, Vol. 1 (London: Collins, 1970), pp. 182–3.

34   Hanbury Williams to Kitchener, 14 June 1915, Lloyd George mss, D/17/6/7.
35   PRO FO 800/58, Bertie to Grey, 3 August 1915.
36   Haig diary entries, 14 and 23 June 1915, Haig mss, Acc. 3155/101; see also PRO 30/57/59, Esher to Kitchener, 20 June 1915; N. Papayanis, 'Collaboration and pacifism in France during World War One', *Francia*, vol. 5 (1977), pp. 429–30.
37   PRO FO 371/2510/88180, Minute by Clerk on Butler to Hurst, 9 July 1915; Baird to Bonar Law, 8 May 1915, Bonar Law mss, 37/2/13; Barrow to Wilson and enc., 17 June 1915, Wilson mss, 73/1/19; Lady Algernon Gordon Lennox (ed.), *The Diary of Lord Bertie of Thame, 1914–1918*, Vol. 1 (London: Hodder & Stoughton, 1924), p. 189.
38   Wilson diary entry, 26 June 1915, Wilson mss (microfilm) reel 6; see also, PRO FO 800/58, Crewe to Bertie, 8 July 1915; PRO FO 800/167, Memorandum by Bertie, 5 July 1915.
39   PRO FO 800/57, Bertie to Grey, 9 June 1915.
40   PRO 37/135/8, Kitchener, supply of heavy guns to the army (and enc.), 6 October 1915; French to Brade, 23 June 1915, Robertson mss, I/5/2; see also Haig to Rothschild, 20 May 1915, Haig mss, Acc. 3155/214A; Brade to Llewellyn Smith, 30 June 1915 and enc., Lloyd George mss, D/17/6/14; R. J. Q. Adams, *Arms and the Wizard: Lloyd George and the Ministry of Munitions, 1915–1916* (London: Cassell, 1978), pp. 165–7; Holmes, *Little Field Marshal*, p. 296.
41   Robertson, Memorandum of a conference at Chantilly, 24 June 1915, Robertson mss, I/5/14.
42   Lennox (ed.), *Bertie*, Vol. 1, p. 190.
43   Wilson diary entries, 30 June, 1, 2 and 3 July 1915, Wilson mss (microfilm) reel 6; French diary entries, 1 and 2 July 1915, French mss, vol. L; Balfour to Asquith and enc., 2 July 1915, Asquith mss, vol. 14, ff. 77–77B [there is a second copy of this memorandum with marginalia by Lansdowne, Harcourt, McKenna and Henderson in Asquith mss, vol. 46, f. 101]; PRO CAB 42/3/7, Minutes of a meeting of the Dardanelles Committee, 5 July 1915.
44   PRO FO 800/167, Memoranda by Bertie, 7 and 10 July 1915; PRO FO 800/58, Crewe to Bertie, 8 July 1915; Hankey, *Supreme Command*, Vol. 1, p. 349.
45   French diary entry, 6 July 1915, French mss, vol. L; Wilson, Chantilly, 7 July 1915, Wilson mss, 73/1/19.
46   C. Mackenzie, *Gallipoli Memories* (London: Cassell, 1929), p. 353; PRO CAB 42/3/3, Hankey, The Dardanelles, 16 June 1915; PRO CAB 19/33, Dardanelles Commission. Minutes of evidence, QQ. 21700–5 (Crewe); Gilbert (ed.), *Churchill*, Vol. 3, *Companion*, pt 1, pp. 1003–4.
47   Hamilton to Churchill, 5 August 1915, Hamilton mss, 5/6; War Office to GHQ, MEF, 22 June 1915, Hamilton mss, 5/17.
48   PRO FO 800/378, Des Graz to Nicolson, 2 June 1915; PRO FO 800/95, Bax-Ironside to Grey, 21 June 1915 and minute by Cecil, 24 June 1915.
49   PRO FO 800/378, Nicolson to Hardinge, 27 May 1915.
50   PRO FO 800/378, Bax-Ironside to Nicolson, 9 June 1915; Stancioff to Howell, 23 June 1915, Howell mss, IV/C/2/152; R. J. Crampton, *Bulgaria, 1878–1918* (New York: Columbia University Press and Eastern European Monographs, 1983), pp. 439–41.
51   PRO FO 800/57, Crewe to Bertie, 10 June 1915; PRO FO 800/95, Crewe to Grey and Grey to Crewe, 14 and 15 July 1915.
52   PRO CAB 19/29, Dardanelles Commission. Notes for evidence on the attempt to secure assistance by diplomatic efforts to help the position in the

peninsula [n.d. but *c.* 1916]; PRO FO 800/378, Chirol to Nicolson, 7 July 1915; PRO FO 800/378, Cecil to Nicolson, 5 August 1915; PRO FO 800/379, O'Beirne to Nicolson, 26 July 1915; K. Robbins, 'British diplomacy and Bulgaria, 1914–1915', *Slavonic and East European Studies Review*, vol. 49, no. 117 (1971), pp. 576–9.

53   R. R. James, *Gallipoli* (London: Pan, 1974) p. 307.
54   PRO FO 371/2505/106006, Sir A. Hardinge to Grey, 28 July 1915; PRO FO 800/378, Howard to Nicolson, 23 July 1915; PRO FO 800/58, Bertie to Grey, 6 August 1915; Wilson diary entries, 23 July and 2 August 1915; Wilson mss (microfilm) reel 6; T. Kaarsted, *Great Britain and Denmark, 1914–1920* (Odense: Odense University Press, 1979), pp. 90–1; F. Fischer, *Germany's Aims in the First World War* (London: Chatto & Windus, 1967), pp. 195–8; A. Nekludoff, *Diplomatic Reminiscences before and during the World War, 1911–1917* (London: John Murray, 1920), pp. 351–2.
55   PRO FO 800/58, Bertie to Grey, 12 and 14 August 1915; PRO FO 371/2364/102589, Nicolson to Grey and forwarded to Kitchener, Asquith and Balfour, 27 July 1915; Sir C. E. Callwell, *Field Marshal Sir Henry Wilson: His Life and Diaries*, Vol. 1 (London: Cassell, 1927), pp. 243–4; Kitchener to French, 28 July 1915 and Wilson, Note, 16 August 1915, Wilson mss, 73/1/19.
56   A. K. Wildman, *The End of the Russian Imperial Army: The Old Army and the Soldiers' Revolt (March–April 1917)* (Princeton, NJ: Princeton University press, 1980), pp. 89–94.
57   PRO FO 371/2454/102165, Curtis to Rendell and the Foreign Office, 4 July 1915 (105582), Buchanan to Foreign Office, 1 August 1915, and (106237), Buchanan to Foreign Office, 3 August 1915.
58   PRO FO 371/2454/115774, Buchanan to Foreign Office, 19 August 1915; see also K. Young (ed.), *The Diaries of Sir Robert Bruce Lockhart*, Vol. 1, *1915–1928* (London: Macmillan, 1973), p. 24.
59   Hamilton to Kitchener, 17 August 1915, Hamilton mss, 5/17.
60   PRO CAB 42/3/16, Minutes of the Dardanelles Committee, 20 August 1915.
61   PRO CAB 41/36/40, Asquith to H.M. the King, 20 August 1915; Kitchener to Hamilton, 20 August 1915, Hamilton mss, 5/17.
62   Holmes, The *Little Field Marshal*, pp. 295–7; R. Blake, *The Private Papers of Douglas Haig 1914–1919* (London: Eyre & Spottiswoode, 1952), p. 100; French diary entries, 24 and 29 July 1915, French mss, vol. M; Clive diary entries, 25, 26, 28 and 30 July, and 3, 4, 5 and 25 August 1915, Clive mss, II/2.
63   Holmes, *The Little Field Marshal*, p. 302.
64   Holmes, *The Little Field Marshal*, p. 300.
65   Blake, *Private Papers*, p. 103.

7

Men, Money and Munitions: Mobilizing the British Economy for War in the Summer of 1915

THE DEBATE inside the Cabinet in the summer of 1915 about how to mobilize the British economy for war was not conducted along ideological lines between exponents of 'freedom' and 'control'. Whatever their public rhetoric no ministers in the privacy of the Cabinet expressed any moral scruples about the right of the state to compel men to fight for their country. Rather the debate was conducted between two groups who supported two different war policies. One faction consisted of Lloyd George, Churchill and most Unionist ministers except Balfour. They championed a powerful Ministry of Munitions and the cause of compulsory military service as the best way to channel Britain's human and economic resources into the war effort. Their opponents, led by McKenna and Runciman and with the hesitant support of Balfour, Grey and Asquith and several other Liberals, suspected that such a single-minded concentration of resources behind the war effort would be dangerous. They feared that compulsory military service would destroy national unity and they were afraid that even if Britain did win the war by throwing all its resources into the war, it would in doing so lose the peace because it would bankrupt itself. Kitchener stood uneasily between the two camps. He resented his loss of control over munitions production but the heavy losses the army sustained at Loos finally convinced him that the voluntary system would not be able to supply the drafts necessary to keep his armies up to strength in 1916.

One of the ostensible causes of the May crisis was the Asquith government's failure to provide the BEF with sufficient shells. One of the coalition government's first priorities was to increase munitions production by establishing the Ministry of Munitions under Lloyd George.

The new ministry did not mark the end of the era of running the war economy according to the tenets of *laissez-faire* because such an era had never really existed. The ministry directed the operations of the engineering industry through an active partnership with the industry's own managers on the model which had already been established by the Railway Executive Committee. The ministry was a businessmen's organization in two senses. Successful managers like G. M. Booth and Eric Geddes were brought into Whitehall to run some of the ministry's central departments. But the day-to-day operations of the ministry's area boards of management were left under the control of local businessmen. The government had no option in this matter. It simply did not have enough civil servants to arrogate this function to itself and the existing managers, as one of them tartly explained to Lloyd George, 'are not going to sit down in an office in London and be clerks either to the War Office or the Munitions Department'.[1]

In the opening months of the war many Liberals and the leaders of the organized labour movement believed that compulsory military service epitomized all that was worst in German society and the very thing which they were fighting against. In December 1914 Fenner Brockway established the No Conscription Fellowship. Liberals like the editor of the *Nation*, H. W. Massingham, thought that any attempt to introduce compulsory military service in Britain would only divide the country at a time when national unity was all-important.[2] Some Unionists had fewer doubts. The Milnerite–tariff reform wing of the party made a positive virute of supporting military conscription. However, they did not have universal support even within their own party. The Unionists' House of Commons army committee were afraid that compulsory military service would only lose the party votes. Bonar Law agreed with them and in late 1914 he tried to restrain its more enthusiastic Unionist supporters.[3] In the spring of 1915 a further complication arose. There was no shortage of recruits but there was a shortage of military equipment of all kinds. The rapid expansion of the New Armies, the BEF's escalating demands for munitions and the indiscriminate recruiting of skilled workers from the engineering and munitions industry meant that there was a serious shortage of skilled labour to meet the army's demands. Lloyd George and Grey had already raised the question of how best to organize the industrial labour force before the Asquith government collapsed.[4] The 'shell scandal' seemed to indicate that the voluntary Treasury agreement of March had failed to solve this problem. Trade unionists were widely blamed for obstructing the war effort by adhering to restrictive practices and bad time-keeping. Some employers believed that the only solution to their labour problems was industrial conscription. Labour had already been organized on paramilitary lines in two places. In April Lord Derby had raised a volunteer battalion of dockers in Liverpool to clear congestion at the port and, on Tyneside, the War Office's representative had organized 6,000 volunteers into King's Squads. Each squad consisted of skilled engineering workers who placed themselves at the disposal of government contractors in the district.[5]

The 'shell scandal' convinced many Unionist politicians that compulsory service was needed, just as much in the factories as in the army. In the new government Walter Long, a prewar supporter of compulsory military service, and Lloyd George took the lead. On 3 June Long presented a draft bill to the Cabinet calling for the compulsory registration of all adults between the ages of 15 and 65. In the first draft of the Munitions of War Bill, Lloyd George toyed with the possibility of introducing industrial conscription into shipbuilding and engineering establishments working on government contracts and he hinted as much at a public meeting in Bristol.[6] Their proposals met with a hostile reception. Since February prominent labour leaders like the MPs George Roberts and J. H. Thomas and James Sexton, the secretary of the National Union of Dock Labourers, had said publicly that they would be willing to consider compulsory military service, but not industrial conscription, if the government said that it was a military necessity. But by coupling military and industrial conscription, Lloyd George made it impossible for the organized labour movement to judge the former solely on its merits as a way of raising troops. Henceforth organized labour saw opposition to compulsory service as part of their wider struggle to improve or at least to preserve their social and economic position. They were suspicious that the Unionist supporters of compulsory service wanted it not simply as a way to win the war but also as a way of breaking their unions by placing their members under military discipline. Their suspicions were further aroused when Lord Northcliffe emerged as the leading public champion of compulsory service. Northcliffe was a red rag to a labour bull and even committed conscriptionists like Lord Milner were dismayed by his intervention.[7]

The Cabinet divided along lines which remained constant until the passage of the first Military Service Act in January 1916. McKenna, Runciman, Harcourt and Grey were suspicious of Long's bill because they saw it as an obvious prelude to compulsion. They were afraid that, with British visible and invisible exports already falling sharply, military conscription might make it impossible for Britain to continue the war long enough to defeat the Germans. If too many men were taken for the army, and too large a proportion of industry were given over to supplying them, Britain's balance of payments would collapse and national bankruptcy would make it impossible for it to support its first line of defence, the Royal Navy, or to meet its financial obligations to its allies.[8] Balfour and Asquith also raised political objections to the bill. Balfour believed that industrial conscription would arouse bitter trade union opposition and the Prime Minister thought that three-quarters of his own party and the whole of the Labour and Irish Nationalist parties would not stomach it.[9]

Neither Lloyd George, Churchill nor the remaining Unionists had any immediate reply to those who objected to compulsion on economic grounds, beyond asserting that the strategic and political penalties of not introducing compulsion would be greater than the economic penalties of doing so. Like Kitchener, Lloyd George was determined that not only would the Entente win the war but that Britain would win the peace and therefore 'it was most important that the eventual victory of the Entente powers should be due to us and to our efforts, and not to Russia, so that we might be in a dominating position when peace terms were discussed'.[10] The compulsionists also swept aside Asquith's and Balfour's political objections by claiming that all would be well if only the government gave the country a clear lead. They were aware that the allies' doubts about Britain's commitment to the war would only be met if they solved the munitions problem and introduced military conscription, and some of them had glimpsed the logic of attrition. If the war lasted into 1916 France would probably reach the limit of its manpower resources and the defensive war of attrition in the West could not be indefinitely prolonged. Ultimately the Entente would have to launch a major co-ordinated offensive and Britain would have to bear a heavier share of the fighting and the casualties as the allies advanced towards Berlin. As Curzon explained on 21 June,

> The war seems to me to be resolving itself largely into a question of killing Germans. For this purpose, viewing the present methods and instruments of war, one man seems to me about the equivalent of another, and one life taken to involve another life. If then two million (or whatever figure) more of Germans have to be killed at least a corresponding number of Allied soldiers will have to be sacrificed to effect that object. I say 'at least', because if we contemplate, as we must do before long, an advance into Germany, the proportion will be gravely deflected against the Allies.[11]

For the time being all parties compromised. Asquith allowed Long's bill to proceed but postponed debate on the real issues involved. In Balfour's words the bill could be seen as 'the guiding of voluntary enlistment, military and industrial, into the channels least hurtful to national production & efficiency'.[12] The National Register Bill became law on 15 July and the Register was taken a month later. Thirty-two Liberal MPs voted against the bill, claiming that it was but one step away from compulsory military service. But another group of Liberals issued a public manifesto arguing that it was a necessity if Britain was to win the war.[13] Lloyd George dropped the idea of industrial compulsion from his bill and substituted voluntary enlistment in the War Munitions Volunteers' scheme, the Tyneside King's Squads writ large. The terms of the Munitions of War Act were very one-sided in their treatment of capital and labour. In an attempt to prevent wage inflation and ensure continuity of production, labour mobility was restricted through a system of leaving certificates, and strikes were banned in controlled establishments which fell under the auspices of the Act. All disputes were to be settled by arbitration. Trade union restrictive practices were to be relaxed under the safeguards negotiated in March. In return all the unions received was a promise that the government would restrict their employers profits to a maximum of 20 per cent above their peacetime levels and some representation on the munitions tribunals established to administer the Act.[14]

In some respects Reginald McKenna, the new Chancellor of the Exchequer, was an improvement on his predecessor. He had served an apprenticeship at the Treasury as Financial Secretary between 1905 and 1907. Even the Unionist Lord Milner, who rarely had a good word to say for any Liberal, conceded that he was well-suited for his new job.[15] Throughout 1915 McKenna was an unrepentent supporter of the notion that Britain's best war policy was to abstain from creating a large conscript army and instead to support its allies by supplying them with money, munitions and ships. In September 1915 Hankey wrote that

> His argument briefly is this – that if we take many more men we cannot hope to supply our allies to whom we are committed to the tune of about a million a day, not in money but in goods or credit. His plan is to limit our army, but to give our doles gratis as a gift and not as a loan.[16]

The most fundamental divisions which emerged in the new Cabinet were not between 'Easterners' and 'Westerners'. All ministers and their senior service advisers were 'Easterners' in the sense that they all recognized that the Entente could not defeat the Central Powers without Russian support. But what they could not agree on was how best to support it. Nor was the Cabinet divided between advocates of *laissez-faire* on the one hand and more state intervention on the other. There was no apparent opposition inside the Cabinet to the principle of state control of the munitions industry embodied in the Munitions of War Bill. In 1916 Runciman and Curzon worked amicably together at the Board of Trade and the Shipping Control Committee to supervise the movement of British tonnage. Sir John Simon, who posed in public as a defender of individual liberty, bracketed together 'Quakers, conscientious objectors, and cranks', in a Cabinet memorandum only days before his resignation over the first Military Service Act in December 1915.[17] The real divisions were between those ministers like McKenna and Runciman on the one hand and Lloyd George, Bonar Law and, after December 1915 the CIGS,

Sir William Robertson, on the other. The first group drew their inspiration from the Napoleonic Wars. They wanted Britain to continue to be the economic powerhouse of the Entente so that it and its allies could survive a long war. As McKenna explained to L. T. Hobhouse, 'We can go on ten years if they will only leave industry alone . . . There are 100 ways of winning the war and only one of losing – conscription'.[18] Conscription was the high road to national bankruptcy. Conversely Lloyd George and his friends were ready to risk bankruptcy in the belief that without a huge British army the Entente would be defeated but with it they might win by the end of 1916. The divisions within the Cabinet were more temperamental than political or ideological. On one side were the cautious, patient and to some extent sanguine men like McKenna, Runciman, Grey and Balfour. On the other were those like Lloyd George, Bonar Law, and Carson, who were temperamentally unwilling and perhaps unable to follow any policy requiring those virtues.

McKenna's financial expedients can only be understood in the light of his preference for a long-haul war policy. He opposed conscription because he feared its economic repercussions, not because it violated sacred Liberal principles.[19] But he remained a partisan Liberal politician throughout his period at the Treasury. In mid-August the government faced three problems. The failure of the Suvla Bay landing ended any lingering hopes that the war would be over by Christmas 1915. Money, therefore, had to be found for a long war. Secondly, the government faced a serious exchange rate crisis in New York. Thanks to Lloyd George the Treasury had little effective control over what the purchasing departments or the allies spent in America. Allied munitions-purchasing, much of which was financed by British credit, was chaotic. In January the New York banking firm of J. P. Morgan had become the sole British purchasing agent in the USA but the French did not agree to work through them until April and the Russians until May, and even after that individual Russian ministries continued to place orders through other agents.

The establishment of the Ministry of Munitions did not solve this problem. In June Kitchener established a War Office committee to buy supplies for Russia in the USA which operated independently of the new ministry. In July Lloyd George and his French counterpart, Albert Thomas, agreed that in future French orders for munitions supplies placed in Britain would bypass the CIR and go straight to the ministry.[20] The need to finance Russian and Italian orders, as well as Britain's own, meant that during the summer the exchange rate turned against Britain in New York. On 14 August Morgans told the Treasury that in the coming week they had only $4m to meet outstanding liabilities of $17m.[21] And thirdly, at home class resentment was growing. The rich complained that while they paid for the war through increased direct taxes, the working classes were spending their new-found wealth on luxuries like pianos.[22] Treasury attempts to impose austerity had failed. Continuity of production had to come first. By June the Committee on Production in Engineering and Shipbuilding had granted increases to 750,000 workers. But it was only by working longer hours and because more family members were in regular employment that most working-class families were able to keep their earnings level with inflation.[23] Discontent in the labour world existed not just because of the threat of compulsory service but because of reports of the sharply increased profits being made by some businessmen.

The exchange rate crisis in New York coincided with the taking of the National Register and made the opponents of conscription all the more determined to resist a policy which they believed would fatally deplete Britain's dwindling economic power. At the same time it made the supporters of compulsion equally determined to insist that the government had to make a more rational use of British manpower. The War Policy Cabinet Committee was established in August 1915, a whole year after the start of the war, to carry out the first complete survey of Britain's human and economic resources. It marked the end of a year of chaotic military expansion and the first attempt to relate Britain's military policy to its economic potential. Members and witnesses fell into three groups. There were those like Lloyd George, Churchill and Curzon who wanted military and industrial conscription at once. Others, like Runciman, McKenna, Grey and Balfour did not oppose military conscription on principle. McKenna was quite ready to see between 5,000 and 10,000 men conscripted each week. But he believed that if more were taken it would wreck the economy and the Entente alliance, because eventually Britain would not be able to meet its economic obligations to the allies. And finally there was Kitchener, who wanted to 'wait and see'. The Committee produced two reports. The main report, signed by all its members, was non-committal. It simply stated what the Committee thought were Britain's military obligations to the Entente – to place seventy divisions in the field throughout 1916 – and showed that the voluntary system as it was then operating would probably be unable to maintain such a force. The government could provide the men by cutting credits to the allies; it could make the main points of the report public and hope that by doing so it would stimulate voluntary recruiting, whilst holding out the threat of military conscription if it did not; or it could move at once to either military conscription or complete national service. Churchill, Curzon, Chamberlain and Selborne signed a minority report supporting an immediate recourse to conscription and possibly also to national service so that Britain could not only maintain 100 divisions in the field throughout 1916 but also continue to subsidize the allies.[24]

McKenna's financial policieis were founded on the assumption that future recruiting would be limited and they were intended not only to safeguard the exchange rate but also to reduce class resentment and inflation and to ensure Britain would be able to finance a long war. In May the Treasury at last awoke to the fact that the free issue of Treasury bills was simply fuelling inflation and that fiscal policy had to be used to check consumption. A forced loan was politically impossible and so Treasury officials urged the issue of a second war loan on terms sufficiently generous not just to attract British but also American investors. They wanted £1,000m of the public's money, because, as J. M. Keynes, who had been brought into the Treasury in 1915, wrote, 'The public is the only ultimate source of command over the material resources of the country; and direct application to them is the only safe way of securing command over these resources, except for temporary periods and for amounts which are not too large'.[25] For the first time since the start of the war the Treasury tried to tap working-class savings. The loan was issued on 21 June and paid 4·5 per cent interest. Small investors were tempted by the issue of £25 and £5 bonds and vouchers for as little as 5s.[26]

But although it was important to attract small investors it was even more important to make the loan a propaganda success. Failure would destroy the government's credit at home and abroad. Therefore, the Treasury was careful to deal generously with holders of the first war loan by offering them generous conversion terms. They were even more solicitous of the clearing banks because, even though they did not want to create more bankers' money, they knew that only the banks could make the loan a financial success. The clearing banks were alarmed that the generous interest rates which McKenna was offering would cause a dangerous drop in the value of all other securities and that depositors would deplete their reserves by investing in the loan. E. S. Montagu, the Financial Secretary, was angry with what he described as the bankers 'shifty, uncandid selfseeking', suspecting that they were only interested in their own profits. But he recognized that 'We cannot do without them now and it is right that you [McKenna] should attempt to conciliate them'.[27] Conciliation took the form of the Bank of England lending the clearing banks money at a half per cent below bank rate on the under-standing that they would lend money to their customers at the same rate to invest in the new loan.[28] The issue of the loan was accompanied by a vigorous patriotic campaign to encourage investors. Politicians never tired of repeating that it was a patriotic duty to reduce consumption by investing in the loan.[29] However, by the middle of July it was apparent that the loan had failed. It had brought in only £570m, well short of the £1,000m McKenna had sought. Investments from small savers were especially disappointing. Much of the money they did invest was simply transferred from existing GPO savings accounts. The Inland Revenue blamed this on two things. The administration of the voucher scheme was too complicated and investments could not be withdrawn quickly in the event of a personal emergency. More fundamentally, the Treasury probably exaggerated the amount of spare cash the working classes had in the first place.[30]

The government's failure to curb consumption was followed by their failure to stop wage rises through the Munitions of War Act. In July the South Wales miners struck for an increase in wages. The Cabinet, desperate for coal, capitulated. Lloyd George and Runciman negotiated a settlement but less than a month later the miners threatened to strike again over its interpretation. Runciman stood by in disgust as Lloyd George made further concessions. Sir George Askwith, chairman of the Committee on Production in Engineering and Shipbuilding, who at one point had been asked to arbitrate in the dispute, believed that Lloyd George's intervention was disastrous because it simply encouraged other groups of workers to press their claims all the harder.[31]

Within a month the government faced another setback, this time in America. To meet the exchange rate crisis the British had rushed gold and securities to New York. To cover their longer-term needs the British and French governments then tried to raise a joint loan in the USA. They hoped to borrow £200m at 4·5 per cent interest without the backing of collateral. But the American investing public, who were far from convinced that the Entente was going to win the war, were unaccustomed to foreign government loans, and normally received 5·5 per cent interest backed by unimpeachable American securities. The best that the allied mission under Lord Reading could do was to raise £100m at 5 per cent. Keynes, who was in charge of American finance at the Treasury, believed that even after mobilizing American securities held in Britain together with the French, Russian and British gold stocks and by 'throwing in our watch chains', the British would face a deficit of £48m in New York by 31 March 1916. By relying on American contractors being unable to meet their delivery dates that deficit might just be covered but 'It would be foolish', he concluded, 'to assert that we have any reasonable security of getting through the six months April–October 1916 without a catastrophe'.[32]

As persuasion had failed both at home and abroad, McKenna was forced to do what he had already threatened and resort to coercion through taxation. The budget of September 1915 is remembered for one thing, the McKenna duties, supposed to have signalled the death knell of the Liberals' commitment to free trade. When the Cabinet discussed them Lloyd George threw a note across the table to Walter Long saying 'So the old system goes, destroyed by its own advocates'.[33] But Lloyd George, who hated McKenna, was always prepared to believe the worst of him and was not privy to his real purposes. By contrast one of the Chancellor's friends, Runciman, was lavish in his congratulations.[34] Furthermore, there was far more to the budget than just these duties. McKenna wanted to reduce domestic consumption on goods not related to the war effort in order to check the trade deficit with the USA and simultaneously he also wished to reduce labour discontent by limiting excess profits. He was in the happy position – for a Chancellor of the Exchequer – of actually being urged by some businessmen to increase taxes. After one deputation had called on him to urge him to do just that, Sir John Bradbury minuted

Now that a deputation had waited upon the Prime Minister and asked for further taxation the Chancellor of the Exchequer can go cheerfully ahead knowing that for the first time in the history of his office he has been invited by the people to lay further fiscal burdens upon them. His task is made all the easier because he has been asked to do this not only with a view to raising revenue, but in order to meet the perhaps still more important problem of reducing personal expenditure. He cannot make a mistake, because if he taxes too much for revenue purposes he will thereby check spending all the more.[35]

But although he might not be able to make a mistake he still had to operate within certain political and economic constraints. These were explained in a memorandum by Keynes. The demand for goods and services was greater than the productive capacity of the country could supply. The only way to reduce prices was to reduce demand. This could be done by òne of two methods. The government could continue to create credits and allow inflation to grow so that and in time price rises would automatically limit consumption. That might be all very well in theory but its short-term consequences would be disastrous. It would stimulate imports, lead to a collapse of the exchange rate and place an intolerable strain on the entire community, especially the poor. The only practical course was for the government to increase taxes or levy loans taken directly from the purchasing power of the consumer. If the loans and taxes were properly constituted they would fall on those best able to bear their burden.[36]

McKenna's initial problem was how to strike the correct balance between direct and indirect taxation. The clearing banks wanted increased duties on sugar, tea, cocoa, and tobacco and a forced loan levied on all classes. A deputation from the city of London asked for a tariff on all luxury imports. Bradbury suggested doubling all existing rates of taxation but, for administrative reasons, leaving the income tax threshold at £160 p.a. To provide what he termed 'some comic relief', he insisted that bachelors should pay 50 per cent more income tax than married men.[37] Montagu, perhaps lacking Bradbury's quirky sense of humour, wanted to bring everyone who earned more than £2 per week within the orbit of the income tax. Both wanted to introduce import duties. Montagu suggested an 'unscientific' 10 per cent duty on all imports balanced by a 10 per cent bounty on all exports. That would help the exchange rate but give no comfort at all to those who clamoured for tariff reform after the war.[38]

Over the income tax McKenna compromised between Montagu's very low threshold and the Board of Inland Revenue's insistence that they did not have the manpower to collect taxes from so many new taxpayers. The threshold was lowered to £130 p.a. Even that increased the number of income tax payers by between 70 and 100 per cent.[39] Rates of income tax were raised by 40 per cent in a full year and the super tax on higher incomes was graduated for the first time.[40] An across-the-board tariff was an administrative impossibility. The Board of Customs and Excise simply did not have the men to administer it just at the moment when the government was doing all it could to shed manpower in favour of the armed forces. The political dangers of increasing the cost of living were readily apparent and made duties on foodstuffs dangerous. That left only tariffs on luxury imports and there the scope for doing anything was strictly limited. Despite lurid press reports about wasteful consumption on luxury imports, their value had in fact fallen between January and June 1915 to only £15·3m. And it was not politic to tax all of those that remained. McKenna refused, for example, to tax ornamental feathers because most came from France and French businessmen were already very bitter about British commercial policy. He therefore restricted his own duties to imported American motor cars.[41]

However, Lloyd George, who had been angered by the Treasury's insistence that his ministry should restrict their purchases in America, criticized McKenna's proposals because they did not raise enough new revenue. Lloyd George wanted the income tax threshold further reduced and the list of articles subject to import tariffs increased. They compromised. The tax threshold stayed where it was but watches, clocks, hats and musical instruments were added to the list of dutiable items. McKenna's concession was more apparent than real. All the new duties together would only save a drop in the ocean compared to the predicted deficit of £400m by March 1916. They certainly did not satisfy Unionist tariff reformers like Walter Long but McKenna had never intended that they would. He never expected that his duties would significantly reduce imports, raise revenue or save tonnage. But he kept that a secret from even his closest colleagues. The McKenna duties had a partisan political purpose. McKenna wanted them to fail as a fiscal measure because, as he privately explained to the Liberal MP, Sir Alfred Mond, it 'would be a good object lesson as to the impossibility of tariffs in this country'.[42]

McKenna's final innovation was the excess profits duty. The Treasury recognized that 'the restlessness of labour in many parts of the country is to a great extent due to the feeling that employers are making huge profits out of the war which they are being allowed to pocket'.[43] The government had already made some concessions to these sentiments by introducing a munitions levy as part of the Munitions of War Act. In June McKenna had announced that the same principle would be extended to other businesses. He levied the duty at 50 per cent on all profits in excess of the annual average of those earned in the three years preceding the war but made certain allowances for capital investments.[44]

The Treasury hoped that the budget would bring in £305m in revenue, compared to only £189m in the 1913 budget. The lion's share of the revenue would come from the new rates of direct taxation and in this respect McKenna was following the Liberals' prewar policy of making the tax system more progressive. But, like all good Chancellors, what he gave with one hand he took with the other. By lowering the income tax threshold he probably brought a considerable part of the working class into the income tax paying class for the first time although many probably escaped from the Chancellor's clutches by claiming abatements. The budget received a mixed reception. Free traders welcomed the new direct taxes but condemned the McKenna duties because they apparently sold the pass to the tariff reformers. Tariff reformers welcomed the duties but wanted far more and complained that the new rates of income tax meant that the middle classes were paying a disproportionately heavy burden of the cost of the war. The most criticized part of the budget was the excess profits duty – criticized at least by those liable to pay it. Together with the new rates of income and super tax it threatened to take 13*s* 10*d* out of every £1 of excess profits.[45] It is difficult to generalize about how heavily it fell in practice. There was certainly some scope for evasion especially because the Inland Revenue was denied the powers to inspect companies' books to assess it.[46]

McKenna still had a deficit of £1,285m to meet and he could do so only by more borrowing. In December the government issued a new tap stock, 5 per cent Exchequer bonds, while in 1916 it again resorted to the large-scale sale of Treasury bills to meet its immediate needs.[47] To stop this burden becoming even larger, the Treasury first tried to disabuse the allies of the notion that the British had a bottomless purse from which they could lend them unlimited amounts. On 30 September 1915 the Treasury signed a milestone agreement regulating Russian loans and purchasing. The British agreed to lend the Russians £25m per month for the next year. Each instalment was to be backed by an equal sum of Russian Treasury bills. For the final six months each allotment was to be provisional on Britain's ability to find sufficient exchange in the USA and Russia promised to hold ready £40m in gold to export to the USA to support the exchange position. The credits were to be used to pay for existing contracts in Britain and North America and a monthly limit of £4·5m was placed on any new contracts. Finally, the British were given *de facto* control of all of Russia's foreign purchasing through a joint committee sitting in London.[48] The Treasury also tried to assert more control over Britain's own spending departments. The Ministry of Munitions in particular had become a law unto itself. It had no idea of the total value of the imports it was purchasing, it granted wage increases without consulting the Treasury and in September Lloyd George embarked upon a new big gun programme without even consulting the War Office. In November the Cabinet insisted that all spending departments should henceforth refer all contracts worth more than £500,000 to the Treasury and Munitions began to put its own house in order by improving its costing procedures.[49]

The compilation of the National Register further polarized opinion about conscription. The failure of the American loan made its opponents within the Cabinet even more determined to resist it while reports of growing French restlessness made its supporters all the more determined to persevere. At the end of July Milner became chairman of the National Service League. Northcliffe's press campaign meant that he could no longer wait and he flung the organization into the campaign for national service. He organized an all-party pressure group consisting of men like the Unionist MP Richard Yerburgh, the Unionist mayor of Birmingham Neville Chamberlain, the Liberal MP Josiah Wedgwood and non-party public figures like Sir Edward Elgar and the Bishop of Birmingham. One of Milner's closest followers, the Unionist MP Leopold Amery, defined national service as giving the government 'the right to make use, to whatever extent it may require, of the lives and property of all its members'.[50]

Milner and his friends like Henry Wilson also engaged in an active campaign of private intrigue to sway opinion in their favour. Wilson tried to influence Bonar Law through Major John Baird, Law's parliamentary private secretary who was serving on the staff at GHQ. The Liberal MP Freddie Guest served as a channel to Carson and H. A. Gwynne, the editor of the *Morning Post*. In late July and early August they formed a cabal to influence the Cabinet. Wilson argued that without compulsory service French goodwill would evaporate. Guest undertook the hopeless task of trying to persuade Sir John Simon of the rightness of their case while Gwynne wrote to Law and Asquith.

> To speak quite plainly; whether we like it or not, if we are to win this war we must have compulsory service. It is the only answer to the capture of Warsaw; it is the only means of satisfying France. Without it we may make a break among the Allies and may find ourselves fighting alone.[51]

Only compulsion would provide the men necessary to make good the losses of a great offensive in the spring of 1916 and without it the war would end on Germany's terms in a peace based on the status quo which in practice would be no more than an armed truce. The cabal wanted to reduce Kitchener to a cipher because 'He is the only man the country believes in' but hoped that real power would come to rest with Wilson, whom they wanted to return to London as CIGS, and Carson.[52]

None of the recipients of this pressure were convinced by it. Law was pulled in two directions. Unionist MPs like Lord Charles Beresford thought that the National Register was simply a poor excuse for avoiding the necessity of national service. Others, like Lord Hugh Cecil, bitterly resented Northcliffe's campaign. Most members of the labour movement outside of the ILP supported the continuation of the war until the Germans had been expelled from occupied Belgium and France. But they thought that the call for national service or conscription was premature and were still suspicious of the class motives of its advocates. J. Bruce Glasier, a leading member of the ILP, described them as 'A dainty dish of gilded patricians to set before the British public, Tories, Tariff Reformers, Anti-Democrats every one'.[53] During the eve of the TUC conference at Bristol early in September, Henderson warned the Cabinet that there was no possibility of the labour movement accepting industrial conscription and that they would only accept military conscription on five conditions. One last attempt had to be tried to find the men through the voluntary system. If that failed, Kitchener had to call in public for conscription and if it were introduced it should be accompanied by universal suffrage, heavy taxes on the rich and the promise that it would be abandoned at the end of the war.[54]

So bitter did the controversy become that at the end of August a group of elder statesmen emerged to counsel a policy of wait and see. Led by the jurist A. V. Dicey, the former imperial pro-consul Lord Cromer, and the former Liberal Prime Minister Lord Rosebery, they sympathized with the objectives of the National Service League but not with its methods. Names like Lord Milner's only served to raise the ire of the organized working classes and, in Cromer's words, 'far from tending to allay class differences of opinion, it would tend to accentuate them, and this is just what above all things we now wish to avoid'.[55] Privately Asquith opposed conscription, fearing it would lead to a labour revolt and the collapse of the government. Publicly both he and Bonar Law sheltered behind Kitchener's prestige. Only when Kitchener said publicly that conscription was a military necessity would the deadlock be broken.[56] There was little the compulsionists could do. Resignation would be futile. The Unionists could not form a government on their own and even if Lloyd George resigned with them he knew that he could not count on sufficient Liberal support to form another coalition.

Kitchener's hand was finally forced in October when the comparative manpower and casualty statistics upon which he had rested his policy of attrition were undermined. But by early October Serbia was in imminent danger of collapse. There was every possibility that the Germans would soon be able to open the road to Constantinople, revitalize Turkey, threaten directly the whole of Britain's eastern empire and add Turkish manpower to their own reserves. And secondly, Loos had done little to help Russia, and Kitchener reluctantly admitted that, with Russia so weak, it would no longer be possible for Britain to withhold its main force from a large-scale offensive in the West in 1916. The BEF's losses at Loos indicated that fighting on the Western front in 1916 would be more expensive than the voluntary system could sustain and so on 8 October he asked for 35,000 men per week up to the end of 1916, a figure well beyond the 5,000 – 10,000 McKenna was prepared to concede.[57]

The result was the first of a series of crises over conscription which were to rock the Cabinet in 1915–16. On this occasion two peacemakers emerged in the shape of Crewe and Long. They suggested that Lord Derby, the Director General of Recruiting, should be given until the end of November to find the men the army wanted. His target was to find 500,000 men who were ready to attest their willingness to serve by 31 March 1916. But that was kept a secret from the public, who were simply told that if an unspecified number were not forthcoming, the voluntary system would have been deemed to have failed and the government would introduce military conscription. The Derby scheme, which was announced on 21 October, involved a personal canvas of every man between the ages of 18 and 45 by the Parliamentary Recruiting Committee. Each man was allotted to one of twenty-three groups according to his age and to one of two classes depending on his marital status. Asquith tried to encourage married men to attest by promising that the unmarried would be called up first.[58]

The shortage of men was only one bottleneck in the war economy. The shortage of shipping was another and on this question the government was much less reluctant to impose physical controls to ensure the more efficient use of resources. By the autumn nearly a quarter of the entire British merchant fleet was already under requisition. In October a Cabinet Committee under Bonar Law discovered that wheat imports had fallen by 21 per cent over the preceding six months and that shipowners were reluctant to employ their vessels on the North Atlantic route because of the high likelihood that their ships would be requisitioned when they docked.[59] Unlike organized labour the shipowners had no powerful supporters inside the Cabinet, press or Parliament. The government therefore rode roughshod over trade interests and despite the protests of many owners established four committees to control the trade. To ensure that Britain's own carrying trade received greater priority, no vessels would in future be permitted to ply between two foreign ports without a license from the Ship Licensing Committee. The Requisition (Carriage of Foodstuffs) Committee was established to find tonnage to carry North American wheat and, much to the disgust of the corn trade, the committee began to accumulate a reserve stock in Britain which they planned to release on to the market if shortages led to very steep price increases. It also gained control of the entire Canadian wheat crop by the simple expedient of persuading the Dominion government to requisition it. To ease the problem of port congestion which was delaying the turn-around of vessels, the Cabinet established the Port and Transit Executive Committee.[60] Finally in January 1916 Curzon became Chairman of the Shipping Control Committee. Its task was to decide on the allocation of requisitioned tonnage between competing interests. Thus, while the degree of state control varied, by the beginning of 1916 every British ship was subject to some form of state direction.[61] The first problem the new committee had to face was how to reduce imports. Despite the strident objections of the businessmen involved, in January they made a start by opening negotiations with distillers and paper manufacturers to impose a temporary ban on the import of their raw materials.[62] By mid-February, faced with a 25 per cent shortfall in tonnage, Curzon recommended a ban on 13m tons of imports to run from March to June. The Board of Trade objected on the grounds that it would lead to resentment from the French and retaliation from neutrals like the Spanish, and the final agreed figure was 4m tons. The British might be able to do without Spanish oranges but they could not do without its iron ore.[63]

In the summer of 1915 the new government pursued two economic strategies. Lloyd George's establishment of the Ministry of Munitions has been seen as symbolizing the commitment of part of the new government to end the *laissez-faire* policies of their predecessors and to organize the war economy through the imposition of physical controls. Lloyd George, Long and their friends wanted conscription because they thought it was the only way the army would get the men it required, because they hoped it would discipline the industrial labour force, because it was necessary to hold the Entente alliance together and because they hoped that if the allies mobilized all their resources quickly they would be able to win the war by the end of 1916. At the Treasury McKenna represented the continuation of the previous government's reliance on fiscal devices to regulate the economy and direct human and material resources to where they were most needed. The opponents of conscription pointed to the grave threat to national unity if conscription were imposed against the wishes of the organized labour movement. McKenna and Runciman were doubtful that the war could be won in 1916 and were prepared to continue fighting for ten years if necessary. They were more ready to ignore the importunities of the allies for more British military support and to insist that what they really wanted was money and supplies. These would only be forthcoming in sufficient quantities if the government did not impose conscription.

Notes

1   HMSO, *History of the Ministry of Munitions*, Vol. 2, pt 2 (London: HMSO, n.d.), pp. 3–13, 25; C. J. Wrigley, 'The Ministry of Munitions: an innovatory department', in K. M. Burk (ed.), *War and the State: The Transformation of British Government, 1914–1919* (London: Allen & Unwin, 1982), pp. 40–1; *Hansard*, 72 HC Deb., 5s. cols 1183–92; R. J. Q. Adams, *Arms and the Wizard: Lloyd George and the Ministry of Munitions, 1915–1916* (London: Cassell, 1978), pp. 62–9; J. Grigg, *Lloyd George: From Peace to War, 1912–1916* (London: Methuen, 1985), pp. 258–62.

2   T. C. Kennedy, 'Public opinion and the conscientious objector, 1915–1919', *Journal of British Studies*, vol. 12, no. 2 (1973), p. 106; J. Hinton, *The First Shop Stewards Movement* (London: Allen & Unwin, 1973), p. 40; M. Bentley, *The Liberal Mind, 1914–1929* (Cambridge: Cambridge University Press, 1977), pp. 26–7; A. F. Havighurst, *Radical Journalist: H. W. Massingham (1860–1924)* (Cambridge: Cambridge University Press, 1974), p. 235; J. Rae, *Conscience and Politics: The British Government and the Conscientious Objector to Military Service, 1916–1919* (London: Oxford University Press, 1970), pp. 11–13.

3   J. Ramsden, *The Age of Balfour and Baldwin 1902–1940* (London: Longman, 1978), p. 113; R. J. Scally, *The Origins of the Lloyd George Coalition: The Politics of Social Imperialism, 1900–1918* (Princeton, NJ: Princeton University Press, 1975), pp. 105–8; A. Sykes, *Tariff Reform in British Politics, 1909–1913* (Oxford: Clarendon Press, 1979), pp. 195–8; Long to Blumenfeld, 7 September 1910 and 11 March 1911, Blumenfeld mss; Bonar Law to Cecil, 10 November 1914, Bonar Law mss, 37/4/27 and Bonar Law to Oliver, 18 December 1914, Bonar Law mss, 37/4/39.

4   D. French, *British Economic and Strategic Planning, 1905–1915* (London: Allen & Unwin, 1982), p. 171; PRO FO 800/100, Grey to Asquith and enc., 14 May 1915.

5   Adams, *Arms*, pp. 90–2; K. R. Grieves, 'The Liverpool dock labour battalion: Military intervention in the Mersey docks, 1915–1918', *Transactions of the Historic Society of Lancashire and Cheshire*, vol. 132 (1982), pp. 139–43.

6   Grigg, *Lloyd George*, pp. 263–4; José Harris, *William Beveridge: A Biography* (Oxford: Clarendon Press, 1977), p. 208; PRO CAB 37/129/8, Long, National Registration, 3 June 1915; Long to Bonar Law, 1 June 1915, Bonar Law mss, 50/4/5; Selborne, Notes on National Organisation, 27 May 1915, Selborne mss, file 80, ff. 1–3; C. J. Wrigley, *David Lloyd George and the British Labour Movement: Peace and War* (Brighton: Harvester, 1976), pp. 115–17.

7   Wrigley, *Lloyd George*, pp. 165–6; S. Koss, *The Rise and Fall of the Political Press in Britain*, Vol. 2, *The Twentieth Century* (London: Hamish Hamilton, 1984), pp. 283–4; Milner to St Loe Strachey, 21 August 1915, St Loe Strachey mss, S/10/11/7.

8   PRO CAB 37/129/24, Harcourt, Compulsion, 8 June 1915; PRO CAB 37/129/20, Runciman, Effect of diminished exports on Foreign Exchange, 2 June 1915.

9   PRO CAB 37/129/30, Balfour, Memorandum for the Cabinet, 9 June 1915; Rae, *Conscience*, pp. 1, 9; Earl of Oxford and Asquith, *Memories and Reflections, 1852–1927*, Vol. 2 (London: Cassell, 1928), p. 109.

10 PRO CAB 42/21/2, Minutes of the War Committee, 5 October 1916.

11 PRO CAB 37/130/19, Curzon, Registration and Military Service, 21 June 1915; PRO CAB 37/129/35, Long, Registration for War Purposes, 11 June 1915; PRO CAB 37/129/36, Lansdowne, Memorandum for the Cabinet, 12

June 1915; PRO CAB 37/129/22, Selborne, Agricultural Labour, 8 June 1915.

12 PRO CAB 41/36/29, Asquith to H.M. the King, 24 June 1915.

13 *The Times*, 28 July 1915; Bentley, *Liberal Mind*, pp. 27–8.

14 Hinton, *Shop Stewards*, pp. 34–7; Wrigley, *Lloyd George* pp. 112–21.

15 J. Barnes and D. Nicholson (eds), *The Leo Amery Diaries*, Vol. 1, *1896–1929* (London: Hutchinson, 1980), p. 118.

16 Hankey diary entry, 3 September 1915, Hankey mss, 1/1.

17 PRO CAB 37/139/53, Simon, Memorandum for the Cabinet, 24 December 1915.

18 T. Wilson (ed.), *The Political Diaries of C. P. Scott, 1911–1928* (London: Collins, 1970), p. 137.

19 McKenna to Asquith, *c.* 30 December 1915, McKenna mss, 5/9.

20 HMSO, *History of the Ministry of Munitions*, Vol. 2, pt 8 (London: HMSO, n.d.), pp. 9–12; K. Neilson, *Strategy and Supply: The Anglo-Russian Alliance, 1914–1917* (London: Allen & Unwin, 1984), pp. 100–4.

21 K. M. Burk, *Britain, America and the Sinews of War 1914–1918* (London: Allen & Unwin, 1985), pp. 63–4.

22 PRO FO 633/24, Cromer to Campbell, 6 February 1915; B. A. Waites, 'The effect of the First World War on class and status in England, 1910–1920', *Journal of Contemporary History*, vol. 11, no. 1 (1976), p. 35.

23 Lord Askwith, *Industrial Problems and Disputes* (Brighton: Harvester Press, 1920/74), p. 384; A. Marwick, *The Deluge: British Society and the First World War* (London: Penguin, 1965), pp. 133–6.

24 Wilson (ed.), *Scott Diaries*, p. 137; PRO CAB 37/134/2, Ashley, Memorandum on the relations between the economic position of the United Kingdom and military service, 1 September 1915; PRO CAB 37/134/9, War Policy Committee: Report, 8 September 1915; PRO CAB 37/134/7, War Policy Committee: Supplementary Memorandum, 7 September 1915; PRO CAB 37/134/25, Balfour, Efficiency in war and compulsion, 19 September 1915.

25 PRO T 170/72, Keynes, The Bank of England in relation to government borrowing and the necessity of a public loan, 14 May 1915; see also PRO T 170/71, Bradbury, War Loan, 7 June 1915; PRO T 170/71, Withers to Bradbury and enc., 14 May 1915; for Keynes's work at the Treasury in 1915–16, see R. Skidelsky, *John Maynard Keynes: Hopes Betrayed 1883–1920* (London: Macmillan, 1983), pp. 297–315.

26 PRO T 170/71, War Loan, 1930–60, June 1915; PRO T 170/72, War loan: Scheme for working class subscriptions, n.d. but *c.* June 1915, and Withers to Waley and enc., 25 June 1916.

27 PRO T 170/78, Montagu to McKenna, 30 June 1915; PRO T 170/76, Bradbury, War loan: Conversion, n.d. but *c.* June 1915, and Turpin, Addendum to memorandum on War Finance dated 27 April 1915, 9 June 1915.

28 PRO T 170/78, McKenna to Martin-Holland, 2 July 1915; Leaf to McKenna, 14 June 1915; PRO T 170/93, Martin-Holland to McKenna, 9 July 1915.

29 See, for example, PRO T 170/97, The National Association of Girls Clubs, *c.* July 1915; PRO T 170/78, Advertising Manager, Lincolnshire, Boston and Spalding Free Press to Treasury, 30 June 1915; see the speeches by Samuel and McKenna in *The Times*, 16 July and 4 August 1915.

30 PRO T 170/78, Bank of England to Bradbury, 13 July 1915; PRO T 170/78, Bradbury, Memorandum, £4 10s War Loan 1925–45, *c.* October 1915; PRO T 170/70, Davis to Waley, 12 July and 4 August 1915, and Waley to Bradbury, 26 June 1915; PRO T 170/97, Stewart to Bradbury, 13 December 1915.

31   Askwith, *Industrial Problems*, p. 395; PRO CAB 41/36/34, Asquith to H.M. the King, 19 July 1915.
32   Elizabeth Johnson (ed.), *The Collected Works of John Maynard Keynes*, Vol. 16 (London: Macmillan, 1971), p. 140; Burk, *Sinews of War*, pp. 69–75; PRO T 170/90, Keynes, Balance sheet between the United Kingdom and North America October 1 1915 to March 31 1916, 5 October 1915; Reading to McKenna, 8 and 25 September 1915, McKenna mss, 5/6.
33   A. J. P. Taylor, *English History 1914–1945* (Oxford: Clarendon Press, 1965), pp. 71–2.
34   Runciman to McKenna, n.d. but *c.* 23 September 1915, McKenna mss, 5/3.
35   PRO T 170/88, Bradbury, Suggestion for further taxation, *c.* July 1915.
36   PRO T 170/73, Keynes, Inflation, *c.* 15 September 1915.
37   PRO T 170/88, Bradbury, Suggestion ... taxation; PRO T 170/81, St Aldwyn to McKenna, 6 June 1915; PRO T 171/118, Marcus Samuel to McKenna, 26 August 1915.
38   PRO T 171/126, Montagu to McKenna, 10 August 1915.
39   PRO T 171/119, Warren Fisher to McKenna and enc., 9 and 31 August 1915.
40   PRO CAB 37/134/14, McKenna, War Taxation, 10 September 1915; PRO CAB 41/36/42, Asquith to H.M. the King, 3 September 1915.
41   PRO T 171/118, Board of Customs and Excise, Import of Ornamental Feathers, 10 September 1915; PRO T 171/117, Board of Customs and Excise to McKenna, 28 August and 11 September 1915.
42   Mond to McKenna, 14 October 1915, McKenna mss, 5/10; PRO CAB 37/136/29, McKenna, Estimate of the adverse balance of foreign trade in the periods 13 October 1915, to 31 March 1916, and 1 April 1916 to 30 September 1916, 22 October 1915; PRO CAB 41/36/43, Asquith to H.M. the King, 10 September 1915; PRO CAB 41/36/44, Asquith to H.M. the King, 16 September 1915; A. J. P. Taylor (ed.), *Lloyd George: A Diary by Frances Stevenson* (London: Hutchinson, 1971), p. 61.
43   PRO T 171/27, Withers, Proposed excess profits tax, 16 July 1915.
44   PRO T 171/126 [McKenna], Note to be read with paragraph eight of the Cabinet paper on war taxation dated September 10 – excess profits tax, *c.* 10 September 1915; PRO T 171/122, Warren Fisher to McKenna, 18 June 1915 and minute by H. P. Hamilton, 26 July 1915; Sir J. Stamp, *Taxation during the War* (London: Oxford University Press, 1932), pp. 148–50.
45   PRO T 171/122, Stamp, War Profits, 1 September 1915, and Warren Fisher to H. P. Hamilton, 12 October 1915; PRO T 172/237, Haworth (Employers Parliamentary Association) to the Treasury, 1 October 1915; PRO T 172/236, Pennefather to McKenna, and encs, 5 October 1915; Stamp, *Taxation*, p. 59.
46   Stamp, *Taxation*, p. 79.
47   E. V. Morgan, *Studies in British Financial Policy, 1914–1925* (London: Macmillan, 1952), pp. 110–11.
48   Neilson, *Strategy and Supply*, pp. 112–14.
49   PRO T 170/73, G. L. B. to McKenna, 6 October 1915 and Bradbury to Lloyd George, 27 August 1915; PRO T 170/89, Danruther to Waley, 26 October 1915; Adams, *Arms and the Wizard*, p. 167; C. Addison, *Politics from Within, 1911–1918: Including Some Records of a Great National Effort*, Vol. 1 (London: Herbert Jenkins, 1924), pp. 97–104; PRO CAB 41/36/54, Asquith to H.M. the King, 8 December 1915.
50   *The Times*, 3 September 1915; some indications of the public activities of the National Service League are recounted in *The Times*, 29 July, 16, 17, 20 and

21 August 1915; see also A. M. Gollin, *Proconsul in Politics: A Study of Lord Milner in Opposition and Power* (London: Blond, 1964).

51 Gwynne to Bonar Law and enc., 27 September 1915.

52 Percy to Wilson, 27 and 28 July 1915, Wilson mss, 73/1/19; Wilson diary entries, 30 and 31 July and 1 August 1915, Wilson mss (microfilm) reel 6; Guest to Simon, 19 July 1915, Simon mss, box 51, ff. 70–5.

53 PRO 38/69/1244, J. Bruce Glasier, The Perils of Conscription, 1915; *The Times*, 22 July 1915, carried a report of a meeting of the Socialist National Defence Committee during which Ben Tillet MP accused anti-war groups of being agents of 'Kaiserdom'.

54 *The Times*, 6–9 September 1915; Wrigley, *Lloyd George*, pp. 166–7; PRO CAB 37/134/5, Henderson, Memorandum for the Cabinet, 7 September 1915.

55 PRO FO 633/24, Cromer to Dicey, 24 August 1915; Wilson, *Scott Diary*, pp. 131–2; Taylor, *Lloyd George*, pp. 59, 67.

56 Asquith to Runciman, 23 September 1915, Runciman mss, WR 302; Asquith to Balfour, 18 September 1915, Asquith mss, vol. 28, ff. 162–7; Bentley, *Liberal Mind*, p. 32; Hankey diary entires, 18 and 20 September 1915, Hankey mss, 1/1.

57 PRO CAB 37/135/15, Kitchener, Recruiting for the army, 8 October 1915; PRO CAB 37/135/26, Kitchener, Memorandum for the Cabinet, 12 October 1915; PRO CAB 41/36/48, Asquith to H.M. the King, 12 October 1915.

58 PRO 30/57/76/WR/62, Asquith to Cabinet, 16 October 1915; PRO CAB 37/136/10, Long, The Recruiting Problem, 14 October 1915; PRO CAB 37/136/11, Crewe, The Question of Recruiting, 15 October 1915; PRO WO 106/365, Cross, Memorandum, 2 June 1916.

59 C. E. Fayle, *The War and the Shipping Industry* (London: Oxford University Press, 1927), pp. 150–1.

60 Fayle, *The War*, pp. 152–61; Bonar Law, Report of Industrial Control Committee on Shipping, 27 October 1915, Runciman mss, WR 96; Rew, Wheat Position, 1915–16, 28 February 1916, Runciman mss, WR 92; President, Corn Trade Association, Liverpool, to Runciman, 29 November 1915, Runciman mss, WR 111; Board of Trade Marine Department to Hill and Hill to Runciman, 29 October and 1 November 1915, Bonar Law mss, box 62.

61 PRO CAB 41/37/4, Asquith to H.M. the King, 19 January 1916; Runciman, The Shortage of Tonnage and High Freights, 16 January 1916, Runciman mss, WR 97.

62 PRO CAB 37/140/33, Port and Transit Executive Committee to Cabinet, 14 January 1916; Hill, Memorandum prepared by the Ship Licensing Committee and the Requisitioning (Carriage of Foodstuffs) Committee: Shortage of tonnage, January 1916, Runciman mss, WR 94.

63 PRO CAB 42/10/8, Minutes of the War Committee, 8 March 1916; PRO CAB 37/145/24, Chamberlain, Suggested exclusion of imports of tea and jute from the UK, 11 April 1916; Fountain, Shipping and Prohibited Imports, 4 April 1916, Bonar Law mss, 57/3/XI/2.

8

Britain and the 'Drang nach dem Osten', 1915–16

McKenna's policy rested on two assumptions, that Britain's continental allies would be ready to continue to bear the brunt of the land war whilst Britain held aloof and that Britain and its empire could be kept safe from direct German attack. Despite periodic invasion scares, the Royal Navy did safeguard the British Isles from invasion but by the end of 1915 the remaining foundations of these assumptions had been badly eroded. In September the Bulgarians joined the Central Powers and Serbia was soon overrun. The Germans thus opened a direct line of communication between Berlin and Constantinople and the collapse of the allied position in the Balkans in the autumn of 1915 meant that the Germans might, if they chose, mount a direct attack on Egypt or India. There were three ways the British could try to check them. They could adopt a forward defensive policy by landing at Salonika, giving succour to Serbia and try to cut the railway line to Constantinople. They could remain on the Gallipoli peninsula throughout the winter and, by threatening the Turkish capital, prevent the Central Powers from sending large bodies of troops to Suez or Baghdad. Or they could evacuate Gallipoli, regroup the Mediterranean Expeditionary Force in Egypt and try to shore up the cracking edifice of their prestige in the Muslim world – always a paramount consideration whenever the war against Turkey was being considered – in Mesopotamia and Arabia. In the West, the Anglo-French autumn offensive failed to break the German line and despite the predictions made in January there were no indications that the Germans were about to sue for peace because their manpower was exhausted. By December McKenna's policy of relying on the allies and waiting on events had become untenable.

Concern about Britain's dwindling prestige in the East and the loyalty of its Muslim subjects had been growing since the start of the war. British intelligence was well-informed about German attempts to support insurrection among the Muslim peoples of the British empire. As soon as the

Indian corps landed in France GHQ counter-intelligence officers began to investigate reports of sedition among the native regiments. The Cabinet was sufficiently worried that it received regular reports from the viceroy of the numbers of deserters from the army. In November 1914 the Foreign Office had learnt that the Germans had dispatched four missions across Turkey and Persia to Afghanistan and in March 1915 they captured the baggage of one of their leaders and discovered that it not only contained pamphlets intended to subvert Indian soldiers but also a plan to raise Persia and Afghanistan against the British. In December 1914 some trans-frontier Pathans deserted to the Turks in Mesopotamia and the local commander thought that the remainder of their regiment were so unreliable that they were withdrawn from the front line and sent to build roads. Fears of a second Indian Mutiny made the military authorities extremely suspicious of all signs of unrest among their native troops. Sir Beauchamp Duff, the commander-in-chief of the Indian army, was doubtful of the loyalty of the Pathans if the Afghans made a serious effort to preach a holy war along the North West Frontier of India.[1] In February 1915 the Turks attacked the Suez Canal and although they were repulsed, Sir Henry McMahon, the new high commissioner in Cairo, believed that it had made the native population more than doubtful of the stability of the new regime.[2] Throughout 1915 his garrison commander, Sir John Maxwell, was also afraid of attacks on Egypt's western frontiers by the Senussi of Libya, who he feared might be capable of starting a serious rising inside Egypt.[3]

But by February 1915 the most serious threat to the internal security of the Eastern empire was in India. In February 1915 Hardinge wanted to reinforce the garrison in Mesopotamia. The Turks were known to be sending a new corps to Mesopotamia and he was afraid that unless the momentum of the British advance was maintained the local Arabs would respond to the Turks' call for a holy war and go over to them. Unless another division were sent to Mesopotamia the British would face a serious setback and 'a disaster in Mesopotamia must inevitably bring into the field against us both Persia and Afghanistan with the frontier tribes, and may seriously effect the Mussulman population and Mussulman troops'.[4] The fear that Mesopotamia might be the domino which could bring down the Eastern empire underlay the whole policy of the government of India in 1915. The garrison of India had been seriously depleted. The North West Frontier was guarded by only four divisions while in the rest of India there was only a motley collection of Indian regiments and half-trained British Territorials deployed on internal security duties. Hardinge asked the War Office to reinforce Mesopotamia with another British brigade but Kitchener refused, insisting that India would have to find the troops itself. Hardinge submitted under protest but the decision from London could not have come at a worse moment. The Indian government had just uncovered an insurrectionary movement apparently involving Sikhs, Hindus and Muslims which, with German support, had plotted to stage a major rising some time between mid-March and mid-June.[5]

This was the background against which the Dardanelles campaign was mounted. It was not originally designed in London to be a prophylactic against revolution in India and Egypt. But it is hardly surprising that the British governments in Cairo and Delhi quickly saw it in that light. The surest way to uphold British prestige in the face of Panislamic nationalism and German subversion was to knock Turkey out of the war quickly. Hardinge was delighted with the plan, writing on 1 March 'since action in the Dardanelles, the success of which I can hardly doubt, will undoubtedly relieve the pressure upon us that has been gradually accumu= lating at Baghdad, while at the same time there is the possibility that the arrival of the fleet before Constantinople in the near future will precipitate a revolution and, possibly, the end of the war with Turkey'.[6] Similarly McMahon wrote on 8 March that 'our activity in the Dardanelles is having a good effect here, and our success there or in Constantinople will impress Egypt more than anything we could do elsewhere in the world'.[7]

It was only to be expected that neither welcomed the news of de Robeck's repulse on 18 March and looked forward with eager anticipation to a renewed attack with military support. Hamilton's failure to carry the peninsula in May was therefore seen as constituting a serious blow to British prestige. Hardinge reported rumours that a holy war would be launched along the North West Frontier when the harvest had been gathered and in July he told Chamberlain, the new Secretary of State, that 'defeat, or the necessity of cutting our losses in the Dardanelles, would be absolutely fatal in this country, since the Mahomedans would then undoubtedly turn their eyes to Turkey far more than towards us, and Pan-Islamism would become a very serious danger'.[8] Maxwell begged Hamilton to send him some good news from the Dardanelles. 'There is more in the Pan-Islamic propaganda than we choose to believe, and reports of disasters to our forces are circulated in the Bazaars and where they see streams of wounded pouring in, they believe them.'[9] Their fears found a receptive audience in the new Cabinet where the Indo-Egyptian party of Crewe, Kitchener and Grey was swelled in the coalition government by the new Secretary of State for India, Chamberlain, and by two former Viceroys, Curzon and Lansdowne. One reason they supported the Suvla Bay landing was because they hoped that a British victory would restore Britain's dented prestige in the eyes of its Muslim subjects.[10]

British diplomats in general, and Grey in particular, subsequently received much criticism for failing to save Serbia. However, some of the blame for the slowness with which the British reacted to events in the Balkans in the autumn of 1915 must be laid at the door of British military intelligence. As early as 9 June Bax-Ironside had reported that in August the Germans would assume the defensive against Russia in Poland and send troops to the Serbo-Bulgarian frontier, and in August this was apparently confirmed by a report emanating from a neutral diplomat in Switzerland. But military intelligence refused to accept these reports at their face value. In mid-July the DMO, Sir Charles Callwell, feared a German attack on Serbia but frankly admitted that 'We can make nothing out of all the conflicting accounts as to what the Germans mean to do'.[11] Throughout August GHQ intelligence staff believed that rumours of German troop movements towards Serbia were merely a bluff designed to intimidate the Balkans whilst the Germans drove towards Riga and Petrograd, and by early September the DMO's office agreed with them.[12] Bax-Ironside was right and the soldiers were wrong. On 6 September the Bulgarians finally signed a treaty of alliance and a military convention with Germany and Sir Francis Elliot, the British minister at Athens, reported that the Central Powers would attack Serbia within a fortnight. He was a little premature. Bulgarian mobilization did not begin until 21 September and right until the end of September the War Office were still in two minds about the accuracy of reports that another major offensive against Serbia was imminent.[13]

This uncertainty about the enemy's intentions made the Dardanelles Committee's task of deciding what to do after the failure of the Suvla Bay landing doubly difficult. They could have responded in one of three ways when Hamilton's request for reinforcements reached them after the failure at Suvla Bay. They could have sent the troops Hamilton wanted, in the hope that they would be sufficient to carry the peninsula. They could have ordered him to evacuate his troops or they could have done nothing. Bonar Law and Carson favoured evacuation, fearing that the dispatch of more troops to Gallipoli would only serve to annoy the French.[14] But others believed that evacuation would be badly received both in the Balkans and in Russia. The Russians had just lost Warsaw and Grey was afraid that if they were deprived of the prospect of gaining Constantinople they 'would give up at once in the situation in which they found themselves'.[15] Kitchener feared that evacuation might also have a disastrous effect on British prestige throughout the Muslim world, especially if, as was widely expected, most of Hamilton's rearguard had to surrender ignominiously on the beaches.[16] But he was equally unwilling to send more than a fraction of what Hamilton had requested because he was not ready to divert troops from France on the eve of Sir John French's offensive.[17]

On 31 August the Dardanelles Committee received a firsthand report of the situation on the peninsula from Hankey who had just returned from

Gallipoli. He argued in favour of sending Hamilton drafts and reinforcements and preparing for a winter campaign. Later the same day the French exploded a bombshell in London. They offered to send four more divisions to the eastern Mediterranean to mount a landing on the Asiatic shore of the Straits. In return they asked the British to send two of their own divisions to replace the two French divisions at Cape Helles.[18] This reversal of French policy was the product of French domestic politics. The Union Sacré was coming under increasing strain as criticisms of Joffre from the left in the Chamber mounted. By March they wanted to replace him with General Maurice Sarrail, the commander of the Third Army and one of the few radical republican generals in the French army. But Viviani knew that Joffre still enjoyed a high reputation with the public and that if he sacked him his own government would probably collapse. Joffre precipitated the crisis by sacking Sarrail on 22 July. If Viviani backed Joffre he would lose the support of the Radicals and Radical Socialists, but if he insisted that Sarrail be reinstated he risked losing the support of the right. He tried to sweep the problem away by offering Sarrail the command of an army corps at the Dardanelles but Sarrail refused to go unless he was given command of an independent army.[19] For the sake of preserving good relations with the French, Kitchener was happy to fall in with this suggestion. But some of his colleagues were more prone to look a gift horse in the mouth especially as it soon became apparent that Joffre was not prepared to allow any troops to leave France until after the Anglo-French autumn offensive. The Cabinet insisted on another Anglo-French conference. It met on 11 September and the participants agreed that if the offensive succeeded there would be no need to send troops to the East, while if it failed Joffre grudgingly agreed that he would begin to dispatch the four divisions on 10 October.[20]

In the meantime the Entente could only fall back upon diplomacy in the Balkans. On 14 September they made one last effort to keep the Bulgarians neutral. Under considerable pressure the Serbs finally agreed to cede to them part of the uncontested zone of Macedonia and the Entente agreed to occupy it with some of their own troops to reassure Ferdinand that the Serbs would not later renege.[21] Five days later the Dardanelles Committee learnt of the German–Bulgarian military convention and they immediately recognized that the collapse of Serbia would give the Germans direct railway communications to Constantinople. Hamilton's position might then become impossible as German heavy artillery would be able to shell his troops out of their narrow beach-heads. The Central Powers would also be able to re-open an active front along the Suez Canal and perhaps open a new one in Persia which would threaten India. The longer-term repercussions might be even more dire. As Lloyd George pointed out on 23 September the Entente's policy of winning the war by wearing-down the Central Powers' manpower reserves would suffer a major, if not fatal setback. Once Germany was at Constantinople

> she would be able to regenerate the Turkish nation. The Turks, according to Enver Pasha, had 2,000,000 fighting men, which was only counting 1 out of 10 of the available population simply waiting to be armed and equipped. We had reckoned to wear out the Central Powers gradually in men, but here was a nation who suddenly bring an accession to our enemies of 2,000,000 men. [22]

When the Bulgarians began to mobilize, Venizelos, who had finally returned to power in Greece in mid-August after his election victory in June, informed the Entente that Greece would stand by its alliance with Serbia and place 150,000 men in the field if the Entente would supply the same number. [23] Lloyd George wanted to save Serbia and prevent the Germans breaking through to Constantinople by taking advantage of this offer and divert the troops earmarked for Hamilton and the Suvla Bay garrison to Salonika. The Dardanelles Committee agreed and on 28 September the government publicly pledged that the allies would do all in their power to help Serbia. [24]

But on the same day Elliot telegraphed that the Greek government had gone back on their offer to allow allied forces to land at Salonika and the decision to send troops was promptly reversed. Despite all his enthusiasm Venizelos had been unable to persuade King Constantine to abandon neutrality. Venizelos was ready to ignore Constantine's objections and on 3 October he told the Entente that their troops would be welcome and the French decided to send one of their divisions from Cape Helles to Salonika. The British matched their offer with a British division from Suvla and on 5 October Kitchener and Joffre agreed that each country would land 75,000 men at Salonika. But any lingering hope that they would be warmly received by the Greeks was dashed the next day when Venizelos resigned. Lloyd George insisted that the landing should proceed. 'There was', he insisted on 6 October, 'no comparison between going through Greece and the German passage through Belgium.' [25] It was a statement with which many Greeks might have disagreed.

The German–Austrian offensive against Serbia began on 6 October. The Bulgarians joined their allies three days later and all the Committee's plans were once again thrown into the melting pot. Lloyd George, Carson and Law wanted to proceed with a landing at Salonika and in the process perhaps save Serbia. Curzon and Crewe wanted to pursue the original French suggestion of an offensive along the Asiatic shore of the Straits and preserve British prestige in Muslim eyes by finally crushing the Turks. [26] The new CIGS, Sir Archibald Murray, who had been Sir John French's former CGS, did not support either plan. He believed that the allies would have to land ten divisions at Salonika to save Serbia. They could not arrive until January 1916 and by then Serbia would have been crushed and the days of Hamilton's force at Gallipoli would be numbered. France should therefore remain the destination for the bulk of the British army and Egypt would have to be defended along the Suez Canal.[27] But Kitchener, who shared Curzon's and Crewe's objections to evacuating the peninsula because evacuation 'would be the most disastrous event in the history of the Empire', forced Murray to alter his advice. He wanted to send eight divisions to Egypt, ostensibly as an imperial fire brigade but in reality because he hoped to use them on the peninsula, either in another attempt to advance or to make the existing position tenable in the face of German artillery reinforcements. Asquith grasped at this as a compromise and on 11 October the Dardanelles Committee agreed that as soon as the present offensive in France was ended the divisions would be sent from there to Egypt without prejudice to their final destination. Carson was disgusted at this decision, which seemed to leave Serbia in the lurch. Asquith tried to placate him by sacking Hamilton and replacing him by Sir Charles Monro, the commander of the Second Army in France, and ordering him to report immediately on whether Gallipoli should be abandoned. But this ploy failed. Carson resigned and returned to the back-benches where he quickly became one of the government's most dangerous critics.[28]

Asquith was not allowed to wait and see for long. On 12 October Delcassé, the French foreign minister, who opposed an expedition to Salonika because he thought that all of France's manpower should be concentrated on the Western front, resigned. Viviani's government survived a subsequent vote of confidence in the Chamber although about a hundred left-wing deputies abstained. The government in London interpreted the abstentions as evidence of a dangerous increase in war weariness in France and the spectre of Caillaux returning to power on a peace platform loomed large in their imaginations. They discovered that his wife had obtained 4m francs from the Germans to spread peace propaganda in France and that Caillaux thought that the French people would accept any reasonable terms the Germans offered them.[29] Viviani played on these British fears. On 17 October he sent Millerand to London to beg the British to send more troops to Salonika to protect the Salonika–Uskub railway, Serbia's main line of communication with the outside world, and to hint that if they did not the alliance might be in jeopardy. Faced by that threat the British agreed that the troops earmarked for Egypt would land at Salonika if, by the time they arrived, the Serbs were still fighting. As Crewe, who was deputizing for Asquith during a short illness, explained on 25 October, 'I can't pretend to judge, but I think it may be necessary even at some disadvantage, to send the division direct to Salonika, so as to keep the Entente well on its legs'.[30] By the end of October the military rationale for the expedition appeared to have evaporated when the Bulgarians isolated the Serbian army by cutting the Salonika-Uskub railway. But on 29 October Joffre, who had become a late convert to the Salonika operation when he realized that if it failed and Viviani fell his own position would be untenable, hurried to London to insist that the Anglo-French landing should continue. He made it clear that 'his own retention of the post of Commander-in-Chief of the French army, and even the permanence of the Alliance itself, might depend on the reply of the British Government'.[31] Under pressure from their ally the British gave in but they agreed to play only a strictly limited role. British troops were to guard Salonika and the southern end of the railway while Sarrail pushed northwards to try to re-open communications with the Serbs. If he failed they insisted that the whole force would be withdrawn.[32]

But in practice they had committed themselves to more than they knew. Joffre's trip had been too late to save Viviani. He was succeeded by Briand, who also held the office of foreign minister, and Millerand was replaced by General Galliéni. Briand had long been a supporter of opening a Balkan front. He saw the expansion of French influence as desirable in its own right because it would protect its Mediterranean interests from the Russians and Italians and facilitate its postwar economic recovery. Henceforth Sarrail was no mere general but the main agent of French policy in Greece. Although he might not be able to do very much to win the war, he might be able to do a great deal to ensure that France won the peace.[33] For the sake of preserving the Entente the British now found themselves forced to fight to secure French war aims in the Balkans in much the same way the Russians had dragged them into underwriting their claim to Constantinople.

On 28 October Monro's staff at Gallipoli told him that they would not be able to take the peninsula until the spring of 1916 and that in the meantime they would need 40,000 reinforcements in addition to the drafts necessary to bring their existing formations up to strength. All the corps commanders except Birdwood, who was worried about the impact evacuation would have on the Muslims of India and Egypt, favoured evacuation. But whilst the operations staff believed that it would lead to the loss of half of their men and two-thirds of their guns, some senior officers on the lines of communications believed that it could be done with few losses.[34] The prospects at Salonika looked little better. On 31 October the senior British officer, Sir Bryan Mahon, reported that the Serbs had been cut off from Salonika and that the allies would need twenty divisions and active Greek co-operation if they wanted to reach Nish.[35]

The longer the government in London prevaricated the more nervous the governments in Cairo and Delhi became that as British prestige dwindled the possibility of serious internal disturbances rose. At the end of August Maxwell intercepted a package of letters from the Senussi in

Libya to Muslim leaders all over India and Arabia calling on them to start a holy war against the British. Apart from the garrison along the Canal and the base troops of the MEF he had only four imperfectly trained battalions of British troops to use on internal security duties. Facing them were some 12 million Muslims 'the majority of whom do not love us'.[36] In India there were continued rumours of native disaffection and intelligence reports of German intrigues. 'Among those who, like myself, are in a position to know, there can be no doubt that the situation in India is slowly but surely deteriorating and, so long as the war lasts, is likely to continue to do so', wrote Hardinge on 10 September. 'The constant repetition of attacks on our frontier, the sulkiness of the Mahomedans, the plots hatched outside with ramifications in India, and the cases of sedition in native regiments, all tend to show steady deterioration.'[37]

It was against this background of the imminent collapse of the British position at Gallipoli, in Egypt and India and in the Balkans that the Dardanelles Committee's successor, the War Committee, took four important decisions. They agreed that the British would remain at Salonika because the allies demanded that they do so. They decided to evacuate Gallipoli, after much hesitation, because continued occupation of the narrow beach-heads would be impossible once German heavy artillery arrived. They decided to capture Baghdad as a way of buttressing their flagging prestige in the East. And finally they sanctioned the negotiations McMahon was conducting with Sharif Hussein of Mecca because they needed his political support as the guardian of the Holy Places of Mecca and Medina as a counterweight to the Turks' call for a holy war against the Entente.

The one bright spot in the Eastern theatre in the summer of 1915 seemed to be Mesopotamia. Hardinge was anxious to deal the Turks a really severe blow in Mesopotamia to ensure the loyalty of the Arabs to the British cause. In April Force D was reconstituted as an army corps and the cautious Barratt was replaced by Sir John Nixon, a cavalryman with 'a well earned reputation for dash'.[38] Nixon's exact mission was confused. On 24 March, without consulting either Hardinge or the India Office, Duff told him that his instructions were to retain complete control of the Basra *vilayet* and any neighbouring territory which might enhance its security. He was also to prepare plans for an eventual advance to Baghdad. Nixon thought that these orders implied an early advance. When he asked the Indian General Staff to clarify the meaning of occupying the Basra *vilayet* he was told that he was to occupy Amara to the north and Nasiriyeh to the south. However, Duff later claimed that these orders were not intended to 'drive him on' but were merely a precaution in case the government did decide to advance in the future.[39] For the next few months the impetus to push on in Mesopotamia came from Nixon, aided by the cautious support of the government of India and the reluctant acquiescence of the home government. The result was that Nixon was grudgingly permitted to advance but not given the reinforcements he requested. On 3 June Nixon's spearhead, Major-General Sir Charles Townshend's Sixth Division, occupied Amara while on 25 July Major-General Gorringe's Twelfth Division occupied Nasiriyeh.[40] Nixon next wanted to move further north because he believed that the Basra *vilayet* would not be really secure until he had occupied Kut. The town stood at the confluence of the rivers Tigris and Hai and a British force there would block any Turkish advance to either Amara or Nasiriyeh and stop any enemy attempt to reoccupy Basra. Hardinge and Duff, who were well-aware of the difficulty of providing Nixon with drafts and supplies, gave their agreement in the belief that once at Kut they would be able to economize on the Mesopotamian garrison. Chamberlain supported them and Townshend occupied the town on 29 September.[41]

But then a far bigger prize beckoned. The occupation of Baghdad would be a propaganda victory which would go far to offset the British failure to occupy Constantinople and by reasserting British prestige it might help to preserve peace in India. On 30 August Nixon asserted that with one division he could advance the hundred or so miles from Kut to Baghdad and with two divisions he would actually hold the city throughout the winter. Hardinge supported him on the understanding that two Indian brigades were sent from Egypt to Mesopotamia. (He later raised this to a complete division.) 'In view of German activities in Persia, increasing pressure on Afghanistan, and the aspect in the Balkans and the Dardanelles', he telegraphed to Chamberlain on 6 October, 'we hold that the capture of Baghdad would have such an effect in the Near East, and offers such important political and strategical advantages as to justify movement, but to do this at least an additional Division would be required.'[42] Opinion in London was divided. Barrow cautioned against a further advance unless Nixon was reinforced. Nixon's present force was too small and scattered and it would do British prestige no good at all if, after taking the city, the Turks forced them to evacuate it.[43] But the temptation to carry out a spectacular propaganda coup was very great. As Chamberlain informed Asquith on 4 October, 'If anything goes wrong in the Dardanelles or in Egypt, the situation in India would no doubt "become critical" to use Hardinge's words. Both he and the C in C in India complain that they have no reserve of strength'.[44] On 4 October the Cabinet established an interdepartmental committee to investigate the situation in India and Persia and to decide whether a further advance really was desirable.

Nixon was ready to take Baghdad on the understanding that another division and a cavalry regiment were on their way to Mesopotamia from France to enable him to hold it. His plan rested on a faulty assumption about the weaknesses of his opponents. He believed that the Turks were demoralized and already beaten and he refused to believe intelligence reports that large numbers of reinforcements were already on their way and brushed aside reports from Townshend that his men were exhausted and would be unable to carry a strong enemy position.[45] On 11 October the interdepartmental committee recommended in favour of taking the city provided that the reinforcements Nixon requested were dispatched. Chamberlain agreed and Curzon argued that the caputre of Baghdad would not only cut German communications with Persia and Afghanistan but also that 'The capture of this city would ring through the East and would cause such an impression that it would partially discount any failure at the Dardanelles'.[46] But Kitchener was not prepared to release more troops from France and so the War Committee once again remitted the question to the experts. The General Staff and Admiralty War Staff thought it was feasible to take Baghdad within the next few weeks but, in view of their estimate that 60,000 Turkish reinforcements were on their way to the city, it would be inadvisable to do so.[47] However, their advice was also ignored. The War Committee agreed that the occupation of Baghdad, even if it were followed by a forced evacuation, would give such a badly needed fillip to British prestige that it would be worthwhile. Occupation might be followed by a proclamation of an Arab state independent of the Turks centred on Baghdad. Nixon was warned that he must not expect immediate reinforcements but that he could advance if he thought his existing force was sufficient to take the city. Nothing had changed to make him alter his mind and he ordered a reluctant Townshend to begin his advance by 14 November.[48]

In the same way that the Indian government tried to reassert its prestige with a propaganda coup in Mesopotamia, the Egyptian government tried to do much the same in Arabia by winning over to the British cause Sharif Hussein of Mecca. A revolt against the Turks led by the Sharif was attractive to the governments in Cairo and Khartoum for four reasons. His territories stretched along the shore of the Red Sea, a waterway vital to Britain's imperial communications. The Sharif and his son Abdullah constituted a link between two groups within the Turkish empire who might rebel against Constantinople, a small group of Arab nationalist army officers in Beirut and Damascus and the semi-independent Arab chiefs of the interior of Arabia over whom the Turks had only the most tenuous control. The British administration in Cairo believed that an agreement might serve the longer term British interest of making Britain's Middle Eastern position more secure from its allies. Since the start of the war against Turkey they had been anxious to discover some way of ousting the French from Syria and Palestine at the end of the war. A British-sponsored Arab revolt might do just that. And, most important of all, as a descendant of the Prophet and the guardian of the Holy Places in Arabia, the Sharif could throw his considerable prestige into the scales to counter the call for a holy war against the Entente.[49] The driving force behind the negotiations, which began seriously in July, was Sir Reginald Wingate. On 18 October McMahon reported that the Sharif would join the British if they accepted him as the ruler of an independent Arabia. In return he agreed to govern with the aid of British advisers, to concede a greater degree of control to the British in the Basra *vilayet* and to make concessions to the French in the area of Aleppo–Damascus–Hama and Homs. Grey accepted these terms with the proviso that the British also required special concessions in the Baghdad *vilayet*. Arab 'independence', at least for the British, meant no more than independence from the Turks. Nicolson, for example, thought that the Arabs were no more than a number of warring tribes and that the notion of an Arab state under one ruler was 'a fantastic dream'.[50]

The McMahon–Hussein agreement was greeted with reservations in two quarters. Hardinge thought that the Sharif had no intention of fighting the Turks, that he merely wanted British gold, and that the agreement would mean that Mesopotamia would be handed over to a corrupt Arab government after the war.[51] And the French colonialists had no intention of being ousted quite so easily as Cairo and Khartoum hoped. In August 1915 Georges Picot, a leading French colonialist who had recently been posted to the London embassy, persuaded Cambon that it was high time that the French and the British defined their interests in the area. The French would not tolerate any infringement of their rights in Syria or Cilicia and the Foreign Office recognized that it would benefit them little if, in winning over the Sharif, they alienated the French.[52] They therefore had to try to square their agreement with the Sharif with the French. Picot was appointed as the French delegate to negotiate the boundaries of the French sphere of influence in the Middle East. He shared Hardinge's scepticism about the Sharif and did not take the British promises to him seriously. He defined the French sphere as stretching from the Egyptian frontier to Mosul.

Grey thought this was excessive and the first round of negotiations, led on the British side by Nicolson, ended in deadlock. Nicolson was then replaced by Sir Mark Sykes, an amateur orientalist and francophile who had just returned from Cairo and found it easier than Nicolson had to sympathize with French aspirations in Syria, and by February 1916 he had reached an agreement with Picot. The Sykes–Picot agreement illustrated the lingering suspicions Britain had of French and Russian postwar ambitions in the Middle East. France abandoned its claims to Syria south of Acre and the British abandoned their claims to establish a naval base at Alexandretta in favour of one at Haifa. Britain would be permitted to establish any form of government it chose in the Basra and Baghdad *vilayets*. An 'independent' Arab kingdom was to be established but it would be divided into spheres of interest. In the south and south east the British would have the exclusive right to appoint advisers to the Sharif while in the north and west the French would do so. France was to enjoy similar privileges along the Syrian coast to those enjoyed by the British at Basra and Baghdad but it was to be kept a safe distance from the Egyptian frontier by placing Palestine under international administration. Similarly the Russians were to be kept away from Mesopotamia by extending French domination from the Gulf of Alexandretta to Kurdistan and the Persian frontier. The Russians acceded to these terms in May 1916 when they were granted Turkish Armenia.[53]

These agreements marked a clear departure from Britain's prewar policy, reformulated by the de Bunsen Committee in June 1915, of upholding the integrity of the Turkish empire in Asia. They also created another obstacle to a separate peace with the Turks. In March and October 1915, it had been the Russians, determined to gain Constantinople, who had vetoed negotiations with Turkish dissidents for a separate peace.[54] But by December 1915 Sazonov appeared to have changed his mind and was not so ready to reject Turkish overtures outright. Armenian circles in Constantinople informed the Russians that Djemal Pasha might be willing to lead a revolution against the Committee of Union and Progress if the Entente would accept his terms. He was ready to give up Constantinople and to grant autonomy to Mesopotamia, Syria, Palestine, Arabia, Armenia and Kurdistan. In return he wanted the Entente to guarantee the integrity of Turkey in Asia and to accept him as Sultan. Sazonov believed that even if Djemal failed the attempt would still weaken the Turks. But this time, in an ironic reversal of roles, it was the British who stood in the way of this admittedly slender chance of a negotiated peace. As Nicolson insisted, Djemal's terms were unacceptable to the British in view of their promises to the Arabs and negotiations with the French. Once again, as in the case of the agreement reached with the Italians in April 1915, the process of winning a new ally, far from hastening an end to the war, threatened only to prolong it.[55]

On 4 November the Cabinet dispatched Kitchener to the eastern Mediterranean. Monro's telegram advising the evacuation of the Gallipoli peninsula had done nothing to settle the issue and ostensibly Kitchener was sent to report personally on the situation. But in reality feeling in the Cabinet had become so intense against him that Asquith had to remove him from the scene if only temporarily to allow tempers to cool. The next day Bonar Law and Lloyd George tried to pre-empt his report by insisting that preparations for evacuation should begin immediately. Sir Rennell Rodd, the British ambassador at Rome, had just reported that the Germans had opened direct communications through Serbia to Constantinople and they were afraid that it was now only a matter of time before Monro's troops were blasted off the peninsula.[56] Both ministers wanted to ship the Gallipoli garrison to Salonika. Although a force of 90,000 Bulgars now lay between Salonika and the Serbian army, and Sarrail's chances of reaching the Serbs had all but disappeared, they hoped that in the short term a large allied force at Salonika would pose such a threat to German communications with Constantinople that they would be afraid to commit large forces to attack Egypt. And in the longer term the Russians proposed to aid the Serbs by mounting a winter offensive in Galicia which would draw off enemy troops and Sarrail's force might then be sufficiently powerful to defeat the Bulgarians.[57]

A major allied offensive from Salonika presupposed that the Greeks were at least benevolently neutral. They were not and on 11 November they threatened to disarm and intern Sarrail's troops. The allies retaliated by threatening to blockade their ports. Grey recognized the absurdity of the allied position in Greece and on 14 November he wrote that

It seems to be comparatively easy to send ships, British and French, to summon the Greek Fleet to surrender; but if the summons falls flat are we really going to massacre the Greek Fleet in harbour, when the Greek government have done nothing worse than qualify their promise of benevolent neutrality by a statement that they ought under certain circumstances to intern and disarm Allied troops, and could not promise that under no circumstances would they do it?[58]

To have acted in such a manner would have done the allied cause untold damage. It would have handed the Germans a propaganda victory comparable in size to their own unprovoked invasion of Belgium, and it would have destroyed the Entente's already tenuous claim to be fighting for the rights of small nations. Fortunately a modicum of common sense prevailed. On 19 November, with reports that the Greeks had mobilized five complete corps and were digging-in around Salonika, the War Committee decided to inform the French that they wanted Sarrail to return to the city and prepare to re-embark.[59]

Before Kitchener arrived at Gallipoli on 10 November he was determined to order a landing in the Gulf of Xeros in conjunction with another naval attack up the Straits. A rapid inspection of the position convinced him that it was impracticable. But evacuation seemed to be equally dangerous. Waiting for him were Monro, McMahon, Maxwell and a memorandum from Sir Reginald Wingate. All expect the former stressed the likely political repercussions of evacuation in India and Egypt. Wingate's memorandum presented a grand allied plan of campaign involving landings at Alexandretta to cut the Turks' railway communications to Egypt and Mesopotamia, a further advance in Mesopotamia, an offensive from Egypt into Palestine and a Russian advance from the Caucasus to Trebizond. Those actually present preferred something a little less ambitious, the retention of Cape Helles, the evacuation of Suvla and Anzac and a landing at Ayas Bay in the Gulf of Iskanderun. It was this scheme which the government in London persisted in wrongly calling Kitchener's Alexandretta scheme.[60] But the French immediately vetoed any British operation in Syria and the War Committee knew that the position at Gallipoli depended on what happened in Greece.[61] Kitchener paid a brief visit to Greece and it left him in no doubt that the Greeks would not join the Entente. He therefore agreed that the Salonika operation would not prevent the Germans moving big guns and ammunition to Gallipoli and on 22 November he recommended to Asquith that while Helles ought to be held, the other beach-heads would have to be evacuated and Egypt would have to be defended along the Suez Canal.[62]

On 23 November the War Committee went one step further and recommended evacuating all three beaches. But when the final decision was remitted to the complete Cabinet, Curzon, Crewe, Lansdowne and Selborne forced another delay. The plans laid in Delhi and Cairo to support their flagging prestige if the peninsula was evacuated were already collapsing. On 16 November the Sharif of Mecca had made it plain that all the British had bought for the time being was his benevolent neutrality.[63] He had no intention of actually rebelling against the Turks until the allies' military position in the East was much more favourable. Townshend's advance on Baghdad had begun on 21 November but by 23 November news had reached London that he had been repulsed at Ctesiphon and was in retreat. By 3 December his men had halted in Kut where they were to remain besieged until they surrendered in April 1916.

The news of the Battle of Ctesiphon cast a pall of gloom over London and Delhi. Nixon reported that he would not be able to advance again until March 1916 and then only if he received reinforcements and sufficient drafts to bring his force up to its proper strength. Balfour believed that 'the effect of the action at Ctesiphon might be in its results comparable to the withdrawal from the Dardanelles and might carry away Persia'.[64] Curzon, the leader of the group in the government who opposed evacuation, bullied a reluctant Hankey into preparing a memorandum rehearsing the arguments against it. On 25 November the War Committee belatedly agreed to bring all units in India and Mesopotamia up to strength and to dispatch two more divisions to Basra as soon as possible.[65]

Kitchener returned to London on 30 November, depressed by what he had discovered and ready to add his voice in favour of evacuating Salonika and sending the troops there to defend the Suez Canal. Only Bonar Law and Lloyd George wanted to remain at Salonika in strength. To Lloyd George, evacuation meant the end of any possibility of forming a Balkan confederation and would condemn the allies to 'the loss of any opportunity of touching the Germans except across immensely defended positions'.[66] However, their colleagues wanted to follow Kitchener and stick to the letter of the agreement they had struck with the French on 29 October. Sarrail's attempt to relieve the Serbs had failed and they wanted his force to withdraw to Salonika. Once there, and provided the Greeks agreed to defend their own frontiers against the Central Powers, the Entente could re-embark their troops. If the Greeks refused to give this assurance the Entente would interpret their refusal as an act of war.[67]

On 4 December Briand and Asquith met at Calais and Asquith believed that he had carried the day. He was wrong. Bonar Law and Lloyd George had two immensely powerful allies in the shape of the French and Russian governments and the Cabinet was thrown into consternation when they discovered that both their allies not only insisted on remaining at Salonika but the French actually wanted to send more troops.[68] Shortly after the Calais conference the French learnt that Sarrail's troops had been attacked by the Bulgarians. There was immediate uproar in the Chamber as the left accused the government of leaving Sarrail in the lurch. Whatever the military reasons in favour of evacuation there was now a strong political reason in favour of remaining. On 6 December Bertie telegraphed that 'I think it quite likely that a withdrawal of Entente allies from Salonika under pressure from His Majesty's Government may cause fall of Briand's Cabinet. We would be considered by French public opinion to have left France in the lurch.'[69] The necessity of preserving harmonious relations with the allies was once again paramount. Bertie's telegram persuaded the War Committee to postpone their decision until they knew the recommendations of a major allied military conference at Chantilly which began on 6 December. That was tantamount to handing the whole decision not only about Salonika, but also Gallipoli and Egypt, over to the allies. The assembled generals accepted Joffre's advice that the allies should remain at Salonika, that they should evacuate Gallipoli and that the British should defend Egypt along the Suez Canal. On 7 December, after reports of blizzards on the peninsula which had caused over 16,000 casualties, the Cabinet finally agreed to evacuate Suvla and Anzac. On 9 December, as a result of the Chantilly conference, Grey and Kitchener were sent to France with *carte blanche* to settle the Salonika dispute. They reached a provisional agreement that the allied force would for the time being simply dig-in around Salonika and await developments. Kitchener believed that this decision saved the French government but it did nothing to bolster Britain's dwindling prestige in the Middle East. A passive policy at Salonika was not likely to stop the Germans if they really did intend to transport men and guns to Turkey to attack the British in Egypt and Mesopotamia. On 20 December Suvla and Anzac were successfully evacuated and three days later, after Birdwood had reported that the Turks had just begun to shell the beaches with newly-arrived Austrian 10 in. howitzers, the War Committee agreed to the evacuation of Helles.

That was successfully completed on 9 January 1916. Henceforth Egypt would have to be defended along its own doorstep and the Turks would be free to send troops to the Canal, the Caucasus or Baghdad.[70]

The Dardanelles campaign had been a dismal failure redeemed only by Italy's entry into the war in May. Much of the blame for this was subsequently laid at Grey's door. Christabel Pankhurst described Grey's Balkans diplomacy, and especially his inability to save Serbia, as a betrayal not only of an ally but of the British empire.[71] Her emotional response betrayed the lack of understanding of Balkan realities demonstrated by many of Grey's critics. They failed to recognize the strength of the competing national ambitions which had divided the Balkan states since before the war and they grossly overestimated Britain's ability to influence events on the mainland of Europe. The allied failure to carry the Dardanelles was only one factor, and probably not the most important, in determining the policy of the Balkan neutrals. Italy signed the Treaty of London in April 1915, just before Hamilton's first failure at Gallipoli, because the Russians were making headway against the Austrians in Galicia. Every major allied coup at the Dardanelles after April was preceded by a Russian defeat on land which meant that pro-Entente politicians in Greece, Romania and Bulgaria carried little conviction when they insisted that the Central Powers would lose the war. The Balkan states, with no naval tradition of their own, were unlikely to be impressed with offers of handfuls of allied troops or naval support or least of all by promises of future territorial gains when they saw the German army overrunning Russian Poland. The fall of Warsaw in August did at least as much as Hamilton's failure at Suvla Bay to keep Romania and Greece neutral. To the extent, therefore, that the British believed that the Dardanelles campaign or the dispatch of an expeditionary force to Salonika would create a Balkan confederation, they were the victims of wishful thinking.

Notes

1   PRO CAB 19/8, Mesopotamian Commission, Private correspondence between General Sir Beauchamp Duff and Earl Kitchener, Duff to Kitchener, 30 August and 25 September 1914; Kirke diary entry, 2 December 1914; Kirke mss; PRO 30/57/47/QQ/9, Wingate to Fitzgerald, 18 January 1915.
2   PRO 30/57/47/QQ/15, McMahon to Kitchener, 4 February 1915.
3   PRO 30/57/47/QQ/25, Maxwell to Kitchener, 24 June 1915; Maxwell to Kitchener, 6, 7, 23 May, 20 and 21 July and 7 August 1915, Hamilton mss, 5/17; Maxwell to Kitchener, 29 May 1915, Hamilton mss, 5/12.
4   PRO CAB 37/124/31, Hardinge to Cabinet, 16 February 1915.
5   PRO WO 106/887, Precis of correspondence, War Office to CGS, India, 16 January 1915, C-in-C India to War Office, 16 January 1915, Hardinge to

Crewe, 25, 26, 27, 30 January and 3 March 1915; PRO 800/375, Hardinge to Nicolson, 3 February 1915; PRO 30/57/69/WQ/10, Hardinge to India Office, 1 February 1915; T. G. Fraser, 'India in Anglo-Japanese relations during the First World War', *History*, vol. 63, no.209 (1978), p. 368; Sir A. Rumbold, *Watershed in British India, 1914–1922* (London: Athlone Press, 1979), p. 32; Lord Hardinge of Penshurst, *My Indian Years, 1910–1916* (London: John Murray, 1948), p. 116; Sir M. O'Dwyer, *India as I Knew it, 1885–1925* (London: Constable, 1925), pp. 200–6.

6   PRO FO 800/377, Hardinge to Nicolson, 1 March 1915.
7   PRO FO 800/377, McMahon to Nicolson, 8 March 1915.
8   PRO CAB 42/3/11, Chamberlain to Cabinet and enc., 27 July 1915.
9   Maxwell to Hamilton, 8 May 1915, Hamilton mss 5/12.
10 See, for example, Kitchener's comments at the War Council on 14 May 1915, PRO CAB 22/1, Minutes of the War Council, 14 May 1915, and PRO CAB 37/130/4, Chamberlain to Cabinet, 30 June 1915.
11 Callwell to Wilson, 13 July 1915, Wilson mss, 73/1/18; PRO FO 371/2503/121282, Picot to Foreign Office, 24 August 1915; PRO FO 800/378, Bax-Ironside to Nicolson, 9 June 1915.
12 Kirke to his wife, 9 August 1915, Kirke mss, vol. 1; French diary entries, 17, 20, 21, 22 August 1915, French mss, vol. M; Percy to Wilson, 4 September 1915, Wilson mss 73/1/19
13 Percy to Wilson, 23, 25, 28 September 1915, Wilson mss, 73/1/19; Elliot to Foreign Office, 6 September 1915, Lloyd George mss, D 19/9/1.
14 PRO CAB 19/33, Dardanelles Commission. Minutes of evidence, QQ. 22526–7 (Carson); Maxse to Percy, 17 July 1915 and Percy to Wilson, 28 July 1915, Wilson mss, 73/1/19; Bonar Law to Selborne, 7 July 1915, Bonar Law mss, 53/6/31.
15 PRO CAB 42/3/15, Minutes of the Dardanelles Committee, 19 August 1915.
16 ibid.
17 PRO CAB 42/3/17, Minutes of the Dardanelles Committee, 9 June 1915.
18 PRO FO 800/58, Nicolson to Grey and enc., 1 September 1915.
19 J. K. Tanenbaum, *General Maurice Sarrail, 1856–1929: The French Army and Left-Wing Politics* (Chapel Hill, NC: University of North Carolina Press, 1974), pp. 52–64; J. C. King, *Generals and Politicians: Conflict between France's High Command, Parliament and Government 1914–1918* (Berkeley, Calif.: University of California Press, 1951), pp. 36–79; D. Dutton, 'The Union Sacré and the French cabinet crisis of October 1915', *European Studies Review*, vol. 8, no. 4 (1978), pp. 411–17; M. M. Farrar, 'Politics versus patriotism: Alexandre Millerand as French minister of war', *French Historical Studies*, vol. 11, no. 4 (1979–80), pp. 589–95; PRO FO 800/58, Bertie to Grey, 3 and 5 August 1915; PRO FO 800/60, Bertie to Grey, 4 August 1915.
20 PRO CAB 42/3/23, Minutes of the Dardanelles Committee, 3 September 1915; PRO CAB 41/36/42 and 43, Asquith to H.M. the King, 3 and 10 September 1915; PRO CAB 28/1, Note of a conference held at the Terminus Hotel, Calais, on Saturday 11 September 1915.
21 K. J. Calder, *Britain and the Origins of New Europe 1914–1918* (Cambridge: Cambridge University Press, 1976), pp. 40–3; PRO CAB 19/29, Dardanelles Commission, Notes for evidence on the attempt to secure assistance by diplomatic efforts to help the position in the peninsula [n.d. but *c.* 1916]; PRO FO 800/379, Nicolson to Hardinge, 15 September 1915.
22 PRO CAB 42/3/28, Minutes of the Dardanelles Committee, 23 September 1915.
23 G. B. Leon, *Greece and the Great Powers, 1914–1917* (Thessaloniki: Institute

for Balkan Studies, 1974), pp. 207–24; PRO CAB 41/36/45, Asquith to H.M. the King, 23 September 1915; PRO CAB 37/134/30, Nicolson to Grey, 23 September 1915.

24 PRO CAB 42/3/28 and 30 and 33, Minutes of the Dardanelles Committee, 23, 24 and 29 September 1915.

25 PRO CAB 42/4/3, Minutes of the Dardanelles Committee and enc., 6 October 1915; K. Robbins, 'British diplomacy and Bulgaria, 1914–1915', *Slavonic and East European Studies Review*, vol. 49, no. 117 (1971), pp. 581–3.

26 PRO CAB 42/4/4, Minutes of the Dardanelles Committee, 7 October 1915; PRO CAB 19/33, Dardanelles Commission. Minutes of Evidence, Q. 21717 (Crewe).

27 PRO CAB 42/4/2, Murray, Appreciation by the General Staff of the actual and prospective military situation in the various theatres of war, 2 October 1915; PRO CAB 42/4/4, Murray, Appreciation by the General Staff of the Balkan and Dardanelles situation, 6 October 1915.

28 PRO CAB 42/4/6, Minutes of the Dardanelles Committee, 11 October 1915; PRO CAB 19/33, Dardanelles Commission. Minutes of evidence, QQ. 22523, 22540–2 (Carson); Carson to Asquith, 12 and 17 October 1915, Asquith mss, ff. 7–8, 15–16, 17–20, 34–7; Bonar Law to Asquith, 15 October 1915, Bonar Law mss, 53/6/44.

29 PRO FO 371/2505/155148, Rodd to Foreign Office, 21 October 1915; PRO FO 800/167, Bertie to Rodd, 21 October 1915; Lady Algernon Gordon Lennox (ed.), *The Diary of Lord Bertie of Thame, 1914–1918*, Vol. 1 (London: Hodder & Stoughton, 1924), p. 245.

30 PRO 30/57/69/WO/30, Crewe to Kitchener, 25 October 1915; Oliver, Viscount Esher (ed.), *Journals and Letters of Reginald, Viscount Esher*, Vol. 3 (London: Ivor Nicholson & Watson, 1934), pp. 266–9; Callwell to Robertson, 20 October 1915, Robertson mss, I/8/26.

31 PRO CAB 28/1, Notes of a Conference held at 4.30 p.m. on Friday October 29, 1915 at 10 Downing Street; Hankey diary entry, 29 October 1915, Hankey mss, 1/1.

32 PRO CAB 28/1, Memorandum by Lord Kitchener, 30 October 1915; Clive diary entry, 3 November 1915, Clive mss, II/2.

33 D. Dutton, 'The Balkan campaign and French war aims in the Great War', *English Historical Review*, vol. 94, no. 370 (1979), pp. 97–112.

34 R. R. James, *Gallipoli* (London: Pan, 1965/74), pp. 322–3; General Staff, Recommendation of the General Staff on the question of action to be taken at Gallipoli, November 1915, Robertson mss, I/9/28; Lt.-Gen. Sir George Macmunn, *Behind the Scenes in Many Wars. Being the Military Reminiscences of Lt.-Gen. Sir George Macmunn* (London: John Murray, 1930), pp. 169–70.

35 PRO WO 32/5122, Mahon, appreciation of the Military situation in Serbia, 31 October 1915.

36 Maxwell to Kitchener, 30 August 1915, Hamilton mss, 5/17; Maxwell to Hamilton, 24 September 1915, Hamilton mss, 5/12; see also PRO 30/57/47/QQ/42, McMahon to Fitzgerald, 5 October 1915; PRO 30/57/47/QQ/43, Graham to Fitzgerald, 7 October 1915.

37 PRO CAB 42/6/5, Chamberlain, The military situation in India, 7 December 1915 and enc., Hardinge to Chamberlain, 10 September 1915; PRO CAB 19/8, Mesopotamian Commission, Proceedings, QQ, 16457–9, 16531–2; Lord Hardinge, *My Indian Years*, pp. 126–7.

38 Maj. R. Evans. *A Brief Outline of the Campaign in Mesopotamia 1914–1918* (London: Sifton Praed, 1926), p. 26; PRO FO 800/377, Hardinge to Nicolson, 8 April 1915.

39 PRO CAB 19/8, Mesopotamian Commission. Proceedings, QQ. 15099 (Duff) 10827, 11477, 11492, and Statement by Sir J. Nixon, 14 November 1915; PRO WO 106/877, Duff to Nixon, 24 March 1915.

40 B. C. Busch, *Britain, India and the Arabs, 1914–1921* (Berkeley, Calif.: University of California Press, 1971), pp. 29–30.

41 PRO CAB 19/8, Mesopotamian Commission. Proceedings, Q. 11477 (Nixon); PRO WO 106/877, Hardinge to Chamberlain and Chamberlain to Hardinge, 27 July and 6 August 1915; J. D. Goold, 'Lord Hardinge and the Mesopotamian expedition and inquiry, 1914–1917', *Historical Journal*, vol. 19, no. 4 (1976), pp. 928–9; J. S. Galbraith, 'No man's child: the campaign in Mesopotamia, 1914–1916', *International History Review*, vol. 6, no. 3 (1984), p. 368.

42 PRO WO 106/877, Hardinge to Chamberlain, 6 October 1915; PRO FO 800/379, Hardinge to Nicolson, 23 September 1915; PRO CAB 42/4/12, Report of an inter-departmental Committee on the strategical situation in Mesopotamia, 16 October 1915; Hardinge to Chamberlain, 17 September 1915, Asquith mss, vol. 15, ff. 13–14.

43 PRO WO 106/877, Barrow to Chamberlain, 4 October 1915.

44 Chamberlain to Asquith, 4 October 1915, Asquith mss, vol. 28, ff. 210–11.

45 PRO CAB 19/8, Mesopotamian Commission. Proceedings QQ. 11499–500, 11516; PRO WO 106/877, Nixon to Duff and Chamberlain and Nixon to Chamberlain, 5 and 8 October 1915.

46 PRO CAB 42/4/9, Minutes of the Dardanelles Committee, 14 October 1915; PRO CAB 42/4/7, Chamberlain to Cabinet and enc., Copy of the conclusions of the Committee to consider the strategical situation in Mesopotamia, 11 October 1915.

47 The present and prospective situation in Syria and Mesopotamia: A paper prepared by the General Staff in consultation with the Admiralty War Staff, 19 October 1915, Robertson mss, I/9/12.

48 PRO CAB 42/4/15, Minutes of the Dardanelles Committee, 21 October 1915; Busch, *Britain, India*, p. 34; PRO WO 106/877, Chamberlain to Hardinge, 21 and 23 October 1915.

49 J. Nevakivi, *Britain, France and the Arab Middle East, 1914–1920* (London: Athlone Press, 1969), pp. 25–8; G. Troeller, 'Ibn Sa'ud and Sharif Husain: A comparison in importance in the early years of the First World War', *Historical Journal* vol. 14, no. 3 (1971), pp. 627–32; R. H. Lieshout, '"Keeping the better educated Moslems busy": Sir Reginald Wingate and the origins of the Husayn–McMahon correspondence', *Historical Journal*, vol. 27, no. 2 (1984), pp. 453–64; I. Friedman, *The Question of Palestine, 1914–1918: British–Jewish–Arab Relations* (London: Routledge & Kegan Paul, 1973), pp. 95–101; PRO 30/57/47/QQ/46, Storrs to Fitzgerald, 12 October 1915.

50 PRO FO 800/380, Nicolson to Hardinge, 11 November 1915; PRO FO 371/2486/34982, McMahon to Grey, 18 October 1915 and Grey to McMahon, 20 October 1915.

51 PRO FO 800/379, Hadinge to Nicolson, 12 November 1915; PRO FO 800/380, Hardinge to Nicolson, 9 December 1915.

52 C. M. Andrew and A. S. Kanya-Forstner, *France Overseas. The Great War and the Climax of French Imperial Expansion* (London: Thames & Hudson, 1981), pp. 75–7.

53 PRO CAB 37/142/6, Nicolson, Arab Question, 2 February 1916; PRO CAB 37/142/10, Arab Question, 4 February 1916; PRO CAB 42/8/1, Minutes of the War Committee, 3 February 1916; Andrew and Kanya-Forstner, *The Climax*, pp. 90–7; V. H. Rothwell, *British War Aims and Peace Diplomacy,*

1914–1918 (Oxford: Clarendon Press, 1971), pp. 29–30; R. Adelson, *Mark Sykes: Portrait of an Amateur* (London: Cape, 1975), pp. 199–202.

54   PRO FO 371/2490/97308, Hamilton to the secretary, War Office, 3 July 1915 and minutes by Harold and Arthur Nicolson and Clerk, and (151514), Elliot to Foreign Office, 15 October 1915 (157132), Elliot to Foreign Office, 24 October 1915, minute by Clerk, 25 October 1915 (161328), Elliot to Grey, 30 October 1915; McMahon to FO, 6 September 1915 and minutes by Clerk, Nicolson and Crewe; PRO FO 800/75, Grey to Buchanan, 16 November 1915 and Buchanan to Grey, 17 November 1915.

55   PRO FO 800/380, Nicolson to Hardinge, 30 December 1915; PRO FO 800/381, Nicolson to Hardinge, 12 January 1916; PRO CAB 37/139/63, Grey to Cabinet, 29 December 1915; PRO CAB 37/139/69, Grey to Buchanan, 30 December 1915.

56   PRO CAB 42/5/3, Minutes of the War Committee, 5 November 1915; PRO CAB 37/137/6, Bonar Law to Asquith, 5 November 1915; Bonar Law to Asquith, 8 November 1915, Bonar Law mss, 53/6/47; Chamberlain to Bonar Law, 7 November 1915; Bonar Law mss, 117/1/22 and 23; Asquith to Bonar Law, 5 November 1915, Bonar Law mss, 51/5/7; Crewe to Bonar Law, 5 November 1915, Bonar Law mss, 51/5/8.

57   PRO CAB 42/5/4 and /8, Minutes of the War Committee, 6 and 12 November 1915; PRO CAB 17/180, Best line of operations for the Russian forces now assembled in Bessarabia, 10 November 1915.

58   PRO FO 800/88, Grey to Balfour, 14 November 1915.

59   PRO CAB 42/5/8, Minutes of the War Committee, 12 November 1915; PRO FO 800/63, Elliot to Grey, 6, 12, 13, 14 and 18 November 1915; PRO CAB 41/36/51, Asquith to H.M. the King, 11 November 1915.

60   PRO 30/57/47/QQ/58, Wingate, Note on the Near East, November 1915; PRO 30/57/66, Lord Kitchener's report to the Cabinet on his eastern Mediterranean mission in November 1915, 2 December 1915; G. H. Cassar, *Kitchener: Architect of Victory* (London: William Kimber, 1977), pp. 421–2; Field Marshal Lord Birdwood, *Khaki and Gown: An Autobiography* (London: Ward Lock, 1941), pp. 279–80.

61   PRO CAB 42/5/14, Minutes of the War Committee, 16 November 1915.

62   Kitchener to Asquith, 22 November 1915, Robertson mss, I/9/28.

63   PRO CAB 42/5/20, Minutes of the War Committee, 23 November 1915; PRO CAB 41/36/52, Asquith to H.M. the King, 24 November 1915; PRO CAB 37/137/36, Balfour, Gallipoli, 19 November 1915; C. J. Lowe and M. L. Dockrill, *The Mirage of Power. British Foreign Policy, 1914–1922* Vol. 2 (London: Routledge & Kegan Paul, 1972), p. 216.

64   PRO CAB 37/138/16, Nixon to CIGS, 26 November 1915; PRO FO 800/380, Hardinge to Nicolson and Nicolson to Hardinge, 25 November 1915; Hankey diary entry, 24 November 1915, Hankey mss, 1/1.

65   Hankey diary entries, 27 November 1915, Hankey mss, 1/1; PRO CAB 42/5/22, Minutes of the War Committee, 25 November 1915, PRO CAB 42/5/25, Hankey, The future military policy at the Dardanelles, 29 November 1915.

66   PRO CAB 42/6/1, Minutes of the War Committee, 1 December 1915; Bonar Law to H. Wilson, 22 November 1915, Bonar Law mss, 53/6/50, 22 November 1915.

67   PRO CAB 42/6/1, Minutes of the War Committee, 1 December 1915.

68   PRO CAB 42/6/2, Minutes of the War Committee, 2 December 1915; PRO CAB 41/36/53, Asquith to H.M. the King, 3 December 1915; PRO CAB 37/139/10, Grey to Bertie, 3 December 1915; PRO 30/57/66, Grey to

Asquith, *c.* 3 December 1915; PRO CAB 42/6/6, Benckendorff to Grey, 7 December 1915; K. Neilson, *Strategy and Supply: The Anglo-Russian Alliance, 1914–1917* (London: Allen & Unwin, 1984), pp. 120–2; D. J. Dutton, 'The Calais conference of December 1915', *Historical Journal*, vol. 21, no. 1 (1978), pp. 143–8.

69   PRO FO 371/2278/185903, Bertie to FO, 6 December 1915; PRO CAB 42/6/4, Minutes of the War Committee, 6 December 1915 and Grey to Cabinet, 6 December 1915; PRO CAB 37/139/15, Notes on the Anglo-French conference at Calais, 4 December 1915; D. J. Dutton, 'The Calais conference', pp. 149–53.

70   PRO CAB 42/6/6, /7, /8 and /13, Minutes of the War Committee, 8, 13, 15, and 23 December 1915; PRO 30/57/64, Birdwood to Kitchener, 27 November, 2 and 20 December 1915 and 9 January 1916; PRO CAB 37/139/24, Conference between Sir E. Grey and Lord Kitchener and M. Briand and General Galliéni, 9 and 11 December 1915; PRO CAB 41/36/54 and /55, Asquith to H.M. the King, 8 and 15 December 1915; PRO CAB 37/139/12, Bonar Law, Memorandum, 4 December 1915; PRO WO 106/391, Dossier de la conference entre les representatives des Armées Alliées tenus à Chantilly les 6, 7, et 8 December 1915; James, *Gallipoli*, pp. 333–47.

71   Christabel Pankhurst to Bonar Law, 18 Decembre 1915, Bonar Law mss, 52/1/56.

9

Britain and the Development of the Entente's Policies in the Winter of 1915–16

SINCE AUGUST 1914 Kitchener's war policy had been based on the assumption that the war would reach its climax at the beginning of 1917. He hoped that between 1914 and 1916 the German, Austrian, French and Russian armies would fight each other to a stalemate in a series of costly battles of attrition. Britain would supply its allies with money and munitions and endeavour to induce neutral states to join the Entente. But its direct military commitment would be limited to taking over more of the line in France to free Joffre's troops for more wearing-down operations. By 1917 Britain would be the only belligerent with a large reserve of fully-equipped and trained manpower and the New Armies would be able to win the war for the Entente and allow Britain to impose its own peace terms on allies and enemies alike. Some of Kitchener's colleagues, notably Lloyd George, had little patience with his policies of wait and prepare. Kitchener himself was partly to blame for their impatience because he persistently refused to take them more fully into his confidence. Indeed in January 1915 he deliberately raised false hopes that the war would end by the autumn of 1915 in order to stop them from interfering with his preparations. Throughout most of 1915 he tried hard not to deviate from his intentions and until the autumn he carried most of the Cabinet with him. On 22 July 1915, after a discussion in the Cabinet about the strength of the enemy forces in the field, Asquith wrote that the 'ap[proximate] crux of the war' would come in December 1916. Kitchener expected that the British would have seventy divisions in the field from April 1916 but they would not be fully equipped with heavy artillery until December.[1]

However, the Russian débâcle, Bulgaria's entry into the war, the collapse of Serbia, the new threat posed to their Eastern empire by the defeats at Gallipoli and Kut, the possible regeneration of Turkey under German tutelage, the failure of the Western allies' autumn offensive to redress the situation, and growing signs of war weariness among the allies, meant that the British could no longer stand so far aloof from the continental land war until the end of 1916. Between December 1915 and April 1916 the government conducted a protracted and agonized debate in which they tried to balance the risks of a complete continental commitment against those of alienating the allies by continuing to wage the war on limited liability principles. Although Kitchener and the conscriptionists were aware that the process of attrition had not sufficiently worn down the German army so that it still remained a formidable force, and that the British army would not be fully equipped until the end of 1916, they none the less argued for its premature deployment in the joint allied offensive of 1916. They feared that if the British held back, their allies might desert them and make peace. The anti-conscriptionists argued that the price and the risks involved in this policy were too high. They pointed out that Kitchener and Robertson could offer no guarantees that the Entente would be able to inflict such a crushing military defeat on the Germans that they would be forced to sue for peace by the end of 1916. The only result of adopting their policies might be to bankrupt Britain by the end of the year. By April 1916 the conscriptionists had won. Bankruptcy seemed preferable to defeat.

As defeat followed defeat in the autumn of 1915, pressure to transform the machinery of government grew. French blamed his difficulties on Kitchener, and like Haig and Robertson, wanted his powers curbed by the establishment of a more powerful General Staff at the War Office. The critics found increasing support inside the Cabinet where dissatisfaction not only with Kitchener but also with the actual way the Cabinet conducted its own business was increasing. The Cabinet and the Dardanelles Committee were criticized for being too big, meeting too infrequently and lacking a proper policy. In September both Cecil and Carson wanted to improve the situation by establishing a small War Cabinet sitting daily and empowered to take all important decisions. Cecil's suggestion included a committee of six, presided over by Balfour but excluding Asquith, ostensibly on the grounds that as Prime Minister he would be too busy to attend its daily meetings.[2] But as the experience of the ensuing months was to illustrate, no amount of tinkering with committee structures was enough. The crux of the problem was that the government was fundamentally divided over a number of issues, most notably compulsory military service, Gallipoli and Salonika. The plethora of new committees which were spawned in the autumn and winter of 1915–16 gave ample scope for policital infighting and far from hastening important decisions they only delayed them. The only way

Asquith could have expedited matters would have been to sack the dissenters, but that was something which he shrank from doing for the very good reason that it would have destroyed his government.[3]

The first round of changes began on 25 September when Sir Archibald Murray replaced Sir James Wolfe Murray as CIGS. Sir James was described by a subordinate as being incapable of 'keeping his end up with K[itchener] or indeed anybody outside the W.O.'[4] On 4 October the Dardanelles Committee was superceded by the War Committee, although the change was in some respects only one of title. On 14 October Hamilton was recalled and replaced by Sir Charles Monro. Criticisms continued and on 21 October his colleagues took advantage of the Prime Minister's temporary absence from the Cabinet due to illness to demand a smaller and more effective War Committee.[5] Asquith was not averse to some changes. He considered that Kitchener was on the verge of a nervous breakdown and even day-dreamed about replacing the Cabinet with a dictatorship. Almost the whole Cabinet wanted to remove Kitchener but Asquith knew that to do so would rock his government to its foundations. Although Kitchener no longer had the confidence of his colleagues he was still held in awe by the public.[6] Asquith, therefore, forged another compromise. He established a new and smaller War Committee consisting of himself, Balfour, McKenna, Lloyd George and Bonar Law. Churchill, who was excluded from the government's new inner sanctum, resigned. Kitchener was removed from the scene by dispatching him on a personal mission to the Mediterranean and Asquith himself took over the War Office.[7]

On 2 October the new CIGS presented the Dardanelles Committee with the clearly defined policy his predecessor's critics had demanded. He warned against any hasty involvement in the Balkans. The poor state of the Nish–Salonika railway made it most unlikely that any British help would reach the Serbs before the Central Powers had crushed them. He was aware that the fall of Serbia would mean that the Germans would be free to rejuvenate Turkey and then threaten Egypt directly. But he argued that it would be wrong to concentrate too many troops in the East. The allies' main objective should be the defeat of the German army, the mainstay of the enemy alliance, and the British could only do that in the West. Therefore the government should avoid sending more than the absolutely bare minimum of troops to the East. The Serbs would have to be sacrificed and Egypt should be protected along the Canal line, not in the Balkans or at Gallipoli. All available divisions other than those absolutely necessary to protect Egypt should be sent to France. Murray was, in the words of one authority, 'the first "Western Front" CIGS'.[8]

But Murray was little better than Wolfe Murray in 'keeping his end up' with Kitchener. Murray privately opposed Kitchener's plan to send eight divisions to Egypt to act as a central reserve in the East but caved in when

Kitchener applied pressure to him. This brought down upon his head the wrath not only of his own subordinate General Staff directors, who mounted a campaign of passive resistance to sending more men to the eastern Mediterranean, but also of Haig and Robertson.[9] They did not take seriously the possibility that a regenerated Turkey would decisively tip the military scales in favour of the Central Powers and anyway believed that such a process would take years not months. 'We will win this war by killing and beating the Germans, not by killing Bulgarians or Turks', Haig wrote on 15 October.[10] Robertson had a more realistic grasp of Balkan politics than most ministers. Between 1901–1904 he had been head of the Foreign Intelligence section of the Directorate of Mobilization and Intelligence and later, between 1905 and 1907, held the same job under the reorganized Directorate of Military Operations. In this capacity he was responsible for collecting intelligence material about the Balkans and he had actually travelled throughout the region in the autumn of 1906. He brushed aside the chimera of a Balkan league. 'Everybody who knows anything about the history of the Balkans is of this opinion. The Balkan States will never, as a whole, be on Germany's side or on the side of any other Great Power, and Germany will never be so foolish as to make her main effort there', he wrote to Murray on 21 October.[11] In the East he wanted to evacuate Gallipoli voluntarily rather than wait to be driven from the peninsula. Only the minimum necessary number of troops should be stationed in Egypt to defend the Suez Canal and he countenanced the capture of Baghdad only if it could be done by Indian troops who had proved to be unsuitable for operations in France.[12]

As Robertson demonstrated in October and November 1915 when he was summoned to London to advise the government he was not the short-sighted 'Westerner' of popular historiography whose strategic myopia would not allow him to see beyond the Western front. Like Kitchener and most of his political colleagues he realized that Britain was fighting the war as part of a coalition. He continually argued that the allies had to adopt a single alliance plan and that the British had to secure a greater measure of control over the alliance. He recognized that hitherto Britain had been the junior military partner but that in 1916 it would be the only ally who had fresh reserves of men and sufficient munitions to equip them.[13] He was less fearful for the solidarity of the alliance than some politicians, especially over the question of Salonika. 'After all', he wrote to Callwell on 23 October, 'the French have a certain interest in this war and we should guard against having our hands forced by semi-threats held out against us by Millerand or any other French politician.'[14] He was also very suspicious of French imperial ambitions in the region. Robertson was a 'Westerner' only in the sense that he believed that Britain could make its most effective contribution to the alliance by concentrating its resources in France. He was a committed supporter of continuing the naval blockade, not because he thought that it alone would be the decisive instrument which would defeat the Central Powers but because anything which added to their difficulties was to be applauded. Like Kitchener he disbelieved in the possibility of breaking the German line in the West and maintained that the Germans would only be defeated when their man-power had been exhausted by the slow process of attrition.[15] Robertson argued that victory for the Entente would not depend on the outcome of any single battle but on the cumulative impact of the national efforts of each of the allies and that each of them had to mobilize all of their national resources behind their joint war effort.[16]

In the autumn of 1915 British intelligence estimates of Germany's likely policy in 1916 were confused. Like the French they received several reports that the Germans might oblige the allies by themselves attacking in the West either towards Paris or at Verdun. Between September and December the Germans moved sixteen and a half divisions from the Eastern to the Western fronts. But until mid-February 1916 these reports were largely discounted because they ran counter to the Western allies' greatest fear, namely that having inflicted such a severe defeat on the Russians in 1915 the Germans might concentrate most of their resources in the East to finish off Russia in the spring of 1916.[17] On 15 November Robertson therefore counselled that it would be dangerous to do nothing except wait for the Germans to attack. He advised that in 1916 the allies should harness all their resources in order to mount a series of co-ordinated offensives in the three principal theatres, France, Italy and Russia, timed so as to offset the Germans' advantage of possessing interior lines of communications.[18]

Asquith's confidence in Sir John French had been declining throughout the summer, and the public row started by the publication of his dispatch after the Battle of Loos was the final straw. On 25 November Esher was sent to France to demand French's resignation and Haig succeeded to the command of the BEF on 19 December.[19] Kitchener refused to remain in exile in Egypt and so Asquith was compelled to find a way of permanently circumventing his control of strategy. He asked Robertson to become CIGS and promised him something Murray had never enjoyed, control over the operational conduct of the war. On 5 December Robertson spelt out what he thought this should mean in a document more like a draft treaty between two sovereign powers than a memorandum a military subordinate might properly send to a Secretary of State. He insisted that the War Committee should be the supreme directing authority able to formulate policy and that it should receive advice about military strategy only from the CIGS. All operational directives were to be signed by CIGS under the War Committee's authority and not by the Secretary of State for War. Kitchener was to confine himself to matters concerned with the raising and equipping of the army. Kitchener's initial reaction was to resign but Asquith and Robertson dissuaded him. He remained at the War Office and promised Robertson his support in the War Committee. He kept his word and the two men worked amicably together until Kitchener's death in June 1916.[20] Murray, initially furious at being superceded by Robertson for the second time in less than a year, was fobbed off with a command in Egypt.[21]

Other changes soon followed to strengthen the General Staff at the War Office. Robertson denuded GHQ of several experienced heads of department. MacDonogh came to London as the head of the General Staff's new directorate of military intelligence, which was now separated from the directorate of military operations. Callwell was replaced as DMO by the erstwhile head of the operations branch at GHQ, Major-General Frederick Maurice. Haig's new heads of department at GHQ were younger and less experienced officers. Haig was refused his first choice as chief of staff and had to make do with Sir Launcelot Kiggell, whom Robertson believed lacked the strength of character for the job.[22] MacDonogh's replacement as head of intelligence at GHQ was Brigadier-General John Charteris, Haig's former head of intelligence in the First Army, a highly intelligent but over-sanguine officer who, like some other senior intelligence officers, was apt to overestimate the rate at which German manpower was being exhausted.[23]

Robertson believed that war should be conducted by one man with one plan and initially it appeared that he might have his way.[24] But in fact his accession to the office of CIGS marked less of sharp break with the past than might be supposed. His preferred policy of attrition differed but little from that favoured by Kitchener and that was one reason why they were able to work together so successfully for the remainder of Kitchener's life. Furthermore, Robertson's ability to make policy was circumscribed by the exigencies of foreign and domestic politics. As Robertson himself was the first to admit, British military policy had to be co-ordinated with the allies and, although he sometimes disliked making them, compromises and concessions to their wishes were unavoidable. The need to harmonize British policy with the allies was forcibly extolled by Grey and his officials. They continued to monitor German peace feelers to the allies and to report any shifts in the latter's political constellations which might be detrimental to the alliance. Although the reputation of Grey and the Foreign Office may have been tarnished by their failures in the Balkans they still retained sufficient influence within the government to quash any of Robertson's policies which seriously threatened to undermine the cohesion of the alliance. And finally, where military policy touched upon domestic politics, as it did over the question of conscription, Robertson was bound to encounter opposition from some of his political colleagues.

A series of allied conferences were held in November and December

1915 which went some way to ensuring that allied policy in 1916 would be better co-ordinated than it had been in 1915. The first priority was to ensure that the allies were better supplied with weapons and munitions than they had been in 1915. The Russians were rapidly losing patience with the inability of the British to provide them with the munitions they had promised and in the autumn they clamoured for large numbers of new rifles. But it was now apparent that there was a limit to what the British could supply. They could not equip the Russians and their own New Armies simultaneously and the War Office was reluctant to meet the Russian demands before their own needs had been fulfilled.[25] An allied munitions conference met in London between 25 November and 1 December. The Russian demands were so large that they have rightly been described by one commentator as 'outrageous.' There was a limit to allied co-operation. Lloyd George was well aware that his own political reputation rested on whether or not he could equip the British army successfully and he had no intention of siphoning-off huge quantities of equipment to send to Russia before Haig had what he wanted. The result was a small victory for Robertson. The BEF's needs were placed before those of the allies.[26]

From 6 to 8 December allied military representatives met at Chantilly to concert their plans for 1916. The British were represented by Sir John French, Murray, Robertson and Henry Wilson. The assembled allied generals assumed that the Central Powers would not sue for peace until the German army had been defeated and they believed that the Germans had enough men to maintain their army at its present size and with its present rate of wastage until August 1916. They agreed to continue the policy of attrition but Joffre insisted that France could no longer conduct the wearing-out operations in the West. It had reached the limit of its manpower reserves and so the British and Italians, both of whom had not yet deployed their full manpower resources, would have to carry a greater share of the burden. The Russians would also have to play their part but their ability to do so would be limited unless the other allies supplied it with munitions. The assembled generals agreed that their proper policy would be for the Italians, British and Russians to mount a series of preliminary wearing-down operations in which the French would play little part so that they could husband their manpower. These would be followed by a co-ordinated offensive on the Eastern, Western and Italian fronts by all four allies designed to crush Germany and Austria–Hungary by the end of the year. They also recommended that to enable the British to concentrate their main efforts in the West, Gallipoli should be evacuated and Egypt held with the minimum number of troops. But, to Robertson's disgust and despite Murray's objections, the allies insisted that allied troops remain at Salonika. The French claimed that it was the cheapest and easiest way of checking German imperial ambitions in the East.[27]

Robertson saw a more sinister reason behind their insistence on remaining in Greece. He was afraid that they were becoming, as he wrote to Murray on 10 February 1916, 'a little wobbly' and searching for the chimera of an easy end to the war.[28] Like many other members of the decision-making elite, Robertson had a low opinion of some of Britain's allies. He had learnt to see the Russians and French as rivals to Britain's imperial position long before the Germans had emerged as a separate threat. The war had done nothing to make him regard any of the allies more highly. Japan had already got what it wanted from the war, namely Tsingtau. The Italians' commitment to the common effort would remain in doubt for as long as Italy refrained from declaring war on Germany. Furthermore, 'France is apt to be swayed more by emotion and sentiment than by cool judgement and common sense, and in Russia the greed and self-interest of the Bureaucracy clog the wheels of the machinery of Government'.[29] Robertson wanted to terminate the war in the East by making a separate peace with Turkey and Bulgaria. This would enable the allies to concentrate their resources against Germany. In February 1916 he suggested to the War Committee that not only should the Russians be persuaded to abandon their claim to Constantinople so that the Entente could make peace with Turkey but that rumours which had been current since December that Bulgaria, having occupied Macedonia, might be ready to negotiate, should be pursued vigorously.[30]

Robertson's recipe of diplomacy by arm-twisting met a frosty response from senior members of the Foreign Office. They were afraid that the alliance might not withstand the rough handling Robertson prescribed. At the end of October 1915, as the Serbian campaign was approaching a victorious climax, the German Chancellor, Bethmann-Hollweg, toyed with the idea of calling Germany's enemies to a peace conference in the hope that it would weaken the Entente by encouraging those groups in the allied countries anxious for an early negotiated peace. Nothing came of it but throughout late 1915 the Germans intensified their efforts to detach one or more of the allies from the Entente. In November 1915 they tested the Belgians' resolve by beginning the first of four conversations with representatives of King Albert in neutral Zurich. Albert was worried that an Anglo-French offensive to liberate his country might simply reduce it to a pile of rubble. The German terms, which fell only just short of outright annexation, were not particularly tempting but when the British heard about the talks they were alarmed. In August 1915 Grey had informed the Belgian government that the full restoration of Belgium's independence would be an essential British condition when the time came to discuss peace terms. If the Belgians accepted the German terms the Germans would not only gain permanent control of the Channel coast but they would also have removed the ostensible reason why Britain was at war in the first place. In February 1916 Haig and Curzon, a personal friend of King Albert, were sent to reassure him that allied plans for 1916 would not devastate his country. The British, French and Russians tried to put a stop to the secret talks by publicly signing the declaration of Sainte Adresse with the Belgians, promising to continue the war until Belgium's political and economic independence had been restored and it had been indemnified for its losses. They did not entirely succeed. Albert hinted to the Germans that if the forthcoming allied offensive failed he might again be willing to talk.[31]

At the end of August 1915 Italy declared war on Turkey but refused to do so against Germany. Italian hopes for swift victories had evaporated by the autumn of 1915 and Rodd reported that the Giolittian anti-war party was gaining support in northern Italy. In January 1916 the Italian C.-in-C. General Cadorna, had to issue a proclamation against defeatism in the army. Salandra's government, with its precarious control over parliament dared not risk its popularity by adding still further to Italy's enemies especially as many Italians were convinced that Germany would win the war.[32] It was against this background of growing neutralism and defeatism in Italy that, in late October, British diplomats in Switzerland, Athens and Rome began to report rumours that the Germans and the Pope were trying to bring about a compromise peace between Austria and Italy.[33] Nothing concrete emerged from these rumours except that they underlined the importance of keeping Salandra in office lest he be replaced by someone more willing to listen to German overtures. As one of MacDonogh's agents in Italy reported to the Cabinet in February 1916, 'As long as the Government can control the popular sentiment, Italy will stand with us, but if it gets out of hand – for example, after a defeat – or if the people get tired of the war, especially in winter, then the same thing will happen as after the battle of Adua in Abyssinia'.[34] Asquith was sufficiently concerned about the state of Italian morale to make a special trip to Rome in April 1916.

In the case of France the Germans channelled funds through Switzerland, to support the defeatist propaganda of Georges Duval's *Bonnet Rouge* and made tentative appeals to French diplomats and businessmen. In December 1915, for example, Cambon told Nicolson that a French industrialist in Moscow had been approached by intermediaries acting on behalf of several German industrialists in Sweden who told the Frenchman that France could have peace on apparently generous terms. Briand rejected such proposals out of hand, insisting that he regarded the very word peace as seditious and Bertie reported that the vast majority of Frenchmen were willing to continue the war until Prussian militarism had been destroyed and the Germans driven from occupied France.[35] But the fact could not be ignored that British commercial policy and Britain's tardiness in participating fully in the land war in France had caused some resentment.[36] And there remained the latent threat posed by Caillaux who, according to Bertie, saw himself as a latter-day Napoleon, hoping for peace with Germany so that together they might turn on Britain. The Salonika episode had already demonstrated the fragility of French parliamentary politics and Bertie believed that Caillaux controlled about 150 deputies in the Chamber, not enough to make himself President of the Council but perhaps sufficient to eject the present government.[37]

Even in Japan, the member of the Entente least touched by the war, there were indications of dissatisfaction with the alliance. In November 1915 the Japanese popular press demanded that Britain should recognize Japan's supremacy in China, abandon its claim to a sphere of influence in the Yangtze valley and remove all barriers to Japanese commerce in India and the Pacific. Sir Conyngham Greene, the British ambassador in Tokyo, believed that German money was behind the campaign and the Foreign Office noted several rumours of an imminent agreement between Germany and Japan. Cecil wanted to confront the Japanese and ask them to clarify their policy but Grey was more cautious. The Admiralty wanted increased Japanese naval assistance and Grey recognized that 'if we had not made it clear that we should not bar Japan's expansion of interests in the Far East it would have been clearly to Japan's advantage to throw in her lot with Germany'.[38]

But the most disquieting news came from Russia. During the summer of 1915 it appeared to be enjoying a period of liberal rule. Many of the reactionary ministers who had governed the country had been dismissed. But the military situation continued to deteriorate and at the end of August Sazonov predicted that the Germans might be in Petrograd within two months. The Russians held the Western allies at least partly responsible for their plight. They had failed to meet their promises to deliver guns and shells and they had failed to attack to draw the Germans westwards until it was too late. The tsar sacked the pro-liberal Grand Duke Nicholas and in September assumed personal command of the army. It was a foolish move because henceforth he would be blamed for any further defeats. He then prorogued the Duma and in October he began to purge some of the more liberal ministers from his Cabinet and replace them with known reactionaries.[39]

This caused disquiet among British observers. The Progressive bloc in the Duma believed that the Grand Duke had been sacked because the empress hated him and that a 'Black bloc', anxious to make a separate peace, now surrounded the tsar.[40] British diplomats were divided in their reaction to these stories. Bertie feared that the court wanted peace but Nicolson believed that they would not dare to make overtures because they knew that to do so would start a revolution. Nicolson was torn between believing that Russian patriotism was so powerful that there could not be a revolution and fear that discontent with the regime was so rife that the country was ripe for one. Lloyd George's comment was succinct. 'Russia done for.'[41] The Foreign Office knew that the peace overtures the Germans had made to Russia in January and July 1915 had been rejected.[42] But with the increasing influence of the pro-Germans there was a growing possibility that future German overtures might not be so brusquely rebuffed. The Germans certainly thought that more efforts were worth making. Count Fredericks, the minister of the imperial court, was approached by his opposite number at Berlin with a suggestion that it was time for them both to bring about a *rapprochement* between their two sovereigns. A similar offer was made to a former lady-in-waiting at the Russian court by the Grand Duke of Hesse and by the German foreign minister. The Germans tried to make their proposals more attractive by hinting that the British had already approached them.[43] As soon as he heard this Crewe, who was again deputizing for Grey, told Buchanan to inform Sazonov that this was another attempt to divide the Entente and that 'Closest unity between us is therefore essential'.[44]

Robertson's proposals for a negotiated peace with Turkey and Bulgaria therefore fell on stony ground. They ran completely counter to Grey's policy of appeasing the allies to ensure their continued loyalty to the Entente. By February 1916 Grey was so concerned that France and Russia believed that hitherto Britain had not borne its fair share of the war effort that he insisted on sending them a complete list of Britain's contributions to the common cause.[45] The Foreign Office also began to improve the dissemination of British propaganda in allied and neutral countries. Grey asked the service departments to invite influential allied representatives to Britain to see just what the nation was doing. 'We cannot wait until the day of victory to convince our Allies that we are doing our best and that we are going to win. We must convince them of that in advance in order to keep their spirits up', he wrote to Balfour and Kitchener on 4 January 1916.[46] This was hardly the time, therefore, to begin to coerce the allies to fall in with Robertson's wishes. Furthermore, there was little possibility of Turkey or Bulgaria making peace just after the allies had evacuated Gallipoli and just when Kut seemed to be about to fall. Buchanan believed that if Russia were deprived of the hope of gaining Constantinople it would materially weaken its war effort. Ministers normally as divergent in their views as Kitchener, McKenna and Lloyd George all believed that the allied peoples would demand some tangible territorial rewards for their sacrifices and looked to Turkey to provide it. As McKenna told the War Committee on 22 February, 'Turkey would pay everyone for the war'.[47]

But Grey's trump card was his knowledge of German peace feelers to the allies. They meant, as he explained in a paper for the War Committee on 18 February, that France and Russia had one advantage which the British lacked. 'Germany has taken care to make it known to our Allies that each one of them individually, or at any rate France and Russia, could have peace tomorrow on comparatively favourable terms, if they would separate themselves from us. Our Allies have, therefore, an alternative to continuing the war which is not open to us.' Although Robertson was right to suggest that in material terms the balance of power within the Entente was shifting towards Britain in early 1916 the German 'peace offensive' meant that Britain could not be the undisputed master of the Entente. Britain should urge strongly the policy it thought was right, 'But, if we cannot make our views prevail by argument and influence, we must be very careful not to proceed to threats or pressure that might alienate our Allies.'[48] At the War Committee on 22 February Grey's position was adopted.[49]

Robertson was more successful in nudging the government towards compulsory military service. The Derby canvass was conducted between 23 October and 12 December. Derby's final report, presented to the Cabinet on 20 December, showed that during the canvass 2·8 million men of military age had either enlisted or attested their willingness to do so. But a further 2·18 million men had neither enlisted nor attested. Derby concluded that when the necessary deductions had been made for starred men and a further 200,000 men were deducted to cover the army's immediate requirements for drafts for existing units, only 522,000 new recruits remained under the voluntary system, enough to meet the War Office's demand of 30,000 recruits per week for only seventeen weeks. Furthermore on 2 November Asquith had promised that attested married men would not be asked to fulfil their promise to enlist until all the single men had been taken. This pledge could not easily be fulfilled under the voluntary system as over 650,000 unstarred single men had refused to attest.[50]

The canvass was conducted amidst increasing political tension. Derby was vague about how the success or failure of the canvass should be judged beyond insisting that large numbers of single unstarred men had to be enlisted.[51] Selborne, Chamberlain and Curzon wanted to measure the success or failure of the scheme by whether or not it would be able to supply enough recruits to maintain seventy divisions in the field. In early November there was a Cabinet row when they began to suspect that Asquith was preparing to abandon the seventy divisions standard.[52] Grey talked of urging Asquith to resign and leave Lloyd George with the political odium of trying to impose compulsory service on the country. Other anti-conscriptionists retaliated by trying to divide their opponents. Hankey provided Asquith and McKenna with arguments to use against the conscriptionists and at the end of September tried to persuade Lloyd George to send rifles earmarked for the British to Russia in the hope that the case for conscription would be undermined because not enough weapons would be left to equip any conscripts. Selborne, who had repeatedly urged Asquith and Kitchener to give a public lead in favour of conscription before the canvass was announced, thought that some Unionists would resign from the government over what they believed was just another example of the Prime Minister's propensity to wait and see.[53]

Wiser heads prevailed and others argued for compromise. Walter Long believed that although the coalition was unpopular among the Unionist party and the London press, it was still popular in the country and any party which was seen to be bent on destroying it would be punished at the polls. The Unionist Chief Whip, Lord Edmund Talbot, argued that a mass resignation of Unionists from the government would either leave the field clear for the opponents of conscription or open the way for something almost as bad. A general election would probably return a conscriptionist majority but, if any semblance of national unity was to be maintained, it would also make Lloyd George the Prime Minister of a predominantly Unionist government. Far better, he thought, for the party to wait until the canvass was completed and keep Asquith, whatever his faults.[54] In December Carson, the most likely leader of any insurgent movement from outside the Cabinet, was rendered ineffective by illness. Work on updating the parliamentary register had been suspended in July and by December it was badly out of date. In early December a bill was introduced to prolong the life of Parliament beyond its normal span. A handful of Unionist MPs and peers opposed prolongation and had they been able to sustain their objections the threat of a general election fought over conscription might have forced Asquith's hand sooner. But Bonar Law, alarmed at the prospect of the breakup of the government followed by a general election, viewed any attempt to prosecute the war without Asquith's support with alarm. 'Unless Asquith goes with us', he wrote to Henry Wilson on 26 December, 'the best we can hope for is to carry on the war with the whole of Ireland hostile & a large minority including the Nationalists as a solid body acting as the Radicals did at the time of the Boer War. If necessary we must face it but I dread it.'[55]

Given the obvious reluctance of many senior Unionists to press the issue so hard that it threatened the survival of the coalition, their success in passing the first Military Service Act was all the more remarkable. Some of their success was attributable to Asquith's propensity to compromise, especially when, as in this case, he was under pressure from Lloyd George. Even before Derby had presented his final report, Asquith had attempted to mollify the supporters of conscription by agreeing to establish a drafting committee to prepare a bill.[56] In addition the anti-conscriptionists failed to maintain a common front. None of the opponents of the measure inside the Cabinet questioned the right of the state to compel men to fight for their country. Simon dismissively bracketed conscientious objectors together with 'cranks'.[57] Their arguments continued to rest on the expediency of doing so. Simon thought that the political turmoil which would be caused by the bill would simply not be worth the handful of extra men who would be found. McKenna insisted that ultimate victory was certain provided that Britain retained command of the sea and continued to supply its allies' economic wants. All its resources were now employed and it could only raise more troops if it reduced the aid it had already promised to its allies. Runciman argued that although conscription might bring military triumph in the short term it would bring national disaster in the longer term. More recruiting would ruin staple industries like shipbuilding upon which Britain's postwar prosperity would depend. It would avail Britain little if it won a military victory only to discover it had suffered a permanent economic defeat at the hands of the Americans or Germans.[58]

Their opposition did not sway the conscriptionists. The latter's arguments were grounded in a different view of history, in a different view of the part Britain had to play within the alliance and, above all, in their different temperaments. Bonar Law, Lloyd George, Curzon and their supporters simply lacked the patience and willingness of men like McKenna and Runciman to wait on events. This was best illustrated by remarks written by Bonar Law in late October 1915. Referring to a memorandum written by Balfour he wrote,

> His paper seems to me to indicate, though it does not expressly formulate, a point of view which I have often heard expressed in the Cabinet, and with which I profoundly disagree. That point of view is that this war can be carried on, as the war against Napoleon was carried on, in such a way that we can face the strain for an indefinite period. That is impossible. In this war we must risk everything, including national bankruptcy, in order to bring it to an early termination. Our financial resources are in the same position as the resources of our Allies and of the enemy in men. The army which France, for instance, keeps in the field is an army which can be kept at the present level only for a short time. Victory will come if the Allies are able to keep a superior force embodied long enough to exhaust and defeat our enemy; and our financial resources must be regarded in the same way.[59]

The architects of the eventual compromise were Herbert Samuel, the Postmaster General, and Maurice Hankey. On 22 December, with Lloyd George and Henderson both absent, the Cabinet split on party lines. But they then accepted Samuel's suggestion that he should draft a bill granting local tribunals the power to investigate the circumstances of all single unattested men of military age and discover why they were unwilling to enlist.[60] While ministers considered this over Christmas they were subject to a variety of external pressures, and opposition to conscription began to crumble. Anti-conscription MPs in the Liberal party like J. H. Whitehouse opposed compulsory service in principle and they believed that McKenna shared their views. But they were wrong. Asquith and the other opponents of conscription were forced to reconsider their opposition by Lloyd George. On 27 December he threatened the Prime Minister with his resignation if he did not accept conscription for single men but promised his complete support if he did. Robertson reminded the anti-conscriptionists of the decision of the Chantilly conference to mount a concerted allied offensive in 1916. He insisted that Britain had to keep sixty-seven divisions in the field throughout 1916 to play its part in the plan and to do so the army needed 130,000 recruits each month.[61]

On 28 December the majority of the Cabinet accepted Samuel's formula that unmarried men of military age who could not persuade local tribunals within three weeks that they had good reasons for not enlisting should be deemed to have enlisted. Lloyd George was satisfied with this modest instalment of conscription. His opponents now had to face the prospect that if they persisted they faced the real possibility of a general election, something they dreaded for, as Runciman wrote, an election fought on the issue of 'round up the slackers' would be a disaster for the Liberal party.[62] Asquith pleaded with some of them for two hours and Samuel scolded them that they would disrupt national unity if they resigned. Hankey reminded McKenna that, if he resigned, policy-making would be entirely under the control of the 'militarists and extremists'.[63] By 29 December Harcourt and Montagu had decided not to resign, McKenna, Runciman and Birrell were hesitating and only Simon and Grey had actually decided to leave the government.[64]

However, Hankey then discovered a second compromise which meant that all but Simon withdrew their resignations. On 29 December he discovered that Robertson was as concerned as McKenna about the sufficiency of Britain's economic resources to support a long war. He immediately suggested that the Military Service Bill might be allowed to proceed but that in the meantime the military and economic authorities should meet to decide how many divisions Britain could afford to maintain. All the dissenters except Simon agreed, Runciman writing to his wife that 'By keeping the Army within limits we make compulsion for *marrieds* unnecessary & therefore that *point* will be saved'.[65] On 31 December the Cabinet accepted Hankey's plan, the draft bill was approved and a Cabinet Committee on the Co-ordination of Military and Financial Effort, consisting of Asquith, Chamberlain and McKenna, was established to determine the size of the army Britain could afford.[66]

Both sides had gained something. The anti-conscriptionists had avoided the breakup of the government and a general election, and the conscriptionists had achieved a first instalment of conscription. But the cost in terms of the government's credibility was very high. The

Cabinet's indecision over a period of months only added to its public image of muddle and irresolution. Those Unionists who already thought that the coalition was ineffective and that Asquith was unfit to be Prime Minister were confirmed in their belief. At the beginning of December, Carson established the Unionist War Committee as a ginger group to pressure the government into conducting the war with greater resolution. It soon boasted 150 Unionist MPs as members and throughout 1916 proved to be a dangerous critic of the administration.[67] Asquith had also placed a high strain on the loyalty of some of his own Liberal followers. H. W. Massingham, editor of the *Nation*, believed that 'Liberalism is for the moment lost'.[68] On 6 January 1916 the Military Service Bill passed its first reading in the Commons against the opposition of 60 Irish Nationalists, 11 Labour MPs and 34 Liberals. John Gulland, the Liberal Chief Whip, had to resort to reminding MPs of their personal loyalty to Asquith and then pointing out to them that if the Government were defeated the alternative would be 'an out-and-out conscriptionist Govt with a double dose of everything we hate', in order to keep the number of defecters so low.[69]

A second obstacle then emerged. In obedience to a resolution of a special Labour conference the Parliamentary Labour Party decided that their members had to leave the government. Henderson explained that the Labour movement believed that the government had acted precipitately and without general assent and that the proposed legislation gave no assurances that conscription would not be extended to married men or to workers in industry.[70] Asquith acted quickly to keep Labour in the government by agreeing to meet Labour MPs to calm their fears about industrial conscription. The necessary assurances about industrial conscription were granted during the committee stage of the bill and on 26 January a special Labour Party conference first voted against the bill and then voted to quash a motion in favour of working to repeal it. Henderson and his colleagues were therefore able to remain in the government.[71]

The size of the army could not be decided in isolation from its intended task. On 23 December Robertson asked the War Committee to accept *in toto* the conclusions of the Chantilly conference, including the recommendation that Britain should participate in the greatest possible strength in combined offensive operations on the Western front with its allies, beginning in the spring of 1916. The War Committee's initial decision appeared to be a triumph for the new CIGS. On 28 December, the committee overruled Balfour's argument that the Western allies should remain on the defensive and allow the Germans to wear themselves out by doing the attacking, and appeared to accept Robertson's main recommendations. They agreed that France and Flanders should be regarded by the British as their main theatre. Only eight divisions should be left in Egypt and, after Townshend had been relieved, the forces in Mesopotamia were ordered to go over to the defensive. However, although they agreed that every effort should be made to prepare to launch an offensive in the spring in the West, they did not decide if or when such an operation should begin.[72]

Robertson and Kitchener were left to plead their case. The CIGS tried to silence the doubters by insisting that the allied assaults against the German line in 1914–15 had been repulsed for want of men and artillery and because the allies had failed to co-ordinate their attacks. The Germans were thus able to rush reinforcements from one threatened front to another. Things would be different in 1916 if the allies adopted the Chantilly plan and if Britain introduced conscription.[73] Kitchener admitted that the setbacks of the summer and autumn of 1915 had falsified his earlier calculations and emphasized the political arguments which made British co-operation imperative. In 1914 he had anticipated that the French and Russians would be able to fight the Germans to a standstill by the end of 1916 and the British army, still comparatively fresh, would be able to administer the *coup de grâce* in the spring of 1917. But the Russians had proven to be a serious disappointment and French manpower and British finances were becoming exhausted more rapidly than he had anticipated. He now doubted whether the Entente would be able to continue the war until the spring of 1917. He was afraid that if the Germans were not forced to the peace table by November 1916 the eventual peace 'would be a bad one, especially for England'.[74] Robertson agreed. 'It was necessary for us to win this year or not at all', he told the Cabinet Committee on the Co-ordination of Military and Financial Effort on 8 January.[75] Their arguments convinced an otherwise reluctant Grey. On 14 January he informed the War Committee that Britain had to make its maximum effort in 1916 rather than wait until 1917 because 'if things remain as they are, I think that there will be a sort of general collapse and inconclusive peace next winter. I believe that the only chance of victory is to hammer the Germans hard in the first eight months of this year.'[76]

These arguments continued throughout the Cabinet Committee's deliberations in January. The anti-conscriptionists replied that the government should hold back men from the army because the allies needed British economic support more than they needed British soldiers and because the Entente was bound to win eventually as long as the British could pay their way. The debate eventually resolved itself into a matter of numbers; how many divisions could Britain maintain in 1916 and how rapidly could men be withdrawn from the economy without doing irreparable harm to vital industries. MacDonogh tried to encourage the waverers by presenting them with figures to show that the Entente could win the war in 1916 because the Germans were rapidly exhausting their own manpower reserves. Chamberlain was convinced. If the British did not raise the maximum possible number of men and take part in a combined allied offensive he predicted that in the spring the Germans would knock out Russia and then turn westwards. McKenna could see only the dangers of staking everything on one great military effort in 1916. If the allies attacked and failed, British credit would collapse, the Entente would have shot its manpower and financial bolts, the Germans would still be in possession of large areas of allied territory and 'this would result in our defeat'.[77]

The path to another compromise was opened by Lloyd George at the War Committee on 13 January. He threw his considerable weight behind Balfour's contention that any Western offensive should at least be postponed from the spring until June. The Chantilly plan required the BEF to be committed to a major offensive prematurely and he knew that he could not supply the BEF with the heavy guns and ammunition it needed before November. The committee was persuaded that whilst preparations for an offensive might continue, they still reserved the right to refuse to sanction its actual launching. Both Kitchener and Robertson were dissatisfied. They believed that the position in which the Entente found itself made it imperative for Britain to participate in the allied offensive even if its preparations were not complete. They also knew that the whole of the spring would be needed to conduct wearing-down operations against the Germans and they therefore tried to overcome Lloyd George's objections by privately telling Haig to scale down his munitions demands.[78]

But in the meantime Hankey had recognized that if the opening of the offensive was postponed it might be possible to effect a compromise between McKenna, Runciman and Robertson. The Board of Trade withdrew their submission to the Cabinet Committee, revised their figures and three days later conceded enough to satisfy the War Office, at least for the time being. The committee's report, completed on 2 February, permitted the War Office to raise enough men to maintain sixty-two divisions in the field by June 1916 with drafts for three months together with five more territorial divisions for home defence with no drafts. As a concession to McKenna the report admitted that this was bound to cause industrial disruption and agreed to review the situation in April.[79] Chamberlain, who drafted the report, was reasonably pleased with it. By contrast Runciman regarded the whole episode as a defeat. 'The undertakings to be given to us by the War Office are worthless for the security of the industrial and financial strength to which we attach importance', adding later in the same letter, *'we have failed'*.[80] Although the War Committee had still not assented to a major offensive on the Western front in 1916, by agreeing to conscript single men and raise sixty-seven divisions they had already gone halfway down the road towards committing Britain to a high-risk policy. They were ready to gamble that Britain's full participation in a combined allied offensive in 1916 might compel the Germans to sue for peace by the end of the year, although that was something Robertson never promised. But, as the anti-conscriptionists feared, it might simply result in either a continuation of the existing stalemate or even in the military defeat of the Entente, followed by the collapse of British credit and an eventual peace on German terms because the over-strained British economy could no longer support a continuation of the war.

Notes

1   [Asquith], Cabinet note, 23 July 1915, Asquith mss, Vol. 28, f. 57; see also PRO CAB 41/36/35, Asquith to H.M. the King, 22 July 1915.

2   M. Gilbert (ed.), *Winston S. Churchill*, Vol. 3, *Companion* pt 1 (London: Heinemann, 1971), pp. 1169–70; PRO CAB 41/36/45 and 51, Asquith to H.M. the King, 23 September and 11 November 1915; PRO CAB 37/136/30, Selborne to Cabinet, 18 October 1915; Haig to Kiggell, 1 July 1915, Kiggell mss, II/2; Haig diary entry, 26 June 1915, Haig mss, Acc. 3155/101; J. Gooch, *The Plans of War: The General Staff and British Military Strategy, c. 1900–1916* (London: Routledge & Kegan Paul, 1974), pp. 316–17; PRO FO 800/95, Cecil to Grey, 20 September 1915; Carson to Bonar Law, 5 September 1915, Bonar Law mss, 51/3/5; Wilson diary entry, 20 May 1915, Wilson mss (microfilm) reel 6; French diary entry, 23 May 1915, French mss, vol. K.

3   John Turner, 'Cabinets, committees and secretariats: The higher direction of the war', in K. M. Burk (ed.), *War and the State: The Transformation of British Government, 1914–1919* (London: Allen & Unwin, 1982), pp. 59–63.

4   Callwell to Wilson, 25 September 1915, Wilson mss, 73/1/18.

5   PRO CAB 41/36/49, Crewe to H.M. the King, 22 October 1915.

6   Hankey diary entries, 9 and 16 October and 1 November 1915, Hankey mss, 1/1.

7   Lord Hankey, *The Surpeme Command, 1914–1918*, Vol. 2 (London: Allen & Unwin, 1961), pp. 439–40; PRO CAB 41/36/51, Asquith to H.M. the King, 11 November 1915.

8   Gooch, *Plans of War*, p. 319; PRO CAB 42/4/2, Murray, Appreciation by the General Staff of the actual and prospective military situation in the various theatres of war, 2 October 1915.

9   Callwell to Robertson, 22 October 1915, Robertson mss, I/8/28.

10   Haig diary entry, 15 October 1915, Haig mss, Acc. 3155/103.

11   Field Marshal Sir W. Robertson, *From Private to Field Marshal* (London: Constable, 1921) pp. 147–50; Robertson to Murray, 21 October 1915, Robertson mss, I/15/1.

12   PRO CAB 24/1/G33, Robertson, Memorandum on the conduct of the war, 5 November 1915; PRO WO 159/4, Robertson to Fitzgerald and Kitchener, 31 October 1915.

13   PRO CAB 28/1 Robertson, Memorandum for the meeting of representatives of the Allied armies furnished by Lt.-Gen. Sir William Robertson, 15 November 1915.

14   Robertson to Callwell, 23 October 1915, Robertson mss, I/8/29.

15   Robertson to Callwell, 16 October 1915, Robertson mss, I/8/24.

16 PRO CAB 24/1/G33, Robertson, Memorandum on the conduct of the war, 5 November 1915.

17 Haig diary entires, 26 December 1915, 1 and 11 February 1916 and L. E. Kiggell, Notes of the conference of Army Commanders held by the General, Commanding-in-Chief, at First Army Headquarters, Aire, at 11 a.m. on 11 February 1916, Haig mss, Acc. 3155/104; PRO CAB 42/8/5, Grey to Cabinet, 3 February 1916; PRO FO 371/2504/180839, Picot to Foreign Office, 26 November 1915; French diary entry, 4 December 1915, French mss, vol. M; Kirke diary entry, 12 December 1915, Kirke mss; J. C. King, *Generals and Politicians. Conflict between France's High Command, Parliament and Government, 1914–1918* (Berkeley, Calif.: University of California Press, 1951), pp. 89–96.

18 PRO CAB 28/1, Robertson, Memorandum for the meeting of representatives of the Allied armies furnished by Lt.-Gen. Sir William Robertson, 15 November 1915.

19 R. Holmes, *The Little Field Marshal: Sir John French* (London: Cape, 1981), pp. 306–13.

20 Robertson, *Private to Field Marshal*, pp. 236–43; Robertson to Wigram, 11 December 1915, Robertson mss, I/12/29.

21 Haig diary entry, 18 December 1915, Haig mss, Acc. 3155/103.

22 Hankey diary entry, 18 December 1915, Hankey mss, 1/1; Haig to Asquith, 10 December 1915, Asquith mss, vol. 15, f. 196.

23 J. Marshal-Cornwall, *Wars and Rumours of Wars: A Memoir* (London: Leo Cooper and Secker & Warburg, 1983), p. 22; W. Kirke to Maj.-Gen. F. S. G. Pigott and enc., 29 July 1947, Kirke mss, WMK 13.

24 Robertson to Murray, 30 November 1915, Robertson mss, I/15/7.

25 Sir G. Buchanan, *My Mission to Russia and other Diplomatic Memories*, Vol. 1 (London: Cassell, 1923), p. 250; PRO CAB 42/5/4 and/5, Minutes of the War Committee, 6 and 8 November 1915.

26 K. Neilson, *Strategy and Supply: The Anglo-Russian Alliance, 1914–1917* (London: Allen & Unwin, 1984), pp. 117, 119–20, 125–33; A. J. P. Taylor (ed.), *Lloyd George: A Diary by Frances Stevenson* (London: Hutchinson, 1971), p. 81; HMSO, *History of the Ministry of Munitions*, Vol. 2, pt 8 (London: HMSO, 1923), pp. 20–3; PRO FO 800/380, Lloyd George to Grey, 27 October 1915.

27 PRO CAB 28/1, Military conference of the allies held at the French Headquarters, December 6–8, 1915; PRO WO 106/1454, Note for the conference of 6 December [1915] held at GQG; PRO WO 106/391, Dossier de la conference entre les representatives des Armées Alliées tenus à Chantilly les 6, 7 et 8 Decembre 1915.

28 Robertson to Murray, 10 February 1916, Robertson mss, I/32/1.

29 PRO CAB 42/9/3, Robertson, Note prepared by the Chief of the Imperial General Staff for the War Committee on the assistance that diplomacy might render to naval and military operations, 12 February 1916.

30 ibid. These ideas were probably suggested to Robertson by MacDonogh and by Philip Howell, the chief of staff of the British force at Salonika; see Howell to N. Buxton, 19 January 1916, Howell mss, IV/C/2/198 and Howell to Robertson and Haig, 27 January 1916, Howell mss, IV/C/2/200a; Rodd to Grey, 6 December 1915, Lloyd George mss, D/19/10/1; MacDonogh to Kirke, 20 May 1924, Kirke mss, WMK 13; PRO FO 371/2804/28967, Percy, Memorandum, 8 February 1916; V. H. Rothwell, *British War Aims and Peace Diplomacy, 1914–1918* (Oxford: Clarendon Press, 1971), p. 50.

31 G. Ritter, *Sword and Scepter. The Problem of Militarism in Germany*, Vol. 3, *The*

Tragedy of Statesmanship – Bethmann-Hollweg as War Chancellor 1914–1917 (Coral Gables, Fla: University of Miami Press, 1972), pp. 91–2, 240–4; PRO CAB 37/142/20, Curzon, Mission to the King of the Belgians, February 1916, 8 February 1916; PRO CAB 37/142/47, Villiers to Grey, 14 February 1916; PRO FO 800/381, Villiers to Nicolson, 24 January 1916.

32   Sir James Rennell Rodd, *Social and Diplomatic Memories*, Vol. 3, 1902–1922 (London: Edward Arnold, 1925), pp. 261, 265, PRO FO 800/66, Rodd to Grey, 1 and 26 August, 2 and 15 September and 1 December 1915; PRO FO 800/66, Mouncey to Russell, 9 November 1915; J. Whittam, *The Politics of the Italian Army* (London: Croom Helm, 1977), pp. 195–6.

33   PRO FO 371/2505/156008, Elliot to Foreign Office, 22 October 1915 (156552), Rodd to Foreign Office, 23 October 1915 (157875), Howard to Foreign Office, 25 October 1915 (161330), Grant Duff to Foreign Office, 30 October 1915 (166254), Howard to Foreign Office, 6 November 1915.

34   PRO CAB 37/142/7, MacDonogh, Note respecting the attitude of Italy, 3 February 1916.

35   PRO FO 800/380, Johnstone to Nicolson, Asquith, Grey, Balfour and Crewe, 2 November 1915; PRO FO 371/2505/185780, Nicolson to Grey and enc., 4 December 1915; P. Renouvin, 'L'Opinion publique en France pendant la guerre 1914–1918', *Revue d'histoire Diplomatique*, vol. 84, no. 4 (1970), p. 302.

36   PRO FO 800/60, Bertie to Grey, 30 November 1915; PRO FO 800/167, Drummond to Bertie and enc., 15 December 1915.

37   PRO FO 800/58, Bertie to Crewe, 12 December 1915 and Bertie to Grey, 25 December 1915; PRO FO 800/60, Bertie to Drummond, 20 December 1915; Lady Algernon Gordon Lennox (ed.), *The Diary of Lord Bertie of Thame, 1914–1918*, Vol. 1 (London: Hodder & Stoughton, 1924), pp. 276–7; T. Wilson (ed.), *The Political Diaries of C. P. Scott, 1911–1928* (London: Collins, 1970), p. 163.

38   C. J. Lowe and M. L. Dockrill (eds), *The Mirage of Power: British Foreign Policy 1902–1922*, Vol. 3 (London: Routledge & Kegan Paul, 1972), p. 640; I. H. Nish, *Alliance in Decline: A Study in Anglo-Japanese Relations 1908–1923* (London: Athlone Press, 1972), pp. 167–9; PRO FO 800/95, Memorandum by Mr Swinge, August 1915; PRO FO 800/96, Jordan to Foreign Office, 7 January 1916 and minutes by Cecil and Drummond, 8 January 1916.

39   PRO FO 371/2454/119784, Buchanan to Foreign Office, 25 August 1915 (149314), Buchanan to Foreign Office, 12 October 1915 (149853), Buchanan to Foreign Office, 2 November 1915 (187979), Buchanan to Foreign Office, 25 November 1915.

40   PRO FO 371/2454/116039, Professor Pares, A short memorandum on Russian internal politics during the war with two notes (a) on the anti-German riots in Moscow, eye witness account of Mr Peters; (b) speech by Mr Alexander Guchkov on munitions and army reform, 20 August 1915; Buchanan, *Mission*, pp. 237–8, 245–6; R. Pearson, *The Russian Moderates and the Crisis of Tsarism, 1914–1917* (London: Macmillan, 1977), pp. 55–60, 65–7; PRO FO 800/75, Buchanan to Grey, 7 September and 13 October 1915; G. Katkov, *Russia 1917: The February Revolution* (London: Longman, 1967), pp. 156–60.

41   Wilson (ed.), *Political Diaries of C. P. Scott*, p. 131; K. Neilson, 'Wishful Thinking: The Foreign Office and Russia, 1907–1917', in B. J. C. McKercher and D. J. Moss (eds), *Shadow and Substance in British Foreign Policy 1895–1935, Memorial Essays Honouring C. J. Lowe* (Edmonton, Alberta: University of Alberta Press, 1984), pp. 160–3; PRO FO 371/2455/176927, Buchanan to

Foreign Office, 16 October 1915; PRO FO 800/379, Nicolson to Hardinge, 1 September 1915; PRO FO 800/380, Buchanan to Grey, 16 October 1915; Lennox (ed.), *Bertie of Thame*, Vol. 1, p. 229.

42 PRO FO 371/2505/121350, Howard to Grey and the Cabinet, 22 August 1915.

43 Buchanan, *Mission*, pp. 251–2; PRO FO 800/75, Buchanan to Grey, 26 November and 19 December 1915.

44 PRO FO 800/75, Crewe to Buchanan, 21 December 1915.

45 PRO CAB 41/37/6, Asquith to H.M. the King, 9 February 1916; PRO CAB 37/142/22, Grey, Memorandum: British services to the Allies, 9 February 1916.

46 PRO FO 371/2580/19541, Grey to Kitchener and Balfour, 4 January 1916; P. M. Taylor, 'The Foreign Office and British propaganda during the First World War', *Historical Journal*, vol. 23, no. 4 (1980), pp. 878–83.

47 PRO CAB 42/9/3, Minutes of the War Committee, 22 February 1916.

48 PRO CAB 42/9/3, Grey, The position of Great Britain with regard to her Allies, 18 February 1916.

49 PRO CAB 42/9/3, Minutes of the War Committee, 22 February 1916.

50 PRO CAB 37/139/41, Derby, Memorandum on recruiting, 20 December 1915.

51 Derby to Asquith, 23, 28 and 31 October 1915, Asquith mss, vol. 15, ff. 56–7, 62–3, 77–8; Derby to Blumenfeld, 28 October 1915, Blumenfeld mss.

52 Chamberlain to Bonar Law, 2 and 3 November 1915, Bonar Law mss, 51/5/3 and 4; Wilson (ed.), *Political Diaries of C. P. Scott*, pp. 154–6.

53 Selborne to Asquith, 6 August 1915, Selborne mss, file 80, ff. 34–8; Long to Bonar Law, 12 October 1915, Bonar Law mss, 51/4/7; Hankey diary entries, 27 and 29 September and 13 October 1915, Hankey mss, 1/1.

54 Talbot to Bonar Law, 16 October 1915, Bonar Law mss, 51/4/15; Long to Bonar Law, 12 December 1915, Bonar Law mss, 52/1/28.

55 Bonar Law to Wilson, 26 December 1915, Wilson mss, 73/1/19; M. D. Pugh, *Electoral Reform in War and Peace, 1906–1918* (London: Routledge & Kegan Paul, 1978), pp. 57–60; L. S. Amery *et al.* to Bonar Law, 2 December 1915, Bonar Law mss, 52/1/6.

56 PRO CAB 41/36/55, Asquith to H.M. the King, 15 December 1915; John Grigg, *Lloyd George: From Peace to War, 1912–1916* (London: Methuen, 1985), pp. 329–31.

57 PRO CAB 37/139/53, Simon to Cabinet, 24 December 1915.

58 PRO CAB 37/139/43, Runciman, Extracts from a report of the committee on merchant shipbuilding, 20 December 1915; Simon to Asquith, 27 December 1915, Simon mss, box 52.

59 PRO CAB 37/136/30, Bonar Law to Cabinet, 25 October 1915.

60 PRO CAB 37/139/45, Samuel, Enlistments, 22 December 1915; PRO FO 800/100, Asquith to Cabinet and enc., 23 December 1915.

61 Whitehouse to McKenna, 24 and 31 December 1915, McKenna mss, MCKN 5/9; Grigg, *Lloyd George*, pp. 331–2; Robertson to Kitchener, 27 December 1915, Robertson mss, I/11/1.

62 Runciman to his wife, 27 and 30 December 1915, Runciman mss, WR 303; PRO CAB 41/36/56, Asquith to H.M. the King, 28 December 1915; Taylor (ed.), *Lloyd George: A Diary*, pp. 89–90.

63 Hankey to McKenna, 28 December 1915, McKenna mss, MCKN 5/9; Runciman to his wife, 29 December 1915, Runciman mss, WR 303; Asquith to Simon, 28 December 1915, Simon mss, box 52.

64   Simon to Asquith, 29 December 1915, Simon mss, box 52; Birrell to
      Asquith, 29 December 1915, Asquith mss, vol. 28, ff. 283–4; Grey to
      Asquith, 29 December 1915, Asquith mss, vol. 28, ff. 287–90; Harcourt to
      McKenna, 28 December 1915 and Montagu to McKenna, 28 December 1915,
      McKenna mss, MCKN 5/9.
65   Runciman to his wife, 30 December 1915, Runciman mss, WR 303; Robert-
      son to Haig, 31 December 1915, Haig mss, Acc. 3155/104; Runciman to [?]
      Harmsworth, 1 January 1916; Hankey diary entries, 29 and 30 December
      1915, Hankey mss, 1/1.
66   Hankey diary entry, 31 December 1915, Hankey mss, 1/1; PRO CAB
      41/37/1, Asquith to H.M. the King, 1 January 1916.
67   B. McGill, 'Asquith's predicament, 1914–1918', *Journal of Modern History*,
      vol. 39, no. 3 (1967), pp. 292–3.
68   Massingham to McKenna, 1 January 1916, McKenna mss, MCKN 5/9.
69   Gulland to Simon, 1 January 1916, Simon mss, box 52.
70   PRO 37/140/17, Henderson, Organised Labour and the military service act,
      10 January 1916; PRO CAB 41/37/3, Asquith to H.M. the King, 11 January
      1916; Henderson, Roberts and Brade to Asquith, 10 January 1916, Asquith
      mss, vol. 16, ff. 7–9, 12–13.
71   Labour party conference at Bristol, 27 January 1916, Asquith mss, vol. 29,
      ff. 208–9; C. Addison, *Politics from Within, 1911–1918: Including Some Records
      of a Great National Effort*, Vol. 1 (London: Herbert Jenkins, 1924), p. 245;
      J. Rae, *Conscience and Politics. The British Government and the Conscientious
      Objector to Military Service, 1916–1919* (London: Oxford University Press,
      1970), pp. 37–9.
72   PRO CAB 42/6/14, Robertson, Note for the War Comittee by the Chief of
      the Imperial General Staff with reference to the General Staff paper dated 16
      December 1915, 23 December 1915; PRO CAB 42/6/14, Minutes of the War
      Committee, 28 December 1915; PRO CAB 37/139/55, Balfour to Cabinet,
      26 December 1915.
73   PRO CAB 42/7/1, Robertson, The question of offensive operations on the
      Western front. Note by the CIGS, 1 January 1916.
74   Clive diary entry, 5 January 1916, Clive mss, II/2; PRO 30/57/76/WR/35,
      Kitchener to Asquith, 11 January 1916; Kitchener to Haig, 14 January 1916,
      Haig mss, Acc. 3155/104.
75   PRO CAB 27/4, Minutes of the 6th meeting of the Cabinet Committee on
      the co-ordination of military and financial effort, 8 January 1916.
76   Grey, memorandum, 14 January 1916, Lloyd George mss, D/22/2/9.
77   PRO CAB 27/4, Report, proceedings and memoranda of the Cabinet
      Committee on the co-ordination of military and financial effort, 1916; PRO
      CAB 42/7/8, Chamberlain, Note by Mr Chamberlain. Military policy, 17
      January 1916; Robertson to Haig, 27 January 1916, Haig mss, Acc. 3155/104.
78   Robertson to Haig, 13 January 1916, Haig mss, Acc. 3155/104; PRO
      30/57/55, Kitchener to Robertson, 18 January 1916.
79   PRO CAB 27/4, Report of the Cabinet Committee on the co-ordination of
      military and financial effort, 4 February 1916; Hankey diary entries, 13, 14,
      and 17 January 1916.
80   Runciman to McKenna, 23 January 1916, McKenna mss, MCKN 5/9;
      Chamberlain to Bonar Law, 2 February 1916, Bonar Law mss, 52/3/2.

10

Verdun to the Somme, February to June 1916

THE 1916 CAMPAIGN was conducted by a government which badly needed some spectacular victories to increase its waning authority. At the end of February Lord Robert Cecil informed Spring-Rice in Washington

> that if a ballot were taken of the House of Commons, on the question of whether they had confidence in the present government, there would be an overwhelming majority against the Government . . . On the other hand if the question was whether this Government was to be replaced by some other Government I believe there would be an equally overwhelming majority in favour of the present Government because, at any rate for the time being, there really is no alternative.[1]

One reason for this curious situation was that their opponents, characterized by C. P. Scott as 'the party of energy and concentration', were divided and without effective leadership for much of the time. The Liberal War Committee numbered only 40 MPs. Carson's Unionist War Committee had 150 members but Carson himself was a sick man and, recognizing that even with the support of Lloyd George and Churchill there was no possibility of forming an alternative government, decided on 23 March that he 'must act tentatively'.[2]

Only a major military success would arrest the government's declining prestige. In December 1915 the Chantilly conference had prescribed that in 1916 the Entente's major offensives should be preceded by a series of operations to wear down the enemy forces. But Haig and Joffre could not agree on how this preliminary phase of their operations should be conducted. Haig's formal orders on assuming command of the BEF were almost as ambiguous as those issued to his predecessor. He was reminded that military victory depended on close co-operation with the French. Thus, for example, if he were forced to retreat, his troops were to conform to the movements of the French, who would presumably fall back on Paris. He was not to retreat westwards to secure the purely 'British' objective of protecting the Channel ports.[3] On the other hand he was also reminded that he was an independent commander and the government made it clear to him that he did not come under Joffre's orders. This left him free to make his own suggestions about the conduct of the wearing-out phase of the campaign. In January he explained to his army commanders that between February and mid-April he hoped that each of the Entente's armies would conduct its own small-scale wearing-out operations. Between mid-April and mid-May they would co-operate to conduct larger-scale operations to weaken the enemy's line and finally, starting about twelve days before the main offensive, he hoped that they would mount preparatory attacks to absorb the enemy's reserves. The main offensive ought to start at the beginning of June.[4]

Three factors forced him to change these plans. The Ministry of Munitions could not meet his requirements until July and it also seemed unlikely that the Russians would be ready until then. But, most important of all, Joffre wanted to conserve French manpower by leaving the wearing-out phase of the campaign to his allies. He wanted the British to launch two preliminary attacks on their own in April and May. Haig was ready to bow to the Russians and the Ministry of Munitions but not to the French. He was afraid that Joffre's plan would expose the BEF to defeat in detail during the preliminary stage of the campaign and might mean that when the moment came to launch the final offensive the British would be too weak to play a proper part in it. Like Kitchener, Haig believed that victory or defeat would be measured at the end of the war by Britain's ability to impose its peace terms, not only on its enemies but on its allies as well. 'There is no doubt to my mind', he confided to his diary on 14 January, 'that the war must be won by the Forces of the British Empire'.[5] Haig and Joffre also disagreed about where the main offensive should be launched. Joffre wanted a combined offensive by the British and French armies north and south of the river Somme. Haig preferred an attack from Ypres to capture the important railway junction of Roulers. If that fell he hoped that he would be able to roll up the entire German line to the coast.[6] Only on 14 February did the two commanders reach a compromise. Haig agreed that the main offensive would be on the Somme in July and Joffre agreed that there would be no large-scale wearing-out operations in April and May.[7]

Since the Chantilly conference the allies had laid their plans on the assumption that the Germans would make their major effort in the spring of 1916 against Russia. On 16 January Robertson told Haig that he expected the Germans to attack Russia in May and try to crush it in the summer.[8] However they were not so obliging. After the 1915 campaign General von Falkenhayn, the Chief of the German General Staff, believed that German hegemony in Europe was assured if only Britain could be persuaded to accept it. He told Bethmann-Hollweg that Britain was Germany's arch enemy because it was the cement which held the Entente coalition together and the only way to compel Britain to accept German domination on the continent was to knock its continental 'swords' from its hands. Russia and Italy had already been weakened and, therefore, the Germans had to turn against France and force it to make peace. He recommended that this could best be done by exhausting France's manpower reserves and thus proving to the French people that they had nothing to gain from continuing the war.[9] Bethmann-Hollweg agreed and the German offensive began at Verdun on 21 February. The French government had earlier accepted Joffre's assurances that the city was completely safe. But it quickly became apparent that it was not. Briand rejected Joffre's request to evacuate Verdun because he knew that if he agreed his government would quickly fall, and instead he threatened Joffre with dismissal if the Germans occupied it. Esher was right to tell Haig on 11 March that Joffre's future now 'rests on the sands of politics'.[10]

Initial British reactions to the German offensive were mixed. Robertson and Kitchener were perturbed by it but Robertson did not think the Germans would breach the French line. However on 24 February he agreed that Haig should take over more of the line to enable the French to reinforce the city. By early March, GHQ's intelligence branch had recognized that the German's purpose was to bleed the French army dry and both they and Robertson initially welcomed this in the expectation that it would use up German troops more rapidly than the proposed allied wearing-out operations.[11] But it quickly became apparent that the offensive might have serious political repercussions which could call into question the military and political cohesion of the alliance. On 5 March Joffre informed Haig that the French position at Verdun was so precarious that it cast in doubt his ability to participate in joint operations in the spring.[12] It was rumoured that the French war minister, General Galliéni, wanted to sack Joffre and restructure the entire Ministry of War. For once rumours were true and Galliéni resigned on 8 March when the Cabinet refused to allow him to carry out his plan. He was replaced by General Roques, nicknamed 'old strawberry'.[13] It was assumed that as he was a former classmate of Joffre's, he would be another Millerand. In fact, as casualties mounted at Verdun, he became one of Joffre's sternest critics.[14] Verdun also had a perceptible impact on the French civilian population. For the first time during the war there were signs that morale in some departments was sagging. On 17 March the British military attaché, Colonel Le Roy Lewis, informed Kitchener that the French public might not be satisfied with anything less than a radical reconstruction of the ministry which might include Caillaux's entry into the Cabinet. 'The outlook', he concluded, 'is not altogether cheerful.'[15]

The Germans accompanied their offensive with fresh efforts to secure a separate peace with France and Russia. French diplomats curtly rejected German overtures but the French chargé d'affaires in London warned

Esher on 18 April, 'that the peace party in France is growing and that there are many influential people in France who are beginning to ask themselves whether twelve months hence France is likely to get better terms from Germany than she would to-day'.[16] The Germans adopted a more roundabout route to approach the Russians. In March German emissaries told the Japanese minister in Stockholm that Germany was prepared to relinquish all its interests in China if the Japanese would make peace and persuade Russia to follow suit. Ostensibly their denouement failed. The Japanese immediately told their allies of the German overtures and Sazonov stood by the letter of the Pact of London and told the Japanese ambassador in Petrograd that if the Germans wanted to negotiate they would have to approach all the allies openly and simultaneously. However the Japanese then used the news of the German peace offer to blackmail their allies into granting them concessions in China. That left a nasty taste in British mouths and provided further evidence that the two allies were drifting apart. Furthermore, the new Russian President of the Council, B. V. Sturmer, was far more receptive to German overtures than was Sazonov. Unbeknown to his allies, at the end of May Sturmer hinted to the Germans that he was ready to negotiate on the basis of granting Germany concessions in eastern Europe if Russia were granted similar concessions at the expense of Austria and Turkey.[17]

On 12 March allied military representatives, including Haig and Robertson, met once again at Chantilly to reassess their plans in the light of Verdun. The Italian representative chipped away further at the idea of a combined allied offensive by pleading that his army had to keep a large number of men on the Swiss frontier and claiming that they had only sufficient machine guns and heavy artillery for a local offensive. Robertson was exasperated and blurted out to one of the British liaison officers at GQG that 'I'd like to have kicked him in the stomach'.[18] The generals failed to agree on the crucial question of the timing of their operation. Lloyd George tried to use this inconclusive meeting to persuade the War Committee on 21 March that they should continue to refuse to sanction the launching of any Western offensive. But Kitchener and Robertson, supported by Asquith, prevailed. Another allied conference was held in Paris between 26 and 28 March at which the British representatives, Robertson, Kitchener, Grey and Asquith, agreed to leave the timing entirely to the generals. On 31 March Robertson formally asked the War Committee to abide by this decision.[19] Four days later Haig explained Joffre's plan to the committee and Briand and Ribot threw their weight behind the cause of allied co-operation.[20] Their pressure was decisive. Asquith, Grey and Bonar Law agreed that the future of the alliance depended upon Britain's active participation in the allied offensive. As Asquith explained, 'M. Ribot said definitely that if France did not get the required assistance, she could not go on. She must put up the shutters.'[21] On 7 April the War Committee finally agreed to the BEF's participating in the offensive and after much further wrangling between Joffre and Haig the final date for their joint offensive was fixed for 1 July.[22]

The General Staff supported the allied offensive on the assumption that attrition of manpower would work in the Entente's favour. On 31 March they presented Kitchener with a minute in which they argued that if a permanent loss of 150,000 men per month could be inflicted on the Germans they would be unable to hold their present line for more than ten months and therefore, 'provided Germany can be made to suffer approximately equal losses, it is in the interests of the Entente Powers to force the fighting on the main fronts to the fullest possible extent'.[23] If the Germans' manpower reserves could be exhausted by the autumn the allies might be able to force the Germans to the peace table by the end of the year. But not all the decision-makers shared their faith. Lloyd George suspected their calculations of enemy manpower reserves were wrong and did not think that the BEF had sufficient shells or heavy guns to make a summer offensive practicable. The opponents of conscription insisted that a major offensive was bound to produce high casualties and these could only be sustained if still more men could be found for the army. But another instalment of conscription might wreck the British economy. They warned that if the generals' plans miscarried the Entente might find itself facing at best a stalemate, or at worst a peace settlement imposed on them by the Germans, at the end of the year. Therefore at the same time as they debated and finally agreed upon a second instalment of conscription, the government also tried to insure themselves with the Americans in case the allied offensive failed and the British found themselves with too few men and too little money to continue the war into 1917.

McKenna's first budget of September 1915 had been based on two assumptions, that the government would not resort to conscription and that the war would be over by the end of 1916 without the need for Britain to sustain heavy losses in a major offensive in France. The first Military Service Act undermined the first assumption and by the spring of 1916 the second also looked increasingly precarious. Henceforth Treasury policy was directed towards postponing national bankruptcy for as long as possible. In January 1916 Keynes estimated that the Second War Loan had reduced bank deposits significantly for a time but that they were now 20 per cent above their prewar levels and unless the government again reduced them, inflation would increase.[24] The failure of the Second War Loan to attract working-class savers led to the establishment of the War Loan (Small Investors) Committee under Edwin Montagu. Montagu's committee rejected a forced loan as politically impossible and premium bonds as an affront to the nonconformist conscience. They recommended instead that the existing limit of £200 on post office savings bank deposits should be raised and that trade unions and friendly societies should be urged to encourage their members to save by establishing their own war savings societies. In February the government therefore established a Central War Savings Committee to conduct propaganda work and issued Treasury bills in small denominations to meet the needs of the various societies.[25]

The Montagu committee also recommended that the rich would have to make greater sacrifices if the poor were to be persuaded to show restraint. McKenna tried to follow their advice when he framed his second budget. He raised the standard rate of income tax to 5s in the pound on earned incomes over £2,500 p.a. and excess profits duty went up to 60 per cent. Controlled firms already paying the munitions levy would henceforth pay the higher of the two imposts. This was the limit of what was politically possible for a Liberal Chancellor. Straws in the wind like the Wimbledon by-election of April 1916 indicated that middle-class Liberal voters were unwilling to pay more. Sugar duty was increased, and there were new duties on matches, mineral waters (on the assumption that teetotallers should pay their share of the war), railway tickets and tickets to places of entertainment. Total expenditure in the coming financial year was estimated to be £1825m, £240m more than in the preceding year and estimated revenue from the new taxes was £500m, £180m more than in the preceding year.[26]

The budget was introduced on 4 April and unlike its predecessor it aroused considerable controversy. Many Unionist MPs thought that McKenna had placed an unfairly heavy burden on the well-to-do. This drove Warren Fisher of the Inland Revenue to minute, no doubt fairly, that 'As a matter of fact the present outcry is – to a considerable degree – being fostered by the wealthy who use the case of their less well-to-do brethren as a screen for an attack on the 5s rate as such, which they themselves dislike'.[27] Tariff reformers in and out of the Cabinet resented the fact that even before the budget McKenna had acted through the Board of Trade to deal with the problem of imports by outright prohibition rather than by the imposition of more tariffs.[28] From February onwards a progressively lengthening list of imports was banned by the newly established Prohibition of Imports department organized at the Board of Trade by Sir Guy Granet, the general manager of the Midland Railway company.[29] By contrast free trade Liberals rejoiced that the Chancellor had raised 'an unprecedented sum on free trade principles'.[30] Controlled firms, with the support of Lloyd George, resented the imposition of the new higher rate of excess profits duty on them. They asked McKenna to take account of the fact that after the war they would have to compete with American companies whose capital reserves had not been depleted by the duty, and disingenuously claimed that the new assessments would place an intolerable strain on their accounting departments. Only later, and in private, did some of their spokesmen admit that many of them had not done as well from the Munitions of War Act as they had expected and that they now preferred to be subject to the munitions levy rather than the heavier excess profits duty. The Treasury eventually granted them some allowances but stuck fast to the 60 per cent rate. Further concessions were impossible in view of the protests they would have evoked from organized labour.[31] The budget was subject to another modification in May. The exchange situation with America was so precarious that the Chancellor placed a penal rate of income tax on owners of American securities but offered them relief if they placed them at his disposal. McKenna believed that this expedient would see Britain through until the autumn but thereafter other, as yet unidentified, expedients would be needed.[32]

The political controversy surrounding the budget was nothing to that caused by Robertson's demand for another instalment of conscription. At the end of February the army was 250,000 men below establishment and expected to be 400,000 men short by the end of April. Too many men who had been called up had received exemptions. By March Robertson was describing the First Military Service Act as 'a farce and a failure'.[33] On 21 March he told the War Committee that more men were vital for victory. He did not underestimate the economic or political repercussions of his demands. 'I daresay this question of men may break up the Government before we have finished, and perhaps that is not altogether to be regretted', he wrote to Haig on 22 March.[34] He was supported not only by ministers like Curzon, Long and Selborne who accepted the need for a major offensive in the West but also by Lloyd George, who did not. Lloyd George was concerned that the French believed that they were bearing a disproportionately heavy share of the common burden and that unless the British made a gesture indicating their willingness to take over some of the burden the alliance might be in jeopardy. Although he still looked to Russia, with its apparently inexhaustible manpower reserves to wear down the Central Powers, it could not do so in 1916 because it lacked adequate munitions. As a result, 'we ought to do our best this year to put our maximum force in the Field, and thus to contain a large proportion of the German reserves. Russia, however, must be told that next year it would be for them to make their maximum effort'.[35]

Asquith was under pressure not only from these sources but from the fact that two by-elections were pending and Bonar Law was concerned that the government's declining reputation might mean that unofficial candidates would defeat the official party nominees. Furthermore both the Unionist and Liberal War Committees threatened to raise the conscription issue in the Commons before Easter.[36] On 7 April, Asquith therefore agreed to re-establish the Cabinet Committee on the Co-ordination of Military and Financial Effort.[37] Robertson prepared his position carefully, lobbying politicians and sympathetic journalists and hinting to Repington of *The Times* on 9 April that he would resign if he did not get his way.[38] Lloyd George received conflicting advice. Leopold Amery, a Milnerite Unionist MP who formed an important link between Lloyd George, Robertson and Carson, urged him to resign from the government unles they agreed to general compulsion, on the grounds that anything less would lead to a negotiated peace. However, Christopher Addison, his parliamentary secretary at the Ministry of Munitions, advised caution. If Lloyd George resigned precipitously he would have the support only of the Northcliffe press and 'the wild men amongst the Tories' and he would completely alienate himself from his own party. Addison's advice was the more realistic. Carson could rely on the support of only 75 Unionists in the Commons, and H. A. Gwynne, the pro-compulsion editor of the *Morning Post*, believed that if Lloyd George resigned he could rely on the support of only 23 Liberal MPs.[39] Bonar Law was at his wits' end to see how the political situation could be improved and he hesitated to push the situation to extremes. If the coalition disintegrated it would be impossible to form a new one in the existing House of Commons and there would have to be a general election. He feared that even if the Unionists won, national unity would be destroyed, there would be a powerful opposition in Parliament similar to that which had opposed the last Unionist government during the Boer War and, as he informed Henry Wilson on 31 March, 'in a very short time we would have to have martial law all over the country; for not only would there be a strong opposition in the House of Commons, but that opposition would encourage every form of opposition outside'.[40]

To Lloyd George's fury, the Cabinet Committee's report of 13 April did not endorse general compulsion. He now insisted that he would not accept the report unless the Army Council first assented to it. The result demonstrated the political power of the General Staff. Although Asquith told the Army Council that general compulsion might mean the collapse of the government, and Chamberlain explained to them at some length the economic arguments against it, they did not deviate from their position.[41] Unionist MPs who were not ready to follow Carson's lead were ready to follow Robertson. A Unionist Whip in the Commons told Bonar Law that only a quarter of the parliamentary party would support their leader if he opposed the General Staff. Law hastily deflected this pistol pointed at his head towards Asquith, telling him on 17 April that his party would oppose any motion in the Commons which did not give them general compulsion.[42] The Cabinet therefore hastily scrapped the report of the Co-ordination Committee and a new committee, of Asquith, Bonar Law, Crewe, Lloyd George and Balfour was convened. They suggested that a bill for general compulsion should be passed immediately, timed to come into force a month later. Its enactment would be suspended if 50,000 men enlisted from among the unattested married men by 25 May and if subsequently recruiting did not fall below 15,000 men per week. Lloyd George agreed because it would avoid the disagreeable necessity of resigning, his Tory enemies agreed because they thought he would do them less harm inside the Cabinet, and Robertson agreed because he thought the men would not enlist and then the government would have exhausted all expedients and would have to introduce conscription for married men.[43]

Asquith introduced their proposal to the Commons during a secret session beginning on 25 April. Law made a powerful speech in its favour. The Commons' initial reaction was muted. Samuel believed that 'The House of Commons is rather proud of itself for holding a secret session, like a man who spends an evening out without his wife knowing what he is doing. But as a matter of fact the proceedings have been very dull, as is usually the case in other instances also – as I understand from hearsay.'[44] But when Long introduced the detailed clauses of the government bill he met a furiously hostile reception. The Cabinet, realizing that the Commons would not vote for their compromise legislation, beat a hasty retreat.[45] There was now no escape from general compulsion. The bill was introduced by Asquith on 2 May, and, despite the opposition of 41 Liberals, became law on 25 May.

The second conscription crisis had three results. It demonstrated how precarious was the government's grip on the House of Commons and how much power their critics could wield. As a result of the way they had mishandled the whole question of manpower the government had, in Cecil's opinion, acquired 'A reputation for "flabbiness" [which] is the most fatal reputation that a war Government can have'.[46] It opened a gulf between Lloyd George and Asquith and it marked a further decline in Asquith's own reputation. Hankey, who witnessed Asquith introducing the bill described the Commons as 'astonishingly cold. The fact was that the people who want compulsory service don't want Asquith, while those who want Asquith don't want compulsory service – so he fell between two stools!'[47] Finally it made it possible for the government to continue with the policy of attrition and for the BEF to participate in the allies' summer offensive.

In 1915 the British tried to keep the Americans friendly but at arm's length. As early as December 1914 the Treasury and Foreign Office recognized that the longer the war lasted the more dependent Britain and its allies would become on American supplies and money. The main concern of British diplomacy was, in Spring-Rice's words, 'that we should be allowed to use this country as a base by the tacit consent of the American people and our principal duty is not to create a state of feeling

which would render the American people hostile'.[48] But as 1915 progressed many Americans became increasingly resentful at the way in
which the Entente, or in most cases, the British, sought to interrupt their
trade with the Central Powers. Grey was well aware of the political capital
the Germans could make out of this in America. By May 1915 even papers
normally friendly to the British were critical of the blockade.[49] Count
Bernstorff, the German ambassador in Washington, repeatedly insisted
that his country would accept the principle of the 'freedom of the seas',
and hinted that it might even be the first step towards successful American
mediation to end the war. In 1915 American mediation was the last thing
Grey or the allies wanted. There was general assent among the allied
governments to Spring-Rice's insistence that the terms the Germans were
offering were designed to break up the Entente alliance and deprive
Britain of its most powerful weapon, the blockade. If Germany's terms
were accepted it would be able to resume the war against Britain a few
years later in a vastly stronger position.[50]

Grey tried to deal deftly with the Americans. Fearing that the President
might succumb to German requests that he place an embargo on all arms
shipments, he insisted that American cargoes be treated leniently. Similarly he did not dismiss the idea of the freedom of the seas out of hand.
Grey believed that the Entente had to do all they could to defeat the
Germans. But his concept of victory went well beyond a simple vision of
victory in the field followed by the establishment of a democratic, and
therefore peace-loving, form of government in Germany and the dividing
up of the territorial spoils among the allies. Like House and Wilson, Grey
thought that one reason why war had started in 1914 was because there
was no international body which could impose effective sanctions against
aggressor states and he believed that such a body was needed if future wars
were to be avoided. He therefore told House that he personally was in
favour of establishing a League of Nations at the end of the war whose
members would be pledged to take a collective action against any
aggressor. In return Britain would sacrifice its right of blockade.

Grey hoped that membership of such an organization would confer
several benefits on Britain. In the long term it would nullify the threat
posed to its seaborne commerce from submarines and it would also bring
about a drastic reduction in its defence estimates. In the short term he
recognized that discussion about a League would dampen American
resentment about the blockade and might also sustain allied morale. Eric
Drummond, Grey's private secretary, believed that the working classes in
France, Britain and Italy supported the war because they hoped that it
would end once and for all the expensive prewar arms race and leave more
money for social reforms. But, he wrote in June 1915, 'if the idea became
prevalent that the present war would not lead to a large reduction on
expenditure on armaments, a considerable waning in enthusiasm would

ensue, and anti-war propaganda would become popular'.[51] Grey tentatively broached the idea to the Cabinet by suggesting on 18 June 1915 that they ought to consider allowing the free import of food into Germany if the Germans in return agreed to abandon their submarine blockade of Britain. But his idea was disregarded and in the second half of 1915 the British began to take tentative steps to tighten their blockade.[52]

In doing so they made a second American mediation attempt inevitable. House and Wilson were afraid that if they did not do something to end the war the Germans might intensify their U-boat warfare in 1916 and, as still more Americans perished, they would be dragged willy-nilly into the conflict.[53] House explained his plan to Wilson in early October. He believed that the Entente should be approached unofficially and asked if they were ready to agree to the Americans demanding an end to the war. If they did so the President would call a peace conference. If, however, the Central Powers refused, America would break off diplomatic relations with them and 'later the whole force of our Government, and perhaps the force of every neutral, might be brought against them'.[54] Wilson gave him permission to proceed and House explained his intentions in a letter to Grey on 17 October in which he hinted that if the Germans rejected the American offer they would probably join the Entente. Grey's reply was ambiguous. He did not reject the proposal out of hand but he did make it clear that the allies were determined to continue the war throughout the winter and that therefore the time was not propitious for mediation. Privately some Foreign Office officials were more scornful of the American proposals. Commenting on a remark made by Wilson in December on the desirability of what he called spiritual mediation, Nicolson minuted, 'What is "spiritual" mediation?' Crowe replied, 'I suppose the Pope, plus the Apb. [sic] of Canterbury, the Free Church Council, and possibly Gen[eral] Booth. I suppose the Dalai Lama would not be of the party.'[55] House and Wilson did not realize that a wide gulf separated them from Grey. They saw the proposed League as a substitute for military victory; Grey saw it as a body which would emerge only after the Entente had gained such a victory. Grey did nothing to enlighten the President about this gap in his understanding because as long as talks could proceed on this ambiguous basis a breach between the Entente and America could be postponed.[56]

In mid-December Wilson agreed that House should go to Europe, but he made it clear to him that he did not agree with House that America might join the Entente if they appeared to be on the point of losing the war. He also emphasized that in any future peace negotiations they would

> have nothing to do with any local settlements, – territorial questions, indemnities, and the like, – but are concerned only in the future peace of the world and the guarantees to be given for that. The only possible

guarantees, that is, the only guarantees that any rational man could accept, are (a) military and naval disarmament and (b) a league of nations to secure each nation against aggression and maintain the freedom of the seas.[57]

Wilson's reservations were soon known to the British. Room 40 at the Admiralty quickly broke the private cipher House used to communicate with the President and furthermore, at a private lunch in London on 11 January, House admitted to Runciman that Wilson 'will not go to war on any account'.[58] With the Germans in occupation of large tracts of allied territory, the Entente leaders could not share Wilson's olympian detachment from the details of the territorial settlement. House arrived in Britain in early January and embarked on a round of talks with British ministers, officials and opinion-shapers. Austen Chamberlain believed that he was without 'a very wide or clear grasp of the European situation' and many of those he met were ready to dismiss the entire exercise as an election manoeuvre designed to allow Wilson to present himself as a great peacemaker in the presidential election which was to be held in November.[59] Asquith, for example, 'appears to regard the whole thing as humbug, and a mere manoeuvre of American politics'.[60] Grey, Balfour and McKenna were outwardly among the most responsive to House's ideas concerning the freedom of the seas but Lloyd George gave him a more forthright impression of allied sentiments. On 14 January he told House that it was far too early for mediation. The allies would not entertain it until September by which time the results of the forthcoming campaign would be apparent and their gains might offset Germany's present advantages.[61]

House's subsequent journeys to Berlin and Paris only demonstrated the wide gulf which separated the belligerents. Bethmann-Hollweg left him in no doubt that when he spoke of peace he meant peace on German terms. Similarly the French made it plain that all they wanted from Wilson was benevolent neutrality.[62] On his return to London in February, House tried to salvage what he could from his mission. On 10 February he and Grey agreed that the best way to proceed would be for Wilson, at some unspecified date, to call a peace conference. The Entente would agree to attend and 'if Germany does not, I have promised', House wrote ambiguously, 'for you that we should throw all our weight [sic] in order to bring her to terms'.[63] The question of timing was left vague but at a dinner on 14 February, House believed that he had persuaded Asquith that the right time to put the plan into operation would be when the allied offensive had dented the German line.[64] Their agreement was embodied in a memorandum which Grey gave to House. When Wilson saw the document he inserted one significant caveat. House had expressed the opinion that if the Germans proved to be unreasonable at the putative peace conference, the United States would leave the conference and join the Entente. The President inserted the word 'probably' so that the relevant passage now read 'Colonel House expressed the opinion that, if such a Conference met, it would secure peace on terms not unfavourable to the Allies: and, if it failed to secure peace the United States would probably leave the Conference as a belligerent on the side of the Allies, if Germany was unreasonable'.[65] The President's insertion did not materially alter the sense of the memorandum. The American commitment to join the allies expressed in House's draft was already ambiguous. It was never clear, for example, just how far House's opinion could commit the President to any particular course of action. Wilson's insertion only added one more ambiguity to a document which already abounded in them.

The British were undecided about what to do with the memorandum. Even if Wilson's initiative were an election stunt, the memorandum might be useful in one of two ways. If the combined allied offensive was successful and the Germans faced exhaustion by the autumn, the memorandum could be dusted off and used as the starting point for negotiations which would produce peace terms broadly acceptable to Britain. If, however, it was not successful and Britain and its allies faced the kind of exhaustion that the opponents of conscription had predicted, the memorandum might be used to induce the Americans either to join them or at least intervene to save them from a peace based on the military status quo. Grey summed up the choices facing them in a letter to Bertie on 5 March.

> As long as the Military and Naval authorities of the Allies say they can beat the Germans there need be no talk of mediation: but if the war goes to a stalemate, the question to be asked will be, not whether the mediation is good electioneering for President Wilson, but whether it will secure better terms for the Allies than can be secured without it. It is therefore in my opinion, a great mistake not to treat Colonel House seriously; though if the Allies can dictate terms of peace in Berlin without the help of the United States, nothing will come of Colonel House's proposals.[66]

Robertson could not predict how long the allies would be able to continue the war, but on 21 March he told the War Committee that 'At the present, however, all his own instincts were opposed to availing ourselves of Col[onel] House's suggestion'. At the end of May he went even further and, together with the rest of the Army Council, threatened to resign if House's offer were taken up. In both March and May the War Committee decided to postpone acting on it.[67] It would be an exaggeration to suggest that in shelving the House-Grey memorandum the British threw away their best chance of achieving a satisfactory negotiated peace settlement in 1916. The possibility of arriving at such a settlement was remote in the first place. House's reception in Berlin had demonstrated that there was no room for compromise in 1916. The Germans had no intention of surrendering sufficient of their gains to satisfy Britain or its allies. British intelligence reports indicated that the Germans believed that one more successful offensive would allow them to impose their own terms on the Entente and the British were still intent on crushing 'Prussian militarism'.[68] As Kitchener explained to the American ambassador on 24 March, a compromise peace would probably only last seven years and 'there would be no real and satisfactory end to the war until the military control of Germany was terminated'.[69] Only a handful of ministers knew about the economic predicament Britain might find itself in at the end of the year if the forthcoming allied offensive failed to force the enemy to sue for peace. The public still had every confidence in the Entente's ability to win the war and any attempt to invite American mediation before the allied offensive would have shaken the coalition to its very foundation.

The House-Grey memorandum therefore became an insurance policy which the government might cash in if their military plans went awry and a military and economic stalemate forced them to seek a negotiated settlement. The possibility that the war might end in a stalemate had also occurred to some French politicians. By the end of 1915 the French minister of commerce, Etienne Clémentel, was afraid that the war might end in an unsatisfactory negotiated settlement which would be no more than an armed truce. If this happened Clémental wanted the Entente to continue their wartime co-operation in order to prevent Germany preparing for another war, by forming a common economic bloc to deprive Germany of access to strategic raw materials. He also wanted them to erect a common tariff barrier to defeat any German attempt to ruin their industries by dumping.[70] At the end of December the French invited their allies to a conference to consider how they might concert their postwar trade policies and liberate their economies from dependence on the Central Powers. The invitation struck a responsive cord among Unionist tariff reformers. Even some businessmen who had been ardent free-traders before 1914 now voted in their chambers of commerce for a ban on German imports after the war. Their change of heart was illustrated by the agonizing of C. P. Scott. Although he was loath to surrender his free trade principles, he insisted in a letter to L. T. Hobhouse in January 1916 that

> we have got to make ourselves independent of all foreign powers for the essentials alike of war and of industry and this must involve special measures to meet the special needs and it will be difficult to prevent these from being a cover for protection.[71]

Walter Runciman remained a free-trader but as President of the Board of Trade he could not ignore the mounting pressure to attend the conference. But before it met he agreed with Clémentel that Britain's relations with its colonies and Dominions, its relations with America and 'our old Fiscal controversies, the revival of which in their old form would divide British opinion', would not be discussed.[72] The inter-allied economic conference finally met in Paris between 14 and 17 June. The British delegation consisted of two free-traders, Lord Crewe and the Canadian minister of commerce, Sir George Foster, and two tariff reformers, Bonar Law and William Hughes, the Prime Minister of Australia. The conference's decisions were closely based on the agenda Runciman and Clémentel had already agreed. The first series of resolutions dealing with the war itself did little more than bring the allies into line with existing British practices about trading with the enemy and the control of enemy business in allied countries. The second series of resolutions, dealing with the immediate postwar period, were designed to help Belgium, Serbia, Russia and France make good the destruction of their economic infrastructure by the enemy. They granted these countries priority of access to raw material stocks and denied Germany most favoured nation status after the war. The final group of resolutions, dealing with the period after reconstruction, were designed to diminish the Entente's dependence on enemy countries for strategic goods. But they were so hedged with qualifications that each signatory would remain free to decide its own fiscal policy.[73]

At the end of September 1915 W. H. Page, the American ambassador to Britain, reported that the mood in London was sombre 'and many men's minds are beginning to adjust themselves to the possible end of the war, as a draw'.[74] The tentative way in which the War Committee reacted to the House–Grey memorandum, combined with the government's readiness to begin planning for postwar reconstruction on the assumption that peace might be concluded before Germany had been convincingly defeated, bear witness to the fact that nine months later, on the eve of the allied summer offensive, ministers too recognized that the war might still end in a draw.

Notes

1 PRO FO 800/242, Cecil to Spring-Rice, 25 February 1916.
2 M. Gilbert (ed.), *Winston S. Churchill*, Vol. 3, *Companion*, pt 2 (London: Heinemann, 1971), p. 1462; T. Wilson (ed.), *The Political Diaries of C. P. Scott, 1911–1928* (London: Collins, 1970), p. 205.
3 PRO 30/57/53, Kitchener to Haig, 28 December 1915.
4 Haig diary entries, 8 and 18 January 1916 and Haig, Some thoughts on the future [n.d. but *c*. January 1916] Haig mss, Acc. 3155/104.
5 Haig diary entries, 14, 20 January 1916, Notes on interview with Gen. Joffre at St Omer on Thursday 20 January 1916, and Haig to Asquith, 26 January 1916, Haig mss, Acc. 3155/104; PRO 30/57/53, Haig to Kitchener, 19 January 1916; PRO WO 106/393, Haig to Joffre, 1 February 1916, GQG

(Third Bureau), Note on the Operation to be carried out on the Western Front in 1916, 10 February 1916, and Haig, Plans for future operations, 10 February 1916.

6   J. Terraine, *Douglas Haig: The Educated Soldier* (London: Hutchinson, 1963), pp. 186–7.

7   Haig diary entry, 14 February 1916, Haig mss, Acc. 3155/104.

8   Robertson to Haig, 16 January 1916, Haig mss, Acc. 3155/104.

9   L. L. Farrar, 'Peace through exhaustion: German diplomatic motivations for the Verdun campaign', *Revue Internationale d'Histoire Militaire*, vol. 8, no. 2 (1972–5), pp. 477–82.

10   Oliver, Viscount Esher (ed.), *Journals and Letters of Reginald, Viscount Esher*, Vol. 4 (London: Ivor Nicholson & Watson, 1938), p. 14; J. C. King, *Generals and Politicians. Conflict between France's High Command, Parliament and Government, 1914–1918* (Berkeley, Calif.: University of California Press, 1951), pp. 89–97.

11   PRO WO 106/393, Robertson to Joffre, 24 February 1916; Brig.-Gen. J. Charteris, *At GHQ*, (London: Cassell, 1931), pp. 140–1; J. Jolliffe (ed.), *Raymond Asquith: Life and Letters* (London: Collins, 1980), pp. 248–9.

12   Haig diary entry, 5 March 1916, Haig mss, Acc. 3155/105.

13   PRO 30/57/59, Esher to Fitzgerald, 23 March 1916.

14   King, *Generals and Politicians*, p. 107.

15   PRO 30/57/57, Le Roy Lewis to Kitchener, 17 March 1916.

16   Esher, *Journals*, Vol. 4, p. 18; PRO CAB 42/12/1, Foreign Office to War Committee, 4 April 1916; PRO CAB 37/146/8, Howard to Grey, 8 April 1916.

17   F. W. Iklé, 'Japanese–German peace negotiations during World War One', *American Historical Review*, vol. 71, no. 1 (1965), pp. 62–73; L. L. Farrar, *Divide and Conquer. German Efforts to Conclude a Separate Peace, 1914–1918* (New York: East European Quarterly and Columbia University Press, 1978), pp. 57–60; PRO CAB 42/12/5, Greene to Grey, 5 April 1916; I. H. Nish, *Alliance in Decline. A Study in Anglo-Japanese Relations, 1908–1923* (London: Athlone Press, 1972), pp. 179–83; PRO CAB 37/148/4, Hirtzel, Japanese policy and its bearing on India, 16 May 1916; PRO CAB 37/148/12, General Staff, Japanese activities in China and India, 14 May 1916.

18   Clive diary entry, 12 March 1916, Clive mss, II/1.

19   PRO CAB 42/11/6, Minutes of the War Committee, 21 March 1916; PRO CAB 28/1, Conclusions of Allied Conference, Paris 26–28 March 1916.

20   PRO CAB 42/12/5, Robertson, Future Military Operations, 31 March 1916 and Haig to Robertson, 4 April 1916; Hankey diary entry, 5 April 1916; Hankey mss, 1/1.

21   PRO CAB 42/12/5, Minutes of the War Committee, 7 April 1916.

22   ibid.

23   PRO 30/57/74/WS/74, General Staff, A note on the resources in men of the Allies and of the enemy, and their effect on the duration of the war, 31 March 1916, quoted in K. R. Grieves, 'The British government's political and administrative response to the man-power problem in the First World War', PhD thesis, Manchester University, 1984, pp. 42–3.

24   PRO T 171/129, Keynes, Deposits of joint-stock banks, 29 January 1916.

25   PRO T 170/97, War Loan (Small Investors) Committee. Report and Suggestions, 1916; PRO CAB 37/142/16, McKenna and Montagu, War Loans for small investors, 7 February 1916.

26   Wilson (ed.), *Political Diaries of C. P. Scott*, p. 296; PRO T 171/134, Finance Act 1916, Vol. 1; PRO T 171/129, Budget 1916; PRO T 171/132, Budget

(1916). Inland Revenue (I); PRO CAB 41/37/12, Asquith to H.M. the King, 23 March 1916.

27 PRO T 171/132, W. Fisher, Memorandum, 26 April 1916.

28 *Hansard*, 81 HC Deb., 5s. cols 1063, 1221–5, 1226–7; Chamberlain to Samuel, 9 April 1916, Samuel mss, A 15 (IV), ff. 150–3.

29 PRO BT 13/68 contains a file of letters about the establishment of Granet's department, and PRO BT 13/69 contains the proclamations it issued banning certain classes of imports.

30 *Hansard*, 81 HC Deb., 5s. cols 1229–30.

31 Lloyd George to McKenna, 1 April 1916, Lloyd George mss, D/17/12/4, and McKenna to Lloyd George, 3 April 1916, Lloyd George mss, D/17/12/5; PRO T 172/310, Murray and Calliard to McKenna, 15 April 1916, Hopkins, Memorandum, 26 April 1916, Deputation from the controlled armament establishments and firms, 27 April 1916, W. Fisher, Memorandum, 7 May 1916, and Controlled establishment deputation, 11 July 1916.

32 PRO CAB 37/148/6, McKenna, British financial liabilities in USA, 17 May 1916; McKenna to Runciman, 4 June 1916, Runciman mss, WR 149.

33 Robertson to Haig, 22 March 1916, Haig mss, Acc. 3155/105; Robertson to Kiggell, 21 March 1916; Robertson mss, I/35/62; Brade to Bonar Law, 26 March 1916, Bonar Law mss, 52/4/30; Robertson to Selborne, 26 February and 8 March 1916, Selborne mss, file 80, ff. 155–6.

34 Robertson to Haig, 22 March 1916, Haig mss, Acc. 3155/105; PRO CAB 42/11/8, Robertson, Memorandum by the CIGS regarding the supply of personnel, 21 March 1916.

35 PRO CAB 27/3, Cabinet Committee on the size of the army, 18 April 1916; Curzon to Bonar Law, 20 March 1916, Bonar Law mss, 52/4/32; Wigram to Wilson, 14 March 1916, Wilson mss, 73/1/20; J. Grigg, *Lloyd George: From Peace to War, 1912–1916* (London: Methuen, 1985), pp. 334–5.

36 Carson to Bonar Law, 3 April 1916, and Long to Bonar Law, 15 April 1916, Bonar Law mss, 53/1/1 and /11; Maxse to Wilson, 20 March 1916 and Milner to Wilson, 12 April 1916, Wilson mss, 73/1/20.

37 PRO CAB 41/37/16, Asquith to H.M. the King, 7 April 1916.

38 Lieut.-Col. C. à Court Repington, *The First World War*, Vol. 1 (London: Constable, 1920), pp. 180–2.

39 C. Addison, *Politics from Within, 1911–1918: Including some Records of a Great National Effort*, Vol. 1 (London: Herbert Jenkins, 1924), pp. 247–8; Gwynne to Wilson, 27 March 1916 and Locker Lampson to Wilson, 13 April 1916, Wilson mss, 73/1/20; Amery to Lloyd George, 6 and 13 April 1916, Lloyd George mss, D/16/2/2 and 4; K. and J. Morgan, *Portrait of a Progressive. The Political Career of Christopher, Viscount Addison* (Oxford: Clarendon Press, 1980), p. 49.

40 Bonar Law to Wilson, 31 March 1916, Bonar Law mss, 53/6/68.

41 PRO CAB 37/145/35, Cabinet Committee on the Co-ordination of Military and Financial Effort, 13 April 1916; Hankey diary entry, 15 April 1916, Hankey mss, 1/1.

42 Bridgeman to Bonar Law, 17 April 1916, Bonar Law mss, 53/1/14 and Bonar Law to Asquith, 17 April 1916, Bonar Law mss, 53/6/73.

43 PRO CAB 27/3, Cabinet Committee on the size of the army, 18 April 1916; Robertson to Haig, 26 April 1916, Haig mss, Acc. 3155/105; Henderson, Proposals negotiated by Henderson with the General Staff and agreed to by the Cabinet, 20 April 1916, Runciman mss, WR 139; A. J. P. Taylor (ed.), *Lloyd George: A Diary by Frances Stevenson* (London: Hutchinson, 1971), pp. 105–6.

44   Samuel to his wife, 26 April 1916, Samuel mss, A/157/815; Addison, *Politics*, Vol. 1, p. 251; Proposal [made by Asquith as the Secret Session of the House of Commons on 25 April 1916], Asquith mss, vol. 30, f. 62.

45   J. Barnes and D. Nicholson (eds), *The Leo Amery Diaries*, Vol. 1 (London: Hutchinson, 1980), pp. 128–9.

46   PRO CAB 37/145/7, Cecil, Memorandum on recruiting, 4 April 1916.

47   Hankey diary entry, 2 May 1916, Hankey mss, 1/1.

48   PRO FO 800/85, Spring-Rice to Grey, 16 April 1915; PRO T 171/107, Blackett, The United States of America, 5 January 1915; Kathleen Burk, *Britain, America and the Sinews of War, 1914–1918* (London: Allen & Unwin, 1985), pp. 11–87 is the definitive account of Anglo-American economic relations during the first two years of the war.

49   PRO FO 800/85, Spring-Rice to Grey, 30 April 1915; PRO CAB 37/128/7, Memorandum, 7 May 1915; PRO CAB 37/130/34, British navalism, June 1915.

50   PRO FO 800/85, Spring-Rice to Grey, 6 and 8 June 1915.

51   PRO FO 800/95, Drummond, Freedom of the seas, 11 June 1915, Drummond to Grey and minute by Grey, 7 June 1915 and Grey to Spring-Rice, *c.* 8 June 1915; A. S. Link (ed.), *The Papers of Woodrow Wilson*, Vol. 34 (Princeton, NJ: Princeton University Press, 1980), pp. 144–6.

52   PRO CAB 37/130/15, Crewe, Memorandum, 18 June 1915.

53   A. S. Link, *Wilson: Confusions and Crises, 1915–1916* (Princeton, NJ: Princeton University Press, 1964), p. 101; C. M. Mason, 'Anglo-American relations: Mediation and Permanent Peace', in F. H. Hinsley (ed.), *British Foreign Policy under Sir Edward Grey* (Cambridge: Cambridge University Press, 1977), pp. 473–4.

54   Link (ed.), *Wilson's Papers*, Vol. 35, pp. 42–4.

55   PRO FO 371/2505/189778, Spring-Rice to FO, 12 December 1915 and minutes by Nicolson and Crewe; Link (ed.), *Wilson's Papers*, Vol. 35, pp. 80–2, 186–7, 254–6; Mason, 'Anglo-American relations', pp. 474–5.

56   G. W. Egerton, *Great Britain and the Creation of the League of Nations* (London: Scolar Press, 1979), pp. 27–8.

57   Link (ed.), *Wilson's Papers*, Vol. 35, pp. 387–8; Link, *Confusion and Crises*, pp. 109–13.

58   Runciman to his wife, 11 January 1916, Runciman mss, WR 303; Hankey diary entry, 21 January 1916, Hankey mss, 1/1.

59   Chamberlain to St Loe Strachey, 15 January 1916, St Loe Strachey mss, S/4/5/5.

60   Hankey diary entry, 16 March 1916, Hankey mss, 1/1; PRO FO 800/181, Bertie to Grey, 2 March 1916.

61   C. Seymour (ed.),, *The Intimate Papers of Colonel House*, Vol. 1 (London: Ernest Benn, 1926), pp. 116–19, 128–31; Link (ed.), *Wilson's Papers*, Vol. 35, pp. 465–6, 484–6; Hankey diary entry, 22 January 1916, Hankey mss, 1/1.

62   Link (ed.), *Wilson's Papers*, Vol. 36, pp. 122–3; D. Stevenson, 'French war aims and the American challenge, 1914–1918', *Historical Journal*, vol. 22, no. 4 (1979), p. 881.

63   Link (ed.), *Wilson's Papers*, Vol. 36, pp. 166–7.

64   Link (ed.), *Wilson's Papers*, Vol. 36, p. 170; Seymour (ed.), *Intimate Papers*, Vol. 1, pp. 181–2.

65   Seymour (ed.), *Intimate Papers*, Vol. 1, p. 202.

66   PRO FO 800/181, Grey to Bertie, 5 March 1916; Hankey diary entry, 16 March 1916, Hankey mss, 1/1; Taylor (ed.), *Lloyd George*, p. 101.

67   PRO CAB 42/11/6, Specially secret addendum to the secretary's notes of the

proceedings of the War Committee, March 21, 1916; Hankey diary entry, 25 May 1916, Hankey mss, 1/1.

68 PRO FO 371/00780, War Trade Intelligence department to Foreign Office, 28 April 1916 and (87505), 8 May 1916; PRO FO 800/171, Bertie, Memorandum, 7 May 1916.

69 Link (ed.), *Wilson's Papers*, Vol. 36, pp. 437, 511–12.

70 M. Trachtenberg, '"A new economic order?": Etienne Clémentel and French economic diplomacy during the First World War', *French Historical Studies*, vol. 10, no. 2 (1977), pp. 317–41; R. E. Bunselmeyer, *The Cost of the War 1914–1918. British Economic War Aims and the Origins of Reparations* (Hamden, Conn.: Archon Books, 1975), pp. 34–6; PRO CAB 37/141/15, Grey to Cabinet and enc., 21 January 1916.

71 Wilson (ed.), *Political Diaries of C. P. Scott*, p. 175; PRO CAB 37/142/29, Grey to Cabinet, 11 February 1916; PRO CAB 37/143/8, Montagu to Cabinet, 21 February 1916.

72 Runciman to Clémentel, 12 February 1916, Runciman mss, WR 149; P. Cline, 'Winding down the war economy: British plans for peacetime recovery, 1916–1919', in Kathleen Burk (ed.), *War and the State: The Transformation of British Government, 1914–1919* (London: Allen & Unwin, 1982), pp. 161–2.

73 Bunselmeyer, *Cost of the War*, pp. 39–40; Economic Conference of the Allies held at Paris, 14–17 June 1916, Runciman mss, WR 143.

74 B. J. Hendrick (ed.), *The Life and Letters of Walter H. Page*, Vol. 2 (London: Heinemann, 1930), p. 94.

11

From the Somme to Bucharest, July–August 1916

In 1916 THE policy of attrition assumed a whole new meaning. In 1915 Joffre had tried repeatedly to break through the German line in France. Although he had failed he remained convinced that the idea was practicable and in 1916 he envisaged the Anglo-French offensive north and south of the Somme as a breakthrough battle.[1] In 1915 Kitchener did not believe that the Western allies would be able to break the German line and his original concept of the policy of attrition was the antithesis of Joffre's policy of mounting a series of large and costly assaults against the enemy's positions. Although by early 1916 Kitchener recognized that the political solidarity of the Entente might depend upon Britain playing its full part in the combined allied offensive planned by the Chantilly conference, he was still not convinced that a breakthrough would be possible. On 21 January he told Balfour that 'he did not intend to make another heavy attack in France, but merely to pursue an intensified policy of attrition in order gradually to use up the German reserves'.[2]

War Office intelligence estimates, perhaps recoiling from their excessive optimism of the previous year, indicated that German military manpower was still not exhausted. MacDonogh arrived at an estimate of German casualty figures by adding 50 per cent to the published German figures and then adding a further 10 per cent for casualties due to sickness. This method of calculation probably inflated German losses but even so on 26 June the Enemy Personnel Committee believed that the Germans still had four million men at the front, supported by one million more in their depots, 700,000 lightly wounded who could be returned to duty and a further 700,000 who could be withdrawn from industry. In France MacDonogh believed that although a large number of enemy divisions had been exhausted by the fighting at Verdun, the Germans had retained three fresh divisions plus one complete corps especially to meet any British offensive. All this persuaded Kitchener that a serious attempt to break the German line in a single battle would probably fail, would certainly be very costly and, most important of all, would defeat his major purpose of conserving British military manpower so that Britain would have the strongest army of all the belligerents when the time came to make peace.

Robertson agreed with his political chief that the Germans remained a formidable enemy and that the BEF was not yet properly ready to meet them. On 8 April Sir Henry Rawlinson, the commander of the Fourth Army on the Somme, informed Robertson that many of the junior officers and noncommissioned officers of the New Armies 'have never had any experience and instruction in tactics and the use of ground'.[3] Robertson had already reached the same conclusion and he also knew that the Ministry of Munitions would not be able to supply Haig's army with enough heavy artillery and ammunition to breach the German line. 'Therefore I do not at my end', he wrote to Haig on 28 May, 'propose to cause the Govt. to think of a great offensive promising far reaching effect, but to show them the necessity of our attacking in some [sic] so as to assist & encourage our allies and to well strafe the Germans [sic].'[4] And two days later he assured the War Committee that in the planning for the offensive 'there was no idea of any attempt to break through the German lines, it would be only a move to *dégager* the French'.[5]

Robertson's assurances were misplaced. In the summer of 1915 Kitchener had propagated a defensive theory of attrition. He hoped that the Germans would obligingly wear themselves out by attacking the strongly entrenched allied lines in the West. But instead they turned eastwards and inflicted such a serious defeat on Russia that they forced Kitchener to recognize that the Western allies dare not stand by in 1916 and permit the Germans to knock Russia out of the war. But Kitchener never explained how attrition could be made to work in the Western allies' favour if they had to leave the comparative safety of their own trenches and attack the Germans. Haig and his staff were given no guidance by the War Office and they did not recognize Kitchener's distinction between a campaign which would intensify the process of attrition and one in which they sought to break through the German line. When Kitchener explained to Brigadier Charteris, Haig's chief intelligence officer, on 9 February that he thought a breakthrough unlikely, the latter dismissed it as 'a distinction in terms'.[6] Haig's army had grown to 45 divisions by May 1916 and he thought that this force was sufficient to justify an attempt to break the German line. Joffre and Charteris fed his optimism. In March Charteris estimated that the BEF had a definite superiority in rifles and guns along the whole front and that this was most marked just north of the Somme opposite General von Below's Second Army. The British knew that the German line contained a large number of deep concrete dug-outs but they had a poor opinion of some of the men garrisoning them. At the end of

April Charteris's staff described two of von Below's divisions as 'indifferent'.[7] On 18 June, when the Russian summer offensive was two weeks old, Charteris predicted that its success would compel the Germans to send a large proportion of their reserves eastwards.[8] He also took a more sanguine view of enemy manpower reserves than MacDonogh, estimating that if the Germans fought throughout the summer, by the autumn their army would be 350,000 men below establishment.[9]

Detailed planning for the Somme offensive began on 1 March when Rawlinson was given command of the Fourth Army and told to submit a plan. However, when Haig examined it he was disappointed. Rawlinson had tried to give some reality to Kitchener's concept of offensive attrition. Rawlinson's 'intention is merely to take the enemy's first and second system of trenches and "kill Germans"', wrote Haig on 5 April. 'He looks upon the gaining of 3 or 4 kilometres more or less of ground immaterial [sic].'[10] Rather than adopt Rawlinson's plan of allowing the Germans to exhaust themselves by counter-attacking the British once they were lodged in the German line, Haig wanted to achieve a clean breakthrough during the first assault by 'getting as large a combined force of French and British across the Somme and fighting the enemy in the open'.[11] On 15 June he explained to Rawlinson that his initial objective was to occupy the Pozières heights. If the German defences then broke, Rawlinson was to occupy the enemy's third line, widen the breach and advance with his cavalry towards Bapaume. Thence he could turn northwards to encircle the German troops around Arras.[12]

However, neither Haig nor Charteris thought that the Somme would be an easy victory, and nor did they assume that the Entente would necessarily win the war by the end of 1916. Haig warned Rawlinson that if the German defences did not crumble under his initial assault, the position around Pozières would be consolidated and a second offensive would be mounted by the Second Army.[13] He also cautioned his army commanders to prepare for another campaign in 1917 and warned them that 'however confident of success, it would not be sound to base our plans on the expectation of definitely destroying the enemy's power in one campaign before the winter'.[14] On 30 June Charteris wrote:

> We are fighting primarily to wear down the German armies and the German nation, to interfere with their plans, gain some valuable position and generally to prepare for the great decisive offensive which must come sooner or later, if not this year or even next year. The casualty list will be big.[15]

Charteris was wrong to assume that the difference between Kitchener's and Robertson's conception of the coming battle and that of GHQ was only a distinction in terms. The sceptics on the War Committee had reluctantly agreed to the offensive believing that Haig would not try to repeat the costly attempts at a breakthrough which had characterized some of the battles of 1915. They believed that attrition was the antithesis of a full-scale frontal assault. They shut their eyes to the problem of how Haig might mount a large offensive against heavily entrenched positions and yet inflict heavier losses on the enemy than he suffered himself. Their myopia was perhaps half deliberate because far more than the lives of hundreds of thousands of men were at stake on the Somme. Robertson insisted that nothing less than the conscription of all available manpower into the army and British participation in the plans prepared by the Chantilly conference in December 1915 was necessary if Britain was to avoid defeat. The politicians on the War Committee agreed in the hope that he was wrong in his estimate of the duration of the war and that the combined offensive would force the Central Powers to sue for peace by the end of the year. But, as the prolonged debate over conscription illustrated, they also knew that if the soldiers were right and if the combined allied offensive was costly but not decisive, it would have immense implications both for the Entente and for Britain's future role as a great power. The Germans might still be in control of large tracts of allied territory, the French army would be shrinking in size, the Russians might be morally and economically exhausted, and Britain might have shot its economic bolt and be no longer able to sustain its allies with money and munitions. In such circumstances the War Committee would be left with two choices. They could disinter the House–Grey memorandum and sue for peace and thus accept German domination of the continent of Europe. Or they could fight on in the hope of achieving an eventual victory but in the knowledge that even if they did finally defeat the enemy in the field, they would leave Britain bankrupt and bereft of men.

The combined allied offensive began inauspiciously. The Central Powers struck first. On 15 May the Austrians launched an offensive on the Italian front and threatened for a time to break into the Lombard plains. General Cadorna blamed his setbacks on a shortage of machine guns and heavy artillery. He demanded that the British make good his deficiencies at once and that the Russians hasten their offensive in Galicia to compel the Austrians to withdraw troops from his front.[16] The War Committee were sufficiently concerned to dispatch 200 machine guns and some elderly howitzers because, as Lloyd George told them on 30 May, 'we ought to help the Italians otherwise they might be knocked out. They might not be of any great assistance, but at any rate they are holding down a large force of Austrians, which [*sic*] then be freed for action elsewhere.'[17]

Russian help, when it came, was altogether more substantial. The main Russian offensive launched north of the Pripyat marshes, was a failure. But a subsidiary operation against the Austrians, began on 4 June along the south-western front by General Brusilov, was an unexpected and spectacular success. Cadorna's predicament had assisted Brusilov because the Austrians had diverted troops from his front to attack the Italians. In less than a week at least a third and perhaps nearly a half of the entire Austro-Hungarian army had been killed or captured. Austrian morale never recovered and increasingly Austrian units had to be stiffened with German officers and noncommissioned officers.[18] It was the most spectacular victory won by any of the allied armies since the start of the war.

The Italians' setbacks were quickly forgotten and GHQ's intelligence branch was delighted with the heavy Austrian losses. Attrition appeared to be working very much in the Entente's favour because as Colonel Walter Kirke, the head of Haig's secret service, wrote on 24 June, 'the Germans will soon begin to feel the want of men – 250,000 Austrians will want some replacing, even though they are only Austrians'.[19] However, Rawlinson's Fourth Army did not enjoy a similar success. His infantry attacked on the morning of 1 July. By the end of the day over 57,000 of them had become casualties and nowhere did the British come even close to breaking the German line and reaching the open country beyond. Success would have depended on Rawlinson's gunners being able to clear a path for his infantry through the enemy's defences. The 'Tactical Notes' issued by Fourth Army headquarters in May spoke of the artillery 'battering down all opposition with a hurricane of projectiles'.[20] The attack was preceded by a spectacular bombardment lasting seven days. It wrecked the German front-line trenches but it left many of their garrisons, sheltering in very deep dug-outs, shaken but physically unscathed. Rawlinson had over 2,200 artillery pieces but four-fifths of them were field guns, field howitzers or small mortars firing shells which were too small to do much damage to troops who were well-entrenched. Furthermore, many of the shells fired during the bombardment were fitted with defective fuses and failed to explode. When the bombardment lifted, the Germans were able to emerge from their dug-outs, mount their machine guns and decimate the advancing British infantry.[21]

This initial failure caused Haig to alter the whole purpose of the battle. On 5 July Robertson wrote to Haig's Chief of Staff, Sir Launcelot Kiggell, deprecating another costly attempt at a breakthrough and elaborating a theory of offensive attrition not too far removed from Rawlinson's original concept. He wanted Haig to mount a series of strictly limited attacks preceded by intense artillery bombardments and encouraged Haig to think that 'the German [sic] is now feeling very hard put to it and all that we have to do is to keep up a deliberate and relentless pressure'.[22] Some members of the government were deeply concerned when they heard of the losses the initial assault had sustained. On 8 July Runciman referred to 'these cruelly heavy losses with only indirect gains . . .'[23] and Robertson had to work hard to reassure the War Committee that all was as it should be in France. The distinction between a battle of attrition and a break-through battle quickly became so blurred that it all but disappeared. Writing to his wife on 10 July, Haig demonstrated that he had in practice reverted to Rawlinson's original concept of killing Germans when he insisted that 'The battle is being fought out on lines which suit us. That is to say the enemy puts his reserves straight into the Battle on arrival to attack us, thus suffering big losses.'[24] On 2 August he told his army commanders that the operation had become 'a "wearing-out" battle' in which they must seek to maximize German losses and minimize their own. He also predicted that it would not reach its climax until late September.[25] His first success had come on 11 July when the Germans suspended operations at Verdun because of the pressure placed on them along the Somme. The same day he informed the War Committee through Robertson that the BEF had already inflicted heavy losses on the Germans 'but they must be prepared to carry on for some weeks, therefore they must have reserves and the necessary flow of drafts'.[26]

This did nothing to silence his critics. By the end of July some members of the government were afraid that he would soon have incurred 200,000–300,000 casualties with little to show for it.[27] On 1 August F. E. Smith, the Attorney General, circulated to his colleagues a memorandum written by Winston Churchill calling for the offensive to be ended on the grounds that the gains had been paltry and if it were continued the British army would be exhausted.[28] Robertson dismissed it as a 'damnable paper', the product of people like Churchill and French who had been passed over or who had a grudge against Haig.[29] In their replies to the War Committee, both Robertson and Haig emphasized that events on the Somme could not be understood in isolation from what the rest of the allies were doing. On 1 August Robertson insisted that attrition was working in the allies' favour. British casualties had been high, an estimated 160,000 in July, but over 50,000 had been incurred on the first day of the battle and they had since dropped to an average of 18,000 a week. Against that he estimated that the Germans and Austrians had suffered about 600,000 casualties on all fronts since 1 July. Haig, in a letter drafted by Esher, pointed out that before the offensive there had been growing criticism in France of British inaction. The opening of the battle had stopped it, but if the British suddenly ceased to participate it would have had an incalculable effect on French morale.[30] In addition he claimed that his offensive had relieved Verdun, helped the Russians by keeping German troops in the West, and had helped to bring Romania to the point where it was ready to join the Entente. For the time being the doubters were silenced.

Romania's entry into the war caused the civilian members of the War Committee to experience new heights of optimism in August 1916. They were able for a short time to discount the mounting casualties on the Somme and to overlook Britain's growing economic problems. Instead they could bask for a brief moment in the belief that, for the first time since the start of the war, the Entente had seized the strategic initiative and they could entertain the false hope that they might indeed be able to impose their own peace terms on the Central Powers by Christmas. In August 1915 the fall of Warsaw had been enough to persuade the Romanian prime minister, Bratiano, that the time was not propitious to join the Entente. In September Bulgaria had mobilized, and although the interventionist party in Romania, led by Také Ionescu, wanted Romania to counter the Bulgarians by mobilizing itself, Bratiano had remained cautious. But he did hint that he might act in the spring when he hoped that the Entente would be ready to launch a general offensive. He had not intended to act alone and thus allow the Central Powers to crush Romania in isolation and even Ionescu had been reluctant to move unless the Russians and the Anglo-French forces from Salonika could concert their operations to protect Romania while it mobilized.[31]

The possibility of Romania joining the Entente had been one reason why Lloyd George wanted the allies to remain at Salonika. To Robertson's chagrin the Chantilly conference of December 1915 had decided against evacuation. He therefore did all he could early in 1916 to limit British involvement in the Balkans. Supporting a large force in Greece would require quantities of shipping and munitions which could be ill-spared from the main fronts. In January 1916, when the question of re-equipping the defeated Serbian army arose, he insisted that the British should limit themselves to supplying clothing and stores. The French could provide the necessary guns and ammunition. When the Serbs were ready he wanted to use them to replace British and French troops at Salonika, not to supplement them.[32] But the allies would not permit Robertson to ignore the Balkans. By February the Russians were afraid that the Germans might be about to persuade Romania to join the Central Powers. If that happened Briand thought his ministry would fall and the Russians doubted whether they would be able to prevent the Germans from reaching Petrograd or Moscow.

Bratiano was ready to trade with the Central Powers but in fact had no intention of joining them. But he remained adamant that he would not join the Entente unless the Russians provided troops to protect his country from the Bulgarians. General Alexieff, the Russian Chief of Staff, insisted that he did not have the troops and instead on 11 February he suggested that the allied forces at Salonika should protect Romania by striking northwards against Bulgaria.[33] Robertson was adamant that his idea was not only impractical but was also bad strategy. Throughout most of 1916 he insisted that the best way to help the Russians and Romanians was to mount a large offensive in the West, not to fritter away men, munitions and increasingly scarce tonnage at Salonika. The allies had nearly 250,000 men at Salonika. When the Serbs arrived they would have another 100,000. On 14 February he agreed with Joffre that a successful offensive against Bulgaria would require at least another 250,000 men. For the time being, therefore, the allies did nothing beyond keeping a bridge to the Romanians open by promising them small quantities of munitions.[34]

Shortly after Robertson and Joffre reached this accord, the Germans struck at Verdun. Briand, the leading French exponent of a Balkan campaign, could not afford to allow France to be defeated at Verdun and see Romania join the Central Powers. Furthermore it was imperative that the allied troops at Salonika act to contain the enemy forces facing them, for otherwise they might be moved to France. At the beginning of March the allied commander at Salonika, General Maurice Sarrail, submitted a plan for either a series of demonstrations to contain the enemy forces facing him or for a combined Anglo-French-Serbian offensive with the ultimate objective of taking Sofia. Robertson was furious when he learnt of these proposals and Joffre hastily ordered Sarrail to forget the idea of marching on Sofia and to confine his operations to a demonstration to contain the enemy.[35] Robertson sought to tie Sarrail's hands still further. At the War Committee on 23 March he insisted that Sarrail's force be reduced by one division on the grounds that his existing garrison was more than sufficient to hold the port and the CIGS also suggested that as the Serbs arrived, more British divisions should be withdrawn to France. Despite the objections of Lloyd George and Balfour, both of whom hinted at the demoralizing impact this would have on Russia and Romania, the committee agreed.[36] But neither the Russians nor Joffre would budge. At a conference in Paris on 27 March Joffre 'beat his chest, stamped about, said that W. R. [*sic*] had promised this and that for the offensive, and now was going back on his promise, and made some cross remarks about the British Army generally'.[37] Joffre's performance only confirmed Kitchener's suspicions that the French were involved in the Balkans not for any sound military reasons but because they had dreams of building an eastern Mediterranean empire.[38]

On 21 April Buchanan reported that the Russian military attaché at Bucharest had prepared a draft military agreement with the Romanian General Staff for Romania's entry into the war. Under it the Russians agreed to send no less than four army corps to protect Romania. Grey was sceptical that this would remove the log-jam in the Balkans. Bratiano still wanted an offensive from Salonika. Briand, however, was more enthusiastic and ordered Joffre to tell Sarrail to begin planning for a general offensive against Sofia. At the War Committee on 29 April Robertson dismissed the entire proposal. The Romanians, and the Greeks if they were induced to join the Entente, were allies of doubtful value. They had insufficient munitions and the British could not make good their deficiencies. The Bulgarians would not surrender Macedonia without a struggle and the Serbs, who were the only reinforcements upon whom Sarrail could rely, were of little use after their defeat in the autumn of 1915. Joffre, already hard pressed at Verdun, had no intention of reinforcing Sarrail with French troops.[39] Even Lloyd George was temporarily convinced by Robertson's argument. He did not want a premature offensive which might simply discredit his policy and recognized that Sarrail did not have the men or munitions to achieve success. On 3 May the War Committee accepted the CIGS's conclusions and added that if the Germans did strike at Russia in the summer, the best way they could help Russia was by mounting a vigorous offensive in France.[40]

However, the French then enlisted the support of the Italians and Russians, both of whom pressed for a Balkan offensive to coincide with their forthcoming operations against Austria.[41] When the War Committee heard at the beginning of June that Sarrail was preparing to attack even without British support, Lloyd George characterized the entire proposal as 'a mad proposition'.[42] Asquith thought that the whole episode could be explained by reference to the precarious position of the Briand government at home where it was under attack from Caillaux for the apparent lack of support it had furnished to Sarrail. The British, therefore, softened their position a little, When a powerful French delegation arrived in London on 9 June, the War Committee still refused to co-operate for the present but they did promise that they would re-equip their troops at Salonika for mountain warfare and would reconsider their position if there were any significant changes in the Balkan situation.[43]

Joffre wilfully misunderstood the concessions the British had offered. On 17 June he told Sarrail to continue with his preparations for a general offensive in concert with the new British commander, Lieutenant-General George Milne. Robertson was again angry at Joffre's apparent duplicity and on 22 June the War Committee again refused to countenance an offensive.[44] But on 4 July Bratiano, much impressed by Brusilov's success against the Austrians, told the Entente that Romania was ready to join them provided that the Salonika army would protect Romania by attacking Bulgaria before his country entered the war. The problem now became who should act first. Robertson did not object in principle to aiding Romania from Salonika but he did object to acting before the Romanians themselves moved. He was ready to mount a limited offensive to pin the Bulgarians facing Sarrail's army, provided Romania had already agreed to join the Entente and was already mobilizing. Its mobilization would draw Bulgarian troops away from Sarrail and thus facilitate his advance.[45] However, the Russians and French were ready to fall in with Bratiano's wishes, and promised an allied offensive from Salonika beginning on 1 August if the Romanians would promise to put

150,000 men in the field against Bulgaria one week later. Robertson's objections were overruled and on 23 July it appeared that an agreement had been reached between Románia and the Entente.[46]

But within two days this plan had collapsed. Bratiano announced that not only did the Romanians need another 10 days to prepare their army but that they also refused to declare war on Bulgaria. Romanian irredentist ambitions were directed towards Austrian Transylvania. They wanted to remain on the defensive along the Danube against Bulgaria whilst they marched westwards into Austria.[47] On 28 July the War Committee told the French that unless Romania attacked Bulgaria, they would not participate in an offensive from Salonika. However the Russians agreed to the Romanians' wishes and the other allies had little option but to follow suit. The Treaty of Bucharest was signed on 17 August. The allies guaranteed Romania's territorial integrity and promised to secure for it at the eventual peace Transylvania, the Banat of Temesvar and Bukovina. If it gained all this, its population and territory would double. The treaty committed the Entente to the eventual breakup of the Austro-Hungarian empire. In return Romania agreed to attack Austria but not Bulgaria by 28 August. Sarrail's army would cover its mobilization by attacking the Bulgarians on 20 August.[48]

The prospect of Romania joining the Entente had a demoralizing effect on the Central Powers. The Austrians had only 30,000 poorly-armed troops in Hungary facing perhaps 300,000 Romanian soldiers. On 2 August the Hungarian Independence Party leader, Count Karolyi, approached the British minister in Berne, E. M. Grant Duff, and left him with the impression that his party wished to negotiate a separate peace between Hungary and the Entente. The Foreign Office were delighted at this evident sign of weakness. Grey immediately informed the allied ambassadors and told Grant Duff to listen carefully to anything Karolyi had to say. A week later Bohemian sources in London indicated that Count Tisza, the Hungarian prime minister, and Count Andrassy, the leader of the Hungarian Constitutional Party, also wanted a separate peace with the Entente to forestall the Romanians.[49] Romania's entry into the war also caused consternation among the German high command. Intercepted Italian diplomatic telegrams had enabled them to follow the course of the Russo-Romanian negotiations in some detail, but Bratiano's long period of indecision led Falkenhayn to believe that Romania's entry would be somewhat delayed. The news that Bratiano had actually committed his country to the Entente came as a considerable shock in Berlin. When the Kaiser heard the news on 27 August he declared that the war was lost and Germany would have to make peace.[50]

Romania's entry into the war had quite the opposite effect on the British government. The start of the Brusilov offensive in June marked the point at which the initiative had passed to the Entente for the first time since August 1914. Indeed the three months between June and August 1916 marked the high point of allied success in the entire period examined by this book. Robertson wrote to the Duke of Connaught on 9 August that 'The general situation is now better than it has ever been since the beginning of the war. The Entente are winning on all fronts and losing nowhere.'[51] Grey told Cambon on 24 August that he believed that the Germans would seek an armistice in October. Even Lloyd George, who was still concerned about the mounting casualty list on the Somme, thought that the war was going better than it had done for some time, and wrote to Haig on 21 September 'that the heartening news of the last few days had confirmed our anticipations and hopes that the tide has now definitely turned in our favour'.[52]

Their optimism was fed by a series of intelligence reports about growing demoralization within the enemy camp. By the end of August the Foreign Office knew that at the end of June, Bethmann-Hollweg had told the king of Bavaria that if the allies did not approach the Germans for terms by the autumn the Germans would be compelled to go to them.[53] An agent's report, which was thought to be sufficiently reliable to be circulated at the begining of September to the Prime Minister, the CIGS and senior Foreign Office officials, described senior German politicians including Bethmann-Hollweg as being depressed by the military situation on both the Eastern and Western fronts.[54] On 28 June Grey reiterated to Colonel House that, in the light of the forthcoming offensive, neither Britain nor its allies were ready to discuss peace terms with their enemies. In late July Drummond, in a letter to Spring-Rice seen and endorsed by Grey, still maintained the policy that Britain would seek American mediation only if one or other of the allies became exhausted and the Entente might hope to get better terms with American assistance than if they faced the Central Powers directly across the negotiating table.[55]

In the summer of 1916 there seemed every possibility that the Entente would be able to make a victorious peace and to impose their terms on the enemy. On 17 July Haig wrote that 'There must be no question of *discussing* peace conditions. We must *dictate* peace terms to the Germans.'[56] Exactly what terms the British would seek remained to be clarified. On 7 August, Lord Crawford and Balcarres, who had joined the Cabinet on 12 July as President of the Board of Agriculture, was surprised to discover that 'the War Committee has not only never discussed the demands to be made at a peace conference (that I can understand): but it has never considered upon what terms we should consent to discuss the matter at all'.[57] In May Grey had told the Russian Kadet leader, Paul Milgukov, that it would be time enough to consider the details of the Entente's peace terms when the Germans were ready to evacuate all occupied territory, including Alsace–Lorraine, and to grant the Straits and Constantinople to Russia.[58] Three months later that moment seemed to be within sight. It therefore appeared reasonable for the government to give the matter serious thought. Their deliberations illustrate more clearly than anything else the ambiguity of their relationship with their allies. On the one hand the Entente had to be preserved until the allies could impose acceptable terms upon the Germans. Therefore the British could demand nothing in advance of Germany's defeat which might so antagonize one or more of their allies that they would slacken their efforts against their common enemy. But Russia and France had once been Britain's bitter imperial rivals. The Ententes of 1904 and 1907 had muted their rivalries and they had to a considerable degree been subsumed by their common antagonism towards Germany. But once the German menace had been eliminated, these old enmities might reappear.

Thus in the summer of 1916 when the decision-makers' thoughts turned to the postwar settlement they sought two things. Their first priority was security against a resurgence of any threat from Germany. But almost as important was their wish to be secure from any threat from France or Russia. It would profit Britain little if it eliminated Germany as a menace to its security only to have it replaced by France or Russia. Nowhere was this better illustrated than in a letter Robertson wrote to Esher on 9 August

> What worries me is the making of peace. I confess that I have anxiety when I think of the day on which we may be seated round the Council Table discussing terms of peace. I am not thinking so much of the enemy as of the Allies. I do sincerely hope that we shall be strongly represented when that day comes, but I do not see how we can be unless certain important changes take place.[59]

Like Lord Hardinge, newly reinstated as permanent under secretary to the Foreign Office, Robertson was concerned that the French already had a fully developed war aims programme and would thus be able to steal a march on the British at the peace conference because they knew exactly what they wanted and the British did not. Their fears were groundless. French war aims in the summer of 1916 were still remarkably vague.[60] But the British did not know that, and in August both the Foreign Office and the War Office tried to rectify the situation by producing two memoranda which embodied the most detailed consideration any British government department had yet given to the postwar settlement. The Foreign Office's report, entitled 'Suggested basis for a territorial settlement in Europe' was completed on 7 August and was written by Sir Ralph Paget, an assistant under secretary and Sir William Tyrrell, Grey's former private secretary.[61] The General Staff's memorandum, signed by Robertson, was completed on 31 August.[62] None of these officials sought to crush Germany. Britain's quarrel was still, as it had been in 1914, with Germany's ruling Prussian military caste, not with the German people. They also shared Kitchener's conviction that the existing grouping of the powers was not permanent and that in the future Russia, rather than Germany, might emerge as Britain's most dangerous enemy. The preservation of a strong, but not an overmighty, Germany in central Europe was therefore a British war aim because a strong Germany was a necessary check to Russian ambitions.

Beyond this their conclusions exhibited some differences of emphasis. Paget and Tyrrell insisted that a durable peace in Europe could only be based on the principle of national self-determination. This probably owed much to the various eastern European émigré organizations which had found a home in London since 1914. They looked with favour upon the new nation states because the émigrés assured them that they would be pro-British. The Foreign Office officials also insisted that no state should be left at a grievous economic disadvantage by being denied access to the sea. The General Staff referred more explicitly to the need to ensure Britain's future security by recreating a balance of power in Europe, depriving Germany of its navy and ensuring that a weak and friendly power controlled the coast of the Low Countries.

These differences of emphasis should not obscure the fact that the specific recommendations put forward by these officials about the territorial settlement of Europe were sometimes remarkably similar. They recognized that Britain's hands were already partly tied by the promises it had made to its allies and by the necessity of not strengthening one state so much that it became a menace to its neighbours. This meant that Britain was already pledged to restore Belgium's political and economic independence and to ensure that it was indemnified for its losses under the terms of the declaration of Sainte Adresse signed in February 1916. Britain's own security demanded that Germany be denied access to the Belgian coast after the war. The events of August 1914 had demonstrated that no international treaty could guarantee the inviolability of Belgium's neutrality and so Britain's only option was to persuade the French to sign a tripartite treaty of alliance to protect it. Luxembourg could be afforded similar security by incorporating it into Belgium. In Alsace–Lorraine the British would have to be guided by what the French wanted but the Foreign Office experts wanted to resist any plea that France should be granted territory on the west bank of the Rhine.

The General Staff wanted all of Schleswig and part of Holstein to be returned to Denmark and were prepared simply to follow Russia's wishes with respect to Poland. But Paget and Tyrrell believed that Holstein's population was German and should be allowed to remain part of Germany. The situation was less clear in Schleswig and a plebiscite of the population might be necessary to decide whether the Duchy should remain part of Germany or be returned to Denmark. But the Foreign Office suggested three possible solutions to the Polish question. The Russians could simply absorb all of German and Austrian Poland. That was objectionable because it would create an over-mighty Russia whose frontier would be only 125 miles from Berlin and 200 miles from Vienna. 'Such an extension would secure for Russia a preponderance that might become a serious menace to the balance of power', they insisted. The second solution, a Polish state enjoying autonomy under the Russian Crown, would probably be unacceptable to the Russian government because their other subject nationalities would demand similar treatment. Paget and Tyrrell's favourite option was to establish an independent Polish state, able to act as a buffer between Germany and Russia and to be governed by a Russian Grand Duke.

In the remainder of eastern Europe and the Balkans both reports favoured the establishment of a series of nation states which would act as a barrier to future German or Russian expansion. Ferdinand of Bulgaria would have to abdicate, but if he did so the General Staff were ready to give Bulgaria the uncontested zone of Macedonia and the Foreign Office was prepared to throw in Thrace as well. As compensation the Serbs would be granted Montenegro – the Montenegrin king was thought to have been in communication with Vienna – and Spalato, Gravosa and San Giovanni di Medna as outlets to the Adriatic. In respect of Austria–Hungary, Britain's hands were already partly tied by the Treaty of London of April 1915 and, if the military situation permitted it at the end of the war, the entire empire should be broken up on the grounds that it violated the principle of nationality. There were little evidence that the Czechs wanted their own state and so they could be joined to the new Polish state. The General Staff wanted to give German-speaking Austria to Germany on the grounds that it would contribute to a stable balance of power in Central Europe and the Foreign Office agreed because they hoped that the supposedly peace-loving Austrians might in the future restrain the warlike Prussians.

Paget and Tyrrell merely mentioned that Britain's extra-European war aims deserved fuller consideration. But the General Staff took it for granted that the breakup of the Turkish empire had already been agreed. Russia would receive Constantinople and the Straits and Britain Mesopotamia, Syria and parts of Asia Minor. Persia remained a bone of contention between Britain and Russia and they suggested that the two countries should avoid bringing it up at the peace conference but try to reach their own private arrangement. Both the Foreign Office and the General Staff recognized that the disposal of Germany's colonies in Africa and the Pacific might cause dissension between the Entente and therefore wanted further careful consideration given to it. Like most British policy-makers, the Foreign and War Office officials who prepared these memoranda simply assumed that German naval disarmament was a major British war aim. They were less concerned with securing German military disarmament, although Paget and Tyrrell were strongly in favour of an international agreement to reduce armaments, a point about which Robertson was silent. Paget and Tyrrell concluded their paper by endorsing the idea of a League of Nations, pledged to use force against any aggressors provided that the USA joined it.

The third department intimately concerned with the conduct of the war, the Admiralty, did not present their war aims until October, by which time the prospects of an early peace on British terms had receded. Their aspirations, drafted by Balfour and the First Sea Lord, Sir Henry Jackson, echoed many of the suggestions already made by Paget, Tyrrell and Robertson. Both Balfour and Jackson sought terms which would not only prevent a resurgence of German power but would also check Russian ambitions. Thus Balfour wanted to establish an autonomous Polish state under Russian sovereignty. The friction this would engender between Germany and Russia would ensure that Germany would never be free to turn westwards against France and Britain, and Russia would not be able to turn south-east against India. Jackson took it for granted that the defeat of Germany would automatically entail the destruction of its fleet. He wanted to retain all of its colonies and either to close or to internationalize the Kiel Canal. If Russia acquired Constantinople he wished to strengthen the Mediterranean fleet, occupy some of the Greek islands and gain direct control of the Persian Gulf to protect the route to India.[63]

Grey described the Paget–Tyrrell memorandum as 'very ably done' and ordered its circulation to the War Committee.[64] He also agreed that it was high time the government decided which German colonies it could afford to give away as bargaining counters at the peace conference. Asquith shared Grey's concern and on 27 August he convened a committee under Sir Louis Mallet of the Foreign Office to examine Britain's extra-European war aims. This represented the first real attempt to define British war aims outside Europe since the Harcourt memorandum of March and the de Bunsen report of June 1915. The War Committee had briefly touched on the question on 1 August 1916 in connection with the campaign being waged by General Smuts in German East Africa. Balfour's insistence that the future security of the empire demanded that after the war Germany should be allowed no ports or colonies in Africa or the Pacific had met with general agreement.[65]

But the Mallet Committee revealed that there were serious differences between the officials of the departments who were involved. The Committee ignored British desiderata in Turkey because that was already the subject of agreements with the allies, and confined themselves to the disposal of Germany's possessions in the Pacific and Africa. The Admiralty and the Indian and Colonial Offices took their lead from

Mallet, who restated the opinion of the War Committee of 1 August, that 'the German colonies and possessions will be retained permanently by the Allies'. All they wanted to do was to decide which allies would get which colonies. This policy rested on the assumption that the allies would be able to impose on Germany any terms they chose. The Admiralty and the India Office saw the German colonies as a threat to the empire. The Colonial Office insisted that if German South West Africa was returned to Germany those Boers who had rebelled against British rule in September 1914 would claim that they had been vindicated. Similarly humanitarian opinion in Britain was bound to object that the Germans were unfit to rule natives.

MacDonogh, the General Staff's representative, was more far-sighted, and questioned whether it would be worth the expenditure of men and treasure to continue the war simply to add a few more colonies to the empire. He also believed that it would be unwise to deprive Germany of all of its colonies because doing so would leave it with a permanent grievance. After the war Germany would need an outlet for its surplus population and a guaranteed source of raw materials. It could seek these in its colonies or in the USA. The German–American community and Germany's trade links with the USA had been a serious source of Anglo-American friction since the start of the war, but their importance to Germany would be diminished if it had colonies of its own. The existing grouping of the powers was not permanent and in a few years time Britain might want a strong and friendly Germany as an ally. 'A policy of hate and revenge is not that of true statesmanship, and any peace that may be concluded should be based upon such principles as tend to render it strong and reliable.'[66] And finally, it was unnecessary to deprive Germany of all its colonies. Thanks to its command of the seas, Britain could gobble up most of them at will. But faced with the fact that the Dominions and allies had to be given their share of the spoils, MacDonogh conceded that German South West Africa and the German colonies and coaling stations in the Pacific could not be returned to it and would have to be retained by the Dominions and Japan.

These memoranda and discussions, together with ministers' earlier public and private utterances went some way towards clarifying what the British government thought they were fighting for. However as neither the Robertson nor Paget–Tyrrell reports nor the work of the Mallet Committee were endorsed by the Cabinet it would be wrong to suggest that they constituted official British war aims. They merely reflected some of the ideas about the postwar settlement which were current in official circles in the summer of 1916 when the government believed that the Central Powers might soon approach them to discuss terms. They accepted almost nonchalantly that the breakup of the Austro-Hungarian empire was inevitable if the Romanians lived up to expectation. They accepted that Britain was already bound by treaty obligations to its allies to a policy which amounted to the dismemberment of the Turkish empire. The discussions demonstrated that most ministers and officials who were involved in formulating war policy believed that Britain was fighting to contain, but not to crush, German power. They wanted to end the dominance of Prussia within Germany and, by destroying 'Prussian militarism' to democratize Germany. The policy-makers wished to end Germany's ambitions to be a world power and to disarm its navy, but few of them sought to disarm its army. Britain had entered the war in 1914 to preserve the European balance of power. A strong, but not an overmighty Germany, was a vital component of that balance. Without a powerful Germany in Central Europe there could be no balance of power in Europe and within a few years Britain might discover that it had simply exchanged enemies, France, or more likely Russia, for Germany.

Notes

1 Col. T. Bentley Mott (translator), *The Memoirs of Marshal Joffre*, Vol. 2 (London: Geoffrey Bless, 1932), pp. 464–5.
2 Hankey diary entry, 21 January 1916, Hankey mss, 1/1.
3 Rawlinson to Robertson, 8 April 1916, Robertson mss, I/21/11; Robertson to Stamfordham, 1 October 1915, Robertson mss, I/12/5; PRO WO 106/1510, MacDonogh, Note by the General Staff on the changes in the German order of battle in the Western theatre since January 1916, 1 June 1916; Lieut.-Col. C. à Court Repington, *The First World War 1914–1918*, Vol. 1 (London: Constable, 1920), pp. 114–15; Enemy Personnel Committee, Inquiry regarding the probable resources of the enemy in Personnel at the present stage of the war, 26 June 1916, Lloyd George mss, D/22/4/14.
4 Robertson to Haig, 28 May 1916, Haig mss, Acc. 3155/105.
5 PRO CAB 42/14/12, Minutes of the War Committee, 30 May 1916.
6 Brig.-Gen. John Charteris, *At GHQ* (London: Cassell, 1931), p. 137.
7 GHQ General Staff (Intelligence), Notes on the German Second Army, 28 April 1916 and photograph captioned 'Captured German trenches showing concrete dug-out', 2 March 1916, Haig mss, Acc. 3155/105.
8 GHQ General Staff (Intelligence), Situation on 18 June 1916, Haig mss, 3155/106.
9 Brig.-Gen. J. E. Charteris, Forecast of state of German resources during the summer of 1916, 24 May 1916, Haig mss, Acc. 3155/215 (I).
10 Haig diary entry, 5 April 1916, Haig mss, Acc. 3155/105.
11 ibid. S. Bidwell and D. Graham, *Firepower: British Army Weapons and Theories of War, 1904–1945* (London: Allen & Unwin, 1982), pp. 70–1, 80–2.
12 Haig diary entry, 15 June 1916, Haig mss, Acc. 3155/106.
13 ibid.
14 Butler, O. A. D. 912/1, 27 May 1916, Haig mss, Acc. 3155/215 (p).
15 Charteris, *At GHQ*, p. 151.
16 PRO FO 371/2804/9706, Rodd to Foreign Office, 22 May 1916 and (180949), Rodd to Foreign Office, 26 May 1916 (182105), Rodd to Foreign

Office, 28 May 1916 (183031), Rodd to Foreign Office, 29 May 1916; G. E. Rothenberg, 'The Habsburg army in the First World War: 1914–1918', in R. A. Kann *et al.*, *The Habsburg Empire in World War One* (New York: Columbia University Press and Eastern European Quarterly, 1977), pp. 79–80; J. Whittam, *The Politics of the Italian Army* (London: Croom Helm, 1977), pp. 198–200.

17   PRO CAB 42/14/12, Minutes of the War Committee, 30 May 1916.

18   N. Stone, *The Eastern Front 1914–1917* (London: Hodder & Stoughton, 1975), pp. 232–55.

19   Kirke to his wife, 24 June 1916, Kirke mss, Vol. II.

20   Fourth Army Tactical Notes, May 1916, Montgomery–Massingberd mss, 92.

21   Haig diary entry, 20 June 1916, Haig mss, Acc. 3155/106; PRO CAB 42/15/10, Ministry of Munitions, Output of Munitions – six weeks ending 10 June 1916; 15 June 1916; PRO CAB 42/16/11, Director General of Munitions Design, Extract from reports on visits to France by representatives of the Ministry of Munitions, June–July 1916, 28 July 1916.

22   Robertson to Haig, 5 July 1916, Haig mss, Acc. 3155/107; Robertson to Kiggell, 5 July 1916, Robertson mss, I/35/65.

23   Runciman to Samuel, 8 July 1916, Samuel mss, A/46.

24   Haig to his wife, 14 July 1916, Haig mss, Acc. 3155/144; Robertson to Haig, 10 July 1916, Haig mss, Acc. 3155/107.

25   Kiggell to Rawlinson and Gough, 2 August 1916, Haig mss, Acc. 3155/107.

26   PRO CAB 42/16/5, Minutes of the War Committee, 11 July 1916.

27   Robertson to Haig, 29 July 1916, Haig mss, Acc. 3155/107; L. H[arcourt] to Lloyd George, 22 July 1916, Lloyd George mss, E/4/3/1; Haking to Wilson, 8 August 1916, Wilson mss, 73/1/20.

28   PRO CAB 37/153/3, Smith to Cabinet and enc., 1 August 1916; D. R. Woodward, *Lloyd George and the Generals* (London: Associated University Presses, 1983), pp. 103–4.

29   Robertson to Haig, 7 August 1916, Haig mss, Acc. 3155/107.

30   Robertson to Haig, 1 August 1916, Haig mss, Acc. 3155/107; PRO CAB 42/17/1, Minutes of the War Committee, 1 August 1916; [Haig], Note on the results of the Battle of the Somme during the month of July, *c.* 1 August 1916, Haig mss, Acc. 3155/107; PRO CAB 42/17/3, Minutes of the War Committee, 5 August 1916.

31   G. E. Torrey, 'Rumania and the belligerents 1914–1916', *Journal of Contemporary History*, vol. 1, no. 3 (1966), pp. 183–8; Ionescu to Lloyd George, 14 and 28 October 1915, Lloyd George mss, D/19/13/7 and D/19/8/8.

32   PRO CAB 42/7/13, Robertson, Note for the War Committee on co-ordination of arrangements for supplying and equipping Serbian Army, 25 January 1916.

33   PRO CAB 42/8/6, Nicolson to Grey, 9 February 1916; PRO CAB 37/142/32, Grey to Buchanan, 11 February 1916; PRO FO 800/102, Grey to Kitchener, 10 February 1916; K. Neilson, *Strategy and Supply: The Anglo-Russian Alliance 1914–1917* (London: Allen & Unwin, 1984), pp. 146–7.

34   PRO FO 800/102, Robertson to Grey, 10 February 1916; PRO WO 106/393, Note of a conversation between General Joffre and General Robertson, 14 February 1916; PRO CAB 42/13/2, Robertson, Assistance for Russia, 1 May 1916.

35   PRO WO 106/393, Robertson to Mahon, 6 March 1916; Robertson to Mahon, 6 March 1916, Robertson mss, I/35/74; J. K. Tanenbaum, *General*

Maurice Sarrail, 1856–1929: The French Army and Left-wing Politics (Chapel Hill, NC: University of North Carolina Press, 1974), pp. 189–90.

36   PRO CAB 42/11/9, Minutes of the War Committee, 23 March 1916 and Robertson, Note by the CIGS on the situation at Salonika, 22 March 1916.

37   Clive diary entry, 27 March 1916, Clive mss, II/3.

38   Haig diary entry, 29 March 1916, Haig mss, Acc. 3155/105.

39   Tanenbaum, *Sarrail*, pp. 192–3; PRO CAB 42/12/12, Buchanan to Grey, 21 April 1916; PRO CAB 42/13/2, Robertson, Offensive operations in the Balkans, 29 April 1916.

40   PRO CAB 42/13/2, Minutes of the War Committee, 3 May 1916; PRO CAB 42/14/1, Robertson, Offensive operations in the Balkans, 16 May 1916; Woodward, *Lloyd George*, p. 89.

41   PRO CAB 42/15/6, Buchanan to Grey, 1 June 1916 and Extract from Gen. Delmé Radcliffe's telegram of 6 June 1916 to CIGS.

42   PRO CAB 42/15/6, Minutes of the War Committee, 7 June 1916.

43   PRO CAB 37/149/19, Proceedings of a conference held at 10 Downing Street, on Friday, June 9, 1916 at 11.30 a.m.

44   PRO CAB 42/15/10, Joffre to Sarrail and Robertson to Joffre, 17 and 21 June 1916; PRO CAB 42/15/11, Minutes of the War Committee, 22 June 1916.

45   Tanenbaum, *Sarrail*, p. 103; Neilson, *Strategy and Supply*, pp. 150–1; Robertson to Esher, 7 July 1916, Robertson mss, I/34/6; Robertson to Haig, 11 July 1916, Haig mss, Acc. 3155/107; PRO CAB 42/16/1, Minutes of the War Committee, 6 July 1916.

46   PRO CAB 42/16/10, Minutes of the War Committee, 20 July 1916; Clive diary entries, 22 and 23 July 1916, Clive mss, II/3.

47   PRO CAB 42/16/11, Barclay to Grey, 26 July 1916; PRO CAB 42/17/1, Rodd to Grey, 31 July 1916.

48   PRO CAB 42/16/11, Minutes of the War Committee, 28 July 1916; Neilson, *Strategy and Supply*, pp. 152–4.

49   PRO FO 371/2602/150294, Grant Duff to Foreign Office, 2 August 1916 and (157810), Foreign Office to Buchanan, 11 August 1916.

50   M. Kitchen, *The Silent Dictatorship: The Politics of the German High Command under Hindenburg and Ludendorff, 1916–1918* (London: Croom Helm, 1976), p. 40.

51   Robertson to Connaught, 9 August 1916, Robertson mss, I/35/13.

52   Lloyd George to Haig, 21 September 1916, Haig mss, Acc. 3155/108; PRO CAB 37/154/18, Grey to Bertie, 24 August 1916.

53   B. J. Hendrick (ed.), *The Life and Letters of Walter Hines Page*, Vol. 2 (London: Heinemann, 1930), pp. 180–2; see also Sir A. Fitzroy, *Memoirs*, (London: Hutchinson, 1923), p. 635.

54   Notes from a reliable source, 9 September 1916, Lloyd George mss, E/3/27/1.

55   A. S. Link (ed.), *The Papers of Woodrow Wilson*, Vol. 37 (Princeton, NJ: Princeton University Press, 1980), pp. 412–3; PRO FO 800/86, Drummond to Spring-Rice, 25 July 1916; PRO FO 800/242, Grey to Spring-Rice, 29 July 1916.

56   Haig to his wife, 17 July 1916, Haig mss, Acc. 3155/144.

57   J. Vincent (ed.), *The Crawford Papers: The Journals of David Lindsay, Twenty-seventh Earl of Crawford and Tenth Earl of Balcarres 1871–1940 during the years 1892–1940* (Manchester: Manchester University Press, 1984), pp. 359–60.

58   PRO CAB 37/147/40, Grey to Buchanan, 15 May 1916.

59   Robertson to Esher, 9 August 1916, Haig mss, Acc. 3155/214f.

60   V. H. Rothwell, *British War Aims and Peace Diplomacy 1914–1918* (Oxford:

Clarendon Press, 1971), pp. 39–40; D. Stevenson, *French War Aims against Germany 1914–1919* (Oxford: Clarendon Press, 1982), pp. 40–4.

61 PRO CAB 42/17/4, Paget and Tyrrell, Suggested Basis for a territorial settlement in Europe, 7 August 1916.

62 ibid; PRO CAB 42/18/10, Robertson, General Staff Memorandum submitted in accordance with the Prime Minister's instructions, 31 August 1916; L. S. Jaffe, *The Decision to Disarm Germany: British Policy towards Postwar German Disarmament, 1914–1919* (London: Allen & Unwin, 1985), pp. 12, 21–5, 44–50; K. J. Calder, *Britain and the Origins of the New Europe, 1914–1918* (Cambridge: Cambridge University Press, 1976), pp. 94–8.

63 PRO CAB 37/157/7, Balfour, Memorandum, 4 October 1916; PRO CAB 42/21/8, Jackson, Note on the possible terms of peace, 12 October 1916.

64 PRO FO 371/2804/180510, Grey, Minute, 7 August 1916.

65 PRO CAB 42/17/1, Minutes of the War Committee, 1 August 1916; PRO CAB 16/36, Committee on territorial changes: T. C. 1, terms of reference, 27 August 1916.

66 PRO CAB 16/36, Committee on territorial changes. Reports and Proceedings, 1916–17; Jaffe, *Decision to Disarm*, pp. 48–9.

12

The Strategic Background to the Collapse of the Asquith Coalition

BY NOVEMBER the hopes, raised by Romania's entry into the war, that the Entente might be able to impose a victorious peace upon the Central Powers by the end of the year had been dashed. The Brusilov offensive was halted. The Somme offensive was continued partly to prevent the Germans sending reinforcements to the Eastern front and partly because GHQ believed that the longer it went on the more likelihood there was of German morale collapsing. But the Germans were able to contain the Western allies and scrape together enough men to crush Romania. The combined allied offensive ended in mid-November amongst signs of growing war weariness in all the allied countries. All the British had to show for their efforts was a lengthy casualty list and the growing realization that not for much longer would they be able to act as the economic mainstay of the Entente alliance. Britain's balance of payments problems and President Wilson's threat of a trade embargo meant that in 1917 the Entente would be dependent on American goodwill for much of the economic wherewithal to continue the war. The Asquith coalition collapsed because its members could not agree on how to meet this crisis.

Robertson and Haig persisted with the British offensive on the Somme despite growing criticisms of their operations for three reasons. Haig had always anticipated that his army would suffer heavy casualties during the battle but he was confident that the Germans would suffer even more heavily. His confidence was fed by Charteris. In July Charteris reported that the Germans were losing the battle because they were using up their manpower reserves in a series of expensive and largely unsuccessful counter-attacks which were broken up by the British artillery.[1] He believed that a breakthrough was imminent and, despite the protests of some of his own subordinates, he began to reorganize his own branch for a period of mobile warfare.[2] But MacDonogh at the War Office had come to a different conclusion. His calculations suggested that although the Germans were losing heavily they still had ample manpower to enable them to continue fighting well into 1917. Charteris accepted MacDonogh's figures but ignored his conclusions, and comforted Haig by distributing captured documents indicative of a sharp drop in German morale. On 10 October, for example, GHQ's intelligence branch issued a translation of an order signed by General von Below, the German commander on the Somme, ordering that no major counter-attacks were to be launched without his express orders.[3]

The second reason why the British continued their offensive throughout the summer was that the allies would not allow Haig to relax his efforts. Although the Germans had all but ceased their attack at Verdun by mid-July Briand insisted on 6 August that 'Verdun is not relieved. The pressure has been taken off that is all.'[4] As Grey told the War Committee on 18 August, 'the French were now very pleased, because they cherished the great expectation of a considerable advance. If however, we went on until October without much advance, there would be a reaction. The French would not like the idea of another winter without a definite advance to our credit.'[5] But although Poincaré wanted another full-scale attack similar to that launched on 1 July, Haig would not be rushed. In August he mounted a series of local attacks designed to inflict the heaviest possible losses on the Germans but refused to mount another major assault until mid-September.[6]

Finally Haig and Robertson wanted to keep the Somme offensive going to contain the German army in the West and prevent the Central Powers sending large reinforcements eastwards to crush Romania or Russia. Since the end of the 1915 campaign the Western allies had feared that if they did not act vigorously to draw the Germans westwards they would turn east to capture Petrograd. Even before Romania joined the war Charteris noted German troop movements through Mons and deduced that they were going to Russia. Romania's entry into the war coincided with the end of the Brusilov offensive. Brusilov's gains had been bought with very high casualties. Their replacements were often untrained youths of 19 or family men of over 40. During the autumn and winter of 1916–17 the Russian army suffered from inflation and food shortages and experienced a collapse in morale probably worse than that which it had experienced during the 'Great Retreat' of 1915. The tsarina was blamed for harbouring pro-German elements in the government. There was a widespread belief, shared by the British embassy, that the imperial favourite, Rasputin, was a German spy and that those ministers thought to be his protégés, like Protopopov, Khvostov and Sturmer, might seek a negotiated peace with Germany. Protopopov was known to have spoken to the German banker Max Warburg in Sweden in June and the Germans were known to be continuing their efforts to open negotiations in October and November. Since 1914 Sazonov had symbolized Russia's commitment to the Entente and his dismissal in July and replacement by Sturmer gave Buchanan particular cause for concern. The British embassy in Petrograd, taking much of its information from Robert Bruce Lockhart, the consul general in Moscow who was in close contact with leading Russian liberals, was only half convinced by Sturmer's assurances that Russia would not opt out of the conflict. Buchanan believed that only three things kept Russia in the war, the allied offensive on the Somme, the knowledge that they would require British and French investment to rebuild their economy after the war, and the reactionaries' awareness that if they acted precipitately there might be a revolution.[7]

The Romanian campaign began badly and ended in disaster for the Entente. Romania's entry could not have come at a worse time for the Russian army. It added to their problems because they had to shore up the Romanians by sending large numbers of troops southwards to protect an extra 350 miles of front.[8] Sarrail was supposed to cover the Romanians' mobilization by attacking the Bulgarians facing him on 20 August. But the Bulgarians struck first and it was Sarrail and not the enemy who retreated. The Romanians launched a badly organized offensive into Transylvania which quickly stalled and Lloyd George reacted by urging the dispatch of more troops to Salonika and the mounting of a bigger offensive. On 9 September Robertson, perhaps encouraged by Haig's prediction that German reserves on the Somme were exhausted and that the battle was about to reach a crisis, argued instead that the best way to help Romania was to continue to exert the maximum possible pressure on the Germans in the West. The War Committee agreed, although with little enthusiasm.[9]

On 6 September the Central Powers stole a march on the Entente by establishing a unified military command under the German Supreme Command (OHL) and the speed with which the Germans reacted made nonsense of British plans. Thanks to their control of the central European railway system, they could mass troops against Romania far more quickly than the Western allies could hope to send troops to Salonika by sea. Within three weeks of the Romanian declaration of war they had assembled on the Romanian frontier a force equal in size to the entire Romanian army. Sarrail's offensive from Salonika, which finally began on 10 September, made little headway. Haig's autumn offensive began five days later. Using tanks for the first time, he attacked at Fleurs Courcelette and captured over 3,000 prisoners. But the operation, and subsequent smaller offensives, did not achieve the breakthrough he sought. Nevertheless, given the deteriorating situation on the Eastern front, the state of French morale and his own conviction that German morale was crumbling he was reluctant to pause and allow the enemy to recover.[10] On 7 October he asked the War Committee for permission to continue his offensive for as long as the weather permitted on the grounds that 'It is not possible to say how near to breaking point the enemy may be but he had undoubtedly gone a long way towards it'.[11] On 15 October he and Foch agreed that 'the general feeling in France and the state of Rumania demand decisive action at an early date'.[12] But the resulting operations on the Somme did little to help the Romanians. By mid-September the Central Powers had already halted the Romanian advance and begun a counter-offensive which allowed them to enter Bucharest on 6 December.[13]

If British policy in Romania ended in tragedy, their policy in Greece ended in farce. In January 1916 British intelligence officers in Greece reported that Venizelos, who was convinced that King Constantine was hopelessly pro-German, was willing to stage a coup against him. At the end of May Constantine allowed the Bulgarians to occupy some Greek frontier fortifications after the Greek army had offered only token resistance. Venizelos asked for French and British support to enable him to establish a provisional government at Salonika which would reverse the king's policies and by June Sarrail, the French and British ministers at Athens, and most of the French Cabinet except Briand, were ready to back him. But Crewe, deputizing for Grey, wanted to wait until the Greek people had made their own wishes known in the forthcoming general election.[14] Grey was also afraid that Anglo-French involvement in an anti-monarchical coup would have adverse repercussions on their relations with the Russians. It would play into the hands of the pro-German reactionaries whom he thought surrounded the tsar.[15] But the Bulgarian invasion of Greece threatened the indefinite postponement of the election, and the situation began to slip beyond British control. On 31 August the French informed the British through their naval attaché in Paris that the safety of Sarrail's forces demanded that the Entente seize control of the Greek ports, railways, telegraphs and post offices. A pro-Venizelos revolution took place in Salonika which led to the establishment of a new provisional government. Sarrail was quick to recognize it and the British had no option other than to follow suit.[16] Greece now had two governments, the king's and Venizelos's, and the Entente thus had a new ally in the shape of the Venizelists but the British were not entirely happy. At the end of September they made one more attempt to bring the whole of Greece into the war. They advised Constantine that if he wanted to unite his country he should install a pro-Entente government and declare war on Bulgaria by 1 October. That was hardly advice which the king, with Bulgarian troops already occupying part of his country, was likely to take. The possibility which the British had cherished for over two years of bringing a united Greece into the war had disappeared.

Since the beginning of 1915 British policy had been based on the assumption that the Entente would be able to wear down the Central Powers because they possessed greater resources in men and money. But by the summer of 1916 three major bottle-necks had emerged within the British economy which together threatened to undermine its role as a major military power and the economic mainstay of the Entente. Ships, money and men were all in short supply and the War Committee was unable to determine an order of priorities which satisfied both its own government departments and the allies.

Until September 1915 British ocean-going tonnage had roughly equal-led what it had been in August 1914. Losses, amounting to 1·4m tons had been made good by new launchings and by adding captured or interned ships to the British register. But by September 1916 tonnage registered in Britain had fallen by 761,000 tons. The shipyards could not make good the shortages because the Ministry of Munitions, which consumed nearly three-quarters of all steel produced in Britain, was reluctant to release the steel and skilled labour needed to build more merchant ships.[17] All British ocean-going tonnage was under some form of government control; 31·25 per cent was requisitioned by the Admiralty, War Office or one of the allied governments; 27·14 per cent was under requisition by other government departments for the carriage of wheat, iron ore, timber or flax for the British or allied governments and the remainder was con-trolled by the Ship Licensing Committee.

At the end of April 1916 the War Committee tried to provide more tonnage for non-military purposes by ordering the War Office and Admiralty to release 200 ships. In fact they only released about 60 and by the autumn the Salonika campaign threatened to wipe out even that modest gain. The shortage seemed likely to become worse. The American wheat crop failed and that meant that grain would have to be carried from Australia to make good the shortfall. That would require the equivalent of another 122 vessels. And on 29 October Jellicoe informed Balfour that if losses from U-boats continued at their present rate, by the summer of 1917 they 'would have such a serious effect upon the import of food and other necessaries into the allied countries as to force us into accepting peace terms which the military position on the Continent would not justify and which would fall far short of our desires'.[18]

Government spending soon rose well above the limits set by the April budget, thanks largely to the extra cost of a new artillery programme for the army and heavier than expected allied demands for money and supplies. The French wanted British pig-iron, the Russians wanted munitions and railway supplies, the Italians wanted wheat, coal and steel and they all wanted money and shipping. All the allies assumed that Britain's purse was bottomless and blamed it for selfishness when their wants were not satisfied.[19] The British retaliated by accusing their allies of waste and of failing to organize their own economies properly. Russian munitions factories were reported to be frequently strike-bound and the Italians were suspected of wanting one million tons of coal so they could continue glass production. On 30 June the War Committee therefore decided to call an allied conference so they could impress upon their partners the need to maximize their own production and to decide on the allocation of munitions, money and ships between them.[20]

The conference began on 13 July. The Russians presented a huge shopping list of heavy artillery, shells, small arms and railway equipment of which the British expected to be able to deliver only one-sixth by June 1917. In comparison the Italians demands were modest, only 100,000 rifles at once, and 36,000 shells per month thereafter. The participants agreed to establish a clearing-house in London for all orders placed in neutral countries and reached an interim agreement about British support for the financing of French and Italian orders in the autumn. At a separate Anglo-Italian conference held a month later, Runciman promised to do all he could to meet Italy's coal demands.[21] But hardly had the ink dried on the July agreement than parts of it had to be renegotiated. The French had assumed that they would be able to raise a $100m loan in the USA and their failure to do so led to another heavy drain on the Bank of England's dollar reserves. On 24 August McKenna hurried to Calais to prop up France's foreign purchasing by agreeing to discount £150m of French Treasury bills in the six months up to March 1917 in return for £50m of French gold.[22] The Russians were much more loath to part with their gold and asked to renegotiate their existing promise to send gold to Britain if the British demanded it. The Treasury remained obdurate and eventually the Russians gave way with ill grace. Exporting gold would only make Russian inflation worse and, according to the Russian finance minister, 'would cause serious discontent amongst all classes and create bad feeling towards us'.[23] In November the Italians asked for more steel and were refused. The British no longer had sufficient for their own requirements.[24]

The effect of conscription on the economy combined with the heavy losses sustained on the Somme meant that manpower again became a bone of contention for the War Committee in the summer. The Adjutant General's branch found itself competing with half a dozen other government departments for men. In February 1916 the Board of Trade had estimated that even allowing for the employment of 11 per cent more women the total industrial labour force had fallen by 11·4 per cent since the start of the war.[25] In May the Cabinet tried to insist that the army release to the Admiralty and the Ministry of Munitions some of the skilled engineering workers who had enlisted. Their order was met with obstruction and then by a blank refusal on the grounds that the army required skilled artificers just as much as other government departments.

Sir Neville Macready, the Adjutant General, was similarly obstructive when the Home Office asked him to release miners so they could increase coal production to meet British and allied requirements. He replied that the army needed their services in its tunnelling companies on the Western Front.[26] Macready found it relatively easy to meet Haig's initial losses during the Somme offensive, but by the end of July he was concerned for the future. He estimated that there were still 3·8 million men of military age who had not been enlisted, of whom 1·5 million were protected from enlistment by one or other government department. On 21 July he informed Robertson that the needs of the army and industry could only be met if four things were done; a greater use had to be made of foreign labour, unfit men should be returned to industry from the home defence forces, exemptions granted by tribunals to men under thirty should be withdrawn, and a definite decision should be made as to which industries should be sacrificed by withdrawing their labour. Lloyd George agreed and on 1 August suggested that a new committee should be established to examine the claims of each government department for manpower.[27] The Manpower Distribution Board, under the chairmanship of Austen Chamberlain, was established on 22 August. It had powers to adjudicate in all questions arising between departments concerning the allocation of labour and any new projects requiring more men were to be referred to it but it had no executive authority to initiate changes in the distribution of manpower.[28]

On 11 September Robertson informed the War Committee that the army needed 400,000 recruits by March 1917 and that it would not get them unless fewer men were exempted.[29] The board's first report, which was presented to the War Committee on 29 and 30 September, broadly supported the army. Tribunals were enjoined to speed up their procedures and the numbers of exemptions and badges granted by them and government departments should be further limited. The board also recommended that the process of dilution be increased as the only alternative to industrial conscription. The army was to be given first choice of the skilled manpower thus made available and the Ministry of Munitions would have to make do with what was left. Perhaps more significantly, it also spelt out the economic and political implications of these recommendations for Britain and its allies. For example, hitherto orders for guns had been placed by the Ministry of Munitions without first consulting the Adjutant General to discover whether the gunners could be found to operate them. That would have to cease. No new munitions factories should be built. And 'The Board are of opinion that it should be made clear to the Allies that demands for supplies in excess of those to which we are already committed may entail a reduction of our military effort.'[30] The board had given a clear warning that the British war economy had reached the limit of expansion unless the government was ready to risk the political repercussions of industrial conscription. Although the War Committee agreed that the Adjutant General would in future be consulted about the manpower implications involved if the allies asked for new credits or supplies, in practice government policy continued to drift and by November the board had failed to resolve the conflict of interest between the War Office and the Ministry of Munitions. However, by compelling those departments who required manpower to quantify their demands, it made the War Committee aware of the fact that departments like the Home Office and the Board of Agriculture which hitherto had been regarded as being of secondary importance to the war effort, were in fact performing vital tasks which had to be sustained.[31]

Shortages of men, money and tonnage undermined the government's policy of preserving social cohesion by maintaining the freest possible entry of imports into Britain and reducing consumption by a combination of loans and taxes. After dropping by half between March and July, Atlantic freight rates began to rise again in August. Currency inflation continued apace. The government preferred to export gold to meet payments in New York rather than keep it in the Bank of England to restrict the issue of paper money. In June a second major round of wage demands had begun. These were coupled with demands from trades councils and the TUC for the government to control all food supplies and to introduce rationing.[32] In September the Board of Trade estimated that the cost of living for the working classes had risen by half since the start of the war. The Cabinet's initial reaction was to establish a committee to investigate the cause of the rising price of basic foodstuffs. But even before it reported, the government was driven to act by the threat of a world grain shortage in 1917 combined with the threat of strikes in strategic industries if they were not seen to be doing something.[33] At the end of August old age pensions were increased by half and the lowest paid government employees were granted a war bonus of between 3 and 4 shillings per week. In October the Royal Commission on Wheat Supplies was established. Importers became government agents and were paid a fixed percentage according to their turnover. William Beveridge was made head of the Board of Trade's new Food Department. However, the government's most successful innovation was an order issued to millers compelling them to extract a larger proportion of flour from the grain by milling it more finely.[34]

On 30 August, only three days after Romania mobilized, Asquith asked all departments to submit a list of their war aims. Like Hardinge and Robertson he was afraid that the French would be able to steal a march on the British unless they prepared themselves. 'Everything indicates', he told his colleagues, 'that M. Briand considered that we should be face to face with this question before the end of the autumn.'[35] On 6 September he left Haig with the impression that he was determined to continue the war 'till Germany is vanquished'.[36] This determination was nourished by Foreign Office reports that the Germans were under so much pressure that they might soon make overtures to the allies. Count Horodyski, a Galician Pole who worked as an agent for the Foreign Office, reported on 18 September that he had been approached by an intermediary of the Bavarian government who was seeking peace. Herbert Hoover, the head of the American relief mission in Belgium, told Lord Eustace Percy of the Foreign Office on 25 September that the Germans had twice approached the Belgians offering them peace on the basis of restoring their independence and hinting that they might also be willing to restore Lorraine to France.[37] With their hopes raised by these reports and Romania's entry into the war, British ministers and officials were, at least for the time being, able to push to one side their growing economic problems. The last thing that Foreign Office officials like Bertie and Hardinge wanted in September was for President Wilson, seeking re-election in the forthcoming presidential election, to pose as a peacemaker by offering mediation. The British and French left the Americans in no doubt that they would not welcome American intervention. Briand told the American ambassador in Paris that the time was not ripe and in Washington Spring-Rice repeated the same message to friends of the administration.[38]

However, Britain's dangerous economic dependence on the USA was underlined when, on 16 September, Spring-Rice reported that Congress had given Wilson the power to retaliate against any country which placed improper restrictions on American trade. The threat of a trade embargo could not be taken lightly because it would hamstring the Entente's ability to continue to prosecute the war into 1917, but the War Committee could not agree on how to reply if the Americans did impose one. Grey counselled caution and the need to prepare a reasoned vindication of British policy, but Lloyd George did not think that sufficient. He had received a secret intercept, probably from the DNI, Captain Hall, of a telegram sent by the American ambassador in Berlin purporting to show that the Germans were seeking American mediation. On 28 September he therefore gave an interview to Roy Howard of the United Press of the United States, insisting that Britain was not ready for peace and that 'The fight must be to the finish – to a knockout'.[39] Reactions to Lloyd George's initiative were mixed. Bertie and Hardinge welcomed it because it appeared to rule out a compromise peace. But, far from rallying national opinion behind the war, it only provoked the government's opponents to fresh demands for a more detailed definition of British war aims. Leaders of the Union of Democratic Control like C. P. Trevelyan refused to accept that the issues at stake were sufficient to warrant the losses the British had sustained since July. On 11 October he told the Commons that

It is not everybody who is blind to the real meaning of that abominable phrase "A war of attrition". They know that rubbing away is not only on one side. It was all very well when the attrition was all on the other side at the time of Verdun, when the principal attrition was hundreds of thousands of Germans; but part of the attrition now is hundreds of thousands of British men.[40]

The UDC did not wage a campaign to stop the war unconditionally. They claimed that the war was being needlessly prolonged even though a negotiated peace which would meet the legitimate aspirations of the French, Belgians and Serbs could be secured. They condemned the government for prolonging the war merely to win territory for Italy and Russia, denounced the idea of a fight to the finish, and demanded that the government should publicly announce their war aims.[41] But Asquith and Grey refused to rise to the bait. Far better to risk the ire of their domestic critics than to accede to their wishes and find themselves at odds with the Americans and their own allies by starting a public discussion of territorial war aims before the enemy had sued for peace. Instead they relied on emotion. Britain and its allies had already suffered so much that they could not allow their losses to be in vain and the war to end in what Asquith described on 11 October as 'some patched-up, precarious, dishonouring compromise, masquerading under the name of peace'.[42]

Lloyd George's interview marked the high point of the government's optimism that they would be soon be able to end the war on their own terms. Hopes of imposing allied peace terms on the Central Powers, which had seemed so bright in August when Romania joined the war, had begun to fade by October. The Russian offensive had stopped, the Germans had checked the Romanian advance and Haig's offensive in mid-September had failed to inflict a decisive defeat on the German army in the West. As the prospect that the war would continue into 1917 became more real, so some ministers began to express doubts about the ability of the economy to sustain a war of attrition for much longer. On 30 September the General Staff tried to demonstrate that attrition was working in the Entente's favour by presenting a memorandum to the War Committee justifying Haig's conduct of the Somme offensive by claiming that the Germans had suffered 200,000 more casualties than the allies during the battle. But Balfour was frankly, and probably correctly, sceptical of their figures. 'We could not go on indefinitely', he told the War Committee on 3 October, 'pouring out capital and suffering heavy casualties which required replacing. He thought that the Germans had now given up all thought of victory, but that they thought that the Allies' resources would fail before we could achieve a victory over them.'[43] McKenna and Grey deprecated Lloyd George's interview because they knew, in the Chancellor's words, that Britain simply could not pay for what Lloyd George proposed, 'an indefinite war'. Grey thought that Lloyd George's impetuosity had only made an American trade embargo more likely and that he had acted unnecessarily because the French had already persuaded Wilson not to attempt mediation for the time being. Grey still wanted to hold the possibility of American mediation in reserve if peace through victory finally became impossible.[44]

Grey and Balfour persuaded the War Committee to conduct a complete survey of British, allied and enemy resources and their respective abilities to continue fighting. The results did not make comforting reading. They demonstrated that McKenna was fast running out of fiscal expedients. On 24 October he informed the War Committee that a survey of Britain's financial liabilities showed that 40 per cent of all the money Britain spent on the war was expended in the USA. Britain was a valuable market for the Americans and one which they might be reluctant to lose, but British supplies of gold and convertible securities were nearly exhausted. Soon 80 per cent of all allied spending in the USA would have to be paid for by American loans. If the American government became irritated with Britain's seemingly unreasonable refusal to negotiate peace, or if American investors lost confidence in the Entente's ability to win the war, the loans could cease overnight. McKenna concluded that by June 1917 President Wilson would therefore be in a position to dictate almost any terms he chose to impose on the Entente.[45] By contrast Max Muller, the Foreign Office's expert on the German economy, told the War Committee on 30 October that the German government was finding little difficulty in paying for its war effort and that by a rigorous system of controls and the use of substitutes the German economy would continue to function for an unspecified time despite the allied blockade. Indeed if the Germans overran Romania their economic position might actually improve.[46] The moral of these two reports was plain. In the short term it was the Entente, whose entire policy since 1915 had rested on the assumption that in a long war they possessed the greater staying power, who were the more vulnerable to economic pressure.

The Asquith coalition collapsed in December 1916 because it seemed to lack the necessary will to overcome these problems. On 31 October Hankey summarized the conclusions of the memoranda which Asquith had requested on 30 August. The Somme offensive had matched Robertson's expectations. He had never suggested that it would bring the enemy to the peace conference but it had inflicted heavy losses on them. After outlining the main allied political and territorial war aims, Hankey then indicated that most of the coveted territory was still occupied by the enemy. It was therefore pointless to discuss these peace terms with the Central Powers until the balance of military advantage had tipped towards the Entente. To achieve this the allies had to mobilize more men and material and safeguard their ability to continue the war. Their weakest points were their reliance on American economic assistance and their mounting shipping losses.[47]

The government began to prepare its plans for 1917 in the light of Hankey's conclusions and also in reaction to events in Germany. Between September and November 1916 the Germans publicly demonstrated their determination to continue the war into 1917 by adopting the Hindenburg Programme and the Auxiliary Labour Law. They hoped that by militarizing their economy, raising the age of military service, reducing the numbers of exemptions, and exploiting the occupied territories more thoroughly they could double their shell production and treble their gun production by the spring of 1917.[48] In the face of this evidence of the Germans' determination to continue fighting, Robertson abandoned Kitchener's assumption upon which all previous plans had been based, that the crisis of the war would be reached early in 1917. In a memorandum presented to Lloyd George and the War Committee on 3 November he flatly stated that although he could not predict when the war would end he estimated that Germany could probably continue fighting until the summer of 1918. The British therefore would also have to prepare to do the same and although he never suggested that the British economy should be militarized to the same degree as the Germans', he did insist once again on a thorough comb-out of the domestic economy and an intensification of the dilution programme to provide the army with the men it required. He also recognized that Britain would have to give up the last shreds of Kitchener's policy of relying on allied manpower to wear-down the Germans. The Russians were corrupt and inefficient, the Italians were unwilling to send troops abroad and 'Rumania runs away'. He still believed that the Central Powers would only be defeated when the German army had been defeated. The Germans had two-thirds of their troops in the West and therefore Britain would have to concentrate as large a proportion of their own forces there after allowing for sufficient detachments to safeguard vital imperial interests. And finally, like Haig he wished to maintain pressure on the Germans on the Western front throughout the winter to prevent them from recovering from the losses they had sustained in 1916 and then to mount another offensive in the spring of 1917.[49]

The summer and autumn of 1916 was a period of growing frustration for Lloyd George. He had become Secretary of State for War on 6 July, a month after Kitchener was drowned on his way to Russia. He had taken the office reluctantly, not least because Robertson was unwilling to relax the constraints which had been placed on Kitchener to rob him of much of his real power.[50] His tenure of the War Office throughout the Somme offensive did nothing to diminish his misgivings. Until the Romanians entered the war he supported the Somme as part of a single concerted allied offensive. He interpreted the coming to power in Germany of Hindenburg and Ludendorff at the end of August as a signal that German policy would shift eastwards. He now feared that the Central Powers would overrun Romania in the same way as they had crushed Serbia and that if they did so, its oil and wheat might enable them to continue the war for another two years. He could only rage impotently while Romania was crushed. Robertson refused to send sufficient reinforcements to Salonika to enable Sarrail to mount an offensive to relieve it. The CIGS insisted that he had no men to spare and that even if some could be found they would arrive too late.[51] A trip to the front in mid-September convinced him that Haig was tactically inept and that his army was suffering needless casualties. However, he soon discovered that it was dangerous to make such criticisms public. Both Robertson and Haig carefully cultivated sympathetic newspapermen. When Haig heard of Lloyd George's criticisms, his staff leaked news of them to Northcliffe, Gwynne and St Loe Strachey. They were amply rewarded. On 26 September Gwynne's *Morning Post* publicly warned Lloyd George not to interfere in the soldiers' business.[52]

By October Lloyd George had lost patience with Robertson and wanted to end his stranglehold on policy-making. He recognized that the soldiers were so popular with the press and public that a frontal assault would never succeed. So he tried to undermine Robertson's position by suggesting first to Asquith on 26 September and then to the War Committee on 31 October that the CIGS should be sent to Russia. He was genuinely anxious to improve Anglo-Russian relations, but he was probably even more anxious to get Robertson out of the way and give himself more control over military policy.[53] At the War Committee on 3 November, in Robertson's absence, he 'proceeded to examine the prospects of the policy of attrition' and found them bleak. The Entente's losses had been heavier than those of the enemy in 1916, the Entente was short of money, ships and food and would soon be faced with a German peace offensive designed to disrupt its cohesion. The civil population needed tangible victories to sustain its morale and he was afraid that another period of heavy casualties would only increase public support for a negotiated peace. He was delighted with his colleagues' response. They agreed that the forthcoming allied military conference to decide strategy in 1917 should be preceded by a political conference at which the political representatives of the Entente would decide policy for 1917 and then present their plans to the soldiers as a *fait accompli*.[54]

Both of Lloyd George's ploys failed. Robertson knew that he wanted him out of the country so he could 'play "hankey-pankey" behind his back' and adamantly refused to be bundled off to Russia.[55] He also learnt of Lloyd George's plan to hold the political conference before the generals met and, by warning Joffre, ensured that the two conferences in fact coincided on 15 November. Lloyd George realized that he had been outmanoeuvred, but hoped to retrieve the situation by presenting Asquith with a draft speech for the conference roundly condemning the policy of attrition. On 9 November he told Hankey that unless Britain and its partners mended their ways, 'We are going to lose this war'. Hankey called his memorandum 'a most lugubrious and pessimistic document, though difficult to answer in detail'.[56] Lloyd George argued that

> As the war drags along its weary and bloodstained path, the sacrifices and sufferings must necessarily increase; the casualties will become heavier, and the gloom cast by the appalling losses over the homes of the country will become darker and deeper. Then food will become scarcer and costlier, the burdens of taxation will be heavier. Efforts will be made perhaps by powerful neutrals to patch up a peace on what would appear to be specious terms, and there is a real danger that large masses of people, worn out by constant strain, may listen to well-intentioned but mistaken pacificators; and, last of all, there is the danger, which one hardly likes to contemplate, but which is ever present in our minds, of one of the four great Allies being offered terms which seem better than indefinite prolongation of the horrors of war. No alliance has ever born the strain of a protracted war without breaking.[57]

He was disappointed, for Asquith only presented a bowdlerised version of the speech to the conference. Joffre and Robertson refused to dispatch significant reinforcements to Salonika, despite Russian, Romanian and Serbian blandishments, and agreed instead that in 1917 the allies should mount another combined offensive on the main fronts.[58] The politicians agreed that they, and not the generals, should decide policy, and that their first priority should be to supply Russia, even if it meant going short themselves. But Asquith refused to fall in with Briand's wish to mount a winter offensive in the east. Asquith instead wanted to call another conference at Petrograd to consult the Russians. The politicians then nullified such agreements as they had reached by adopting the conclusions of the military conference lock, stock and barrel.[59]

By 18 November there was, according to Crawford and Balcarres, 'a wave of anxiety spreading through the inner circles at home, which will soon be reflected in the public mind'.[60] But, despite this growing anxiety about the military and economic situation, only Lord Lansdowne, in a memorandum of 13 November which was a belated reply to Asquith's request for his colleagues' views on war aims, expressed any defeatist sentiments. He questioned whether Lloyd George's policy of the 'knock-out blow' was either practical or desirable and suggested that Britain might be heading for a pyrrhic victory. 'We are slowly but surely killing off the best of the male population of these islands.'[61] Several generations would have to pass before the human and economic losses which had already been sustained could be made good. He recommended that unless Robertson could confidently predict when the allies would win it would be better to make peace sooner rather than later. Lloyd George agreed with Robertson that it was 'the wail of a tired old man' but he feared that Lansdowne might become the leader of a peace party within the government.[62] Robertson wrote a harshly critical reply insisting that a military victory, no matter how long it took, was preferable to a premature peace. The latter would place an intolerable stain upon future generations and dishonour the memory of those already dead.[63] Cecil and Grey agreed that as long as the naval and military authorities believed that Germany could be defeated and satisfactory peace terms achieved, a negotiated peace would be premature and a betrayal of the interests of Britain and its allies. On 28 November the War Committee discussed their response if Wilson should try once again to mediate and Asquith concluded that 'the time has not yet come for peace feelers'.[64]

In November Lloyd George's frustration centred on the fact that neither the machinery of government nor many of the personnel seemed able to cope with the manifold problems which they were encountering. Many of the Liberal ministers had been in office for ten years and were tired, and the entire administration lacked any energetic central control. Asquith failed to impose himself on his colleagues and by the summer he was, according to the American ambassador who lunched with him on 1 August, 'a spent force, at once nimble and weary'.[65] His energy further declined after the death of his eldest son on the Somme in September. The Cabinet was 'a huge gathering, so big that it is hopeless for more than one or two to express an opinion on each detail – great danger of side conversation and localised discussions'.[66] Much the same criticisms could be made of the War Committee, which had steadily grown in size in 1916 and whose business was, by November, badly congested. But in the final analysis defective machinery was only a secondary reason why the government was failing to cope. The basic reason was, as Lloyd George told Sir George Riddell on 26 November, 'the number of able men with strong opinions which it comprises. The clash of ideas is too great.'[67]

Throughout November Lloyd George tried, with some success, to break through the inertia which threatened to undermine Britain's war effort. It was only when he was balked at the last moment that he turned his back on reforming the machinery of government and embarked upon a palace coup against the Prime Minister. On 6 November the coalition's chief whips warned the Cabinet that anti-war speakers were drawing growing audiences in cities like Glasgow and Leicester when they condemned the government's economic policies for causing high food prices and demanded a negotiated peace. Runciman was reluctant to introduce food rationing because it had been tried and failed in Germany. Instead he tried to expedite future deliveries by summoning two civilian shipping experts to help him make more efficient use of the available tonnage and to increase launchings. He also wanted to use the Defence of the Realm Act to enable the Board of Trade to control the price and distribution of food. But Lloyd George thought that was too mundane. Unless the government was seen to be doing something dramatic to stop the rise in the cost of living, 'there might be a terrible upheaval in the country, which would inevitably effect the conduct of the war', he told the War Committee on 13 November.[68] He therefore recommended the appointment of a Shipping Controller to control the distribution of tonnage, and a food dictator to control the purchase, domestic culti-vation, distribution and price of all home-grown and imported food-stuffs. The War Committee agreed to appoint a Food Controller but the post could not be filled. Both the Speaker of the House of Commons and Lord Milner rejected the job and it was still vacant when the government collapsed. Hankey described the post of Shipping Controller as 'stupid' as it would simply duplicate the work of the Curzon Committee and it came to nothing until after the formation of the Lloyd George coalition.[69]

For a time Lloyd George had more success in persuading the govern-ment to accept national service. The latest munitions programme required 300,000 workers above and beyond the manpower allocated to the Ministry of Munitions by the Cabinet Committee on the Co-ordination of Military and Financial Effort in April. At the same time the Army Council wanted another 940,000 recruits for the 1917 campaign. On 9 November the Manpower Distribution Board recommended another comb-out of inessential men and hinted that some form of national service for men and women was necessary to make proper use of the labour available.[70] The problems likely to be caused by this were quickly illustrated by a two-day strike in the Sheffield engineering industry resulting from the call-up of a skilled man who had lost his badge. The strike demonstrated that debadging would only work with the co-operation of trade unionists at a local level, and therefore the government promised to introduce a trade card scheme which gave local union officials much greater control over the call-up of their own members.[71] On 21 November the War Committee agreed to another comb-out of industry but balked at introducing national service until the Army Council unanimously demanded it. Robertson was delighted. 'I have managed', he wrote to Haig on 30 November, 'to frighten the Government pretty badly the last few days, and today, within an hour, they decided to place every man up to 60 years of age at the disposal of the Govt. for *national service.*'[72] But he rejoiced too soon.

The government's political authority had never really recovered from the conscription crises of 1915–16 and the Easter Rising in Dublin. In July they were forced to establish two Royal Commisions to inquire into what had gone wrong at Gallipoli and Kut, and by November the only London paper which supported the coalition was the *Daily Telegraph*.[73] Even before the allied conference in Paris, Lloyd George had been discussing with Carson the necessity of taking the real power to conduct the war out of the hands of Asquith and placing it in those of a smaller and more effective War Committee. Carson and his associates, Milner, the members of the Unionist War Committee and their press allies, shared Lloyd George's conviction that the existing administration lacked the energy and determination to lead the country. In March Leo Maxse, the editor of the *National Review*, believed that it was 'the very worst Government we have ever had in this country for the particular business in hand, namely war'.[74] But their solutions differed. Milner, Carson and their friends wanted to drive Asquith from office completely. Lloyd George wanted to retain him as titular Prime Minister and as a symbol of national unity but wished to ensure that the real power to decide war policy passed to a small committee of which he would be the chairman.[75] After weeks of grumbling at the inefficiency of the government, he finally decided to act in mid-November because he foresaw that the final collapse of Romania would so discredit Robertson that Asquith would be forced to bow to his wishes and because he was afraid that Wilson might follow his re-election as President with another mediation attempt.

Bonar Law's position in all this was unenviable. Unionists outside Westminster felt cheated of their fair share of power by the coalition, and by the summer they were beginning to share Maxse's belief that Law and his Unionist colleagues within the Cabinet had been suborned by Asquith.[76] Just how precarious his position had become was demonstrated on 8 November when Carson's Unionist War Committee demanded a more vigorous prosecution of the economic war against Germany under the guise of a resolution in the Commons demanding that enemy property in British colonies and protectorates should only be sold to natural-born British subjects. A third of the Unionists present voted for the resolution, a third abstained, and only a third supported their titular party leader and the government.[77]

The shock administered by this vote persuaded Law to agree with Lloyd George that the government had to be reconstructed to enable it to prosecute the war more vigorously. On 20 November he met Carson and Lloyd George and the latter explained to him his scheme for a small war committee to run the war. On 25 November Law proposed a similar scheme to the Prime Minister, drafted by his close friend Sir Max Aitken. Asquith considered it over the weekend and dismissed it as an attempt by Lloyd George to displace him.[78] But he was not deaf to all suggestions to improve the Cabinet's efficiency and on 29 November he agreed to Cecil's suggestion to establish a Committee of National Organization to be chaired by Lloyd George to take charge of war organization on the home front.[79] But if Asquith hoped that he could placate Lloyd George in this way, he was quickly disabused. Runciman was to be a member of the new committee but immediately showed himself to be opposed to a more thorough-going organization of manpower. He was absent from the War Committee on 30 November which agreed to introduce national service but as soon as he learnt of the decision he refused to accept it.[80] His refusal was instrumental in persuading Lloyd George on 1 December to try to cut through the endless debate by insisting that a new War Committee should be established consisting of himself, Bonar Law and Carson. Subject to the final decision of the Prime Minister, they would have control over all questions connected with the war.

But although Asquith's reply was conciliatory in tone he still insisted on retaining the substance of power within his own hands.[81] On 30 November Law had told his Unionist colleagues that he was in league with Lloyd George. They deprecated the new War Committee in the belief that it would only serve to aggrandize Lloyd George and on 3 December the leading Unionists in the Cabinet told Bonar Law that they wished to resign. They probably expected that Asquith would in turn be forced to resign and Lloyd George would be confronted with the consequences of his own temerity. He might then become Prime Minister and Asquith might be Lord Chancellor or Chancellor of the Exchequer, but he would be so dependent on Unionist support that he would become their prisoner.[82] Neither Asquith nor Lloyd George took kindly to the idea of being dictated to by Chamberlain, Curzon, Cecil and Long and so they quickly patched up an agreement. The new War Committee would be established but Asquith was to see its daily agenda and could veto any of its decisions.[83] Law agreed to this and although there was still some uncertainty about the personnel of the new committee, the crisis appeared to be well on its way to being settled.

However on 4 December *The Times*, the *Manchester Guardian* and the *Morning Post* all carried stories suggesting that the terms of the reconstruction meant that Lloyd George had defeated Asquith and that the latter would henceforth be Prime Minister in name only. Asquith was furious and believed that Lloyd George had deliberately leaked the story to the press. In fact the actual source was Carson, who seeing his opportunity to smash the coalition slipping away, had leaked news of the new arrangements to Geoffrey Robinson, the editor of *The Times*. Carson believed that another compromise would not endure and that Lloyd George had to replace Asquith and he was even prepared to fight a general election if the Commons would not support a new government.[84] On the evening of 4 December Asquith's Liberal colleagues insisted that Lloyd George's terms were humiliating and advised Asquith to call his bluff by resigning. Few of them expected Lloyd George to be able to form a government or, having formed one, to make it last.[85] They were wrong. On 5 December the entire government resigned. The king asked Law to form a new administration but refused him a dissolution. Another coalition was therefore inevitable. Law agreed to try but insisted that he could not succeed unless Asquith joined the new administration. The latter refused and so the king had to call for Lloyd George.[86] On 7 December Lloyd George found himself Prime Minister by default.

Notes

1   Brig.-Gen. J. Charteris, *At GHQ* (London: Cassell, 1931), p. 156.
2   Kirke diary entries, 8 and 31 August 1916, Kirke mss.
3   Charteris, *At GHQ*, pp. 162, 171, 175; General Staff (Intelligence) GHQ [S.S. 485], Translation of a German Document. Army Order regarding the execution of counter attacks, Gen. von Below, 23 August 1916, Mont-gomery–Massinberd mss, 49/III; Lieut.-Col. C. à Court Repington, *The First World War, 1914–1918*, Vol. 1 (London: Constable, 1920), pp. 278–9.
4   Oliver, Viscount Esher (ed.), *Journals and Letters of Reginald, Viscount Esher*, Vol. 4 (London: Ivor Nicholson & Watson, 1938), p. 45.
5   PRO CAB 42/17/11, Minutes of the War Committee, 18 August 1916.
6   Clive diary entries, 22 and 30 August 1916, Clive mss, II/3; Haig to Robertson, 23 August 1916, Haig mss, Acc. 3155/107.
7   Sir G. Buchanan, *My Mission to Russia and other Diplomatic Memories*, Vol. 2 (London: Cassell, 1923), pp. 3, 15–25; Brig.-Gen. H. H. Waters, *Secret and Confidential. The Experiences of a Military Attaché* (London: John Murray, 1926), p. 360; A. K. Wildman, *The End of the Russian Imperial Army: The Old Army and the Soldiers' Revolt (March–April 1917)* (Princeton, NJ: Princeton University Press, 1980), pp. 95–6, 105–116; PRO FO 371/2746/21068, Buchanan to Foreign Office, 2 February 1916 and (23490), Buchanan to Foreign Office, 6 February 1916 and (143483), Buchanan to Grey, 23 July 1916 and (145612), Buchanan to Grey, 25 July 1916 and (19624), Buchanan to Foreign Office, 29 September 1916 and (197548), Howard to Foreign Office, 3 October 1916; PRO FO 800/75, Buchanan to Grey, 4 August 1916; PRO FO 371/2803/147690, Buchanan to Foreign Office, 28 July 1916 and (149263), Howard to Foreign Office, 31 July 1916 and (223716), Findlay to Foreign Office, 7 November 1916; PRO FO 371/2805/226058, Rumbold to Foreign Office, 9 November 1916; PRO CAB 37/155/4, Buchanan to Grey and enc., 8 September 1916; Buchanan to Hardinge, 20 October 1916, Lloyd George mss, E/3/23/2.
8   G. E. Torrey, 'The Rumanian campaign of 1916: Its impact on the bel-ligerents', *Slavic Review*, vol. 39, no. 1 (1980), pp. 36–7.
9   N. Stone, *The Eastern Front 1914–1917* (London: Hodder & Stoughton, 1975), p. 265; PRO CAB 42/19/6, General Staff, Possible action of the Central Powers during the autumn and winter of 1916, 9 September 1916; PRO CAB 42/19/3 and /6, Minutes of the War Committee, 5 and 12 September 1916.
10   Kiggell to 3, 4 and Reserve Armies, 29 September 1916, Haig diary entries, 30 September and 2 October 1916, Haig to Robertson, 7 October 1916, Haig, mss, Acc. 3155/108.
11   PRO CAB 42/21/3, Haig to CIGS, 7 October 1916.

12 Haig diary entry, 15 October 1916, Haig mss, Acc. 3155/108.

13 Torrey, 'The Rumanian campaign of 1916', pp. 32–3.

14 D. Dutton, 'The deposition of King Constantine of Greece, June 1917: An episode in Anglo-French diplomacy', *Canadian Journal of History*, vol. 12, no. 3 (1978), pp. 325–8; Asquith to War Committee and enc., 24 January 1916 Asquith mss, vol. 29, pp. 204–5; PRO CAB 42/15/4, Crewe to Bertie, 2 June 1916, Vice-Adm. Mediterranean to Admiralty, 3 June 1916, Elliot to Foreign Office, 30 May 1916; PRO CAB 800/63, Elliot to Grey, 28 June and 30 August 1916.

15 PRO FO 800/59, Grey to Bertie, 30 August 1916.

16 PRO CAB 42/18/8, Minutes of the War Committee, 30 August 1916 and Kelly to Admiralty, 31 August 1916; PRO CAB 42/19/1, Minutes of the War Committee, 1 September 1916 and Bertie to Grey, 31 August 1916, Elliot to Grey, 31 August 1916, Grey to Elliot, 1 September 1916.

17 PRO CAB 42/22/6, Runciman, Merchant Shipping, 24 October 1916.

18 A. Temple Patterson (ed.), *The Jellicoe Papers*, Vol. 2 (London: Navy Records Society, 1968), p. 89; Jones to Runciman, 26 July 1916, Runciman mss, WR 149.

19 PRO CAB 42/15/15, Minutes of the War Committee, 30 June 1916 and CIR, Italian coal requirements, 21 June 1916 and Knox to Foreign Office, 1 June 1916; Thomas to Lloyd George, 2 and 25 June 1916, Lloyd George mss, D/19/6/29 and 33; Le Roy Lewis to Lloyd George, 18 August 1916, Lloyd George mss, E/3/14/4; K. Neilson, *Strategy and Supply: The Anglo-Russian Alliance, 1914–1917* (London: Allen & Unwin, 1984), pp. 171–202.

20 PRO CAB 42/15/15, Grey to Bertie, 30 June 1916; PRO CAB 28/1, Asquith, Finance Committee. Conclusions of a meeting held at 10 Downing Street, 3 July 1916; Lloyd George, Memorandum of the Secretary of State for War for the consideration of the Munitions Conference at the War Office, 12 June 1916.

21 Conference between the Secretary of State for War, the Minister of Munitions and representatives of the French, Italian and Russian governments, 13 July 1916, Lloyd George mss, E/7/3/2; PRO CAB 28/1, Inter-ally conference on finance, held in London, 15 July 1916 and Second supplementary financial agreement between the British and Italian governments, 15 July 1916; PRO CAB 42/16/11, Montagu, Memorandum on the allocation of heavy artillery to Russia, 17 July 1916; PRO CAB 37/154/15, Rodd to Grey, 23 August 1916.

22 PRO CAB 42/18/4, Minutes of the War Committee, 22 August 1916; PRO CAB 28/1, Protocol of the financial conference held at Calais, 24 August 1916; K. Burk, *Britain, America and the Sinews of War 1914–1918* (London: Allen & Unwin, 1985), pp. 78–80.

23 PRO CAB 42/19/6, FO to Buchanan, 12 September 1916; PRO CAB 42/17/11, Buchanan to Grey, 11 August 1916; PRO CAB 42/21/2, Waters, Financial agreement between British and Russian governments, 3 October 1916; Neilson, *Strategy and Supply*, pp. 202–4.

24 Dallolio to Lloyd George, 10 November 1916 and Lloyd George to Dallolio, 11 November 1916, Lloyd George mss, E/3/16/1 and /2.

25 K. R. Grieves, 'The British government's political and administrative response to the man-power problem in the First World War', PhD thesis, Manchester University, 1984, pp. 35–7.

26 PRO CAB 41/37/20, Asquith to H.M. the King, 10 May 1916; PRO CAB 37/149/16, Samuel, Coal supply distribution, 8 June 1916; PRO CAB 37/149/25, Memorandum by Mr Hugesson, 10 June 1916; PRO CAB

37/149/29, Harcourt, Coal supplies, 13 June 1916; PRO CAB 42/15/11, Minutes of the War Committee, 22 June 1916 and Younger, Report on the allocation of men released from the colours under the bulk release scheme for the United Kingdom, *c.* 20 June 1916; PRO CAB 42/15/8, Minutes of the War Committee, 16 June 1916; PRO CAB 42/16/8, Macready, Release of miners, 1 July 1916; PRO CAB 42/22/10; Return of miners transferred to class 'W' Army Reserve under Army Council Instruction 1377 up to 30 September 1916, 26 October 1916.

27   Grieves, 'The man-power problem', pp. 35–7; PRO CAB 42/17/1, Minutes of the War Committee, 1 August 1916.

28   Grieves, 'The man-power problem', p. 44; PRO CAB 42/17/3, Minutes of the War Committee, 5 August 1916; PRO CAB 42/18/4, Minutes of the War Committee, 22 August 1916 and Derby, Terms of reference of the Man-power Distribution Board, 15 August 1916.

29   PRO CAB 42/19/6, Robertson, Memorandum, 11 September 1916.

30   PRO CAB 42/21/2, Fawcett, First report of Manpower Distribution Board, 30 September 1916; PRO CAB 42/21/1, Fawcett, Manpower Distribution Board, 29 September 1916.

31   Grieves, 'The man-power problem', pp. 44–75; PRO CAB 42/21/2, Minutes of the War Committee, 5 October 1916.

32   C. E. Fayle, *The War and the Shipping Industry* (London: Oxford University Press, 1927), p. 168; Lord Askwith, *Industrial Problems and Disputes* (Brighton: Harvester, 1920/74), pp. 409–10; R. Harrison, 'The war emergency workers' national committee', in A. Briggs and J. Saville (eds), *Essays in Labour History, 1886–1923* (London: Macmillan, 1971), pp. 245–6; PRO T 170/106, Bradbury to Chalmers, 20 April 1916 and Bradbury to McKenna, 25 August 1916.

33   Fayle, *The War*, pp. 195–6; Board of Trade, The rise in the cost of living of the working classes from the commencement of the war up to 1 September 1916, Runciman mss, WR 103.

34   PRO CAB 41/37/31, Asquith to H.M. the King, 25 August 1916; PRO CAB 37/157/11, Crawford and Balcarees, Standard bread and wheat economy, 5 October 1916; P. E. Dewey, 'Food production and policy in the United Kingdom, 1914–1918', *Transactions of the Royal Historical Society*, 5th series, vol. 30 (1980), pp. 71–88.

35   PRO CAB 42/18/8, Minutes of the War Committee, 30 August 1916.

36   Haig diary entry, 6 September 1916, Haig mss. Acc. 3155/108.

37   PRO FO 800/96, Drummond, Memorandum, 18 September 1916; PRO CAB 37/155/38, Memorandum by Lord E. Percy, 26 September 1916.

38   PRO FO 800/168, Bertie to Hardinge, 4 September 1916; C. P. Anderson diary entry, 15 September 1916, C. P. Anderson mss, box 1, folder 3. [I am most grateful to Dr Kathleen Burk for bringing this document to my attention.]

39   J. Grigg, *Lloyd George: From Peace to War, 1912–1916* (London: Methuen, 1985), p. 425; A. J. P. Taylor (ed.), *Lloyd George: A Diary by Frances Stevenson* (London: Hutchinson, 1971), p. 114; the telegram in question was probably Gerard to Lansing, 25 September 1916, reprinted in A. S. Link (ed.), *The Papers of Woodrow Wilson*, Vol. 38 (Princeton, NJ: Princeton University Press, 1982), pp. 313–14.

40   *Hansard* 86, HC Deb., 5s. col. 145; PRO FO 800/181, Bertie to Hardinge, 6 October 1916.

41   PRO FO 371/2803/204461, Morel to Grey and encs, 11 October 1916; M.

Swartz, *The Union of Democratic Control in British Politics during the First World War* (Oxford: Clarendon Press, 1971), pp. 78–82.

42 *Hansard* 86 HC Deb., 5s. col. 103.

43 PRO CAB 42/21/1, Minutes of the War Committee, 3 October 1916 and General Staff, German casualties in the Somme fighting, 30 September 1916.

44 T. Wilson (ed.), *The Political Diaries of C. P. Scott 1911–1928* (London: Collins, 1970), pp. 227–8; Grey to Runciman, 30 September 1916, Runciman mss, WR 300.

45 Burk, *Sinews of War*, pp. 81–3; PRO CAB 37/157/40, McKenna, Our financial position in America, 24 October 1916; PRO T 170/95, Interdepartmental Committee to consider dependence of the British Empire on the United States, 13 October 1916; PRO CAB 37/158/3, Grey to Cabinet and enc., 30 October 1916.

46 PRO CAB 42/22/9, Muller, The economic position in the Central Empires, 30 October 1916; PRO CAB 42/22/11, War Trade Intelligence Department, The economic position of Germany, 30 October 1916.

47 PRO CAB 42/22/14, Hankey, The general review of the war, 31 October 1916.

48 M. Kitchen, *The Silent Dictatorship: The Politics of the German High Command under Hindenburg and Ludendorff 1916–1918* (London: Croom Helm, 1976), pp. 41. 68–79, 95–8.

49 PRO CAB 42/23/4, Minutes of the War Committee, 3 November 1916; Robertson to Milne, 7 November 1916, Robertson mss, I/34/10; Haig diary entry 22 October 1916, Haig mss, Acc. 3155/108.

50 Grigg, *Lloyd George*, pp. 356–60; Wilson (ed.), *The Political Diaries of C. P. Scott*, pp. 216–8; Lloyd George to Asquith, 17 June 1916, Lloyd George mss, D/18/2/19; Robertson to Lloyd George, 24 June 1916, Robertson mss, I/19/1; Lloyd George to Robertson, 26 June 1916, Robertson mss, I/19/3.

51 Grigg, *Lloyd George*, pp. 386–9; PRO CAB 42/21/3, Minutes of the War Committee, 9 October 1916; PRO CAB 42/21/6, Minutes of the War Committee, 12 October 1916 and Robertson, Further reinforcements for the allied powers at Salonika, 11 October 1916, Milne to CIGS, 11 October 1916, and Robertson to Joffre, 12 October 1916; PRO CAB 42/22/1 and 5, Minutes of the War Committee, 17 and 24 October 1916.

52 D. R. Woodward, *Lloyd George and the Generals* (London: Associated University Press, 1983), pp. 98–113; J. M. McEwen, '"Brass-Hats" and the British press during the First World War', *Canadian Journal of History*, vol. 18, no. 1 (1983), p. 55.

53 Grigg, *Lloyd George*, p. 389; Taylor (ed.), *Lloyd George: A Diary*, p. 120.

54 PRO CAB 42/23/4, Minutes of the War Committee, 3 November 1916 and FO to Bertie and Rodd, 3 November 1916; Hankey diary entry, 3 November 1916, Hankey mss, 1/1.

55 Hankey diary entry, 7 November 1916, Hankey mss, 1/1; Robertson to Asquith, 13 November 1916, Robertson mss, I/13/21; Robertson to Haig, 8 November 1916, Haig mss, Acc. 3155/109.

56 Hankey diary entry, 12 November 1916, Hankey mss, 1/1.

57 PRO CAB 28/1, Statement drafted by Mr Lloyd George as a basis for the Prime Minister's statement at the Paris Conference on November 15, 1916.

58 [Kiggell], Conference at Chantilly, November 1916, Kiggell mss, VI/2; Clive diary entries, 14 and 16 November 1916, Clive mss, II/3; Haig diary entry, 15 November 1916, Haig mss, Acc. 3155/109.

59 PRO CAB 28/1, Note by the secretary of the War Committee on the results of the Paris conference, November 15 and 16, 1916.

60   J. Vincent (ed.), *The Crawford Papers: The Journals of David Lindsay, Twenty-seventh Earl of Crawford and Tenth Earl of Balcarees 1871–1940 during the years 1892–1940* (Manchester: Manchester University Press, 1984), p. 365.

61   PRO CAB 37/159/32, Lansdowne, Memorandum, 13 November 1916.

62   Robertson to Lloyd George, c. 13 November 1916, Lloyd George mss, E/8/4/2(a); Taylor (ed.), *Lloyd George: A Diary*, p. 127.

63   PRO CAB 37/160/15, Robertson, Memorandum, 24 November 1916.

64   D. Lloyd George, *The War Memoirs of David Lloyd George*, Vol. 1 (London: Odhams, 1938), p. 531; PRO CAB 37/160/20, Grey, Memorandum, 27 November 1916; PRO CAB 37/160/21, Cecil, Memorandum, 27 November 1916.

65   Link (ed.), *Wilson's Papers*, Vol. 38, p. 256.

66   Vincent (ed.), *Crawford Papers*, p. 365.

67   Lord Riddell, *Lord Riddell's War Diary, 1914–1918* (London: Ivor Nicholson & Watson, 1933), p. 223; Hankey diary entry, 10 November 1916, Hankey mss, 1/1.

68   PRO CAB 42/24/5, Minutes of the War Committee, 13 November 1916; PRO CAB 37/159/12, Gulland *et al.*, The need for public meetings, 6 November 1916; PRO CAB 37/159/22, Crawford and Balcarees, Home food supplies, 9 November 1916; PRO CAB 37/159/29, Runciman to Cabinet, 11 November 1916; Vincent (ed.), *Crawford Papers*, p. 364.

69   Hankey diary entry, 10 November 1916, Hankey mss, 1/1.

70   PRO CAB 42/25/1, Fawcett, Third report of the Man-power Board, 9 November 1916.

71   C. J. Wrigley, *David Lloyd George and the British Labour Movement: Peace and War* (Brighton: Harvester, 1976), pp. 171–3; PRO CAB 37/159/41, Henderson, The man-power distribution board and labour, 16 November 1916; PRO CAB 42/24/10, Minutes of the War Committee, 17 November 1916 and Chamberlain, Method of dealing with men of the skilled engineering trades. Draft proposals, 17 November 1916.

72   Robertson to Haig, 30 November 1916, Haig mss, Acc. 3155/109; PRO CAB 37/160/25, Supply of men for the army. Memorandum by the military members of the Army Council for the Secretary of State for War, 28 November 1916; PRO CAB 42/25/1, Minutes of the War Committee, 21 November 1916; PRO CAB 42/26/4, Minutes of the War Committee, 30 November 1916.

73   St Loe Strachey, Memorandum, 13 November 1916, St Loe Strachey mss, S/18/3/38; J. M. McEwen, 'The press and the fall of Asquith', *Historical Journal*, vol. 21, no. 4 (1978), pp. 865–9.

74   Maxse to Bonar Law, 8 March 1916, Bonar Law mss, 52/4/7.

75   Hankey diary entry, 22 November 1916, Hankey mss, 1/1.

76   Doyle, Memorandum, 6 June 1916, Beaverbrook mss, C/203; Maxse to Wilson, 3 April 1916, Wilson mss, 73/1/20; R. J. Scally, *The Origins of the Lloyd George Coalition: The Politics of Social Imperialism, 1900–1918* (Princeton, NJ: Princeton University Press, 1975), pp. 280–335.

77   R. Blake, *The Unknown Prime Minister: The Life and Times of Andrew Bonar Law 1858–1923* (London: Eyre & Spottiswoode, 1955), pp. 298–9.

78   Asquith to Law, 26 November 1916, Bonar Law mss, 53/4/24; Blake, *Unknown Prime Minister*, pp. 302–8; Taylor (ed.), *Lloyd George: A Diary*, p. 128.

79   PRO CAB 37/160/21, Cecil, Memorandum, 27 November 1916; Lord Hankey, *The Supreme Command 1914–1918*, Vol. 2 (London: Allen & Unwin, 1961), p. 564; Vincent (ed.), *Crawford Papers*, p. 368.

80 Runciman to Asquith, 1 December 1916, Runciman mss, WR 149; PRO CAB 42/26/6, Minutes of the War Committee, 1 December 1916.

81 Taylor (ed.), *Lloyd George: A Diary*, p. 130; Lloyd George, Memorandum to the Prime Minister, 1 December 1916, Lloyd George mss, E/2/23/9.

82 J. M. McEwen, 'The struggle for mastery in Britain: Lloyd George versus Asquith, December 1916', *Journal of British Studies*, vol. 18, no. 1 (1978), pp. 140–2; Lord Newton, *Lord Lansdowne. A Biography* (London: Macmillan, 1929), pp. 452–3; Lansdowne to Bonar Law, 1 December 1916, Bonar Law mss, 117/1/29; Drummond to PM [n.d. but *c.* 3 December 1916], Resolution passed by Unionist Ministers on Sunday, December 3 but not shown to the Prime Minister by Mr Bonar Law, and Curzon to Asquith, 4 December 1916, Asquith mss, vol. 31, ff. 8–12, 15 and 33; Vincent (ed.), *Crawford Papers*, pp. 369–70.

83 Asquith to Lloyd George, 4 December 1916, Lloyd George mss, E/2/23/12.

84 Carson to Bonar Law, 4 December 1916, Bonar Law mss, 117/1/31; Grigg, *Lloyd George*, pp. 458–60.

85 Samuel, Resignation of Asquith government, 5–6 December 1916, Samuel mss, A/56.

86 ibid; Bonar Law to Asquith and Asquith to Bonar Law, 5 December 1916, Asquith mss, vol. 31, ff. 43–4, 49; Cecil to Asquith, 5 December 1916, Asquith mss, vol. 17, ff. 182–3; H. Nicolson, *King George V. His Life and Reign* (London: Constable, 1952), pp. 287–91; Taylor (ed.), *Lloyd George: A Diary*, pp. 131–2.

13

Conclusion Victory or Bankruptcy?

IN THE LATE eighteenth century and throughout the nineteenth century, Britain had been numbered amongst the great powers of Europe not because it possessed a large population or a significant standing army but because it was the world's first industrial nation and because its economic power enabled it to maintain a pre-eminent navy. But in the second half of the nineteenth century its relative economic power began to slip as its continental rivals began to industrialize. By 1914 Britain still possessed formidable economic and naval power but its main rival Germany was not only a formidable land power but possessed the economic potential to build a fleet sufficiently large to pose a serious challenge to Britain's naval security in the North Sea. The Liberal government's determination to wage the war on limited liability principles, either through relying on the policy of 'business as usual' or by pursuing Kitchener's policy of persuading Britain's allies to exhaust the Central Powers' (and their own) manpower reserves, was a recognition of the fact that if Britain wished to retain its great power status in a world of mass conscript armies, it would have to husband carefully its economic and human capital.

Such methods were fully compatible with one of the government's major war aims, namely to ensure that at the end of the war Britain would be the strongest of the belligerents. Germany was not Britain's only serious rival in 1914. Although the rise of the Anglo-German antagonism had temporarily eclipsed Britain's imperial rivalries with Russia and France, it had not eliminated them. Once they had entered the war in August 1914 British policy-makers hoped that at the end of the fighting Britain would be in a position to impose its own peace terms on friends and enemies alike. Between 1914 and 1916 the British sought simultaneously to control the world's oceans, to act as paymaster for the Entente, to persuade neutral states to throw their forces into the military balance against the Central Powers and, under Kitchener's guidance, to raise a continental-scale army.

Kitchener's reputation suffered after the war. Unlike Churchill, Lloyd George, Grey or Asquith, Kitchener never had the opportunity to defend himself in print after the war. As a result he has sometimes been made to bear an unfairly heavy share of the blame for mistakes which were not solely his own. There is no better scapegoat than a dead scapegoat. Simultaneously his political and strategic insights into the nature of the coalition war upon which Britain had embarked in August 1914 have sometimes been overlooked. Kitchener was far more than just a great poster. He originally intended that the New Armies would win the peace for Britain after the French and Russian armies had won the war for the Entente. By the late 1920s attrition had come to symbolize the epitome of fruitless assaults in which the British invariably gained little or no ground and suffered far heavier casualties than the Germans.[1] But when the British government originally conceived it in early 1915 it meant something very different. Kitchener believed that it would be practical for the allies to remain on the defensive and allow the Germans to dash themselves to pieces in attacking well-prepared allied positions. He anticipated that by the spring of 1917 the French and Russian armies and the forces of the Central Powers would have fought each other to a standstill and the British, with their army still intact, would be able to administer the *coup de grâce* and impose their own terms on allies and enemies alike.

However, it proved to be impossible to pursue this policy of protecting the British economy and people from the ravages of the war. Britain's other major war aim was the destruction of Prussian militarism. In practice that meant the overthrow of the domestic status quo within Germany. Such a far-reaching purpose could only be effected after the Entente had inflicted such a crushing military defeat on the Central Powers that they were beyond all hope of retrieving the situation by continuing the war. Thus in 1914–1915 Britain had, paradoxically, embarked upon a limited war and yet hoped to achieve war aims which could only be imposed upon the Germans after total military defeat had been inflicted upon them. Coincidentally with the formation of the Asquith coalition and the entry of the Unionists into the government in the summer of 1915, it became apparent that Kitchener and his colleagues had overestimated both the resilience and the patience of their allies. The French and Russians were not prepared to wait patiently and perhaps indefinitely while the enemy remained in occupation of large parts of their territory without attempting to expel them. Nor, as the losses the French and Russian armies suffered in 1914–16 demonstrated, were their own manpower reserves as bountiful as the British believed. Britain fought the war as a member of a coalition. The need to hold the Entente together from November 1914 onwards in the face of German overtures to the allies meant that the British had to persuade their friends that they had more to gain by continuing to fight in alliance with the British than by listening to German peace overtures. This was the paramount consideration which led the Asquith coalition between August 1915 and April 1916 reluctantly to concede that the allies were not strong enough to inflict a crushing military defeat upon the Central Powers without large-scale British military assistance on the continent of Europe. That in turn meant that during the Battle of the Somme, Kitchener's policy of defensive attrition was abandoned and replaced by a new policy of offensive attrition.

Grey did survive to write his memoirs but they give a somewhat misleading impression of his role in guiding government policy during the war. He did not abdicate his role as Foreign Secretary and allow the soldiers to make war policy although, after the human tragedies of Gallipoli, Loos and the Somme, it served his political reputation well to make the reader think that he did. His claim that 'As far as Europe was concerned diplomacy in war counted for little', was manifest nonsense.[2] Grey successfully exerted all his diplomatic skills in pursuit of his one overriding aim, to keep the Entente united in the face of military setbacks and enemy attempts to inveigle one or more of the allies into a separate peace. The search for new allies among the minor powers was an important but secondary consideration, which he did not allow to threaten the solidarity of the Entente. The negotiations with the Italians and the Balkan neutrals were so prolonged because he recognized that it would avail Britain little if, in gaining another minor ally, it alienated one of its major partners. Grey drew a sharp dividing line between the proper roles of the soldiers and the statesmen and insisted that neither should stray into the others' territory. Strategy – the movement and operational conduct of armed forces – was the job of soldiers and sailors and, as he wrote to St Loe Strachey of the *Spectator* in January 1917,

> A Secretary for Foreign Affairs who attempted to decide the movement of troops & to overrule the Military authorities about strategy in war time ought to be turned out of the Government at once as a public danger.[3]

But equally, as for example his decisive rejection of Robertson's plan to make a separate peace with Turkey and Bulgaria in the spring of 1916 demonstrated, policy-making was the proper province of the politicians.

The cost of the war in terms of human lives and treasure was horrendous for all the belligerents. The Balkan neutrals were right to hesitate before deciding to enter the war because in human terms they did suffer more heavily than the great powers. Approximately 12·5 per cent of all men mobilized in Britain during the war were killed, a figure slightly in excess of the losses suffered by Germany and Austria–Hungary. The

French lost 16·7 per cent but the Romanians suffered a staggering 33 per cent fatal casualties and the Serbs 40 per cent.[4] On 1 December 1916 Robertson complained that it was common knowledge that 'the Nation is not really at war as yet and that until it is we cannot expect to win. Not only do we conduct "business as usual" but in many respects we are doing much more business than usual'.[5] He was grossly exaggerating. The prewar policy of 'business as usual' had never really been implemented. Its foundations were kicked aside by Kitchener when he decided to raise the New Armies. In 1915–1916 the party of caution, led by McKenna and Runciman, fought a valiant rearguard action to salvage what they could of this policy. 'Our ultimate victory', McKenna assured his collegues on 20 December 1915, 'is assured if, in addition to our naval and military activities, we retain unimpaired our power to assist in financing, supplying and carrying for the Allies, but the retention of that power is probably the most indispensable element of success.'[6] This policy had served Britain well in the past and they saw no reason why it should not do so in the existing conflict. But their critics, who were at bottom temperamentally unsuited to the pursuit of such a fabian policy, saw it only as a recipe for a prolonged and indecisive stalemate. As Robertson astringently commented in January 1916 during the deliberations of the Cabinet Committee on the Co-ordination of Military and Financial Effort,

> The attitude of some ministers is rather to find out what is the smallest amount of money & smallest number of men with which we may hope, some day, to win the war, or rather not to lose it, whereas the proper attitude is to see what is the greatest number of men we can put into the field in the shortest possible period of time, after thoroughly organising labour, eliminating all occupations not essential to the vigorous prosecution of the war, & making full & appropriate use of every man & woman in the country.[7]

Although Lloyd George was often critical of the way in which Robertson and his military colleagues used the men and munitions he helped to provide, he agreed with the CIGS that the war would be won by the side who could mobilize its human and economic resources most efficiently. As the Minister of Munitions informed Asquith in May 1916, 'It was quite clear even to the civilian mind soon after the war began that this war would ultimately be decided by superiority in quality and quantity of material, and by the wearing down of the enemy in numbers'.[8] Thanks to the conscriptionists' efforts and the importunities of Britain's allies who wanted money, munitions and men, Runciman's and McKenna's warnings that the complete concentration of the British economy behind the war effort might spell national bankruptcy were cast aside. The exponents of conscription won the day. One of their leading spokesmen outside the Cabinet, the Unionist MP Leopold Amery, believed that in scrapping the navalist policies of his opponents the government was quite properly bowing to reality. 'You and the political principles and traditions you most cherish', he wrote to Sir John Simon on 8 January 1916, 'have come up against the facts of a new world which is incompatible with them.'[9] But the facts of this new world, a world in which Britain no longer enjoyed an effortless superiority because of its industrial pre-eminence and a world in which Germany showed itself able to withstand economic blockade and military assault for four years, was equally incompatible with Amery's cherished dream that Britain should and could remain an independent great power in the twentieth century.

The cost of the conscriptionists' victory was high. The effort of being both the paymaster and economic powerhouse of the Entente and of raising a continental-scale army exposed British claims to be a great power by eroding its economic independence. After 1914 Britain became increasingly dependent upon the USA for money and materials. By November 1916 the end of British credit was within sight but victory was not. The Germans still controlled large tracts of allied territory and the British had apparently made little progress in ridding themselves and Europe of the menace of Prussian militarism. Indeed the passage of the Auxiliary Labour Law and the enactment of the Hindenberg Programme could be understood as showing that Prussian militarism was fastening itself upon German society more firmly than ever. Grey explained Britain's predicament to the Italian minister of finance on 21 November.

> I said that everyone was making great demands on us. In previous wars we had given our Allies the full support of our fleet and of our money. In this war, for the first time we were giving the fullest possible support, not only naval and financial, but also in merchant shipping and material, and we had for the first time created a large army. We had the utmost good-will, and we were giving in all these respects – in navy, in army, in finance, in material, and in merchant shipping – the utmost that we could. Our resources were very considerable, but they were not inexhaustible.[10]

On 28 November a powerful group of American bankers advised their clients not to lend any more money to the belligerents. Two days later the Federal Reserve Board repeated their warning. When the War Committee heard the news, Bonar Law realized that it meant that Britain 'must face victory or bankruptcy'.[11] In August 1914 the British government anticipated that the French and Russian armies would be able to checkmate the Central Powers on land and that Britain's economic and naval power would decisively tip the balance of power in favour of the Entente. The events of the next two years showed that these assumptions were mistaken. By the end of 1916 it was apparent that, even though Britain had transformed itself into a great land power, the Entente could not defeat the Central Powers without external assistance. When the Asquith coalition collapsed, Britain could not afford to lose the war but nor could it afford to win it. Henceforth it was only able to continue fighting at its present scale on American sufferance.

Notes

1   Maj.-Gen. the Rt Hon. J. E. B. Seely, *Adventure* (London: Heinemann, 1930), pp. 229–30.
2   Grey, Viscount, *Twenty-Five Years, 1892–1916*, Vol. 2 (London: Hodder & Stoughton, 1925), p. 154.
3   Grey to St Loe Strachey, 17 January 1917, St Loe Strachey mss, 8/7/8/32.
4   J. M. Winter, 'Britain's "Lost Generation" of the First World War', *Population Studies*, vol. 31, no. 3 (1977), pp. 451–2.
5   Robertson to Lansdowne, 1 December 1916, Robertson mss, I/21/47.
6   PRO CAB 37/139/40, McKenna, The freight question, 20 December 1915.
7   Robertson to Wigram, 12 January 1916, Robertson mss, I/12/30.
8   Lloyd George to Asquith, 30 May 1916, Lloyd George mss, D/18/2/11.
9   Amery to Simon, 8 January 1916, Simon mss, box 52, ff. 91–3.
10 PRO CAB 37/160/9, Grey to Rodd, 21 November 1916.
11 PRO CAB 42/26/2, Minutes of the War Committee, 28 November 1916; PRO CAB 37/160/28, Spring-Rice to Grey, 29 November 1916; PRO CAB 41/47/42, Asquith to H.M. the King, 30 November 1916; Kathleen Burk, *Britain, America and the Sinews of War 1914–1918* (London: Allen & Unwin, 1985), pp. 83–6.

Bibliography

1 Departmental Records in the Public Record Office, London

Board of Trade
Cabinet
Foreign Office
Ministry of Reconstruction
Treasury
War Office

2 Private Papers

C. P. Anderson mss (Library of Congress, Washington).
H. H. Asquith mss (Bodleian Library, Oxford).
Lord Beaverbook mss (House of Lords Record Office, London).
Lord Bertie mss (Public Record Office, London).
R. B. Blumenfeld mss (House of Lords Record Office, London).
A. Bonar Law mss (House of Lords Record Office, London).
Lt.-Col. J. H. Boraston mss (Imperial War Museum, London).
Sir J. Bradbury mss (Public Record Office, London).
Lord Carnock (Sir A. Nicolson) mss (Public Record Office, London).
Lt.-Gen. Sir S. Clive mss (Liddell Hart Centre for Military Archives, King's College, London).
H. A. Creedy (Kitchener) mss (Public Record Office, London).
Lord Cromer mss (Public Record Office, London).
Lord Esher mss (Churchill College, Cambridge).
Lt.-Col. B. Fitzgerald mss (microfilm, Imperial War Museum, London).
Viscount French mss (Imperial War Museum, London).
Lord Gainford mss (Nuffield College, Oxford).
Viscount Grey of Fallodon mss (Public Record Office, London).
H. A. Gwynne mss (Bodleian Library, Oxford).
Earl Haig mss (National Library of Scotland, Edinburgh).
Viscount Haldane mss (National Library of Scotland, Edinburgh).
Sir Ian Hamilton mss (Liddell Hart Centre for Military Archives, King's College, London).
Lord Hankey mss (Churchill College, Cambridge).
Col. P. Howell mss (Liddell Hart Centre for Military Archives, King's College, London).
Admiral F. W. Kennedy mss (Liddell Hart Centre for Military Archives, King's College, London).

Lt.-Gen. Sir L. Kiggell mss (Liddell Hart Centre for Military Archives, King's College, London).
Gen. Sir W. Kirke mss (Imperial War Museum, London).
Earl Kitchener mss (Public Record Office, London).
Earl Lloyd George mss (House of Lords Record Office, London).
R. MacDonald mss (Public Record Office, London).
Sir G. MacDonogh mss (Public Record Office, London).
R. McKenna mss (Churchill College, Cambridge).
Maj.-Gen. Sir F. B. Maurice mss (Liddell Hart Centre for Military Archives, King's College, London).
Maj.-Gen. A. A. Montgomery mss (Liddell Hart Centre for Military Archives, King's College, London).
Lt.-Gen. Sir A. Murray mss (Public Record Office, London).
Field Marshal Sir W. Robertson mss (Liddell Hart Centre for Military Archives, King's College, London).
Lord Runciman mss (University of Newcastle upon Tyne Library).
J. St Loe Strachey mss (House of Lords Record Office, London).
Lord Samuel mss (House of Lords Record Office, London).
Earl Selborne mss (Bodleian Library, Oxford).
Lord Simon mss (Bodleian Library, Oxford).
Maj.-Gen. Sir E. Spears mss (Liddell Hart Centre for Military Archives, King's College, London).
Sir C. Spring-Rice mss (Public Record Office, London).
Field-Marshal Sir H. Wilson mss (Imperial War Museum, London).

3 Official Publications

General Staff, War Office, *Report on Foreign Manoeuvres* (London: 1907).
General Staff, War Office, *Report on Foreign Manoeuvres* (London: 1912).
General Staff, War Office, *Report on Foreign Manoeuvres* (London: 1913).
General Staff, War Office, *Handbooks of the Armies of Bulgaria, Greece, Montenegro, Rumania and Servia* (London: 1904).
General Staff, War Office, *Handbook of the Greek Army* (London: 1906).
General Staff, War Office, *Handbook of the Rumanian Army* (London: 1907).
General Staff, War Office, *Handbook of the Rumanian Army* (London: 1910).
General Staff, War Office, *Handbook of the Bulgarian Army* (London: 1909).
General Staff, War Office, *Handbook of the Bulgarian Army* (London: 1910).
General Staff, War Office, *Handbook of the Servian Army* (London: 1909).
HMSO, *Hansard Parliamentary Debates*, Fifth Series.
HMSO, *The Foreign Office List*.
HMSO, *The War Office List*.
HMSO, *Dardanelles Commission: First Report* [Cd. 8490], 1917.
HMSO, *Dardanelles Commission: Final Report* [Cmd. 371], 1919.
HMSO, *Mesopotamian Commission Report* [Cd. 8610], 1917.
HMSO, *Field Service Regulations (Operations)*, 1909.
HMSO, *Field Service Pocket Book*, 1914.
HMSO, *History of the Ministry of Munitions*, 12 Vols (London, 1920–4).
HMSO, *National War Savings Committee. First Annual Report* [Cd. 8516], 1917.
HMSO, *Departmental Committee on Prices. Second and Third Reports* [Cd. 8483], 1916.

4   *Memoirs, Collections of Documents, etc.*

Addison, C., *Politics from Within, 1911–1918*, Vol. 1 (London: Herbert Jenkins, 1924).

Amery, L. S., *My Political Life: War and Peace*, Vol. 2 (London: Hutchinson, 1953).

Arthur, Sir G., *Not Worth Reading* (London: Longman, Green, 1938).

Askwith, Lord, *Industrial Problems and Disputes* (Brighton: Harvester, 1920/74).

Asquith, Earl of Oxford and, *Memories and Reflections, 1852–1927*, 2 Vols (London: Cassell, 1927).

Barnes, J., and Nicholson, D. (eds), *The Leo Amery Diaries, 1896–1929*, Vol. 1 (London: Hutchinson, 1980).

Bentley Mott, Col. T. (translator), *The Memoirs of Marshal Joffre* (London: Geoffrey Bless, 1932).

Birdwood, Field Marshal Lord, *Khaki and Gown: An Autobiography* (London: Ward Lock, 1941).

Blake, R. (ed.), *The Private Papers of Douglas Haig 1914–1919* (London: Eyre & Spottiswoode, 1952).

Brock, M. and E. (eds), *H. H. Asquith: Letters to Venetia Stanley* (London: Oxford University Press, 1982).

Buchanan, Sir G., *My Mission to Russia and other Diplomatic Memories*, 2 Vols (London: Cassell, 1923).

Callwell, Maj.-Gen. Sir C., *Experiences of a Dug-out 1914–1918* (London: Constable, 1920).

Cecil, Viscount, *All the Way* (London: Hodder & Stoughton, 1949).

Charteris, Brig.-Gen. J., *At GHQ* (London: Cassell, 1931).

Churchill, R. S., *Winston S. Churchill*, Vol. 2, *Companion*, 2, *1907–1911* (London: Heinemann, 1969).

Churchill, W. S. C., *The World Crisis, 1911–1918* (London: Mentor, 1923/68).

Cooper, D., *Old Men Forget* (London: Hart-Davis, 1953).

David, E. (ed.), *Inside Asquith's Cabinet: From the Diaries of Charles Hobhouse* (London: John Murray, 1977).

Esher, Viscount O. (ed.), *Journals and Letters of Reginald, Viscount Esher*, Vols 3–4 (London: Ivor Nicholson & Watson, 1934–8).

Fitzroy, Sir A., *Memoirs*, Vol. 2 (London: Hutchinson 1923).

Gooch, G. P., and Temperley, H. W. V. (eds), *British Documents on the Origins of the War, 1898–1914* (London: HMSO, 1926–38).

Gregory, J. D., *On the Edge of Diplomacy: Rambles and Reflections, 1902–1928* (London: Hutchinson, 1928).

Grey, Viscount, *Twenty-Five Years, 1892–1916*, 2 Vols (London: Hodder & Stoughton, 1925).

Hachey, T. E. (ed.), *Anglo-Vatican Relations, 1914–1939* (Boston, Mass.: G. K. Hall, 1972).

Halpern, P. G. (ed.), *The Keyes Papers: Selections from the Private and Official Correspondence of Admiral of the Fleet Baron Keyes of Zeebrugge*, Vol. 1, *1914–1918* (London: Navy Records Society, 1972).

Hankey, Lord, *The Supreme Command, 1914–1918*, 2 Vols (London: Allen & Unwin, 1961).

Hardinge, Lord, *The Old Diplomacy* (London: John Murray, 1947).

Hardinge, Lord, *My Indian Years, 1910–1916* (London: John Murray, 1948).

Hendrick, B. J. (ed.), *The Life and Letters of Walter Hines Page*, 2 Vols (London: Heinemann, 1930).

Howard, C. H. D. (ed.), *The Diary of Sir Edward Goschen, 1900–1914* (London: Royal Historical Society, 1980).

James, R. R. (ed.), *Memoirs of a Conservative. J. C. C. Davidson's Memoirs and Papers, 1910–1937* (London: Weidenfeld & Nicolson, 1969).

Johnson, E. (ed.), *The Collected Works of John Maynard Keynes*, Vol. 16: *Activities, 1914–1919* (London: Macmillan and the Royal Economic Society, 1971).

Jolliffe, J. (ed.), *Raymond Asquith: Life and Letters* (London: Collins, 1980).

Jones, T., *A Diary with Letters, 1931–1950* (London: Oxford University Press, 1954).

Karolyi, M., *Memoirs of Michael Karolyi: Faith without Illusion* (London: Cape, 1956).

Lennox, Lady A. G. (ed.), *The Diary of Lord Bertie of Thame, 1914–1918*, 2 Vols (London: Hodder & Stoughton, 1924).

Link, A. S. (ed.), *The Papers of Woodrow Wilson*, Vols 31–8 (Princeton NJ: Princeton University Press, 1980–2).

Lloyd George, D., *War Memoirs*, 2 Vols (London: Odhams, 1936–8).

Lockhart, R. H. B., *Memoirs of a British Agent* (London: Macmillan, 1974).

Macarthy, D. (ed.), *H. H. A. Letters of the Earl of Oxford and Asquith to a Friend* (London: G. Bless, 1933).

MacKenzie, C., *Gallipoli Memories* (London: Cassell, 1929).

Macmunn, Lt.-Gen. Sir G., *Behind the Scenes in Many Wars* (London: John Murray, 1930).

Marder, A. J., *Fear God and Dreadnought: The Correspondence of Admiral of the Fleet Lord Fisher of Kilverstone*, Vol. 3 (London: Cape, 1959).

Marshal-Cornwall, Gen. Sir J., *Wars and Rumours of Wars: A Memoir* (London: Leo Cooper and Secker & Warburg, 1983).

Maurice, N. (ed.), *The Maurice Case: From the Papers of Major General Sir Frederick Maurice* (London: Leo Cooper, 1972).

Morgan, K. O. (ed.), *Lloyd George Family Letters 1885–1936* (Cardiff and London: University of Wales Press and Oxford University Press, 1973).

Nekludoff, A., *Diplomatic Reminiscences before and during the World War, 1911–1917* (London: John Murray, 1920).

O'Dwyer, Sir M., *India as I Knew it, 1885–1925* (London: Constable, 1925).

Patterson, A. T. (ed.), *The Jellicoe Papers*, Vol. 2 (London: Navy Records Society, 1968).

Percy, Lord E., *Some Memories* (London: Eyre & Spottiswoode, 1958).

Ramsden, J. (ed.), *Real Old Tory Politics: The Political Diaries of Robert Sanders, Lord Bayford* (London: The Historians Press, 1984).

Repington, Lieut.-Col. C. à Court, *The First World War, 1914–1918*, 2 Vols (London: Constable, 1920).

Richards, F., *Old Soldier Sahib* (London: Faber, 1936).

Riddell, Lord, *Lord Riddell's War Diary, 1914–1918* (London: Ivor Nicholson & Watson, 1933).

Robertson, Field Marshal Sir W. R., *From Private to Field Marshal* (London: Constable, 1921).

Robertson, Field Marshal Sir W. R., *Soldiers and Statesmen, 1914–1918*, 2 Vols (London: Cassell, 1926).

Rodd, Sir J. R., *Social and Diplomatic Memories, 1902–1922*, Vol. 3 (London: Edward Arnold, 1925).

Samuel, Viscount, *Memoirs* (London: Cresset Press, 1945).

Seely, J. E. B., *Adventure* (London: Heinemann, 1930).

Seely, J. E. B., *Fear and be Slain* (London: Hodder & Stoughton, 1931).

Seymour, C. (ed.), *The Intimate Papers of Colonel House,* 2 Vols (London: Ernest Benn, 1926).

Simon, Viscount, *Retrospect* (London: Hutchinson, 1952).

Storrs, Sir R., *Orientations* (London: Ivor Nicholson & Watson, 1937).

Taylor, A. J. P. (ed.), *Lloyd George: A Diary by Frances Stevenson* (London: Hutchinson, 1971).

Townshend, Maj.-Gen. Sir C., *My Campaign in Mesopotamia* (London: Thornton Butterworth, 1920).

Vansittart, R., *The Mist Procession: The Autobiography of Lord Vansittart* (London: Hutchinson, 1958).

Vincent, J. (ed.), *The Crawford Papers: The Journals of David Lindsay, Twenty-seventh Earl of Crawford and Tenth Earl of Balcarees 1871–1940 during the Years 1892–1940* (Manchester: Manchester University Press, 1984).

Webb, Beatrice, *The Letters of Sidney and Beatrice Webb,* Vol. 3, *Pilgrimage 1912–1947* (Cambridge: Cambridge University Press, 1983).

Wilson, T. (ed.), *The Political Diaries of C. P. Scott 1911–1928* (London: Collins, 1970).

Young, K. (ed.), *The Diaries of Sir Robert Bruce Lockhart,* Vol. 1 (London: Macmillan, 1973).

5   Printed Secondary Sources

Adams, R. J. Q., *Arms and the Wizard: Lloyd George and the Ministry of Munitions, 1915–1916* (London: Cassell, 1978).

Adelson, R., *Mark Sykes: Portrait of an Amateur* (London: Cape, 1975).

Ahmad, F., *The Young Turks, 1908–1914* (London: Oxford University Press, 1969).

Ahmad, F., 'Great Britain's relations with the Young Turks, 1908–1914', *Middle Eastern Studies*, vol. 2, no. 4 (1966), pp. 302–25.

Allen, Capt. G. R. G., 'A ghost from Gallipoli', *Journal of the Royal United Services Institute*, vol. 108 (1963), pp. 137–40.

Andrew, C. M. and Kanya-Forstner, A. S., *France Overseas. The Great War and the Climax of French Imperial Expansion* (London: Thames & Hudson, 1981).

Arnold, T. W., *The Caliphate* (London: Oxford University Press, 1924).

Aspinall-Oglander, Brig.-Gen. C. F., *History of the Great War. Military Operations. Gallipoli*, Vol. 1 (London: Heinemann, 1929).

Atkin, J., 'Official regulation of British overseas investment, 1914–1931', *Economic History Review*, vol. 23, no. 2 (1970), pp. 324–35.

Bailes, H., 'Technology and imperialism: A case study of the Victorian army in Africa', *Victorian Studies*, vol. 24, no. 1 (1980), pp. 84–104.

Balfour, M., *The Kaiser and his Times* (London: Cresset Press, 1964).

Ballhatchet, K., *Race, Sex and Class under the Raj: Imperial Attitudes and Policies and their Critics, 1793–1905* (London: Weidenfeld & Nicolson, 1980).

Barnett, C., *The Collapse of British Power* (London: Eyre Methuen, 1972).

Beesly, P., *Room 40: British Naval Intelligence 1914–1918* (London: Hamish Hamilton, 1982).

Bentley, M., *The Liberal Mind, 1914–1929* (Cambridge: Cambridge University Press, 1977).

Bidwell, S., and Graham, D., *Firepower: British Army Weapons and Theories of War, 1904–1945* (London: Allen & Unwin, 1982).

Birn, D. S., *The League of Nations Union, 1918–1945* (Oxford: Clarendon Press, 1981).

Blake, R., *The Unknown Prime Minister: The Life and Times of Andrew Bonar Law 1858–1923* (London: Eyre & Spottiswoode, 1955).

Bodger, A., 'Russia and the end of the Ottoman Empire', in M. Kent (ed.), *The Great Powers and the End of the Ottoman Empire* (London: Allen & Unwin, 1984), pp. 76–110.

Bolt, Christine, *Victorian Attitudes to Race* (London: Routledge & Kegan Paul, 1971).

Bond, B., *Liddell Hart: A Study of his Military Thought* (London: Cassell, 1977).

Bonham-Carter, V., *Soldier True: The Life and Times of Field Marshal Sir William Robertson* (London: Frederick Muller, 1963).

Boraston, Lt.-Col. J. H., and Dewar, G. A. B., *Sir Douglas Haig's Command, December 19th., 1915 to November 11th., 1918*, 2 Vols (London: Constable, 1922).

Bosworth, R., *Italy and the Approach of the First World War* (London: Macmillan, 1983).

Boyce, D. G., 'British opinion and Ireland and the War, 1916–18', *Historical Journal*, vol. 17, no. 3 (1974), pp. 575–93.

Bridge, F. R., *Great Britain and Austria–Hungary, 1906–1914* (London: : Weiden-field & Nicolson, 1972).

Bridge, F. R., 'The British declaration of war on Austria–Hungary', *Slavonic and East European Studies Review*, vol. 47, no. 117 (1969), pp. 401 ff.

Brown, Judith, 'War and the colonial relationship: Britain, India and the war of 1914–1918', in M. R. D. Foot (ed.), *War and Society: Historical Essays in Honour and Memory of J. R. Western, 1928–1971* (London: Paul Elek, 1973).

Bunselmeyer, R. E., *The Cost of the War, 1914–1918. British Economic War Aims and the Origins of Reparations* (Hamden, Conn.: Archon Books, 1975).

Burk, E., 'Moroccan resistance, pan-islam and German war strategy, 1914–1918', *Francia*, vol. 3 (1975), pp. 434–64.

Burk, K. M., *Britain, America and the Sinews of War 1914–1918* (London: Allen & Unwin, 1985).

Burk, K. M., 'The Treasury: From impotence to power', in K. M. Burk (ed.), *War and the State: The Transformation of British Government, 1914–1919* (London: Allen & Unwin, 1982), pp. 84–107.

Burk, K. M., 'The diplomacy of finance: British financial missions to the United States, 1914–1918', *Historical Journal*, vol. 22, no. 2 (1979), pp. 351–72.

Burk, K. M., 'The mobilisation of Anglo-American finance during World War One', in N. F. Dreisziger (ed.), *Mobilisation for Total War. The Canadian, American and British Experience, 1914–1918, 1939–1945* (Waterloo, Ontario: Wilfrid Laurier University Press, 1981), pp. 23–43.

Busch, B. C., *Britain, India and the Arabs, 1914–1921* (Berkeley, Calif.: University of California Press, 1971).

Busch, B. C., *Hardinge of Penshurst: A Study in the Old Diplomacy* (Hamden, Conn.: Archon Books, 1980).

Calder, K. J., *Britain and the Origins of the New Europe 1914–1918* (Cambridge: Cambridge University Press, 1976).

Callan, R., 'What about the Dardanelles?', *American Historical Review*, vol. 73, no. 3 (1973), pp. 641–8.

Callwell, Maj.-Gen. Sir C., *Field Marshal Sir Henry Wilson: His Life and Diaries*, 2 Vols (London: Cassell, 1927).

Calvert, P. A. R., 'Great Britain and the New World, 1905–1914', in F. H. Hinsley (ed.), *British Foriegn Policy under Sir Edward Grey* (Cambridge: Cambridge University Press, 1977), pp. 382–94.

Cassar, G. H., *The French and the Dardanelles* (London: Allen & Unwin, 1971).

Cassar, G. H., *Kitchener: Architect of Victory* (London: William Kimber, 1977).

Challener, R. D., *The French Theory of the Nation in Arms* (New York: Columbia University Press; 1955).

Churchill, R. S., *Lord Derby: King of Lancashire* (London: Heinemann, 1959).

Cline, P., 'Winding down the war economy: British plans for peacetime recovery, 1916–1919', in K. M. Burk (ed.), *War and the State: The Transformation of British Government, 1914–1919* (London: Allen & Unwin, 1982), pp. 157–81.

Clinton, A., 'Trades Councils during the First World War', *International Review of Social History*, vol. 15, no. 2 (1970), pp. 202–34.

Cohen, S. A., 'The genesis of the British campaign in Mesopotamia, 1914', *Middle Eastern Studies*, vol. 12, no. 2 (1976), pp. 119–26.

Cooper, J. M., 'The British response to the House–Grey memorandum: New evidence and new questions', *Journal of American History*, vol. 59 (1973), pp. 958–71.

Corp E., 'Sir William Tyrrell: The eminence grise of the British Foreign Office, 1912–1915', *Historical Journal*, vol. 25, no. 3 (1982), pp. 697–708.

Corrigan, H. S. W., 'German–Turkish relations and the outbreak of war in 1914: a reassessment', *Past and Present*, vol. 36 (1967), pp. 144–52.

Crampton, R. J., *The Hollow Detente: Anglo-German Relations in the Balkans, 1911–1914* (London: George Prior, 1979).

Crampton, R. J., *Bulgaria, 1878–1918* (New York: Columbia University Press and Eastern European Monographs, 1983).

Crangle, J. V., and Baylen, J. O., 'Emily Hobhouse's peace mission, 1916', *Journal of Contemporary History*, vol. 14, no. 4 (1979), pp. 731–44.

Darwin, J., *Britain, Egypt and the Middle East. Imperial Policy in the Aftermath of War, 1918–1922* (London: Macmillan, 1981).

Dayer, Roberta A., 'Strange bedfellows: J. P. Morgan & Co., Whitehall and the Wilson administration during World War One', *Business History*, vol. 18, no. 2 (1976), pp. 127–51.

Dewey, P. E., 'Food production and policy in the United Kingdom, 1914–1918', *Transactions of the Royal Historical Society*, 5th series, vol. 30 (1980), pp. 71–88.

Dewey, P. E., 'Military recruiting and the British labour force during the First World War', *Historical Journal*, vol. 27, no. 1 (1984), pp. 199–223.

Douglas, R., 'Voluntary enlistment in the First World War and the work of the Parliamentary Recruiting Committee', *Journal of Modern History*, vol. 42, no. 4 (1970), pp. 564–85.

Dutton, D., 'The Union Sacré and the French cabinet crisis of October 1915', *European Studies Review*, vol. 8, no. 4 (1978), pp. 411–24.

Dutton, D., 'The Balkan campaign and French war aims in the Great War', *English Historical Review*, vol. 94, no. 370 (1979), pp. 97–113.

Dutton, D., 'The deposition of King Constantine of Greece, June 1917: An episode in Anglo-French diplomacy', *Canadian Journal of History*, vol. 12, no. 3 (1978), pp. 325–45.

Dutton, D., 'The Calais conference of December 1915', *Historical Journal*, vol. 21, no. 1 (1978), pp. 143–56.

Edmonds, Brig.-Gen. Sir. J. E., *Military Operations: France and Belgium*, 14 Vols (London: Heinemann, 1922–48).

Egerton, G. W., *Great Britain and the Creation of the League of Nations* (London: Scolar Press, 1979).

Ehrman, J., 'Lloyd George and Churchill as War Ministers', *Transactions of the Royal Historical Society*, 5th series, vol. 11 (1961), pp. 101–16.

Ekstein, M. G., 'Russia, Constantinipole and the Straits', in F. H. Hinsley (ed.),

British Foreign Policy under Sir Edward Grey (Cambridge: Cambridge University Press, 1977), pp. 423–35.

Englander, D., and Osborne, J., 'Jack, Tommy and Henry Dubb: The armed forces and the working class', *Historical Journal* vol. 21, no. 3 (1978), pp. 593–621.

Erickson, J., '*Koalitsionnaya Voina*: Coalition warfare in Soviet military theory, planning and performance', in K. Neilson and R. A. Prete (eds), *Coalition Warfare: An Uneasy Accord* (Waterloo, Ontario: Wilfrid Laurier Press, 1984), pp. 79–122.

Evans, Maj. R., *A Brief Outline of the Campaign in Mesopotamia 1914–1918* (London: Sifton Praed, 1926).

Eyck, F., *G. P. Gooch: A Study in History and Politics* (London: Macmillan, 1982).

Farrar, L. L., 'Peace through exhaustion: German diplomatic motivations for the Verdun campaign', *Revue Internationale d'Histoire Militaire*, Vol. 8, no. 2 (1972–5), pp. 477–94.

Farrar, L. L., *Divide and Conquer. German Efforts to Conclude a Separate Peace, 1914–1918* (New York: Columbia University Press, 1978).

Farrar, M. M., 'Politics versus patriotism: Alexandre Millerand as French minister of war', *French Historical Studies*, vol. 11, no. 4 (1979–80), pp. 577–605.

Fayle, C. E., *The War and the Shipping Industry* (London: Oxford University Press, 1927).

Feldman, G. D., *Army, Industry and Labour in Germany, 1914–1918* (Princeton, NJ: Princeton University Press, 1966).

Fergusson, T. E., *British Military Intelligence 1870–1914: The Development of a Modern Intelligence Organisation* (London: Arms and Armour Press, 1984).

Fest, W. B., *Peace or Partition: The Habsburg Monarchy and British Policy, 1914–1918* (London: George Prior, 1978).

Fischer, F., *Germany's Aims in the First World War* (London: Chatto & Windus, 1967).

Fraser, P., *Lord Esher: A Political Biography* (London: Hart-Davis, McGibbon, 1973).

Fraser, P., 'British policy and the crisis of Liberalism in May 1915', *Journal of Modern History*, vol. 52, no. 1 (1982), pp. 1–26.

Fraser, P., 'The impact of the war of 1914–1918 on the British political system', in M. R. D. Foot (ed.), *War and Society: Historical Essays in Honour and Memory of J. R. Western 1928–1971* (London: Paul Elek, 1973).

Fraser, T. G., 'Germany and the Indian revolution, 1914–1918', *Journal of Contemporary History*, vol. 12, no. 2 (1977), pp. 255–68.

Fraser, T. G., 'India in Anglo-Japanese relations during the First World War', *History*, vol. 63, no. 209 (1978), pp. 366–82.

French, D., 'The military background to the "shell crisis" of May 1915', *Journal of Strategic Studies*, vol. 2, no. 2 (1979), pp. 192–205.

French, D., *British Economic and Strategic Planning, 1905–1915* (London: Allen & Unwin, 1982).

French, D., 'The origins of the Dardanelles campaign reconsidered', *History*, vol. 68, no. 223 (1983), pp. 210–24.

French, D., 'Sir John French's secret service on the Western front, 1914–1915', *Journal of Strategic Studies*, vol. 7, no. 4 (1984), pp. 423–40.

French, D., 'The Edwardian crisis and the origins of the First World War,' *International History Review*, vol. 4, no. 2 (1982), pp. 207–21.

French, D., 'Sir Douglas Haig's reputation: A note', *Historical Journal*, vol. 28, no. 4 (1985), pp. 953–60.

French, D. W., 'Some aspects of social and economic planning for war in Great Britain, c. 1905–1915', PhD thesis, London University, 1978.

Friedman, I., *The Question of Palestine, 1914–1918: British–Jewish–Arab Relations* (London: Routledge & Kegan Paul, 1973).

Friedman, J. R., Bladen, C., and Rosen, S., *Alliances in International Politics* (Boston, Mass.: Allyn & Bacon, 1970).

Fry, M. G., *Lloyd George and Foreign Policy. The Education of a Statesman*, Vol. 1 (London and Montreal: McGill, Queens University Press, 1977).

Galbraith, J. S., 'No man's child: the campaign in Mesopotamia, 1914–1916', *International History Review*, vol. 6, no. 3 (1984), pp. 358–85.

Gilbert, B. B., 'David Lloyd George: the reform of British land holding and the budget of 1914', *Historical Journal*, vol. 21, no. 1 (1978), pp. 117–41.

Gilbert, M., *Winston Spencer Churchill*, Vol. 3 and *Companion Volumes* (London: Heinemann, 1971).

Gollin, A. M., *Proconsul in Politics: A Study of Lord Milner in Opposition and Power* (London: Blond, 1964).

Gooch, J., *The Plans of War. The General Staff and British Military Strategy, c. 1900–1916* (London: Routledge & Kegan Paul, 1974).

Gooch, J., 'Soldiers, strategy and war aims in Britain, 1914–1918', in B. Hunt and A. Preston (eds), *War Aims and Strategic Policy in the Great War 1914–1918* (London: Croom Helm, 1977).

Goold, J. D., 'Lord Hardinge and the Mesopotamian expedition and inquiry, 1914–1917', *Historical Journal*, vol. 19, no. 4 (1976), pp. 919–45.

Gowen, R. J., 'Great Britain and the twenty-one demands of 1915: co-operation versus effacement', *Journal of Modern History*, vol. 43, no. 1 (1971), pp. 76–97.

Grand, A. J. de, 'The Italian nationalist association in the period of Italian neutrality, August 1914 to May 1915', *Journal of Modern History*, vol. 43, no. 3 (1971), pp. 395–412.

Greenhut, J., 'Race, sex and war: the impact of race and sex on the morale and health services of the Indian Corps on the Western front, 1914', *Military Affairs*, vol. 45, no. 2 (1981), pp. 71–4.

Greenhut, J., 'The Imperial Reserve: The Indian Corps on the Western front, 1914–1915', *Journal of Imperial and Commonwealth History*, vol. 12, no. 1 (1983), pp. 54–73.

Greenhut, J., 'Sahib and sepoy: an inquiry into the relationship between British officers and native soldiers of the British Indian Army', *Military Affairs*, vol. 48, no. 1, (1984), pp. 15–18.

Grieves, K. R., 'The British government's political and administrative response to the man-power problem in the First World War', PhD thesis, Manchester University 1984.

Grieves, K. R., 'The Liverpool dock labour battalion: Military intervention in the Mersey docks, 1915–1918', *Transactions of the Historic Society of Lancashire and Cheshire*, vol. 132 (1982), pp. 139–58.

Grigg, J., *Lloyd George: From Peace to War, 1912–1916* (London: Methuen, 1985).

Guinn, P., *British Strategy and Politics 1914 to 1918* (Oxford: Clarendon Press, 1965).

Haggie, P., 'The royal navy and war planning in the Fisher era', *Journal of Contemporary History*, vol. 8, no. 3 (1973), pp. 113–33.

Hamilton, C. I., 'Naval power and diplomacy in the nineteenth century', *Journal of Strategic Studies*, vol. 3, no. 1 (1980), pp. 74–86.

Hamilton, K. A., 'Great Britain and France, 1905–1911', and 'Great Britain and France, 1911–14', in F. H. Hinsley (ed.), *British Foreign Policy under Sir Edward Grey* (Cambridge: Cambridge University Press, 1977), pp. 113–31 and 324–33.

Hanak, H., 'The Union of Democratic Control during the First World War', *Bulletin of the Institute of Historical Research*, vol. 36, no. 94 (1963), pp. 168–80.

Hancock, W. K., and Gowing, M. M., *British War Economy* (London: HMSO, 1949).

Hardach, G., *The First World War 1914–1918* (London: Allen Lane, 1977).

Hardy, P., *The Muslims of British India* (Cambridge: Cambridge University Press, 1972).

Harnetty, P., 'British and Indian attitudes to the Indian problem at the end of the nineteenth century', *Canadian Historical Association. Report of the Annual Meeting* (1959), pp. 48–55.

Harries-Jenkins, G., *The Army in Victorian Society* (London: Routledge & Kegan Paul, 1977).

Harris, José, *William Beveridge: A Biography* (Oxford: Clarendon Press, 1977).

Harris, José, 'Bureaucrats and businessmen in British food control', in K. M. Burk (ed.), *War and the State: The Transformation of British Government, 1914–1919* (London: Allen & Unwin, 1982), pp. 135–56.

Harrison, R., 'The war emergency workers' national committee', in A. Briggs and J. Saville (eds), *Essays in Labour History, 1886–1923* (London: Macmillan, 1971).

Harvey, A. D., 'European attitudes to Britain during the French Revolutionary and Napoleonic eras', *History*, vol. 63, no. 209 (1978), pp. 356–65.

Haste, C., *Keep the Home Fires Burning: Propaganda in the First World War* (London: Allen Lane, 1977).

Havighurst, A. F., *Radical Journalist: H. W. Massingham (1860–1924)* (Cambridge: Cambridge University Press, 1974).

Hazlehurst, C., *Politicians at War, July 1914 to May 1915: A Prologue to the Triumph of Lloyd George* (London: Cape, 1971).

Hazlehurst, C., 'Asquith as Prime Minister, 1908–1916', *English Historical Review*, vol. 85, no. 336 (1970), pp. 502–31.

Heller, J., 'Sir Louis Mallet and the Ottoman empire: The road to war', *Middle Eastern Studies*, vol. 12, no. 1 (1976), pp. 3–34.

Hiley, H. P., 'The failure of British espionage against Germany', *Historical Journal*, vol. 26, no. 4 (1983), pp. 867–89.

Hinton, J., *The First Shop Stewards Movement* (London: Allen & Unwin, 1973).

Holmes, R., *The Little Field Marshal: Sir John French* (London: Cape, 1981).

Hopkins, D., 'Domestic censorship in the First World War', *Journal of Contemporary History*, vol. 5, no. 4 (1970), pp. 151–69.

Howard, C., 'MacDonald, Henderson and the outbreak of war, 1914', *Historical Journal*, vol. 20, no. 4 (1977), pp. 871–91.

Howard, C. H. D., 'The policy of isolation', *Historical Journal*, vol. 10, no. 1 (1967), pp. 77–88.

Howard, C. H. D., *Britain and the Casus Belli 1822–1902* (London: Athlone Press, 1974).

Howard, M., *The Continental Commitment* (London: Pelican, 1972).

Howard, M., *War and the Liberal Conscience* (London: Temple Smith, 1978).

Howard, M., 'The British way in warfare – a reappraisal', in M. Howard, *The Causes of War* (London: Temple Smith, 1983).

Iklé, F. W., 'Japanese–German peace negotiations during World War One', *American Historical Review*, vol. 71, no. 1 (1965), pp. 62–76.

Jaffe, L. S., *The Decision to Disarm Germany: British Policy towards Postwar German Disarmament, 1914–1919* (London: Allen & Unwin, 1985).

James, R. R., *Gallipoli* (London: Pan, 1965/74).

Jeffery, K., 'The eastern arc of empire: A strategic view, 1850–1914', *Journal of Strategic Studies*, vol. 5, no. 4 (1982), pp. 531–45.

Jervis, *The Logic of Images in International Relations* (Princeton, NJ: Princeton University Press, 1970).

Johnson, D., Crouzet, F., and Bedarida, F., *Britain and France: Ten Centuries* (Folkstone: Dowson Press, 1980).

Joll, J., *The Origins of the First World War* (London: Longman, 1984).

Jones, R. A., *The British Diplomatic Service 1815–1914*, (Gerrards Cross: Colin Smythe, 1983).

Kaarsted, T., *Great Britain and Denmark, 1914–1920* (Odense: Odense University Press, 1979).

Katkov, G., *Russia, 1917: The February Revolution* (London: Longman, 1967).

Kedourie, E., 'Cairo, Khartoum and the Arab question', in E. Kedourie, *The Chatham House Version and other Middle Eastern Studies* (London: Weidenfeld & Nicolson, 1970).

Kedourie, E., *England and the Middle East: The destruction of the Ottoman Empire, 1914–1921* (London: Bowes, 1956).

Keiger, J. F., 'Jules Cambon and the Franco-German detente, 1907–1914', *Historical Journal*, vol. 26, no. 3 (1983), pp. 641–59.

Keiger, J. F., *France and the Origins of the First World War* (London: Macmillan, 1983).

Kemp, P. (ed.), *The Papers of Admiral Sir John Fisher*, Vol. 2 (London: Navy Records Society, 1964).

Kennedy, P. M., *The Rise and Fall of British Naval Mastery* (London: Allen Lane, 1976).

Kennedy, P. M., *The Rise of the Anglo-German Antagonism, 1860–1914* (London: Allen & Unwin, 1980).

Kennedy, P. M., *The Realities Behind Diplomacy: Background Influences on British External Policy, 1865–1980* (London: Fontana, 1981).

Kennedy, P. M., 'The First World War and the international power system', *International Security*, vol. 9, no. 1 (1984), pp. 7–40.

Kennedy, T. C., 'Public opinion and the conscientious objector, 1915–1919', *Journal of British Studies*, vol. 12, no. 2 (1973), pp. 105–19.

Kent, M., 'Constantinople and Asiatic Turkey, 1905–1914', in F. H. Hinsley (ed.), *British Foreign Policy under Sir Edward Grey* (Cambridge: Cambridge University Press, 1977), pp. 148–63.

Kent, M., 'Asiatic Turkey, 1914–1916', in F. H. Hinsley (ed.), *British Foreign Policy under Sir Edward Grey* (Cambridge: Cambridge University Press, 1977), pp. 436–51.

Kihl, M. R., 'A failure of ambassadorial diplomacy', *Journal of American History*, vol. 57, no. 3 (1970), pp. 636–52.

Kimche, J., *The Second Arab Awakening* (London: Thames & Hudson, 1970).

King, J. C., *Generals and Politicians: Conflict between France's High Command, Parliament and Government 1914–1918* (Berkeley, Calif.: University of California Press, 1951).

Kitchen, M., *The Silent Dictatorship: The Politics of the German High Command under Hindenburg and Ludendorff, 1916–1918* (London: Croom Helm, 1976).

Klein, I, 'The Anglo-Russian convention and the problems of central Asia, 1907–1914', *Journal of British Studies*, vol. 11, no. 1 (1971), pp. 126–47.

Klieman, A. S., 'British war aims in the Middle East in 1915', *Journal of Contemporary History*, vol. 3, no. 3 (1968), pp. 237–51.

Koblik, S., *Sweden: The Neutral Victor: Sweden and the Western Powers, 1917–1918* (Laromedelsforlagen: Scandinavian University Books, 1972).

Koss, S., *Asquith* (London: Allen Lane, 1976).

Koss, S., *The Rise and Fall of the Political Press in Britain*, Vol. 2 (London: Hamish Hamilton, 1984).

Kumar, P., 'The records of the Government of India and the Berlin–Baghdad railway', *Historical Journal*, vol. 5, no. 1 (1962), pp. 70–9.

Langhorne, R., 'Anglo-German negotiations concerning the future of the Portuguese colonies, 1911–1914', *Historical Journal*, vol. 16, no. 24 (1973), pp. 361–87.

Lebzelter, G., *Political Anti-Semitism in England, 1918–1939* (London and Oxford: Macmillan and St Anthony's College, Oxford, 1978).

Leon, G. B., *Greece and the Great Powers 1914–1917* (Thessaloniki: Institute for Balkan Studies, 1974).

Liddell Hart, Capt. B. H., 'Economic pressure or continental victories', *Journal of the Royal United Services Institute*, vol. 76, no. 503 (1931), pp. 486–503.

Lieshout, R. H., ' "Keeping the better educated Moslems busy": Sir Reginald Wingate and the origins of the Husayn–McMahon correspondence', *Historical Journal*, vol. 27, no. 2 (1984), pp. 453–64.

Lieven, D. C. B., *Russia and the Origins of the First World War* (London: Macmillan, 1983).

Lieven, D. C. B., 'Pro-Germans and Russian foreign policy 1890–1914', *International History Review*, vol. 2, no. 1 (1980), pp. 34–53.

Link, A. S., *Wilson: Confusions and Crises, 1915–1916* (Princeton, NJ: Princeton University Press, 1964).

Link, A. S., *Wilson: Campaigns for Progressivism and Peace, 1916–1917* (Princeton, NJ: Princeton University Press, 1965).

Liska, G., *Nations in Alliance: The Limit of Independence* (Baltimore: Johns Hopkins Press, 1962).

Lockwood, P. A., 'Milner's entry into the War Cabinet, December 1916', *Historical Journal*, vol. 7, no. 1 (1964), pp. 120–34.

Louis, W. R., *Great Britain and Germany's Lost Colonies* (Oxford: Clarendon Press, 1967).

Louis, W. R., 'Australia and the German colonies in the Pacific, 1914–1919', *Journal of Modern History*, vol. 38, no. 4 (1966), pp. 407–21.

Lowe, C. J., and Dockrill, M. L., *The Mirage of Power*, 3 Vols (London: Routledge & Kegan Paul, 1972).

Lowe, C. J., 'Italy and the Balkans, 1914–1915', in F. H. Hinsley (ed.), *British Foreign Policy under Sir Edward Grey* (Cambridge: Cambridge University Press, 1977), pp. 411–22.

Lowe, C. J., 'Britain and Italian intervention, 1914–1915', *Historical Journal*, vol. 12, no. 3 (1969), pp. 533–48.

Lowe, C. J., 'The failure of British diplomacy in the Balkans, 1914–1916', *Canadian Journal of History*, vol. 4, no. 1 (1969), pp. 73–99.

Lowe, C. J., *The Reluctant Imperialists: British Foreign Policy 1878–1902* (London: Routledge & Kegan Paul, 1967).

Mackay, R. F., *Fisher of Kilverstone* (Oxford: Clarendon Press, 1973).

Mallet, B., and George, C. O., *British Budgets: Second Series 1913/14 to 1920/21* (London: Macmillan, 1929).

Mannasker, F. M., 'East and West: Anglo-Indian racial attitudes as reflected in popular fiction, 1890–1914', *Victorian Studies*, vol. 24, no. 1 (1980), pp. 33–51.

Marder, A. J., *The Anatomy of British Sea Power: A History of British Naval Policy in the Pre-Dreadnought Era 1880–1905* (Hamden, Conn.: Archon Reprints, 1964).

Marder, A. J., *From the Dreadnought to Scapa Flow: The Royal Navy in the Fisher Era, 1904–1919*, Vols 1 and 2 (London: Oxford University Press, 1961–5).

Marquis, A. G., 'Words as weapons: Propaganda in Britain and Germany during the First World War', *Journal of Contemporary History*, vol. 13, no. 3 (1978), pp. 486–98.

Marwick, A., *The Deluge: British Society and the First World War* (London: Penguin, 1965).

Mason, C. M., 'Anglo-American relations: Mediation and "permanent peace"', in F. H. Hinsley (ed.) *British Foreign Policy under Sir Edward Grey* (Cambridge: Cambridge University Press, 1977), pp. 466–87.

Matthew, H. C. G., *The Liberal Imperialists: The Ideas and Politics of a Post-Gladstonian Elite* (London: Oxford University Press, 1973).

Mayer, A. J., *Political Origins of the New Diplomacy 1917–1918* (New York: Vintage Books, 1970).

McDougall, W. A., *France's Rhineland Diplomacy, 1914–1924: The Last Bid for a Balance of Power in Europe* (Princeton, NJ: Princeton University Press, 1978).

McEwen, J. M., 'Northcliffe and Lloyd George at war, 1914–1918', *Historical Journal*, vol. 24, no. 3 (1981), pp. 651–72.

McEwen, J. M., 'Lloyd George's Liberal supporters in December 1916', *Bulletin of the Institute of Historical Research*, vol. 53 (1980), pp. 265–72.

McEwen, J. M., 'The press and the fall of Asquith', *Historical Journal*, vol. 21, no. 4 (1978), pp. 863–85.

McEwen, J. M., 'The struggle for mastery in Great Britain: Lloyd George versus Asquith, December 1916', *Journal of British Studies*, vol. 18, no. 1 (1978), pp. 131–56.

McEwen, J. M., '"Brass-Hats" and the British press during the First World War', *Canadian Journal of History*, vol. 18, no. 1 (1983), pp. 43–67.

McGill, B., 'Asquith's predicament, 1914–1918', *Journal of Modern History*, vol. 39, no. 3 (1967), pp. 283–303.

McKibbin, R., 'Arthur Henderson as Labour Leader', *International Review of Social History*, vol. 23, no. 1 (1978), pp. 79–101.

McLean, I, 'Popular protest and public order: Red Clydeside, 1915–1919', in J. Stevenson and R. Quinault (eds), *Popular Protest and Public Order: Six Studies in British History, 1790–1920* (London: Allen & Unwin, 1974).

Metcalf, T. R., *The Aftermath of Revolt: India, 1857–1870* (Princeton, NJ: Princeton University Press, 1965).

Middlemas, K., *Politics in Industrial Society: The British Experience since 1911* (London: Andre Deutch, 1979).

Milward, A., *War, Economy and Society, 1939–1945* (London: Allen Lane, 1977).

Monger, G., *The End of Isolation: British Foreign Policy 1900–1907* (London: Nelson, 1963).

Morgan, E. V., *Studies in British Financial Policy, 1914–1925* (London: Macmillan, 1952).

Morgan, K. and J., *Portrait of a Progressive: The Political Career of Christopher, Viscount Addison* (Oxford: Clarendon Press, 1980).

Morgan, K. O., 'David Lloyd George', in J. P. Mackintosh (ed.), *British Prime Ministers in the Twentieth Century*, Vol. 1 (London: Weidenfeld & Nicolson, 1977), pp. 118–30.

Morris, A. J. A., *The Scaremongers: The Advocacy of War and Rearmament 1896–1914* (London: Routledge & Kegan Paul, 1984).

Murray, B. K., *The People's Budget 1909–10: Lloyd George and Liberal Politics* (Oxford: Clarendon Press, 1980).

Neilson, K., 'Kitchener: A reputation refurbished?', *Canadian Journal of History*, vol. 15, no. 2 (1980), pp. 207–27.

Neilson, K., *Strategy and Supply: The Anglo-Russian Alliance, 1914–1917* (London: Allen & Unwin, 1984).

Neilson, K., 'Wishful thinking: The Foreign Office and Russia, 1907–1917', in B. J. C. McKercher and D. J. Moss (eds), *Shadow and Substance in British Foreign Policy 1895–1935. Memorial Essays Honouring C. J. Lowe* (Edmonton, Alberta: University of Alberta Press, 1984).

Neilson, K., 'Russian foreign purchasing in the Great War: a test case', *Slavonic and East European Studies Review*, vol. 60, no. 4 (1982), pp. 572–90.

Neilson, K., '"Joy-rides"? British intelligence and propaganda in Russia, 1914–1917', *Historical Journal*, vol. 24, no. 4 (1981), pp. 885–906.

Nevakivi, J., *Britain, France and the Arab Middle East, 1914–1920* (London: Athlone Press, 1969).

Nevakivi, J., 'Lord Kitchener and the partition of the Ottoman Empire 1915–1916', in D. C. Watt and K. Bourne (eds), *Studies in International History: Essays Presented to W. N. Medlicott* (London: Longman, 1967), pp. 316–27.

Newton, Lord, *Lord Lansdowne: A Biography* (London: Macmillan, 1929).

Nicolson, H., *Diplomacy* (London: Oxford University Press, 1939/1969).

Nicolson, H., *King George V. His Life and Reign* (London: Constable, 1952).

Nish, I. H., *Alliance in Decline: A Study in Anglo-Japanese Relations, 1908–1923* (London: Athlone Press, 1972).

Offer, A., 'Empire and social reform: British overseas investment and domestic politics, 1908–1914', *Historical Journal*, vol. 26, no. 1 (1983), pp. 119–37.

d'Ombraine, N., *War Machinery and High Policy* (Oxford: Clarendon Press, 1973).

Osborne, J. M., *The Voluntary Recruiting Movement in Britain 1914–1916* (New York: Garland, 1982).

Paléologue, M., *An Ambassador's Memoirs*, Vol. 1 (London: Hutchinson, 1923).

Papayanis, N., 'Collaboration and pacifism in France during World War One', *Francia*, vol. 5 (1977), pp. 425–51.

Patterson, D. S., 'Woodrow Wilson and the mediation movement', *The Historian*, vol. 33, no. 1 (1970–1), pp. 535–52.

Pearson, R., *The Russian Moderates and the Crisis of Tsarism, 1914–1917* (London: Macmillan, 1977).

Petrie, Sir C., *The Life and Letters of the Rt Hon. Sir Austen Chamberlain*, 2 Vols (London: Cassell, 1939).

Prior, R., *Churchill's World Crisis as History* (London: Croom Helm, 1983).

Pugh, M. D., *Electoral Reform in War and Peace, 1906–1918* (London: Routledge & Kegan Paul, 1978).

Pugh, M. D., 'Asquith, Bonar Law and the first coalition', *Historical Journal*, vol. 17, no. 4 (1974), pp. 813–36.

Rae, J., *Conscience and Politics: The British Government and the Conscientious Objector to Military Service 1916–1919* (London: Oxford University Press, 1969).

Ramsden, J., *The Age of Balfour and Baldwin 1902–1940* (London: Longman, 1978).

Rees, J. F., *A Short Fiscal History of England 1815–1918* (London: Methuen, 1921).

Renouvin, P., 'L'Opinion publique en France pendant la guerre 1914–1918', *Revue d'histoire Diplomatique*, vol. 84, no. 4 (1970), pp. 289–336.

Renzi, W. A., 'Who composed "Sazonov's Thirteen Points": A re-examination of Russia's war aims of 1914', *American Historical Review*, vol. 88, no. 2 (1983), pp. 347–57.

Renzi, W. A., 'Great Britain, Russia and the Straits, 1914–1915', *Journal of Modern History*, vol. 42, no. 1 (1970), pp. 1–19.

Renzi, W. A., 'Italy's neutrality and entry into the Great War: A re-examination', *American Historical Review*, vol. 73, no. 2 (1967–8), pp. 1414–31.

Renzi, W. A., 'The Entente and the Vatican during the period of Italian neutrality, August 1914–May 1915', *Historical Journal*, vol. 13, no. 3 (1970), pp. 491–506.

Ritter, G., *Sword and Scepter: The Problem of Militarism in Germany*, Vol. 3 (Coral Gables, Fla: University of Miami Press, 1972).

Robbins, K., 'British diplomacy and Bulgaria, 1914–1915', *Slavonic and East European Studies Review*, vol. 49, no. 117 (1971), pp. 565 ff.

Robbins, K., *Sir Edward Grey: A Biography of Lord Grey of Fallodon* (London: Cassell, 1971).

Robbins, K., 'Sir Edward Grey and the British Empire', *Journal of Imperial and Commonwealth History*, vol. 1, no. 2 (1972–3), pp. 213–21.

Ronaldshay, Earl of, *The Life of Lord Curzon*, Vol. 3 (London: Ernest Benn, 1928).

Rose, N., *Vansittart: Study of a Diplomat* (London: Heinemann, 1978).

Roskill, S., *Hankey: Man of Secrets*, Vol. 1 (London: Collins, 1970).

Rothenberg, G. E., 'The Habsburg army in the First World War', in R. A. Kann, B. K. Kiraly and P. S. Fichtner (eds), *The Habsburg Empire in World War One* (New York: Columbia University Press and Eastern European Quarterly, 1977), pp. 73–86.

Rothwell, V., 'Mesopotamia in British war aims, 1914–1918', *Historical Journal*, vol. 13, no. 2 (1970), pp. 273–94.

Rothwell, V., 'The British government and Japanese military assistance, 1914–1918', *History*, vol. 57, no. 186 (1971), pp. 35–45.

Rothwell, V. H., *British War Aims and Peace Diplomacy 1914–1918* (Oxford: Clarendon Press, 1971).

Rumbold, Sir A., *Watershed in British India 1914–1922* (London: Athlone Press, 1979).

Sanders, M., and Taylor, P. M., *British Propaganda during the First World War 1914–1918* (London: Macmillan, 1982).

Saunders, D. B., 'Stepniak and the London emigration. Letters to Robert Spence Watson, 1887–1890', *Oxford Slavonic Papers*, vol. 13 (1980), pp. 80–93.

Sayers, R. S., *The Bank of England*, Vol. 1 (Cambridge: Cambridge University Press, 1976).

Scally, R. J., *The Origins of the Lloyd George Coalition: The Politics of Social Imperialism, 1900–1918* (Princeton, NJ: Princeton University Press, 1975).

Schneer, J., 'The war, the state and the workplace: British dockers during 1914–1918', in L. E. Cronin and J. Schneer (eds), *Social Conflict and Political Order in Modern Britain* (London: Croom Helm, 1982).

Scott, F. D., 'Gustaf V and Swedish attitudes towards Germany, 1915', *Journal of Modern History*, vol. 39, no. 2 (1967), pp. 113–18.

Seager, F., 'Joseph Caillaux as Premier 1911–1912: The dilemma of a Liberal reformer', *French Historical Studies*, vol. 11, no. 2 (1979), pp. 239–57.

Searle, G. R., 'The Edwardian Liberal Party and business', *English Historical Review*, vol. 98, no. 386 (1983), pp. 28–60.

Searle, G. R., *The Quest for National Efficiency* (Oxford: Blackwell, 1971).

Shaw, C. I., 'The ambassadorship of Sir Francis Bertie in Paris between 1905–1914', MA thesis, London University, n.d.

Simpkins, P., 'Lord Kitchener and the expansion of the army', in I. F. W. Beckett and J. Gooch (eds), *Politicians and British Defence Policy 1845–1970* (Manchester: Manchester University Press, 1981).

Skidelsky, R., *John Maynard Keynes: Hopes Betrayed 1883–1920* (London: Macmillan, 1983).

Smith, C. J., 'Great Britain and the 1914–1915 Straits agreement with Russia: The British promise of November 1914', *American Historical Review*, vol. 70, no. 4 (1964–5), pp. 1015–34.

Smith, G., 'The British government and the disposition of the German colonies in Africa, 1914–1918', in P. Gifford and W. R. Louis (eds), *Britain and Germany in Africa: Imperial Rivalry and Colonial Rule* (New Haven, Conn.: Yale University Press, 1967).

Spiers, E. M., *Haldane: An Army Reformer* (Edinburgh: Edinburgh University Press, 1980).

Spender, J. A., and Asquith, C., *Life of Herbert Henry Asquith, Lord Oxford and Asquith*, Vol. 2 (London: Heinemann, 1932).

Stamp, Sir, J., *Taxation during the War* (London: Oxford University Press, 1932).

Steiner, Z., 'The Foreign Office, 1905–1914', in F. H. Hinsley (ed.), *British Foreign Policy under Sir Edward Grey* (Cambridge: Cambridge University Press, 1977), pp. 22–67.

Steiner, Z., 'The Foreign Office at war', in F. H. Hinsley (ed.), *British Foreign Policy under Sir Edward Grey* (Cambridge: Cambridge University Press, 1977), pp. 516–31.

Steiner, Z., *Britain and the Origins of the First World War* ((London: Macmillan, 1977).

Steiner, Z., 'Elitism and foreign policy: the Foreign Office before the Great War', in B. J. C. McKercher and D. J. Moss (eds), *Shadow and Substance in British Foreign Policy 1895–1935. Memorial Essays Honouring C. J. Lowe* (Edmonton, Alberta: University of Alberta Press, 1984), pp. 19–55.

Stevenson, D., 'Belgium, Luxemburg and the defence of Western Europe, 1914–1920', *International History Review*, vol. 4, no. 4 (1982), pp. 504–23.

Stevenson, D., 'French war aims and the American challenge, 1914–1918', *Historical Journal*, vol. 22, no. 4 (1979), pp. 877 ff.

Stevenson, D., *French War Aims against Germany, 1914–1919* (Oxford: Clarendon Press, 1982).

Stone, N., *The Eastern Front 1914–1917* (London: Hodder & Stoughton, 1975).

Stone, N., *Europe Transformed, 1878–1919* (London: Fontana, 1983).

Strachen, H., 'The British way in warfare revisited', *Historical Journal*, vol. 26, no. 2 (1983), pp. 447–61.

Summers, A., 'Militarism in Britain before the Great War', *History Workshop Journal*, vol. 2 (1976), pp. 104–23.

Swartz, M., *The Union of Democratic Control in British Politics during the First World War* (Oxford: Clarendon Press, 1971).

Sykes, A., *Tariff Reform in British Politics, 1909–1913* (Oxford: Clarendon Press, 1979).

Tanenbaum, J. K., *General Maurice Sarrail, 1856–1929: The French Army and Left-Wing Politics* (Chapel Hill, NC: University of North Carolina Press, 1974).

Taylor, A. J. P., 'Politics in the First World War', in A. J. P. Taylor, *Politics in Wartime* (London: Hamish Hamilton, 1964), pp. 11–45.

Taylor, A. J. P., *English History 1914–1945* (Oxford: Clarendon Press, 1965).

Taylor, P. M., 'The Foreign Office and British propaganda during the First World War', *Historical Journal*, vol. 23, no. 4 (1980), pp. 875–98.

Terraine, J., *Douglas Haig: The Educated Soldier* (London: Hutchinson, 1963).

Thurbon, Wing Commander M. T., 'The origins of electronic warfare', *Journal of the Royal United Services Institute*, vol. 122 (1977), pp. 56–62.

Torrey, G. E., 'Rumania and the belligerents 1914–1916', *Journal of Contemporary History*, vol. 1, no. 3 (1966), pp. 171–91.

Torrey, G. E., 'The Rumanian campaign of 1916: Its impact on the belligerents', *Slavic Review*, vol. 39, no. 1 (1980), pp. 27–43.

Towle, P., 'The European balance of power in 1914', *Army Quarterly and Defence Journal*, vol. 104 (1974), pp. 333–42.

Trachtenberg, M., ' "A new economic order": Etienne Clémentel and French economic diplomacy during the First World War', *French Historical Studies*, vol. 10, no. 2 (1977), pp. 315–41.

Travers, T. H. E., 'The hidden army: structural problems in the British officer corps, 1900–1918', *Journal of Contemporary History*, vol. 17, no. 3 (1982), pp. 523–44.

Travers, T. H. E., 'The offensive and the problem of innovation in British military thought, 1870–1915', *Journal of Contemporary History*, vol. 13, no. 4 (1978), pp. 531–53.

Trevelyan, G. M., *Grey of Fallodon* (London: Longman, 1937).

Troeller, G., 'Ibn Sa'ud and Sharif Husain: A comparison in importance in the early years of the First World War', *Historical Journal*, vol. 14, no. 3 (1971), pp. 627–33.

Trumpener, U., *Germany and the Ottoman Empire, 1914–1918* (Princeton, NJ: Princeton University Press, 1968).

Trumpener, U., 'Suez, Baku and Gallipoli: The military dimensions of the German–Ottoman Coalition', in K. Neilson and R. A. Prete (eds), *Coalition Warfare: An Uneasy Accord* (Waterloo, Ontario: Wilfrid Laurier University Press, 1984), pp. 29–52.

Trumpener, U., 'Turkey's entry into World War One: An assessment of the responsibilities', *Journal of Modern History*, vol. 34, no. 4 (1962), pp. 369–80.

Trumpener, U., 'German military aid to Turkey in 1914: a historical re-evaluation', *Journal of Modern History*, vol. 32, no. 2 (1960), pp. 145–9.

Turner, J., 'Cabinets, committees and secretariats: The higher direction of the war', in K. M. Burk (ed.), *War and the State: The Transformation of British Government, 1914–1919* (London: Allen & Unwin, 1982), pp. 57–83.

Vincent, R. J., 'Race in international relations', *International Affairs*, vol. 58, no. 4 (1982), pp. 658–70.

Waites, B. A., 'The effect of the First World War on class and status in England, 1910–1920', *Journal of Contemporary History*, vol. 11, no. 1 (1976), pp. 27–48.

Waites, N. (ed.), *Troubled Neighbours: Franco-British Relations in the Twentieth Century* (London: Weidenfeld & Nicolson, 1971).

Waley, S. D., *Edwin Montagu: A Memoir and an Account of his Visits to India* (London: Asia Publishing House, 1964).

Warman, R. W., 'The erosion of Foreign Office influence in the making of foreign policy 1916–1918', *Historical Journal*, vol. 15, no. 1 (1972), pp. 133–59.

Waters, Brig.-Gen. H. H., *Secret and Confidential. The Experiences of a Military Attaché* (London: John Murray, 1926).

Watt, D. C., *Personalities and Policies: Studies in the Formation of British Foreign Policy in the Twentieth Century* (London: Longman, 1965).

Watt, D. C., 'The British reaction to the assassination at Sarajevo', *European Studies Review*, vol. 1, no. 3 (1971), pp. 233–47.

Watt, D. C., *Succeeding John Bull: America in Britain's Place, 1900–1975* (Cambridge: Cambridge University Press, 1984).

Whittam, J., *The Politics of the Italian Army* (London: Croom Helm, 1977).

Wildman, A. K., *The End of the Russian Imperial Army: The Old Army and the Soldiers' Revolt March – April 1917* (Princeton, NJ: Princeton University Press, 1980).

Williams, B. J., 'The strategic background to the Anglo-Russian Entente of August 1907', *Historical Journal*, vol. 9, no. 3 (1966), pp. 360–73.

Williamson, S. R., *The Politics of Grand Strategy: Britain and France Prepare for War, 1904–1914* (Cambridge, Mass.: Harvard University Press, 1969).

Wilson, K. M., 'The opposition and the crisis in the Liberal cabinet over foreign policy in November 1911', *International History Review*, vol. 3, no. 3 (1981), pp. 399–413.

Wilson, K. M., 'To the western front: British war plans and the "military entente" with France before the First World War', *British Journal of International Studies*, vol. 3, no. 2 (1977), pp. 151–67.

Wilson, K. M., 'The Foreign Office and the "education" of public opinion before the First World War', *Historical Journal*, vol. 26, no. 2 (1983), pp. 403–11.

Wilson, K. M., 'The War Office, Churchill and the Belgium option, August to December 1911', *Bulletin of the Institute of Historical Research*, vol. 50 (1977), pp. 218–28.

Wilson, K. M., 'British power in the European balance, 1906–1914', in D. Dilks (ed.), *Retreat from Power: Studies in British Foreign Policy in the Twentieth Century*, Vol. 1 (London: Macmillan, 1981), pp. 21–41.

Wilson, K. M., 'The British Cabinet's decision for war, 2 August 1914', *British Journal of International Studies*, vol. 1, no. 2 (1975), pp. 148 ff.

Wilson, K. M., 'Imperial interests in the British decision for war, 1914: the defence of India in Central Asia, *Review of International Studies*, vol. 10, no. 3 (1984), pp. 183 ff.

Wilson, T., *The Downfall of the Liberal Party, 1914–1935* (London: Fontana, 1968).

Wilson, T., 'Lord Bryce's investigation into alleged German atrocities in Belgium, 1914–1915', *Journal of Contemporary History*, vol. 14, no. 3 (1979), pp. 369–83.

Wilson, T., 'Britain's "moral commitment" to France in August 1914', *History*, vol. 64, no. 212 (1979), pp. 380–90.

Winter, J. M., 'The impact of the First World War on civilian health in Britain', *Economic History Review*, vol. 30, no. 3 (1977), pp. 487–503.

Winter, J. M., 'Britain's "Lost Generation" of the First World War', *Population Studies*, vol. 31, no. 3 (1977), pp. 449–65.

Wohl, R., *The Generation of 1914* (London: Weidenfeld & Nicolson, 1980).

Woodward, D. R., 'Britain's "Brass-hats" and the question of a compromise peace, 1916–1918', *Military Affairs*, vol. 4 (1971), pp. 63–8.

Woodward, D. R., 'Britain in a continental war: The civil–military debate over the strategical direction of the Great War', *Albion*, vol. 12 (1980), pp. 37–65.

Woodward, D. R., *Lloyd George and the Generals* (Newark, NJ: University of Delaware Press, 1983).

Woodward, D. R., 'Did Lloyd George starve the British army of men prior to the German offensive of 21 March 1918?', *Historical Journal*, vol. 27, no. 1 (1984), pp. 241–52.

Wrigley, C. J., *David Lloyd George and the British Labour Movement: Peace and War* (Brighton: Harvester, 1976).

Wrigley, C. J., 'The Ministry of Munitions: an innovatory department', in K. M. Burk (ed.), *War and the State: The Transformation of British Government, 1914–1919* (London: Allen & Unwin, 1982), pp. 32–56.

Index